THIS
OUR
CHURCH

The People and Events
That Shaped It

Volume Five
Basics of Christian Thought
Todd Brennan, General Editor

THIS
OUR
CHURCH

William A. Herr

THE THOMAS MORE PRESS
Chicago, Illinois

Most of the material in this book appeared in different form in the newsletter of the same title published by the Thomas More Association.

ISBN 0-88347-193-0

Contents

Publication of this volume of
BASICS OF CHRISTIAN THOUGHT
is made possible in part by a
ROBERT E. BURNS GRANT
from the Claretian Fathers and Brothers

Chapter 1
PAUL AND THE PRIMITIVE CHURCH

ABOUT seventy years before the birth of Christ, an overly-ambitious Roman general named Cneius Pompeius Magnus, more familiarly known as Pompey, was given command of a Roman army and ordered to clear the Mediterranean of pirates. Pompey accomplished that task in short order and then proceeded to conquer what is now eastern Turkey. Then he continued south along the Mediterranean coast, through modern-day Syria, Lebanon, and Jordan, until finally he reached Palestine.

Following these victories Pompey returned home in triumph and made the mistake of playing power politics with Julius Caesar. Outmaneuvered, outgeneraled, and just plain outwitted, Pompey eventually fled to Egypt, where he was promptly and unceremoniously murdered.

But his legacy to Christianity was secure. Palestine and Asia Minor, including the territory of Cilicia at the northeast corner of the Mediterranean, had been brought into the Roman Empire. And several decades after Pompey's death an ultraconservative Jewish family, Pharisees of the tribe of Benjamin, decided to take advantage of the economic opportunities available in the Roman world outside Palestine. They moved from their home near the Lake of Genasseret in northern Galilee to the capital of Cilicia, Tarsus. There they prospered and became Roman citizens. And there they had a son, whom they named Saul.

When the followers of Jesus began to preach the gospel after Pentecost, they were convinced that the end of the world was imminent. They therefore were anxious to carry the Christian message as quickly as possible to as many of the children of Israel as they could. This included not only the Jews of Palestine but also the far more

9

numerous Jews of the *diaspora*. And in reaching toward this latter group of Jews, the apostles, whether they realized it at first or not, also were reaching toward an enormous number of Gentiles who already were predisposed to accept their message.

For it is a fact—and a fact of the utmost importance for understanding the early development and spread of Christianity—that at the start of the Christian era Palestine was the home of only about twenty percent of the Jewish people. The remainder, the *diaspora* (literally, "dispersion"), were scattered throughout the rest of the ancient world, particularly in Rome and in the larger cities of the eastern and southern Roman empire. And the Jews of the *diaspora,* unlike those in Palestine, were enthusiastic proselytizers—enthusiastic and enormously successful.

They were successful in making converts partly because of the example they set. Jews were greatly respected for their high moral standards, their reverence for human life, their extensive network of charities and social services, their devotion to their families. But they also were successful because people's perception of religious obligation was changing. Religion, which from time immemorial had generally meant little more than ritualistic participation in a tribal cult—a duty more patriotic than spiritual—was rapidly becoming a matter of individual commitment.

With hundreds of different cults and subcults circulating within the Roman Empire, people were beginning to feel free, for the first time in history, to change religions: to follow a particular cult not because they had been born into it but because they were personally convinced of its superiority to others. As men and women began to ask themselves which of the many competing religions was "right"—a question which never would have occurred to a Roman of the early Republic—religious affiliation began to change from a question of social conformity to a question of conscience.

And to the conscientious person, the person seeking something more meaningful to believe in than gods with crocodile heads or anthropomorphic Olympian deities, Judaism had a great deal to recomend it. It was montheistic, which appealed to those schooled in Greek metaphysics; it was based on a personal relationship with God; and it contained a divinely revealed moral law.

This last was a point of no small importance. One might consult a Greek or Roman priest about the most auspicious day on which to begin a journey; but no would think to ask him, let us say, how much of an effort one was obliged to make to return lost goods to their owner—or to consult him about any other moral problem. But one could certainly ask a rabbi. Judaism was more than just a means of warding off evil or obtaining the assistance of supernatural powers. It was a religion to which a person could make an intellectual and moral commitment.

In the climate of the times, Judaism would have been almost irresistibly attractive, except for two irremovable and insurmountable obstacles: circumcision and a set of excruciatingly detailed rules for the conduct of everyday life.

So the converts of the *diaspora*—most of them, at least —did not become full-fledged Jews. Instead, something quite remarkable happened. Large numbers of people from all social and economic classes adopted a modified form of Judaism, not submitting to circumcision or to the Mosaic Law but accepting Jewish beliefs, customs, rituals, and prayers. Greek-speaking Jews called them *sebomenoi,* or "God-fearers;" and they were welcomed into *diaspora* synagogues.

The first known Gentile convert, the Roman centurion Cornelius, is described in *Acts* as a God-fearer; and there is strong evidence that Nero's second wife, Poppaea, also was. At the time of Christ's birth there were an estimated one million Jews and God-fearers in Egypt alone.

These God-fearers were looking for something like Jewish religion without Jewish law, and when Christianity appeared many of them quickly converted. Perhaps the most important reason Christianity was able to spread with such incredible speed was that even before Jesus was born, *diaspora* Jews—albeit unwittingly—were energetically preparing the way. And the church, also unwittingly, quickly took advantage of this preparation. *Acts* records that when the apostles preached on Pentecost, they were heard by people from such places as Rome, Libya, Crete, Arabia, Iran, Iraq, Turkey, and Egypt—in other words, *diaspora* Jews and God-fearers from all over the Mediterranean world.

On the very first day of its existence, the church already was establishing a foundation for its growth beyond Palestine. And on that same day it began to sow the seeds of its first great crisis. The issue was whether or not Christianity would become just another Jewish sect, of which there already were perhaps two dozen at the time. That would have meant, to all intents and purposes, going out of existence. And it was in grave danger of doing precisely that.

For even after Pentecost, the apostles remained well within the somewhat nebulous limits of orthodox Judaism. They continued to worship daily in the temple. Their preaching made no mention of what we would consider the essential core of the Christian faith, probably because they themselves did not yet clearly understand that essential core. The message they proclaimed after Pentecost—repent and be baptized, for the kingdom of God is at hand —was virtually identical to that of John the Baptist. From a theological perspective, it was almost as if Jesus had never been born.

It is no wonder that the Romans had difficulty for so long in distinguishing Christians from Jews: Jews and Christians had difficulty doing it themselves. In Jerusalem, Pharisees and even Jewish priests were joining the Christian community, seeing no conflict between Christian baptism and Jewish orthodoxy.

But if this ambiguity was aiding the primitive church in attracting Jewish converts, it also was making Christian baptism of Gentiles a threat to Judaism. Eventually it led to the first anti-Christian persecution. To understand why this happened one must view the situation not from the Christians' perspective, as the story is usually told, but from that of the Jews.

For if even the apostles were acting as though Christianity were still a part of Judaism, it certainly must have appeared to be a part of Judaism to Jewish leaders as well. Indeed, it would have been virtually impossible for them to think of it as anything else.

But if Christianity was considered part of Judaism, then when it became known that a considerable number of Gentiles were being baptized without undergoing circumcision or submitting to the Mosaic Law—this first happened, apparently, in the Syrian city of Antioch—it must have looked as though Christians were teaching that one could become a Jew without circumcision and that the Law was unnecessary for Jews as well as for Gentiles. In Jewish eyes, therefore, Christianity appeared not merely as a heresy but also as a direct attack on almost everything Judaism stood for.

This was the issue which led to the stoning of Stephen, the first Christian martyr, no more than ten years after

the death of Christ. It also led to a general persecution of
the church in Jerusalem. This caused many Christians to
flee the city, spreading knowledge of their new religion as
they went, and thus resulted in the baptism of still more
Gentiles.

The apostles were not greatly affected by this persecution (*Acts* 8:11), at least in part because, as we already
have seen, they did not represent any obvious deviation
from orthodox Judaism. But the church in Jerusalem,
under the leadership of James and Peter, remained conscious of the threat of violence. The greater the number of
uncircumcised Gentiles who were baptized, the more uncomfortable things became for Jewish Christians in Jerusalem. And the number of Gentile converts kept rising.

That part of the church which was centered in Jerusalem
was trying, in effect, to remain exclusive, while that part
which was centered among the *diaspora* was trying to
become universal. An absolutely crucial question had not
yet been resolved; in all probability it had not yet even been
asked. What, specifically, distinguished Christianity from
Judaism? This, of course, was simply one way of asking
what it really means to be a Christian; and the answer was
the beginning of all Christian theology.

The question had to be addressed in Jewish terms, but it
involved issues which could be clearly perceived only from
a Gentile perspective. And so it took a Jew with a Gentile
perspective to answer it.

Saul of Tarsus—or Paulus, as the Romanized young
rabbi preferred to call himself—had been trained in the
Law of Moses by the renowned teacher Gamaliel, and he
was scrupulous almost to the point of fanaticism in its
observance. This is an important point. To understand the
overpowering force of his conversion experience, one must
remember that Paul was proud of the fact that he was a
thoroughly virtuous man by Jewish standards.

For that experience on the road to Damascus totally shattered Paul. In an instant he became convinced that what he had held most important all his life—his fidelity to the Law of Moses, in defense of which he had helped to arrest and kill innocent people—had been totally useless. It had not justified him in the eyes of God. Paul, who had self-righteously taken it upon himself to enforce the Law, suddenly saw himself as a sinner—and a far worse sinner than most.

But there also was a positive aspect to this traumatic revelation. Contained within it were the basic elements of what would come to be known as Pauline theology, elements which he would struggle for the rest of his life to understand and synthesize more fully.

Paul's sudden conviction that by persecuting Christians he had been at the same time persecuting Jesus, for example, implied that the church—the Christians whom he had hunted down and imprisoned—must be identical in some sense with Jesus. This was the germ of the conception which, thanks in no small part to Paul's own writings, developed into the doctrine of the Mystical Body.

And when Paul concluded, based on his own experience, that not even the most meticulous observance of the Mosaic Law, not the most painstaking attention to ritual observances—indeed, absolutely nothing at all that a person can do on his or her own behalf—can make one righteous in God's sight, he had found the key to answering the fundamental question of what it means to be a Christian.

Paul was the first person to realize clearly that the essence of Christian faith is the belief that one can be justified solely through the merits of the crucified Jesus Christ. And if justification cannot be earned, then it must be a gift. This conception freed God as well as man from legalistic restraints. No longer obliged by his own law to judge his creatures solely on their merits, God now could be seen as freely offering the salvation which no one truly deserves, in spite of the inescapable and universal sinfulness of humanity. Paul, in short, introduced into Christian theology the concept of grace.

There was one more effect of Paul's conversion experience which had far-reaching consequences. It convinced him that he had been directly commissioned as an apostle by the risen Christ. He did not receive the gospel from other men, as he pointed out in *Galatians,* but from Jesus himself; and he recognized no earthly authority higher than his own.

It was characteristic of him that immediately after being baptized he went, not to visit the church's leaders in Jerusalem, but into the desert for three years of solitary prayer and meditation. When Paul was uncertain about something he consulted no one but God; when he was certain, he consulted no one at all. This unshakable confidence that he spoke with an authority at least equal to that of anyone else in the church would prove important in the conflict over Gentile Christians.

For Paul—who alone of the apostles was born outside Palestine and who tended, perhaps because of the Roman citizenship he had inherited from his father, to see the world as one large empire rather than as many separate nations and races—was to become the theoretician of the universalist wing of the early church. He also was the most energetic evangelist of apostolic times.

At about the age of forty-five, or some thirteen years after his conversion, Paul began the first of his three missionary journeys, the first formal efforts to spread the gospel in the church's history. Most of his time was spent in what is now southern Turkey, particularly in Ephesus (near the modern city of Izmir); but he also founded churches in Cyprus and in a number of Greek and Macedonian cities including Philippi, Thessalonica and Corinth.

His strategy was to concentrate on major Greek and Roman population centers, preaching whenever possible in the *diaspora* synagogues. This undoubtedly was the most effective way to present his message to those most likely to accept it—that is, to the God-fearers—but it also meant exposing himself to violent Jewish opposition.

Paul, by his own account, was flogged eight times during these journeys; and once he was stoned and left for dead. This was in addition to the normal hazards of long-distance travel in the ancient world: hunger, thirst, cold, and no less than three shipwrecks. So it is not difficult to imagine Paul's indignation when he discovered that his fledgling congregations, founded and nurtured literally at the cost of his own blood, were being thrown into confusion, not by unbelievers, but by representatives of the mother church in Jerusalem. They were teaching, in effect, that the Gentiles whom Paul had baptized would have to convert to Judaism in order to become true Christians.

This crisis was especially acute at Antioch, the largest Christian community outside Palestine.

Emissaries from James were demanding not only that the Gentile converts in Antioch be circumcised and submit to the Mosaic Law, but also that Jewish Christians stop eating with Gentile Christians. Even Peter, who had been the first to baptize a Gentile, accepted these instructions from Jerusalem and refused to eat with uncircumcised converts.

But Paul absolutely refused to yield on this point, and he did not hesitate to upbraid Peter publicly for denying (as Paul saw it) the basic teaching of the gospel. Almost singlehandedly, Paul fought against the authorities in Jerusalem for the future of the Gentile church—which is to say, the future of the Christian church.

Two issues were intertwined in this dispute, one concerning the nature of the church and one concerning the mechanism of salvation.

Jerusalem Christians prided themselves on being an elite and exclusive group. They called themselves "the elect," "the chosen ones," "the Israel within Israel;" and they were concerned (with excellent reason) that the Jewish character of the church would be totally submerged if circumcision were not required of converts. They also feared a renewed persecution by Jewish leaders over this issue. But if circumcision were required, then Christianity would not be accepted by the non-Jewish world and could never become a universal religion—as Paul was convinced that the logic of the gospel required it to be.The church could not be both Jewish and universal. And if it chose to be Jewish, what would keep it from being reabsorbed into mainstream Judaism?

But the key issue for Paul was theological. He felt, as we have seen, that the belief that justification comes solely through the merits of Christ was the very cornerstone of the Christian religion. That belief had to be safeguarded and strengthened at all costs, and to teach that anything besides baptism is required to become a Christian threatened to weaken it. Paul put the matter in typically blunt terms. If the Law of Moses (or, by implication, anything else) can justify us, then Christ died in vain.

Acts contains an edifying account of how this dispute was resolved. Paul came to Jerusalem, the matter was discussed by the church's leaders, and a compromise solution was announced by James. But the story is of questionable accuracy. Paul does not mention any such compromise—indeed, he says in *Galatians* that he did not yield an inch at this meeting, even to "those who were reputed to be somebody"—and it would have gone totally against his character to give ground on what was for him the most fundamental of all Christian beliefs.

(Whether or not the meeting actually took place in the way that Luke described it, the story in *Acts* became important in its own right. It established a precedent for the settling of doctrinal disputes—a precedent which, unfortunately, was not always followed. The "Council of Jerusalem," as this meeting became known, was the prototype of the ecumenical council.)

In any event, extremists from Jerusalem continued to harass Paul's converts; and the struggle over circumcision of the Gentiles, with all that it implied for the future of Christianity, raged on.

Two groups of missionaries, preaching two different interpretations of the gospel, were competing to evangelize the same communities. One group was accredited by the church of Jerusalem—a church with apostolic foundations, led by people who had been personally taught by Jesus, including some of his blood relations. The other group could appeal only to the authority of Paul's private vision on the road to Damascus. It was an unequal contest, and it became even more unequal after Paul was executed in Rome during the reign of Nero.

What finally insured that Paul's teaching would prevail was neither the correctness of his doctrine nor the force of his logic, but the Roman legions which destroyed Jerusalem about six years after his death, in 70 A.D. Sixty years later emperor Hadrian forbade Jews to set foot in the city under pain of death. The church of Jerusalem simply ceased to exist, and with it disappeared the issue of Gentile circumcision. Jewish Christianity eventually withered away. Had it not been for Paul, the entire church might have withered as well.

Chapter 2
THE RISE OF THE HIERARCHY

MOST Christian communities of the first century bore very little resemblance to their modern counterparts. They had no church buildings and needed none, for they reenacted the Lord's Supper in the houses of friends as part of a common evening meal. They had almost no liturgy of their own. Their forms of worship were adapted from the services of *diaspora* synagogues, and consisted primarily of readings from scripture and commentaries on those readings.

Even the scriptures they read from might not be recognizable to us, for the gospels had not yet achieved their final written form—the earliest patristic writings actually predate them—and apocryphal literature abounded. (It is worth noting, while we are on the subject, that it was the church which produced the New Testament and not the New Testament which produced the church.)

They had no established body of doctrine. The most basic of all Christian dogmas, the divinity of Christ, was not formally defined until 325. Their professions of faith were not affirmations of theological propositions but expressions of praise and gratitude. Thanksgiving, in fact, was the very heart of early Christian worship and belief. "Gratitude" is the literal meaning of the word "Eucharist."

The earliest Christians made no distinction between clergy and laity—Peter's first epistle, for example, calls the entire church "a royal priesthood"—and they had virtually no ecclesiastical structure. This latter was something about which Paul, in his concern to preserve the absolute freedom of those baptized in the name of Jesus, had been particularly adamant.

Although the congregations which he founded adopted

the Jewish practice of establishing councils of elders ("presbyters," from the comparative form of the Greek word meaning "old man"), Paul had insisted again and again that it is the Spirit of God which governs the church. The Spirit would indicate which offices were necessary in a given church, and the Spirit would make manifest which persons were to hold them. Thus it happened that, at least in many of the Gentile churches, these presbyters were not so much administrators as possessors of various gifts. They were charismatics.

That the early Christians lacked much of what we might expect to find in a religious body should not be surprising. They were convinced, as all the apostles seem also to have been, that the destruction of the universe was imminent—an expectation which tended to make the formulation of precise doctrinal statements and construction of elaborate ecclesiastical hierarchies seem rather superfluous. As time went on, however, people began to realize that the world was showing no signs of ending and that the church might continue to exist for generations, perhaps even centuries. This realization led to far-reaching changes in the character of Christianity.

It meant in particular that steps had to be taken to preserve orthodoxy. For the Christian church was founded not on a ritual or a set of rules but on a faith, a belief; and thus it was absolutely essential to ensure that this fundamental faith was not lost or corrupted as it was handed on from one person to another. This was Christianity's overriding concern in the second and third centuries, and it goes a long way toward explaining why the early church developed in the way that it did.

It was this desire to safeguard the faith, for example, which gave rise to the concept of apostolic succession. For whom was one to consult about whether or not a particular doctrine was in harmony with what Jesus had taught, or about how a passage of scripture should be interpreted from the Christian perspective? The most reliable authorities, obviously, were the apostles. But after the last apostle died, the best that one could do was to ask someone who had been taught by the apostles—or, if that were impossible, someone who had been taught by someone who had been taught by them, and so on.

It was for this reason, and not originally because of any concern about the validity of ordination—a fuzzy concept, at best, in those days—that it was considered important for church officials to be able to trace an unbroken link between themselves and the apostles. Already in the year 96, Clement of Rome was writing that presbyters had teaching authority because they stood in apostolic succession. But the authority of presbyters—or, rather, the authority of most of them—was about to be preempted.

It probably was inevitable that in each of the churches one presbyter, whether because of natural leadership ability, a reputation for learning or sanctity, or some other reason, tended to acquire a certain preeminence. He was the person called on most often to settle disputes, to distinguish erroneous teachings from correct ones, to act as the community's spokesman, to take the leading role in its ceremonies. Eventually this preeminence became institutionalized.

By about the year 150, one person had acquired primary responsibility for overseeing religious affairs in most Christian communities, and he actually was called "overseer"—in Greek, *episcopos,* a word which in medieval Latin was corrupted to *biscopus* and which eventually became our word "bishop."

As time went on, the offices of *episcopos* and presbyter, originally indistinguishable, underwent some drastic transformations. Presbyters, whose responsibilities after the emergence of the *episcopoi* consisted mainly of preaching, developed into a priestly class. And the *episcopoi* gradually assumed a virtual monopoly over ecclesiastical authority.

So long as there was only one Christian congregation in a community (which generally was the case, except in the great metropolises of Rome and Alexandria, until about the year 100), an *episcopos* ordinarily presided over the Eucharist and administered baptism and penance for each congregation, although a presbyter could perform these functions in his absence. But as Christianity continued to grow it became necessary to establish additional congregations—new parishes, as it were—and one *episcopos* could not care for them all.

So a decision had to be made. Should each congregation have its own *episcopos*, or should the existing *episcopoi* share some of their responsibilities and create a kind of second-level ministry? In most cases the latter course was followed. And it was only natural that presbyters, who already were administering sacraments on extraordinary occasions, should be chosen to head the new congregations.

Early Christians avoided using the term "priest." It had unpleasant associations with Temple sacrifice and with the Jewish leaders who had opposed Jesus. Besides, Christ was considered to be the only priest of the New Covenant. The primary duty of a Christian leader had been not to conduct ceremonies but to preach—this was only natural in a new religion which was attempting to convert the world, and it reflected Christ's own instructions to his apostles. As late as the fifth century, in fact, John Chrysostom was insisting on the primacy of what is now called the ministry of the word. (It was this tradition to which Luther was appealing when he taught that a priest forfeits his priesthood if he does not preach.)

But eventually the character of the ministry began to change. As the liturgy became longer and more elaborate, more attention was focused on the ritualistic aspects of Christian worship. And a gradual ebbing of missionary fervor, coupled with the shift from adult to infant baptism—which meant that people were becoming Christians without being preached to—lessened the importance of preaching.

Bishops and presbyters became not so much people who taught the Word of God as people who offered sacrifice and who mediated sacramentally between humanity and God. They became, in fact if not in name, priests. This meant that they became a group of people distinct from the rest of the community. By the middle of the third century the Bishop of Rome had to forbid them to wear priestly vestments as everyday clothing. And the distinction between clergy and laity was steadily reinforced.

It began to seem imprudent, for example, particularly in view of the critical need to maintain doctrinal purity, simply to acknowledge as presbyters and bishops those of the laity who already manifested the gifts of the Holy Spirit. Instead, the church chose suitable candidates itself and bestowed the Spirit upon them through the ceremony of ordination. But the idea that the Spirit might sometimes select a lay person to fill a particular ecclesiastical office was not forgotten, and occasionally it reasserted itself. Thus Fabian (236) and Ambrose (374), to cite but two examples, are said to have been chosen by acclamation to be pope and bishop, respectively, while still laymen.

When the clergy agreed to accept salaries and began devoting their full time to the ministry—which from the fourth century on they were required to do—they tended to estrange themselves even more from their fellow Christians. And Constantine, as we shall see, carried this estrangement a step further by granting the Christian clergy, as a class, numerous privileges and exemptions.

In the first century, the entire church had seen itself as a holy group, surrounded by a secular world; by the end of the fourth century the clergy constituted a holy group within the church, surrounded by a secular laity. And within this holy group, bishops, by virtue of their status as successors of the apostles and custodians of the apostolic teaching, came to form the inner core of the church. This development, as might be expected, was looked upon with great favor by the bishops themselves.

Ignatius, Bishop of Antioch, writing in the first decade of the second century, taught that no valid ecclesiastical decisions could be made without the bishop's concurrence. The primary reason, here again, was the necessity of preserving the integrity of the faith. The best way to guard against heresy, Ignatius insisted, was for each church to remain united under its bishop. Cyprian, Bishop of Carthage, wrote a century and a half later that all church functions must be carried out through a bishop and that each bishop is master within his own diocese.

The Holy Spirit was still seen as governing the church in an ultimate sense. But for practical purposes ecclesiastical administration was increasingly carried on by bishops, who provided the link back to the apostles which was necessary in order to keep the church in touch with its origins. And since they alone possessed the power of administering all the sacraments and they determined which teachings conformed with apostolic belief, the bishops had become, in a manner of speaking, the conduits through which the Spirit communicated with the church and sanctified its members. It was in this way that the institutional church, represented by the bishops, became a kind of intermediary between the faithful and God.

In a sense, the "overseers" were—and are—the sole inheritors of that total freedom in grace which Paul had envisioned as belonging to all Christians. Still to be determined, however, was who was going to oversee the overseers.

It was quite natural for the church located in the capital and largest city of the Roman Empire to exert some kind of leadership over other Christian communities. Part of this was due to sheer force of habit. People in the provinces had been accustomed to looking to Rome for instructions and advice since before the birth of Christ. The wealthy Roman congregation had from its earliest days contributed generously to less fortunate churches; this tended to make the recipients listen with even greater attentiveness when Rome spoke. But the decisive factor in establishing Rome's preeminence was, yet once more, the importance of preserving the church from error.

For the same line of reasoning which supported the bishops' claim to authority—that is, their role as preservers of the apostolic tradition—logically implied that the Bishop of Rome possessed authority of a special kind. He was, after all, not merely a successor to the apostles but the successor and doctrinal heir of the two most important apostles, Peter and Paul, both of whom had taught and died in Rome. After the destruction of Jerusalem, no other church had anywhere near as direct an association with the apostles as did Rome.

The original theological basis for Rome's claim to a special status among the churches, therefore, was not the "Thou art Peter" text of *Matthew* 16:18-19 but the Roman congregation's unique reputation for doctrinal purity. Thus Irenaeus, bishop of Lyons, referred around the year 185 to Rome's faithful transmission of the teachings of Peter and Paul from the apostles' own time down to his own. And Irenaeus drew the logical conclusion: Other churches should make certain that their doctrines agreed with the teaching of Peter and Paul as preserved by Rome. The Roman Church, in other words, established the criterion of orthodoxy for all other churches. It was difficult for a bishop to argue with this conclusion without at the same time calling into question the source of his own authority.

As befit its role as the faithful guardian of apostolic belief, Rome was the first Christian church to eliminate minority doctrinal tendencies—in other words, to purge itself of heresy. Ironically enough, two of the minority tendencies involved, Marcionism and Montanism, both represented theological traditions which could be found in the writings of Paul.

Marcionism began as an attempt to determine which of the many contradictory epistles, gospels, and pious histories circulating in the early church accurately reflected the teachings of Jesus. And Marcion, a wealthy shipowner from what is now northern Turkey who died around 160, used a remarkably straightforward method.

Since Paul's epistles are the earliest Christian documents, Marcion accepted their teaching as authentic; anything which conflicted with Paul he considered spurious. This was a rigorous criterion—even some of the writings attributed to Paul himself, such as *Hebrews* and the Pastoral Epistles, failed to meet it—and Marcion's New Testament consisted merely of seven Pauline epistles, parts of *Acts,* and a portion of Luke's gospel. And that was only the beginning.

Unable to reconcile the Law of Moses with justification through Christ, Paul had rejected the Law of Moses; Marcion, seeing no way to reconcile the God about whom Jesus had spoken with the God of the Old Testament, rejected the entire Old Testament—which Christians had more or less automatically accepted as part of their Jewish heritage—and its God along with it. The God of Jesus, Marcion taught, was a God of mercy and love, an entirely different being from the vengeful and violent God of the Jews.

From one point of view, Marcion merely carried the process of separating Christianity from Judaism a step or two further. And his version of Christianity enjoyed great popularity, both because it was relatively uncomplicated (Marcion having removed the conflicting elements) and because many potential Christian converts, particularly among the educated classes, had found the bloodthirsty God of Abraham to be even less appealing than the gods of Homer and Ovid. Even though Marcion was excommunicated in 144 and left Rome for the eastern provinces, his ideas quickly spread throughout the Empire and survived in some areas until the Middle Ages.

Marcion forced the church to face some difficult questions. It was due in large measure to a desire to mediate some of the contradictions which he pointed out that Christian theologians began developing allegorical interpretations of the Old Testament. And it was primarily because of the success of his movement that the church established a definitive list of contents, or "canon" (the word originally meant "measure" or "standard"), of the New Testament—those epistles and gospels which it believed to be of apostolic origin.

This was a highly significant event, for it ensured that there would be both diversity and continuity in the development of Christian theology. Marcion had attempted to eliminate the inconsistencies in Christianity, to reduce it to a single theological perspective. By recognizing the authenticity of many of the documents Marcion had rejected and

by reaffirming that the Old Testament is indeed a part of
divine revelation, the church accepted the fact that there
are conflicting elements within the Christian message. This
meant that there would be room for the growth of different theological schools.

At the same time the "closing of the canon," as it is
sometimes referred to, meant that orthodox Christian
theology would be based solely on the teachings handed
down by the apostles. Christianity would be a religion in
which issues were settled not by new revelations or by vi-
sions but by appealing to an already received and approved
tradition.

This decision naturally called into question the status of
charismatics. In I *Corinthians* 12:28, Paul had described
Christian prophets as having a role second only to that of
apostles. But people who received direct communications
from God were not only a threat to the unique teaching
authority claimed by bishops; they also were highly unpredictable. There was no way of knowing what they might
say or whom they might follow. This issue came to a head
in the latter half of the second century when many
charismatics began to follow Montanus, a native of what is
now central Turkey, who declared himself to be the incarnation of the Holy Spirit.

Montanus led a movement which might best be described as Pentecostal. Its members experienced ecstatic
convulsions and other manifestations of religious hysteria,
and they saw themselves as restoring the pure beliefs and
practices of primitive Christianity. (The appearance of a
major reform movement little more than a century after
Paul's death gives some idea of how rapidly the church was
changing.) They denounced the establishment of a separate
order of clergy and declared that they were subject only to
the Holy Spirit. They also believed that the utterances of

their prophets superseded the teachings of the New
Testament, and they set up their own churches to revive the
Christianity of Paul's epistles. That meant, among other
things, religious equality between the sexes.

Paul's churches had been radically democratic because
they saw themselves as governed by the Holy Spirit, and
the Spirit bestowed its gifts on whomever it wished—rich
or poor, male or female, free or slave. Women voted
equally with men in the selection of bishops, and they were
elected to the deaconate at a time when deacons in many
places had almost complete administrative control over
church property and were, after bishops, the most important Christian officials.

Women may have enjoyed more equality in the primitive
church than they did anywhere else at any time in history
until our own day. And Montanism restored that early
equality. One of its most notable features was the authority and responsibility it gave to women, both as prophet-
esses and in the ministry.

This had important consequences. For the Roman
church moved quickly not merely to oppose but to utterly
discredit Montanism, whose triumph would have meant
the end of institutional Christianity. And, in an era when
religious polemics seldom were confined to substantive
issues, the prominence of women in the Montanist church
was one of the things which orthodox writers attacked
most savagely.

Tertullian, for example, the most outspoken apologist
of the early church, ridiculed the fact that Montanists
allowed women to preach, to conduct exorcisms, and to
baptize—functions which even male members of the orthodox laity were not allowed to perform. It was impossible, he insisted, for any woman to be active in the ministry.
There is bitter irony in this, for Tertullian eventually

became a Montanist himself and praised the spiritual powers granted to Montanist women just as fervently as he had previously denounced them. But by that time the damage could no longer be undone. Women's status in the church already had suffered a serious decline, in general because of the increasing restrictions placed on the role of the laity and in particular because of the decreasing importance of the deaconate. But it was the aftereffects of the fight against Montanism, more than anything else, which ensured that the church would not open its ministry to women.

In their role as leaders of the most important Christian community, the bishops of Rome soon began to interest themselves in the affairs of other churches. At first this interest took the form of advice and exhortations, and it was welcomed. When Rome tried to impose its will on other churches by force, however, it met with determined opposition.

The earliest attempt to influence another church seems to have been the letter written around the end of the first century by Clement, third successor to Peter in the traditional listing of Roman bishops, to a congregation in Corinth which had deposed its presbyters. Clement urged reconciliation and advised the rebellious party, although they were a majority in the Corinthian church, to reinstate the presbyters and to do penance. Not only was Clement's advice followed, but his letter was preserved and read during the services of the Corinthian community for many years thereafter.

But the outcome was different a hundred years later when the bishop of the Roman church, Victor, tried to force other churches to change the date on which they celebrated Easter.

The passion, death and resurrection of Jesus were commemorated by the primitive church on the same day that the Jews observed Passover. (There is a reminder of this ancient practice in the fact that our word "paschal" is derived from the Hebrew word for Passover, *pesach*.) This seemed appropriate, both because that was the day on which Jesus had completed his redemptive mission and because the crucifixion became symbolically related to the death of the Passover lamb. But as time went on many churches, particularly in the West, began to emphasize the resurrection over the crucifixion and to commemorate the Easter events on the Sunday following Passover. Thus it happened that at times some Christians were celebrating Easter while others still were enduring the penances of Lent. This led to confusion, and occasionally to ill feelings.

Victor thought he had the solution: all Christians should celebrate Easter on the same day that the Roman Church did. Many agreed with his suggestion. But the churches of Asia Minor, which claimed to be following a tradition dating back to John the Apostle, refused to change. And when Victor threatened them with excommunication, his fellow bishops, including St. Irenaeus, quickly intervened. Victor, apparently realizing that he had gone too far, backed down.

Something similar happened about fifty years later when the Roman bishop, Stephen, threatened to excommunicate St. Cyprian for continuing to teach that baptism administered by heretics is invalid. Stephen was opposed by many other bishops, and apparently never carried out his threat.

By the end of the third century, no one denied the preeminence of the bishop of Rome. But it was not yet clear what the nature of that preeminence was to be, since primacy in the teaching of doctrine does not necessarily imply any right to interfere in the administrative affairs of other churches. The first recorded use of the "Thou art

Peter'' text to support Rome's claim to supremacy was made by Stephen during his conflict with Cyprian. But other bishops did not necessarily agree with his interpretation of the passage. As late as a hundred and fifty years after Stephen's death, Ambrose, bishop of Milan, wrote that what Jesus had said to Peter on that occasion had in fact been said to all the apostles.

It remained to be determined whether the bishop of Rome was to be merely the first among equals, the most respected and influential of bishops, or whether he would become in some sense the ruler of the entire church.

Chapter 3
CONSTANTINE AND THE
CHURCH TRIUMPHANT

BY the time Diocletian ascended the imperial throne in 284, the Roman Empire was beginning to disintegrate. The army had been installing and deposing emperors at a mind-numbing rate for almost a hundred years, ever since Publius Helvius Pertinax was murdered by his own body-guards—who then auctioned off the emperorship. Inflation was driving the value of currency so low that eventually the government refused to accept its own money and demanded that taxes be paid in kind. But Diocletian was both shrewd enough to devise a strategy for restoring unity and stability to the Empire and ruthless enough to carry that strategy out.

To achieve stability Diocletian nearly doubled the number of provinces, thereby diluting the power of provincial governors. Then he combined provinces into larger group-ings called dioceses. (Diocletian was the first to use the word "diocese" to designate an administrative unit—it is derived from a Greek term meaning "to manage a house-hold.") He divided the overall government of the Empire, taking charge of the Eastern portion himself; and in order to keep the military from influencing the selection of emperors he designated an heir apparent for each half.

To promote unity Diocletian attempted, among other things, to destroy the church—not so much because of Christians' religious beliefs as because of the threat they were beginning to pose to the Empire's political cohesion. Until this threat arose, the policy of Rome toward the practice of religion—to the extent that it can be said to have had a policy—had been one of toleration. There was very little official persecution of Christianity for the first two hundred years of its existence, except for one brief outbreak during the reign of Nero which was confined to the city of Rome itself.

The popular image of the primitive church as an outlawed secret organization, whose members were systematically hunted down and killed for their religion and who escaped persecution by hiding in catacombs, has no basis in fact. It is contradicted by the testimony of many writers of the first and second centuries, including those pagans who commented on the charity practiced by early Christians—something they could hardly have noticed if Christians had kept their religious affiliation secret. And the catacombs were built not as hiding places but as ordinary communal cemeteries, a common practice among Romans of modest means. (The rich were entombed above ground along the sides of major highways.) So far were they from being secret that Roman officials issued building permits for their construction.

One of the reasons Rome was tolerant was that Roman religion was polytheistic, and polytheism by its very nature tends toward toleration. At least one of the pagan emperors, for example, unwilling to risk offending any powerful deity, placed a statue of Jesus in the same shrine where he kept representations of all the other gods whose favor he sought. No one thought any less of the Christians for worshipping a strange God. Almost everyone in the Empire was worshipping a strange god of some sort, and many worshipped several of them.

Also contributing to an atmosphere of toleration was the fact that Roman law was designed not to preserve any particular ideology but simply to maintain public order. It regulated people's behavior and punished them for illegal acts, but it ordinarily did not concern itself with their personal convictions. Romans generally could believe whatever they wished, so long as they behaved themselves.

But although the early Christians seldom were persecuted because of their religion, they sometimes did suffer violence for other reasons.

Despite their reputation as peace-loving people, for example, Christians were widely believed to engage in secret ceremonies of the most revolting type, during which they were said to practice incest, ritual murder, and cannibalism. The fact that they permitted only baptized persons to witness the celebration of the Eucharist naturally served to encourage these rumors. This made Christians convenient scapegoats whenever plague, drought, famine, or any other disaster occurred. Particularly in the rural areas, pagans would sometimes attempt to assuage their own misery by torturing and killing Christians, just as Christians in similar circumstances would later make a practice of torturing and killing Jews. Many of the early martyrs met their deaths in pogroms of this type, which increased in number and in severity as economic conditions grew more and more unbearable.

Other Christians ran afoul of the law not because of their religion but because they stirred up mass hysteria. This was particularly true of prophets and charismatics, who had a disconcerting habit of announcing to their superstitious followers that the world was about to end and ordering everyone to stop working and move out into the desert. That sort of thing was a menace to public safety, and the Roman state punished it severely. So did the Roman Church, which was no more anxious to become associated with trouble-makers than the church of Jerusalem had been. Fear that the wrath of civil government might descend upon its own head was one of the reasons why the orthodox church excommunicated the more unruly of the charismatics. There is some irony in the fact that a majority of the early Christian martyrs—those killed before the advent of widespread general persecution in the

middle of the third century—belonged to groups like the
Montanists, groups which would be regarded as heretical
today.

What finally brought Christianity into direct conflict
with Rome was the issue of emperor worship. For while
Rome had no laws restricting the private practice of
religion, it did insist, as all governments do, on the political
loyalty of its subjects. And it established, as all governments do, specific rituals by which its subjects were to
demonstrate that loyalty. Sacrificing to the spirit of the
emperor was the Roman equivalent of saluting a flag or
reciting a pledge of allegiance, and refusal to offer such a
sacrifice was regarded as an unpatriotic act.

Since Christians considered sacrificing to the emperor
equivalent to adoring a pagan god, they found themselves
on a collision course with the state.

In theory there was a precedent for compromise.
Emperor worship was just as abhorrent to Jews as to
Christians. And Rome, recognizing the right of every people to follow the religious practices of their ancestors, had
exempted Jews from making the legally prescribed sacrifices. One might expect that Christians could have been
granted a similar exemption. But Christianity was a different sort of religion, and now it was about to pay a heavy
price for its decision not to remain part of Judaism but to
become a universal faith.

If Christianity had been content to remain a small sect,
or if it had been the ancestral cult of some specific na-
tionality, Rome might have been willing to make some sort
of accommodation with it. But monotheistic Christianity
was as intolerant as polytheistic paganism was tolerant. It
did not intend to exist alongside other religions, but to
replace them. This included the Roman state religion, of
which the emperor as *pontifex maximus* (literally, "chief

bridge-builder,'' the highest religious official of Rome) was head.

And any attempt to change the religious system of their society appeared as threatening to most Romans as an attempt to change the economic system of American society would appear to most of us. Since the primary purpose of pagan religion was to influence the forces of nature—to ensure a good harvest, or prevent infertility, or secure victory in war—many people were convinced that to abandon Rome's traditional religion would be to invite disaster of catastrophic proportions. Besides, as we have seen, Christians refused to declare their allegiance to the established government.

Especially under the chaotic conditions of the third century, no government could sit quietly by while a large group of its citizens set up what appeared to be a state within a state. Once it had become clear that Christianity might succeed in converting a large part of the Empire, Rome was faced with the choice of either neutralizing the new religion or destroying it.

Emperor Decius (249-251) began the first widespread, systematic persecution of Christians; and after his reign periods of repression alternated with periods of toleration until Diocletian, in 302, initiated the longest and most brutal sustained effort to crush the church. All Christian places of worship and sacred books were ordered destroyed, and every Christian was commanded to offer sacrifice to pagan gods and to obtain a certificate from local authorities stating that he or she had done so. Those who refused were subjected to the most excruciating tortures before being executed. As might be expected, a black market in these certificates was soon established; and some Christians attempted to save both their lives and their souls by purchasing one without actually offering sacrifice.

Diocletian's policies were successful to some extent, just as those of Decius had been. A large number of Christians, including many bishops, abjured their faith when faced with the very real and immediate alternative of being burned alive or being eaten by wild animals. But these persecutions came too late: by the time they began in earnest, Christianity was too widely accepted to be uprooted by force. Christians already were a majority in parts of North Africa and Asia Minor, and about ten percent of the total inhabitants of the Empire had been baptized—roughly the same as the percentage which *diaspora* Jews and God-fearers had represented when Jesus was born. Roman society simply was not stable enough to survive the extermination, or even the active persecution, of that large a portion of its population.

(Because of the way in which the gospel had first been spread, there was a far greater concentration of Christians in some parts of the Empire than in others. Many more people had been baptized in the East, for example—in places like Turkey and Syria—than in Western areas like France and Spain, in large part because there had been few *diaspora* synagogues in the Iberian mountains or the forests of Gaul. This uneven geographical distribution of Christianity would have important consequences later on.)

In 305 Diocletian abdicated, the first Roman emperor to do so. Six years later his successor in the East, Galerius, ordered an end to the persecutions. He realized that the church had become too large to destroy.

At the same time, however, something else had been happening which neither Diocletian nor Galerius had been perceptive enough to realize. As it became more and more difficult to destroy Christianity, it also became less and less necessary. The larger, more centralized, and better disciplined the church became, the more its interests and those of the state began to coincide. Christianity wanted to become the sole religion of the Empire, and the Empire wanted to establish ideological homogeneity. Both were striving for organizational unity; neither countenanced unpredictable and uncontrollable splinter groups. These were elements out of which a statesman of genius could—and did—create an extraordinary synthesis.

Diocletian's life's work began to unravel almost as soon as he abdicated. A general named Constantius Chlorus became emperor in the West in 305 and died the following year, whereupon his troops acclaimed Constantine, his son by a tavern servant named Helena, as his successor. But Galerius recognized as emperor a general named Severus, who was soon overthrown by Maxentius. Licinius, meanwhile, had succeeded Galerius in the East. This meant that there were three generals claiming to be the sole Roman emperor, precisely the kind of thing which Diocletian's reforms had been designed to prevent.

In 312 Constantine moved to resolve this impass by marching against Maxentius, who controlled the city of Rome. The two armies met at the Tiber River just outside the city in the famous Battle of the Milvian Bridge, before which Constantine is said to have had a vision promising him victory. The following year Licinius and Constantine met in northern Italy and, in the midst of much other business, agreed upon a series of declarations establishing complete religious freedom which collectively became known as the Edict of Milan. Much subsequent unpleasantness might have been avoided if matters had been left at that, but they were not.

Constantine inherited Diocletian's problem of how to establish unity among the various peoples of the Empire, but his solution was the exact opposite of the one Diocletian had tried. Realizing that Christianity was not tied to any particular nation or culture—thanks primarily to the efforts of Paul—and thus was much better suited to serve as a unifying force than any of the national cults, including those of Rome itself, he not only tolerated Christianity but promoted it as vigorously as Diocletian had tried to destroy it. Constantine utilized the enormous financial and military resources of the Empire to encourage mass conversions, and he employed every means at his disposal to integrate Christian beliefs into Roman cultural life. In the process he may have done more to shape the external character of the institutional church than anyone else in history.

Realizing that much of the popular appeal of the pagan cults derived from their splendid temples and colorful public ceremonies, Constantine insisted that the Christian church acquire the most magnificent symbols of earthly grandeur which money could buy—an idea which many church leaders for centuries afterward found enormously appealing.

Early Christians had scoffed at pagans for building temples to house their gods. Now Constantine subsidized the construction of huge Christian places of worship which he modeled on the *basilica,* a rectangular Roman assembly hall. The type favored by Constantine had a semicircular apse at one end. This was an imitation of the imperial audience hall, in which the apse was designed to accommodate the emperor's throne; and it became the prototype of most subsequent Christian churches in the West. As another symbol of the kind of outward pomp and majesty which he felt the church should display, Constantine gave the bishop of Rome as his official residence not merely a mansion but the enormous Lateran Palace, which remained the headquarters of the Roman Church until 1308.

This desire to counteract the emotional and psychological appeal of paganism proved contagious. It led the Roman bishop Damasus, some thirty years after the death of Constantine, to change the celebration of the Lord's Supper from a simple, relatively unstructured ceremony into a much longer, much more formal and elaborate ritual. It also was Damasus who decreed that Latin should be used during the mass, which previously had been said in Greek.

As part of his attempt to use Christianity to promote unity within the Empire, Constantine did his best to absorb the church's administrative structure into that of the state. On one hand he gave Christian bishops many of the powers enjoyed by secular rulers, particularly in matters involving social welfare, and permitted them to resolve civil lawsuits. On the other hand he used the penalties of civil law to enforce ecclesiastical decisions, and he exiled bishops who opposed him in theological matters. The complex and troublesome mutual dependence of church and state which lasted almost to our own time was one of the legacies of Constantine.

Another was the transformation of ecclesiastical offices, particularly important bishoprics, into prizes worthy of the attention of greedy and ambitious men. Numerous cases of bribery to obtain episcopal appointments were reported, and the efforts of some bishops to advance their careers by moving from minor sees to more prestigious (and more remunerative) ones became a major scandal.

The see of Rome, naturally enough, was the most sought-after prize of all. An episcopal election in that city in 366 was so hotly contested that over a hundred people reportedly were killed, and the last recorded decree of the Roman Senate was a futile prohibition against the use of bribery to influence the election of bishops in the capital. No one had been nearly that eager to become bishop of Rome in the days when the successful candidate was likely to end his life as a slave in the Sardinian lead mines.

Constantine's policies led to a phenomenal increase in the number of baptisms. Within a half-century of his accession the great majority of the inhabitants of the Empire were Christians, which means that the church grew more than four times as much in that fifty years as it had in the previous two hundred and eighty. And, as often happens when large numbers of people are suddenly converted from paganism, this growth was accompanied by a great influx of pagan beliefs and customs into Christianity.

Some of these, such as the practice of genuflection during liturgical ceremonies, were deliberate adaptations from the rituals of the imperial court. Others, like the transformation of minor pagan deities into Christian saints, may have occurred more or less spontaneously. One of the most important sources of pagan influence, particularly during Constantine's reign, was the widespread practice of sun worship.

That Constantine was converted to Christianity is well known; less well known is what he was converted from. Like many other Roman soldiers, Constantine worshipped Mithra, the *Sol Invictus* ("Unconquered Sun"), whose cult had been made an official army religion. Sun worship, in fact, was so popular in the Roman world that in 274 the emperor Aurelian declared the sun god to be the chief deity of the Empire.

Even after his acceptance of Christianity, Constantine retained an attachment to at least the external forms of sun worship. His triumphal arch, constructed after his conversion, honored the *Sol Invictus;* his coins featured sun symbols; and he set up enormous statues of himself in the costume of a sun god. He retained the pagan title *pontifex maximus* throughout his reign. It was Constantine who decreed that the nativity of Jesus should be commemorated on the winter solstice, December 25, the same day

Mithraites celebrated the birthday of the Unconquered Sun. And it was he who initiated the practice of making the first day of the week—which the Romans, like ourselves, called "the day of the sun" *(dies solis)*—a legal holiday and day of rest.

The example set by Constantine reinforced an already existing syncretism between Christianity and sun worship, evidence of which can be found in Christian art and literature. "Sun of Justice" was a popular term for Christ, and Christians sometimes referred to Jesus as "driving his chariot across the sky." A statue discovered beneath (of all places) St. Peter's in Rome portrays Christ as the sun god Apollo.

In 324 Constantine defeated his Eastern counterpart, Licinius, and from then until his death in 337 he ruled as undisputed master of the entire Roman world. In the same year he began to transfer the capital of the Empire to an entirely new city of his own construction on the edge of Asia Minor, a city which Constantine called "New Rome" and which was destined to become the center of a Christian civilization and a theological tradition much different from that of the West.

A more immediate result of Constantine's acquisition of the Eastern Empire was that it involved him in a major theological controversy. For Christianity, unlike paganism but like Judaism and every other religion which demands an intellectual and moral commitment, tended to fragment into bitterly opposed factions. (When Julian the Apostate, Constantine's nephew, attempted to restore paganism, he shrewdly granted complete equality to all Christian sects and splinter groups in the hope that they would destroy one another. "No wild beasts," wrote the historian Ammianus Marcellinus in the fourth century, "are as hostile to humans as Christians are to one another.")

But Christianity hardly could serve as a unifying force within the Empire if it were divided against itself. And so Constantine, who often referred to himself as "the bishop of things outside the church," took an active—sometimes hyperactive—role in maintaining church unity. Since his primary interests were more political than theological, he preferred to negotiate compromises whenever possible rather than insisting on doctrinal purity at the risk of creating dissident factions.

When Athanasius, the bishop of Alexandria, refused to admit certain persons to church membership, Constantine threatened to depose and exile him on the spot unless he relented. On the occasion of a major schism in North Africa he tried every means he could think of to reconcile the two parties and ended by granting the dissident faction an amnesty. A church which was not all-inclusive did not serve Constantine's purposes.

Now he was faced with the case of Arius, a presbyter from Alexandria who maintained that since Christ was the "only begotten Son of God" there must have been a time before he was begotten when he did not exist. This was considered by many bishops, especially those in the West, to be shocking heresy.

Constantine's first response, characteristically enough, was to command both sides to stop arguing over what seemed to him to be a trivial point. When this failed he ordered some three hundred bishops to discuss the matter in his palace at Nicaea, about seventy-five miles southeast of Constantinople.

From start to finish there was no doubt about who was in charge at the Council of Nicaea. Constantine gave the opening address, presided over the deliberations, promulgated the council's final decrees as civil laws, and threatened to depose any bishop who refused to accept them. It was Constantine who proposed that the council use the word "consubstantial" to define the relation between the first two persons of the Trinity, a suggestion which he had no difficulty in getting the bishops to accept but which was destined to lead to much confusion and controversy. True to his word, he exiled those few bishops who refused to endorse the use of the term.

Yet here as always Constantine's foremost objective was unity, and he had no intention of allowing theological differences to divide his empire. Eleven years after Nicaea he assembled his bishops again and announced that he had revoked the excommunications of Arius and his followers and had readmitted them to the church. In the end it was an Arian bishop, Eusebius, who baptized the emperor on his deathbed.

Augustus Caesar reportedly boasted that he had found Rome a city of brick and left it a city of marble. Constantine could be said to have found Christianity a religion which considered itself not of this world and to have left it a religion with an enormous worldly investment.

He, more than anyone else, was responsible for making the church a temporal as well as a spiritual power, for giving it a vision of itself as responsible for bringing about the kingdom of God on earth through political, economic, and military means. That vision was to prove perhaps the greatest obstacle down through the centuries to the accomplishment of the church's spiritual mission. Dante summed it up well: "Alas, Constantine!" he wrote in despair, "What evil you brought into the world!"

Paganism remained the Roman state religion until 380, when Theodosius gave Christianity that status and made the practice of paganism illegal. (Perhaps because of religion's close association with political allegiance, it seems never to have occurred to anyone simply not to have a state religion at all.) Emperor Gratian already had renounced the title of *pontifex maximus,* which was subsequently assumed by the bishops of Rome.

Constantine's successors continued his policy of constant interference in religious affairs, and the church seemed destined to remain subservient to secular authority. What finally allowed it to become independent, at least in the West, was the fact that secular authority in the West disintegrated.

Chapter 4
ARIANISM, DONATISM, AND
AN EMPIRE'S END

MORE than four hundred years before the birth of Christ, at about the same time that the Roman Republic was being founded, several groups of Germanic tribes began to drift southward from Scandinavia along the valley of the Oder river.

By the time of Constantine one group, the East Goths ("Ostrogoths"), had settled north of the Black Sea in what is now the Ukraine, while the West Goths ("Visigoths") were living north of the Danube near what is now Romania and the Vandals occupied an area in the general vicinity of modern Hungary.

Perhaps because it had identified itself so closely with the Roman Empire, the church showed no great interest in expanding its missionary activities beyond the imperial borders. In particular, it made little or no effort to convert any of the Germanic tribes. But the day was not far off when it would wish that it had.

By the end of the fourth century a majority of Rome's soldiers were Germanic tribesmen—"joining the barbarians" had become a common expression for enlisting in the army—and the commander-in-chief of the Roman forces in the West was a Germanic general named Stilicho. Whole tribes of barbarians had been allowed to settle in Roman territory on condition that they aid in defending it against other barbarians: the Franks had been admitted under these terms into what is now Belgium in 358. Rome had allowed these peoples into the Empire for the simple reason that it was no longer able to keep them out.

As its borders grew more and more porous, Rome, like a fortress preparing to withstand a siege, organized itself to meet the threat of invasion. In 395, strategic considerations prompted Theodosius to split the Empire once more into Eastern and Western portions. His military instincts were sound: although the Western Empire would soon be overwhelmed, the Eastern Empire would survive for another thousand years. But the division reinforced the tendency of the Latin and Greek worlds to drift apart, a tendency which would have grave consequences for Christianity.

In 402, the capital of the Western Empire was moved to Ravenna, a small town on Italy's eastern coast with nothing to recommend it but the fact that it could easily be defended and was relatively close to the crucial northern frontiers. Rome still had a population of a million and a half, but it was no longer even the capital of its own empire. From a military point of view it was expendable—another fact which was to have an important impact on the church. Meanwhile, the forces which would decide Rome's fate had already been set in motion.

Constantine had hoped that his council at Nicaea would restore doctrinal unity to the empire. In point of fact, however, the century following Nicaea was marked by some of the bitterest, longest-lasting, and most divisive theological disputes in the church's history.

Nicaea did not even accomplish the objective for which it had been convened, for some of the issues raised by Arius involved delicate philosophical and linguistic problems which defied Constantine's attempt to impose a solution by force.

All Christians agreed that Jesus was, as he himself put it, "the Son of God." The problems began when people asked questions for which Jesus had provided no answers. Was Jesus God in the same sense that the Father is God? Was he equal to the Father? If he was, how could one

explain his statement that "the Father is greater than I"
(*John* 14:28)? If Jesus was God, did God die on the cross?

Arianism and the other great Christological controversies might best be understood as attempts to reconcile three
deceptively simple statements: Jesus was God; Jesus was
man; and no man is God. The ordinary rules of logic, obviously, do not apply here; neither do the ordinary metaphysical rules. What made the problem even more difficult
to resolve was the necessity of maintaining at the same time
that Jesus was distinct from the Father, that they were
both divine, and that there is only one God.

Many previous attempts to explain the relation between
Jesus and the Father had failed to meet one or more of
these exacting criteria, either by inadequately distinguishing between Father and Son or else by not placing sufficient stress on Christ's humanity. Theologians who concentrated on avoiding one of these errors frequently were
accused of having fallen into the other.

Arius, however, managed to slight both Christ's divinity
and his humanity. He taught that the body of Jesus had
been united not to a human soul but to the divine Logos,
and that this Logos had been created by the Father. Jesus,
then, was not truly human; nor was he God in the same
sense that the Father is God. This was theologically unacceptable for several reasons, and Arius was condemned
first by a local synod in Alexandria and then by the entire
Egyptian episcopate.

Had events been allowed to follow their natural course,
Arianism might quickly have slipped into the same obscurity which enveloped previous Christological heresies. But
Constantine was persuaded by his theological advisor, Hosius of Cordoba, to turn the dispute into an affair of state
by having the Council of Nicaea declare the teachings of
Arius to be incompatible with orthodox belief. Even this

did not satisfy Hosius, who suggested that Constantine's goal of doctrinal unity would best be served if the bishops supplemented their rejection of Arianism by adopting a creed (from the Latin word *credere*, "to believe"), a statement expressing official church teaching. This was a momentous step. For the first time, the church would not merely be declaring that certain beliefs are not orthodox; it also would be defining precisely what orthodox belief is.

This official statement of beliefs did not, as a matter of fact, promote Constantine's objectives at all. By reducing the opportunity for doctrinal compromise, it increased the chances that future controversies would result in permanent divisions within the church—which was exactly what Constantine was determined to avoid, and precisely what eventually happened. But Hosius had his way.

A number of creeds already existed. They originated, apparently, as summaries of the responses given by candidates during the ceremony of baptism. The best known of these summaries, for example, the Apostles' Creed, was adapted directly from the baptismal rite used in Rome. The bishops at Nicaea took one of these creeds, modified it by inserting various anti-Arian formulas, and adopted it as an authoritative statement of Christian belief. One of the formulas they inserted was the description of the Son as "consubstantial" with the Father: *homoousios* in Greek.

Constantine was able to browbeat most of the bishops into signing the Nicene Creed, as this statement became known. Many of them, however, later attacked it. They preferred to leave the matter undefined, since it was not treated in scripture; and they particularly objected to the word *homoousios*.

Part of the problem was that *homoousios* ("of the same substance") had connotations and associations which its Latin equivalents lacked, both because Greek is intrinsically a more subtle language than Latin and because Greek had been used for technical metaphysical speculation for at least a thousand years. *Homoousios* could be interpreted to mean that the Son is identical to the Father. For this reason its use had been condemned almost sixty years earlier by a synod in Antioch. Some claimed the word suggested that God is a material being. Still others objected that *homoousios* had been used by the Manicheans to mean that Father and Son had a common origin.

These objections were not necessarily motivated by pro-Arian sympathies. Even Athanasius, who was exiled five times from his see in Alexandria because of his staunch opposition to Arianism, recommended against insisting on the use of *homoousios*. In the political conditions created by Hosius and Constantine, however, opposition to the word *homoousios* meant opposition to the Nicene Creed; and it had the practical effect of strengthening the Arian position.

Constantine was succeeded by his sons, Constantius II in the East and Constans in the West. After the death of his brother in 350, Constantius ruled alone. Like his father, Constantius insisted on religious unity in his empire, and he used the same methods as his father to obtain it. Unlike his father, however, Constantius sided with the Arians.

Now the shoe was on the other foot. Synod after synod, at the new emperor's behest, condemned the Nicene Creed. The bishop of Rome, Libellus, protested and was exiled; Hosius, then over a hundred years old, was imprisoned in the imperial palace. (Both eventually obtained their freedom by signing conciliatory statements.) Soon every see in the Empire was controlled by an Arian bishop. St. Jerome, who had a gift for producing memorable phrases, wrote that the world was amazed to discover that it suddenly was Arian.

Councils in the West (Rimini, 359) and the East (Constantinople, 360) solemnly proclaimed that the Son was not, after all, of the same substance as the Father, but of a similar substance—*homoiousios* rather than *homoousios*. These two words became the slogans of the Arian and Nicene parties respectively, and the fact that they were identical except for the single Greek letter *iota* is said to have been the origin of our expression "only an iota of difference."

But the triumph of Arianism was short-lived. Theodosius, the last ruler of a united Empire, came to power in 379 and almost immediately ordered all Christians to profess the Nicene Creed, which became a kind of religious loyalty oath. In 381 Theodosius convened a general council in Constantinople which reaffirmed all the declarations of Nicaea. All Arian bishops were deposed; and Theodosius, with the aid of the imperial police apparatus, effectively crushed Arianism within the Empire.

The underlying Christological problems remained unresolved, however; and, as we shall see, they continued to exacerbate relations between East and West for centuries. In addition, the assumption by Constantine, Constantius, and Theodosius that religious unity was a necessary means to political unity, and their blatant manipulation of religion to further their secular ambitions, set unfortunate precedents.

Arianism itself, thanks to an accident of history, was granted a new lease on life. Ulfilas, a Goth who had been baptized in Constantinople and who converted his people to Christianity, had himself been converted by an Arian. Thus it happened that the Goths, then the Vandals, then the Lombards and Burgundians, adopted Arianism as their national religion. When the Germanic tribes conquered the Western Empire, therefore, they were, in the eyes of the church, worse than barbarians, worse even than pagans: they were heretics. This was to have far-reaching consequences.

While the Christological theories of Arius were occupying the energies of the bishops in Europe and Asia Minor, the church in North Africa was being torn apart by a complex dispute about the forgiveness of sin and the nature of the sacraments, a dispute whose roots went back to apostolic times.

Because Jesus was expected to return to earth within the lifetime of the Apostles, there had been little need for a theory of penance in the early church. People who committed serious sins were simply separated from the rest of the community, as the epistles of Peter and Paul had recommended, usually by requiring them to leave worship services before the reenactment of the Lord's Supper began. They were excluded, in other words, from the celebration and reception of the Eucharist. This was intended to be a temporary expedient, until the Christ of the *parousia* resolved these cases himself.

As time went on, however, it became apparent that this procedure was not satisfactory as a long-term solution. Exclusion might be considered merely temporary from the viewpoint of eternity, but it was turning out to be permanent from the viewpoint of those involved. Here the church faced a problem similar to the one which Paul had addressed: Was the church to be universal, or was it to be restricted to a select few? If it was intended to be universal, it could hardly countenance the permanent estrangement of large numbers of sincere and repentant members.

By at least the third century, if not earlier, a public reconciliation procedure—"ordeal" might be a better word —had been developed. Penitents confessed their sins to the bishop; then their hair was cut short and they were dressed in goat skins and covered with ashes to symbolize their having strayed from the fold of Christ's sheep. During the period of their rehabilitation, which might last for years, they were expected to fast and to practice other mortifications, while in some areas they were obliged to stand outside the church each week and beg for reinstatement or to prostrate themselves before the congregation while prayers were said over them.

This forgiveness of sin through penance was considered analogous to the forgiveness of sin through baptism. Penitents who, in the opinion of the bishop, had made sufficient atonement were restored to full church membership on Holy Thursday, the same day on which the bishop baptized catechumens. Just as a person could be baptized only once, so no one was allowed to undergo the ritual of penence more than once in his or her lifetime.

Even after reinstatement, former sinners were not permitted to run for public office, operate a business, join the army, or have sexual relations for the rest of their lives. As might be expected, many people put off this once-in-a-lifetime penance as long as possible, or avoided it entirely by postponing baptism until just before death. It was not until the early Middle Ages that the practice of repeatable and private confession, first developed by Celtic monks, became widespread.

But the church's claim that it could forgive even the most grievous sins did not go unchallenged. This, in fact, was the issue which led Tertullian to become a Montanist: distinguishing between mortal and venial sins, he denied that anyone but God could forgive the former. Tertullian —who, as we have seen, wanted to preserve the democratic church of Paul's epistles—also saw that acknowledging the power of the clergy to forgive or not to forgive serious sin would widen even more the gulf between clergy and laity. Dissident factions who refused to accept the idea that the church could forgive mortal sin set up their own champions as bishops of Rome—Hippolytus around 220 and Novatian in 251.

The persecutions of Decius and Diocletian intensified this dispute by greatly increasing the number of mortal sinners. The period following these persecutions was something like the aftermath of a military occupation: everyone was concerned with the denunciation and punishment of collaborators, of whom there were many. Particularly in the strict, somewhat fanatical churches of North Africa, where even hiding to avoid martyrdom sometimes was considered tantamount to apostasy—and where, as a consequence, almost everyone who was still alive could be suspected of having sinned to some degree —the question of how to deal with apostates was bitterly debated. Among the most detested of all apostates were *traditores,* clergymen who had handed over sacred books to be destroyed by the persecutors.

The issue came to a head in 311 when an admitted *traditor,* Caecilian, was elected bishop of Carthage and was consecrated by a man who was himself suspected of having been a *traditor.* A group of outraged Christians led by Donatus, the bishop of a small diocese near the Sahara, and by Secundus, the Archbishop of Numidia, contended not merely that Caecilian himself was unworthy but also —and this was the crucial issue—that his consecration was invalid because the bishop who had performed it was unworthy. A synod of Numidian bishops deposed Caecilian; then Donatus and his followers appealed to Constantine to support them.

The emperor instructed the Roman bishop, Miltiades, to hold three synods; all three found for Caecilian. But Donatus, who by now had taken over the see of Carthage himself, already was consecrating bishops for the other North African dioceses and teaching that only they could validly administer the sacraments. Donatus, in fact, was not merely propagating a religious theory: he was building a distinctly anti-Roman national church, with a gospel of social revolution. Armed bands of landless Berbers, inspired by the teachings of Donatus, took their revenge against absentee Roman landlords by burning crops, freeing slaves, and generally terrorizing the wealthy.

Executions and floggings eventually dulled the Donatists' taste for rebellion, but refutation of their theological arguments required twenty years of work by the most influential Christian writer after St. Paul: Aurelius Augustinus.

What the Donatists were claiming was, in essence, that the efficacy of a sacrament depends upon the personal holiness of the one who administers it, a holiness which can be acquired only through union with the church. And since they denied that those who had been excluded from the church ever could be readmitted, it followed that those who had committed a serious public sin, such as the *traditores,* could not validly administer sacraments.

To this Augustine replied that the human minister is not the cause of sacramental grace but merely the instrument through whose actions this grace is transmitted, and thus that the worst sinner can administer a sacrament just as effectively as the greatest saint. The holiness of the church, in other words, does not depend upon the holiness of its ministers or even of its leaders. This theory was to prove extremely helpful as time went on, for it allowed the Roman Church to insist that it was still the true church of Jesus Christ in spite of the scandalous and sacrilegious behavior which many priests, bishops and popes were to engage in during the centuries to come.

But the Donatist controversy was more than an argument about the sacraments. It also was a conflict between two different conceptions of the Christian church. The Donatists, like Tertullian, saw themselves as keeping alive the church of apostolic times—a small community, governed by the Holy Spirit, which purged itself of sinful influences and kept itself aloof from the secular world around it.

It was in the process of attacking this notion that Augustine developed his idea of the church as the City of God. Just as the Donatists' vision of the church as an elite group of the righteous was based on their denial of the forgiveness of sin, so the possibility of forgiveness was the foundation of Augustine's view of the church as a universal society containing sinners as well as saints. Christianity could no longer reject the world, as the Donatists proposed. It must transform the world, perfecting and sanctifying its institutions. And if the church was to be a universal society, it could no longer simply exclude sinners and heretics. It must forgive those who repented, and compel those who persisted in their errors to recant. This meant that the church was no longer considered to be a voluntary association.

It was Augustine who first expounded the right—indeed, the obligation—of the state to promote orthodox belief through the use of force. He gave several arguments to support this policy, including the gratitude which former Donatists allegedly expressed for having been compelled to renounce their erroneous beliefs. But Augustine's main reason for advocating the persecution of heretics was his theory of original sin, a concept which he did so much to develop that he was accused of having invented it himself. Since he believed that we are naturally attracted to evil for its own sake, Augustine concluded that most of us can do good only under the constant threat of punishment. Just as God chastised the Israelites in the Old Testament, he

taught, so the state has the responsibility to prepare people, forcibly if necessary, to make a free choice to accept
salvation.

While the Donatists' vision of a small, unworldly church
had been diametrically opposed to the ideas of Constantine, Augustine's conception of a universal church which
relies on the state to impose doctrinal purity would have
been quite in harmony with Constantine's interests—and
with the interests of many other powerful rulers. It was
Augustine more than anyone else who provided the rationale under which countless heretics were tortured and
burned down through the centuries, persecuted by the state
because they threatened political unity and persecuted by
the church for the good of their own souls.

The fall of Rome, one of the few events of ancient times
of which almost everyone is aware, is an event which never
really took place. The Roman Empire did not fall. It merely softened, slowly but inexorably, into helplessness, while
barbarian tribes wandered across it. What caused them to
begin wandering was the sudden arrival in Eastern Europe,
late in the fourth century, of a fearsome Asiatic people
who called themselves *Hioung*. These newcomers quickly
subjugated the Ostrogoths and extracted a yearly tribute
from Constantinople. The Visigoths escaped them by fleeing south across the Danube, where they destroyed a Roman army. Later they moved up the Yugoslavian coast and
down into Italy. Twice they besieged Rome and were
bought off with immense ransoms. At last, in 410, they
forced their way into the city and plundered it, while the
Western emperor, Honorius, remained safe behind Ravenna's fortified walls.

Even though Rome had lost its military significance its
violation still was a devastating shock to all people of
learning and culture. Even Jerome, no lover of earthly

glory, wrote from Bethlehem that the light of the world had been extinguished. But Jerome, as was his custom, was exaggerating. By the standards of the time the pillaging of the Visigoths had been quite restrained, and after two years they left Italy entirely to establish a kingdom of their own in Spain and southern Gaul. The events of 410 were nothing compared to what followed.

It had long been Rome's policy to use one barbarian tribe to fight another. Now a Roman general named Aetius reached for the ultimate weapon to hold back the German invaders. He brought the *Hioung,* the Huns, into Western Europe to fight as his mercenaries. And the Huns served Rome faithfully—putting down a slave revolt in Gaul, halting the advance of the Burgundians, attacking the Visigoths—until the new Western emperor, Valentinian III, foolishly decided to stop paying them.

Valentinian, like his predecessor Honorius, was safe at Ravenna; but his subjects were not. In 451 Attila and some half million of his followers began exacting a merciless revenge, ravaging dozens of cities including Basle, Strasbourg, Rheims, Padua, Metz, Verona, Mantua, and Cremona. Four years later the Vandals, who had entered the Empire in 406 by simply walking across the frozen Rhine and had swept through Gaul to Spain and then to North Africa, captured and plundered Rome. Three decades after that the Ostrogoths conquered Italy at the instigation of the Eastern emperor.

Had a single one of these tribes been religiously orthodox, the church might have been able to forge the same kind of alliance with it in the fifth century that it eventually made in the eighth century with Charlemagne. As it was, however, the church—which from the accession of Constantine in 312 until the death of Theodosius in 395 had enjoyed the patronage and protection of sympathetic emperors—now found itself abandoned by what little imperial authority remained in the West and totally surrounded by barbarian chieftains whom it regarded as heretics. It therefore had to make do for more than three hundred years without the support of a powerful secular ruler, a circumstance which greatly encouraged it to become a secular power in its own right.

While one barbarian tribe after another poured into Italy, the formality of crowning powerless Roman emperors continued at Ravenna. Finally, in 476, a Germanic chief named Odoacer ended this charade by quietly deposing the incumbent emperor and ruling in his own name. This is considered by historians to have been the end of the Roman Empire in the West.

As a sign that the line of Western emperors had ended, Odoacer sent the imperial insignia to Constantinople; and he pledged his loyalty to the Eastern emperor, Zeno. These two symbolic actions were to become extremely important later, for they amounted to an admission that the emperor in Constantinople now had jurisdiction over both East and West and that no one else could be made emperor in the West without his permission. In theory the Empire was reunited, although the emperor had effective control only of the Eastern half.

Nothing in the long history of Rome's empire was quite so pathetic as its ending. Even the name of its last ruler suited the tragio-comic occasion: Romulus Augustulus, after the mythical founder of Rome and its greatest ruler —but in the diminutive form. Romulus, "the little Augustus," was not important enough to be killed: Odoacer sent him back home to live with his family. He was fifteen years old.

But as the ancient empire flickered to an end, the church was stepping into the vacuum left by the evaporation of civil authority in the West. It was, in fact, already in the initial stages of orchestrating the creation of Europe.

Chapter 5
EPHESUS AND CHALCEDON:
THE EAST-WEST FEUD BEGINS

THE hierarchical organization of the early church closely paralleled the imperial administrative structure established by Diocletian. "Metropolitan" bishops—the approximate equivalent of archbishops—were appointed for the capital cities of most of Diocletian's provinces. And when additional sees were established in a province, their bishops were made subordinate (or "suffragan," from a Latin word meaning "having the right to vote") to that province's metropolitan. This organizational model was officially ratified at the Council of Nicaea.

At the same time, a few particularly important sees acquired a more general jurisdiction over larger areas of the Empire: Rome over Italy and the Latin West, Alexandria over Egypt, Antioch over Syria and Palestine, Caesarea and Ephesus over Asia Minor, and Heraclea over what is now Bulgaria and Western Turkey. This also was confirmed at Nicaea. But the rise of Constantinople led to radical changes.

Byzantium, the small town on the western side of the Bosphorus which Constantine chose as the site of his new capital, originally was an obscure suffragan see of Heraclea. Only fifty years after the new city's establishment, however, its bishop was acknowledged by the first Council of Constantinople as second in honor and dignity to the Roman bishop, since Constantinople had become "the new Rome."

This involved a loss of prestige for Alexandria, traditionally the second city of the Empire. And it was bitterly contested by the bishops of Rome, who refused to accept the principle that a see's ecclesiastical importance should be determined by the political status of the city in which it was located—a principle which, they feared, might one day be used against them, now that Rome had lost its own status as imperial capital.

But these protests had little effect. The see of Constantinople quickly extended its authority over the territory previously governed by Heraclea, Caesarea, and Ephesus; and before long its bishops, along with those of Alexandria and Antioch, were universally recognized as the "patriarchs" of the Eastern church, a title originally applied to any bishop of special influence or dignity.

They also were recognized as being the three most jealous and vindictive rivals in Christendom, enemies *ex officio* who welcomed every opportunity to embarrass, to denigrate, and—if at all possible—to depose and excommunicate each other. This had important doctrinal consequences, because, in an era when Christology was the most controversial of theological topics, Alexandria and Antioch happened to be the centers of rival Christological schools.

Antiocene Christology insisted on clearly distinguishing between the humanity of Jesus and his divinity, while the theologians of Alexandria stressed the unity between them. In practice this meant that Antioch emphasized Christ's complete humanity and resisted any attempt to identify the Son and the Father. Alexandria, on the other hand, tended to concentrate on his divinity and to treat the Father and the Son as virtually interchangeable—by teaching, for example, that Christ had created the world.

These were primarily differences of emphasis or phraseology, not conflicts over basic doctrine; and under ordinary circumstances they might have been peacefully resolved to everyone's satisfaction. Largely because of the personal ambitions and animosities of the patriarchs, how ever, they erupted into full-scale political crises throughout the fifth, sixth, and seventh centuries—with ultimately catastrophic consequences.

In order to emphasize the fact that Christ was fully human as well as fully divine, several Antiocene theologians had proposed that the description of Mary as the Mother of God, *theotokos* in Greek, should be balanced by describing her also as the Mother of Man. Better yet, they said, would be to call her *christotokos:* Mother of Christ. This aroused considerable opposition, particularly in the West. And when Nestorius, the patriarch of Constantinople, began to advocate the use of *christotokos* in the early part of the fifth century, he provided the Alexandrian patriarch Cyril with an irresistible opportunity to attack both Antioch and Constantinople at the same time by charging Nestorius with heresy.

While the appropriateness of the term *theotokos* was the immediate occasion for this conflict, the underlying issue was the fact that Cyril and Nestorius each believed that the other's position made the concept of redemption inexplicable. Both held that if one and the same person had not been both true God and true man, then the death of Jesus could not have adequately atoned for our sins. But Cyril was convinced that by refusing to assert that Mary had given birth to a divine person, Nestorius was denying the real unity of Christ's divinity and his humanity, which would imply that the person who died on the cross was not the same as the person who was the Son of God. And Nestorius believed that Cyril's formula "one incarnate nature of God the Word" denied the full reality of Christ's human nature, which suggested that his death could not have fully redeemed our humanity.

In 430 both patriarchs appealed to the bishop and patriarch of Rome, Celestine I. After a Roman synod confirmed Cyril's accusations, Celestine ordered Nestorius to recant—and then, for reasons which defy rational explanation, he chose as his representative in reconciling Nestorius to the church none other than Cyril, the one person least interested in producing an amicable settlement.

Nestorius asked Emperor Theodosius II to convene a general council to resolve this impasse. It met in 431 at Ephesus, some three hundred miles southeast of Constantinople. Celestine, who was not the most brilliant diplomat the Vatican ever produced, sent representatives with instructions to give Cyril their complete support.

Theodosius had appointed John, patriarch of Antioch, to preside at Ephesus. But the delegation from Egypt arrived first. And Cyril, ignoring the protests of imperial legates and bishops alike, opened the council without bothering to wait for the Eastern delegates—many of whom supported Nestorius—or even for the representatives of Celestine. He then ordered Nestorius to present himself and be judged.

The Byzantine patriarch was not foolish enough to appear before a court dominated by his enemies and presided over by his chief accuser. But the Egyptian bishops wasted no time. On the very first day of their deliberations they deposed and excommunicated Nestorius *in absentia,* ratified the legitimacy of the title *theotokos,* and approved Cyril's Christological doctrine. Four days after this, John of Antioch and the Syrian bishops arrived and convened their own council, reinstating Nestorius and excommunicating Cyril.

While the two rival councils of Ephesus were busy anathematizing each other and exchanging personal insults—Cyril's bishops sent Nestorius a letter addressed to "the new Judas," while John of Antioch sardonically referred to his Egyptian counterpart as "Pharaoh"—the representatives of Celestine arrived. Faithful to their instructions, they approved the doctrinal declarations of the Egyptian bishops and confirmed the condemnation of Nestorius.

Finally Theodosius, whose patience was not without limit, dissolved both councils and had Nestorius and Cyril both arrested. Cyril, by bribing members of the imperial court, managed to escape. Nestorius was exiled to Arabia and then to Libya, where he died. Bishops from both Syria and Egypt finally dispersed, leaving historians with the unenviable task of deciding whether John's or Cyril's had been the true Council of Ephesus.

Someone had to pick up the pieces after this debacle. Some means had to be found to reunite the Syrian and the Egyptian churches. And despite Cyril's personal shortcomings, which were many, the central core of his position was capable of being developed into a universally acceptable doctrine. Once he took the trouble to explain what he meant in terms which the theologians of Antioch could accept, the door to compromise was opened.

Nestorius had distinguished between the divine Logos, on one hand, and Christ, whom he saw as a union of humanity and divinity, on the other. Cyril, however, insisted that Christ was identical to the Logos—he was the Logos incarnate. Cyril's basic contention was the Scripture does not say that the Word of God was united to a human body. It says that the Word itself was made flesh. It was, therefore, truly the divine Word which was born of Mary, not merely the human aspect of a composite being. On the basis of this explanation, and after Cyril agreed to use the Antiocene phrase "one union of two natures" rather than continuing to speak of a single nature, the Eastern bishops agreed to the excommunication of Nestorius and accepted the use of *theotokos*.

Ephesus may have been a triumph for orthodoxy—the *theotokos* issue, at least, was resolved—but the victory, if there was one, was Pyrrhic. Before long it became apparent that Nestorianism really had been by far the lesser of two evils. And Ephesus turned out to be only the first battle of a long and very nasty war.

What brought the Western Empire to an end in a practical sense was not the defeat of its armies or the overthrow of its emperors but the disappearance of its bureaucrats: the tens of thousands of nameless functionaries who repaired the roads and aqueducts, collected taxes, kept the peace, and ran municipal governments.

As conditions continued to deteriorate during the barbarian invasions, many of these people were killed and others simply ran away. Gradually the intricate administrative web which bound the scores of different provinces into one organic whole fell apart. The mighty empire slowly decomposed into isolated city-states, and even within these minor principalities there frequently was no one to provide municipal services, feed the poor, dispense justice, and man the fortifications.

In time, the network of bishoprics which the church had built in imitation of the empire's civil administration began to take over the functions of that administration. There really was little choice. Someone had to make things work; and the bishops, long recognized as authority figures, generally were the only people who could handle the job. This was as true in Rome as anywhere else. And if bishops became princes in the provincial city-states, in Rome the bishops were becoming kings.

For the two halves of the Empire were evolving in totally different directions. The Byzantine world was turning into a theocratic state, headed by an emperor-priest who personally selected his patriarchs, while the Eastern church was becoming little more than a branch of the imperial bureaucracy. The bishops of Rome, however, unlike their counterparts in Constantinople, had no powerful ruler close at hand to oppose them. Not only had the Western emperors become powerless figureheads, they also had barricaded themselves behind the walls of Ravenna, more than two hundred miles from Rome, and were quite determined to stay there. While the anarchy which accompanied the barbarian invasions caused unimaginable suffering throughout Europe, it also created conditions conducive to the development of a strong, independent Western church.

But favorable conditions, by themselves, never made anything happen. Someone had to capitalize on this opportunity, to step into the extraordinary power vacuum created by the collapse of imperial authority in the West. And, in the middle of the fifth century, an extraordinary man did.

One may argue about which of the bishops of Rome was the first to enjoy the full powers and prestige which the title "pope" generally connotes today. But there can be no doubt that Leo I was a pope by anyone's definition of the word. Leo the Great, the first of the three popes traditionally granted that honorific title completely reorganized ecclesiastical administration in the West. In the process he made claims and imposed demands far beyond those of any of his predecessors. He also took an important step toward establishing the Latin church as a power independent of the state.

Since the Western Empire no longer possessed an army capable of holding back the barbarians, Leo took it upon himself to defend Rome without one. In 452 he rode north on a mule, unarmed, to singlehandedly ward off an attack by Attila's Huns—and, incredibly, he succeeded. Four years later he was able to persuade Gaiseric, king of the

Vandals, not to burn Rome or to kill its inhabitants. It is possible, of course, that Rome might have been spared without Leo's efforts. But what mattered for history was that people believed the pope had saved them when the emperor was unwilling or unable to do so.

Constantinople I had prohibited any bishop from interfering in the affairs of another diocese. But Leo taught that the bishop of Rome, as the successor of St. Peter, is "the ruler of the whole church"—that he alone possesses the fullness of ecclesiastical power and that other bishops merely share in his authority to a limited extent—and he did not hesitate to impose his will far beyond the borders of his own bishopric, using the penalties of civil law to back up his decisions whenever necessary. While the churches of the East, under the jurisdiction of their individual patriarchs, were developing the collegial structure and spirit which characterize them to this day, the Western church, under the influence of Leo, was becoming a highly centralized institution.

Leo also played a leading role in the Christological disputes which followed the Council of Ephesus. For Ephesus had created more problems than it had resolved, particularly since the Egyptian bishops, whose actions the representatives of Celestine had dutifully confirmed, had endorsed Cyril's "one nature" formula. And although Cyril himself had later abandoned that teaching, many of his followers remained faithful to it. Now a Byzantine theologian named Eutyches, determined to prevent a recurrence of Nestorianism, revived Cyril's doctrine in a novel form. While Christ's divine and human natures may have been separate before the Incarnation, Eutyches proposed there was only one nature following it.

History quickly began to repeat itself. Eutyches was excommunicated by Flavian, who had succeeded Nestorius as patriarch of Constantinople. Flavian in turn was excommunicated by Dioscorus, Cyril's successor as patriarch of Alexandria. The Eastern emperor, who was still Theodosius II—and who must have been suffering from a severe case of *deja vu*—was persuaded in 448 to call a general council to settle the matter. And this council, like the council at which Cyril had opposed Nestorius, met at Ephesus. Dioscorus presided over the assembly, as Cyril had in 431; and Flavian was deposed and sent into exile, just as Nestorius had been.

But the council of 448 had more in common with a lynch mob than with a theological conference. Bishops who supported Flavian were not allowed to speak; neither were Leo's representatives. (The latter would have had some difficulty in speaking anyway. Whether through an oversight or as part of some subtle diplomatic strategy, Leo sent to Ephesus delegates who did not know Greek, the language in which the debates were conducted.) When some of the bishops protested these conditions, soldiers and street brawlers were brought in to beat them into submission.

Leo angrily referred to this assembly as a *Latrocinium,* a Council of Robbers—the name by which it is still known. He refused to acknowledge it as a legitimate church council, and he tried to get Theodosius to invalidate its decisions. But the emperor refused. So the pope waited. And while he waited he began negotiating with the emperor's sister, Pulcheria. Two years later Theodosius was killed in a fall from his horse. Pulcheria then married a senator named Marcian and had him crowned as her brother's successor. Almost immediately Marcian announced the convocation of a new general council, the church's fourth, which was held in 451 just across the Bosphorus from Constantinople at Chalcedon.

The first order of business at Chalcedon—and all that most of the bishops really were interested in accomplishing—was the excommunication of the leaders of the *Latrocinium* and the deposition of Dioscorus as patriarch of Alexandria. And there things would have ended, with the Christological controversy in the same confused state in which Ephesus had left it, had not Marcian insisted, like Hosius and Constantine at Nicaea, that the council agree on a definitive statement of doctrine.

Ephesus had upheld the unity of the person of Christ, upon which Alexandria had insisted; but it had not stressed the Antiocene distinction between his divine and human natures. The doctrinal work of Chalcedon can best be understood as an attempt to supplement the declarations of Ephesus so as to produce a clearer and more balanced Christological definition. And the voice which spoke most authoritatively in establishing this clarity and balance was that of Leo, speaking through the pages of the *Tome* which he had written to Flavian when the teachings of Eutyches first were brought to his attention.

Dioscorus had prevented that statement from being read at the *Latrocinium,* but the bishops of Chalcedon hailed it enthusiastically and eventually made it the basis of their final declaration—in large part because Leo's position was supported by the entire Latin church, whereas the Greek bishops were too divided among themselves to agree on an alternative.

Leo's *Tome* was impressive not so much for the originality of its basic ideas as for the clarity and precision with which it expressed them. The elusive balance between unity and diversity was achieved by distinguishing between diversity at the level of nature and unity at the level of person—by declaring that Christ was, in his humanity, identical to us in all respects except sin and was born for our salvation of the Virgin Mary, whereas in his divinity he had been begotten of the Father from all eternity. In one and the same person, therefore, the same Christ, there are two distinct, unchanged, unconfused natures.

This was a masterful synthesis of the insights of the Alexandrian and Antiocene schools, and it might easily have reconciled both Nestorius and Cyril had they still been alive. But it did not reconcile their followers. Indeed, like the creed of Nicaea, it had precisely the opposite effect. Promulgation of an official statement of Christological orthodoxy threw those for whom the triumph of the Antiocene or the Alexandrian position had become almost a religion in itself into paroxysms of rage. Proterius, successor to Dioscorus as patriarch of Alexandria, was literally torn apart by a street mob for having agreed to the definition of Chalcedon.

So intense and deep-rooted was this opposition, and so important to the political and economic stability of the Empire were Syria and Egypt, the two areas in which it was most widespread, that appeasing the Monophysites (those who held fast to the "one nature" doctrine) remained a top-priority objective Byzantine diplomacy for the next two centuries.

In 484, or six years after Odoacer deposed Romulus Augustulus, Emperor Zeno issued the *Henotikon* ("Decree of Union"), a document composed under the guidance of the Byzantine patriarch Acacius which was intended to placate the Monophysites of Egypt. The *Henotikon* caused controversy more for what it did not say than for what it did. While it reaffirmed the condemnation of both Nestorius and Eutyches and upheld the doctrinal teachings of Nicaea, Constantinople I, and Ephesus, it also deliberately avoided using the Chalcedonian terms "person" and "nature" in speaking of the divinity and humanity of Christ.

While this was not an explicit repudiation of Chalcedon, it clearly could be interpreted in an anti-Chalcedonian sense. Pope Felix III replied by excommunicating Acacius. And Acacius responded by excommunicating Felix.

This was the first official rupture of normal relations between the churches of Byzantium and Rome. It was occasioned by an event which was itself futile, since the *Henotikon* failed completely to reconcile the Monophysites. And it could have been brought to a speedy conclusion, since there was no real doctrinal difference between the two sides, had not Rome refused to reestablish relations with the East until Constantinople agreed to formally condemn Acacius and his five successors as heretics. As it was, the "Acacian Schism" dragged on for thirty-five years, poisoning relations between Eastern and Western churches, until in 519 the Byzantine patriarch, under pressure from the emperor, finally agreed to Rome's demands. Almost immediately a far more serious conflict arose.

When Flavius Petrus Sabbatius Justinianus became emperor in 537 he faced problems similar to those which had confronted Diocletian. And, like Diocletian, he moved quickly and ruthlessly to resolve them. He was determined in particular to recapture the Western empire from the Germanic invaders and to secure religious unity throughout his realm—which meant, above all else, ending the Monophysite controversy.

Justinian's generals retook North Africa, Italy, and eastern Spain. But establishing religious uniformity proved far more difficult, even within the imperial household. Justinian, perhaps because he needed Western support to achieve his political objectives, supported the Chalcedonian party, while his wife and equal coruler, Theodora, sided with the Monophysites. Theodora, in fact, went so far as to depose and exile the uncooperative Pope Silverius and to have elected in his place an ambitious deacon named Vigilius, who had promised her that he would soften Rome's stand toward Monophysitism.

Justinian's strategy for pacifying the Monophysites without compromising orthodoxy was to make a symbolic attack on their archenemy, Nestorius. He issued an edict anathematizing three theologians (all of whom had been dead at least a hundred years) whose writings had manifested Nestorian tendencies. Since this document cited specific chapters of the three theologians' work, it—and subsequently the works themselves—became known as the Three Chapters. Like the *Henotikon,* Justinian's edict was not explicitly anti-Chalcedonian—indeed, it expressly upheld the authority of Chalcedon—but it was an obvious concession to anti-Chalcedonian sentiment and, as such, was considered quasi-heretical in the West.

Justinian then had Pope Vigilius brought from Rome to Constantinople. There, no doubt mindful of the fate of his predecessor, Vigilius reluctantly fulfilled his pledge to Theodora and condemned the Three Chapters. This caused the churches of Gaul, North Africa, and Northern Italy to break off relations with Rome. Vigilius then changed his mind and retracted his condemnation, for which Justinian placed him under house arrest.

In 533 Justinian convened the church's fifth ecumenical council, Constantinople II, whose function was to officially find the three pro-Nestorian theologians to have been guilty of heresy. It met in Constantinople's cathedral, the Hagia Sophia, which Justinian himself had constructed. Pope Vigilius, who was still being detained in the capital, refused to attend, whereupon the council voted to declare him a heretic until he agreed to endorse the emperor's edict.

Six months later Vigilius surrendered completely, again denouncing the Three Chapters and explaining in a pitiful letter that he had defied Justinian only because the devil

had made him do so. He died during the voyage back to
Rome, having lost the respect of friends and enemies alike.
As his successor Justinian chose Pelagius, a deacon who
had been outspoken in his criticism of Vigilius' weakness.

As a result of the Three Chapters controversy, the province of Milan remained in schism until 572; and the province of Aquileia, near Trieste, was cut off from communion with Rome for more than a hundred and twenty-five
years. The doctrinal authority and prestige of the Roman
Church were seriously eroded. Meanwhile, no Monophysites were reconciled.

In 633 another attempt at compromise was made. Constantinople proposed that Christ's actions be described as
proceeding from "one theandric ('god-man') operation."
This was an equivocal expression, and it enjoyed a measure
of equivocal success. "One operation" could mean either
that Christ's human and divine wills were so completely in
harmony that in effect they acted as one—an interpretation approved by Pope Honorius I—or it could mean that
Christ possessed only one will, an interpretation inconsistent with Chalcedon.

The "one operation" formula proved acceptable to
Alexandria and to Antioch, but it stirred up so much resentment in the West that there was real fear that Italy
might secede from the Empire. It finally was rejected by
the sixth ecumenical council, Constantinople III, which
also declared Pope Honorius to have been a heretic for
having tolerated it.

Arguments about how to explain in technical terms that
the Word of God had been made flesh now had been
disrupting political life in the Empire for more than two
hundred years. In 648 Emperor Constans II, who was
fighting desperately to defend his territories against the
seemingly invincible Arabs, decided that this distraction

could no longer be tolerated. He issued a decree which forbade any further discussion of Christ's wills, natures, or operations. Constans wanted his subjects to concentrate on fighting the invaders, not each other. In the West, however, this decree was interpreted as an implicit endorsement of the Monophysite position and an affront to the teaching authority of the church. A Roman synod organized by Pope Martin I denounced it.

Constans, with his empire collapsing around him, was not inclined to tolerate clerical opposition. He made one attempt to have Martin assassinated; then he ordered him arrested and tried for treason. (The specific charge was that, by continuing Christological polemics in defiance of the emperor's ban, Martin had contributed to the loss of Sicily to the Arabs.) Martin was found guilty and sentenced to death. Constans commuted this to exile in the Crimea, where Martin died. By this time, ironically enough, the Monophysite problem finally had been solved —not by Christians but by Muslims.

The ultimate result of the Nestorian and Monophysite controversies, and of the persecutions which accompanied them, was that much of the Middle East welcomed Arab armies as liberators from Byzantine oppression. Egypt and Syria in particular, once they had been guaranteed freedom of belief, preferred to submit to Mecca rather than to Constantinople. Within less than twenty years the entire Roman Empire south and east of the Mediterranean, except for the area which is now Turkey and a part of North Africa, was pledging its allegiance to Islam.

Chapter 6
THE NEW CHRISTIAN EMPIRE

JUSTINIAN'S armies had succeeded in recapturing Italy from the Ostrogoths. But the struggle lasted more than two decades, and it destroyed the political and economic cohesion of the country it was intended to save. When the killing finally stopped, Italy found itself unable to resist the advance of a new invader, one who proved far more ruthless than the Ostrogoths had been.

The Lombards, a Germanic tribe which .had migrated southward from the Elbe valley, had received permission from Justinian to settle in what is now Hungary and eastern Austria. When the Byzantine general Narses, conqueror of the Ostrogoths, was recalled to Constantinople after the Italians had protested against his rapaciousness, the Lombards took advantage of his absence to pour down into Italy, overwhelming the imperial troops. The emperor's viceroy, or exarch, took refuge behind the walls of Ravenna, just as his Ostrogothic and Roman predecessors had done.

Justinian died in 565, and his successors sent no new army to oppose the Lombards. But they ordered the exarch not to agree to a truce, lest this be construed as legitimizing their occupation. As a result of this craven policy, most of Italy could neither defend itself nor sue for peace. To make an already unbearable situation worse, shortly after the invasion the Lombard king was murdered; and for the next decade leadership of the tribe was split among three dozen petty dukes who preyed not only upon the civilian population but also upon each other. For ten years Italy was subjected to the only thing in the world worse than war: war with no one in charge.

In the midst of this orgy of destruction, when no one

seemed able to exert any control over the flow of events, Pope Gregory I stood like a solitary mountain rising out of a turbulent sea. Gregory the Great was the ancient world's last outstanding figure, and the first outstanding figure of the Middle Ages.

Born into the nobility and thoroughly trained in the law, Gregory was quick to demonstrate an unusual combination of political acumen and administrative skill. By the time he was thirty he was running the largest city in Europe—presiding over Rome's Senate, supervising its finances and food supplies, commanding its military and police forces. Then, at about the age of thirty-five, he suddenly retired from public life. He turned his family's home into a monastery, and devoted himself to meditation and to fasts so severe that they permanently ruined his health. A few years later he was ordained.

But Gregory was not permitted to enjoy the luxury of seclusion for long. His talents were too rare, and they were needed too desperately. In 579 he was made papal ambassador to Constantinople and entrusted with the absolutely crucial and totally impossible mission of persuading the emperor to help repel the Lombard invasion. When Pope Pelagius II died in 590, Gregory was chosen by acclamation to succeed him as bishop of the city whose governor he once had been.

Circumstances called for a fearless diplomat, an iron-fisted administrator, and a visionary statesman. Gregory was all of these—and a great deal more. Quickly he assumed total civil and military power. It was he who repaired the fortifications and aqueducts; he saw to it that the people were fed. In defiance of the emperor he concluded a truce with the Lombards. And when the exarch violated this truce, causing the enraged Lombards to march against Rome, it was Gregory who fortified the city

against them and then negotiated an agreement whereby
Rome was spared in exchange for an annual ransom which
he himself provided. In 598 he succeeded in arranging a
general peace.

Once again a pope had personally assumed responsibility
for saving Rome after it had been abandoned by its emper-
or. Far more significant, though, in what it portended for
the future was the fact that the powers Gregory had assumed made him the *de facto* civil ruler of central Italy.

Like Pope Leo I, Gregory strongly asserted Rome's
claim to jurisdiction over the entire church. He pledged to
respect the rights of his fellow bishops, and he did not interfere directly in the affairs of other patriarchates. But at
the same time he insisted that every bishop in the world,
including the patriarch of Constantinople, was subject to
the authority of Rome; and he heard and sometimes upheld appeals from the decisions of other patriarchs.

He overhauled the administration of church estates,
which he took an active part in running; and he reorganized and greatly expanded the papal bureaucracy. It was
primarily Gregory who gave to the Roman church the
administrative structure which enabled it to survive the
Dark Ages.

But perhaps the most important thing Gregory did was
to commit the resources of the papacy to the conversion of
the Germanic North, to set in motion forces which would
make its integration into Christian Europe inevitable. In
597 he sent thirty missionaries to evangelize the Anglo-
Saxons, an investment which paid spectacular dividends.
In little more than a hundred years England not only had
been converted, it was sending missionaries of its own to
convert the other Germanic-speaking pagans, with Wyn-
frith (Boniface) establishing Christianity in Germany and
Willibrord bringing it to the Netherlands.

Western culture had developed from Eastern roots, and it had grown to maturity in countries which bordered the Mediterranean. Gregory must be given a large share of the responsibility for shifting the focus of Western attention northward, toward lands which faced the Atlantic and the North Sea. As a consequence, the Latin-speaking West, whether it realized it or not, began to turn its back on the Greek-speaking East.

Gregory succeeded in holding back the Lombards temporarily, but after his death they continued their southward advance. Finding some way to stop that advance became the overriding diplomatic objective of Gregory's successors, an objective which finally led them to create an extremely important new alliance—and to abandon an old one.

The Frankish nation, a federation of Germanic tribes which had occupied what is now Belgium and northern Holland in the third century, followed a pattern of development different from that of the other barbarian tribes. The Ostrogoths, Visigoths, Vandals, and Lombards all migrated into the heart of the Roman Empire, where eventually they dispersed and were absorbed by the indigenous population. And all of them were Arian. But the Franks had remained pagan. And rather than migrating, they simply expanded south and east of their homeland, consolidating their gains as they went. By 446 they had reached the Somme, in northern France. Forty years later, under the leadership of a ferocious king named Clovis, and with some help from an unusual source, they gained control of everything north of the Loire.

As Clovis carried his wars of expansion southward, into territory controlled by Arian tribes, he found an unexpected ally in the Catholic bishops—many of whom, preferring to be ruled by a pagan rather than by heretical

Christians, opened the gates of their cities to him. It must have occurred to the ambitious king that if the church would do that much to aid an unbeliever, it might do considerably more to help one of its own.

In 496 Clovis was baptized a Catholic along with three thousand of his followers, and the entire Frankish nation soon followed suit. This conversion may have been brought about through the influence of the king's Catholic wife, Clotilde, or it may have been motivated by political considerations. Whatever its cause, it was one of the major turning points in the history of Europe and of the church.

Clovis, following the example of Constantine and the Byzantine emperors, took an active part in ecclesiastical affairs, convening and presiding over the first national synod of the Frankish church. And he continued his conquests—which now, at least for Catholics, assumed the character of a crusade against heresy. At his death in 511 he controlled an area stretching from the Pyrenees to the Alps to the Rhine, or roughly modern France plus the Low Countries. And he had moved the Frankish capital from the Belgian city of Tournai, his birthplace, to Paris.

By 700 the Arian tribes all had been converted, and the Franks were no longer unique in their adhesion to Catholicism. But they were still by far the strongest military power in Europe, and it was to them that the Roman church naturally looked when it needed protection.

Unfortunately for the church (or fortunately, perhaps, in the long run), Clovis left behind a royal line containing a remarkable number of hopeless incompetents. King Dagobert, who died in 638, was the last of his descendants to wield any real power. After that date the throne was occupied by a succession of impotent figureheads, while the "mayors of the palace," who originally managed the royal estates but had evolved into officials somewhat resembling permanent and hereditary regents, governed the kingdom for them.

The anomaly of having one person reign while another ruled was dramatically underscored when Charles, nicknamed Martel ("The Hammer"), became mayor of the palace in 714. Charles ruled the Franks for twenty-seven years, putting down numerous insurrections by rebellious nobles. In 732 he and the Frankish army stood alone against the Muslim forces sweeping northward out of Spain, met them about a hundred and fifty miles south of Paris, and utterly crushed them.

Charles was the savior of Europe, and easily the most powerful person in it. He had, at no small risk to himself, laid the foundation for a strong, stable, and relatively centralized kingdom. And yet he was not and could not be its king, for a long-established and rigidly enforced Frankish custom decreed that only descendants of Clovis could claim the throne. Charles's own great-uncle had been murdered for attempting to violate that custom.

And yet, as always, there could have been a way. Near the end of his life Charles received an appeal from Pope Gregory II for assistance against the Lombards, who were ravaging the area north and east of Rome. For one reason or another, he sent no help. What The Hammer possessed in the way of generalship seems to have been compensated for by a deficiency of political imagination.

But his son Pepin was far more clever. No sooner had he succeeded Charles as mayor of the palace in 741 than he undertook a project dear to the heart of Rome, a thorough reform of the Frankish church. This not only gave Pepin an opportunity to remove corrupt bishops and replace them with men of his own choice, thus strengthening his own political position, but it also established for him a reputation as a supporter of the papacy.

This reputation was a valuable asset, for Pepin was determined to succeed where his father had failed. Since there was no way for him to become king under tribal law, he had decided—with encouragement and assistance, no doubt, from the Frankish clergy—to carry his case to a higher authority. In 749 he posed a carefully worded question to Pope Zachary: Is it better for one who has power to rule, or one who has no power? This is hardly a question Pepin would have asked without having been assured in advance of the answer, for an unfavorable response would have dealt a death-blow to his ambitions.

He was not disappointed. Zachary gave his approval to the proposed coup, and in 751 Pepin used this approval to have the lawful king deposed and himself elected in his place. This action by the Frankish nobles set an extremely important precedent, for it amounted to an acknowledgment that the pope had the power to make kings—and, even more important, to unmake them.

The bill for this favor quickly came due. In the very year of Pepin's accession the Lombards seized what little remained of the Exarchate of Ravenna and threatened Rome itself. Constantinople was powerless to intervene, so Pope Stephen II, Zachary's successor, traveled across the Alps and all the way to France in the middle of winter to beg the Franks for help.

Pepin and his army marched into Italy, defeated the Lombards, and restored Ravenna to the Byzantine exarch. They they marched back to France, whereupon the Lombards took Ravenna again. So the Franks marched back and defeated the Lombards once more.

Pepin now possessed something which he did not particularly want: a strip of territory along Italy's eastern coast which legally belonged to the Byzantine emperor. He was not enthusiastic about returning it yet again to the imperial exarch, who twice in four years had proven himself incapable of defending it. Nor was he enthusiastic about annexing a territory so far removed from his own kingdom, especially at the cost of antagonizing Constantinople.

His brilliant solution was to donate Ravenna and its environs, along with the duchy of Rome, to the church, thus keeping them well within the sphere of Frankish influence while avoiding the headache of administering them and the unpleasantness of a quarrel with their rightful owner. Thus came into existence the Papal States, or States of the Church; and thus the pope became a temporal ruler in law as well as in fact.

It now was clear to the world that the pope, who was legally a subject of the Byzantine emperor, was entrusting himself to the protection of a new champion. Rome was betting that the future would belong not to the Byzantines but to the Franks. And, for a time, it did.

Pepin died in 768 and was succeeded by both of his legitimate sons, Charles and Carloman. When Carloman died in 771, Charles quickly took possession of his half of the kingdom, thus becoming sole ruler of the Franks. This effectively disinherited Carloman's widow and children, who fled to the court of Desiderius, the Lombard king. Desiderius supported their claims, and began pressing Pope Adrian to recognize Carloman's sons as his rightful heirs.

This led to the final resolution of the Lombard problem. Charles invaded Italy and took Pavia, the Lombard capital, by siege. Desiderius was forced to enter a monastery; Carloman's sons were taken prisoner and never heard from again. And Charles annexed all Italy north of Rome, becoming king of the Lombards as well as of the Franks. Having gained control of almost all the Christian lands of Europe, most of which he ruled himself, he then turned against the non-Christians.

Charles launched a massive assault against the pagan

Saxons living south of Denmark, finally subduing and forcibly converting them after a series of savage wars which lasted more than thirty years and which saw the slaughter of thousands of Saxon captives and the deportation of thousands more. He destroyed the empire of the Avars in what is now Hungary and annexed much of their land. He marched several times into Muslim-held Spain and established a Frankish buffer-zone across the Pyrenees. (It was while returning from one of these Spanish campaigns that the rearguard of his army, under the command of Roland, governor of Brittany, was ambushed by the Basques, leading to a struggle which inspired one of the greatest literary works of the Middle Ages.)

Within seven years of the death of Carloman, Charles had carved out an immense domain, pushing the borders of Pepin's kingdom far to the east and south. In the remaining thirty-six years of his reign he endeavored to provide it with an efficient, just, and stable government. For Charles was more than an incomparably gifted warrior. He summed up in himself and in his court everything which the Middle Ages held dear. And it is important to remember this, for he became the archetype of the Christian prince, the model whom many great medieval rulers, particularly German ones, strove to imitate—sometimes with disastrous results.

Although he himself never learned to read, he established a splendid court library and invited Alcuin of York, the most learned man in Europe, to take charge of his palace school and to promote learning throughout his realm. He subsidized the work of scholars, teachers and artists from all of his dominions, many of whom resided at his court in Aachen; and he sponsored a cultural revival such as Europe had not seen, and would not see again, for hundreds of years.

The title "Charlemagne," Charles the Great, does not do him justice. Other rulers were great; this one was overwhelming. He seemed literally larger than life, at least six and a half feet tall at a time when in much of Europe five and a half feet was considered exceptional; and when his seventy-two years came to an end, he was buried sitting upright with sword in hand, as though eager to return to life at the earliest possible instant. Far more suitable is the name by which he is called in the *Song of Roland:* "Golden Charles."

As though conquering, governing, and educating Europe were not enough, Charlemagne, like all powerful Christian rulers before him, also took upon himself the responsibility of promoting religious orthodoxy. Sometimes, unfortunately, he reacted to dangers which were not really there. Such was the case with the second Council of Nicaea.

It is not clear why the Byzantine emperor Leo III, some time in the first third of the eighth century, decided to abolish pictorial representations of Jesus and of the saints. He may have been influenced by the rise of Islam, which considered veneration of religious images idolatrous. Or he may have acted under pressure from the Byzantine army, which became fanatically addicted to image-breaking. However it began, iconoclasm remained imperial policy for more than half a century, during which time one patriarch was beheaded and many lesser clergy either executed or mutilated for opposing it. In 731, or the year before Charles Martel's victory over the Muslims, Pope Gregory III excommunicated everyone who practiced iconoclasm, thus severing relations between the Greek and Latin churches.

Then, in 780, ten-year-old Constantine VI became emperor, with his mother Irene as regent and co-ruler. Six years later Irene convened an ecumenical council, the church's seventh and the last one to be recognized by both East and West, to condemn iconoclasm and restore normal relations with Rome.

The first session opened in Constantinople; but when the militantly iconoclastic palace guard mutinied and stormed the church in which it was being held, the council adjourned and reconvened the following year, 787, in Nicaea. Under the close supervision of Patriarch Tarasius, Nicaea II solemnly upheld the honoring of icons and religious statues, carefully distinguishing this veneration from the adoration which is due only to God. That should have settled matters, at least as far as the Roman church was concerned.

But Charlemagne, like Emperor Leo III sixty years earlier, was personally opposed to the cult of sacred images, perhaps because it was practiced by the tribes in Eastern Europe whose pagan religious beliefs he was trying to stamp out. And he was gravely offended by an account of Nicaea II's proceedings which indicated, because of a faulty translation from the Greek original into Latin, that Tarasius and his bishops had decreed that icons should be worshipped. For these reasons he ordered Pope Adrian not to approve the council's decrees; and although Adrian protested that the condemnation of iconoclasm was entirely orthodox, the ecumenical status of Nicaea II was not confirmed by the West for nearly a hundred years.

It also was Charlemagne who magnified the *filioque* dispute into a major theological crisis. This controversy was another legacy of the rivalry between Alexandria and Antioch. The issue was whether, granted that the Holy Spirit proceeds from the Father, he proceeds "also from the Son" (in Latin, *filioque*). The Alexandrian tradition, which emphasized the unity and uniqueness of God, asserted that the Spirit does, indeed, proceed also from the Son; Antioch, which stressed the distinction of the divine persons, denied it. Most Western theologians had accepted the Alexandrian teaching, while the Eastern churches generally followed Antioch. Tarasius, the patriarch who had presided over Nicaea II, taught that the Spirit proceeds not *from* the Son but from the Father *through* the Son.

Charlemagne, for some reason, was passionately committed to the use of *filioque*. He ordered his theologians to condemn Tarasius and the Byzantines for using the phrase "through the Son"—this they did at a council held in Frankfurt in 794, despite Adrian's insistence that "from the Son" and "through the Son" were both acceptable— and he commanded that *filioque* be inserted into the Nicene Creed in masses said in his dominions, although Adrian urged him not to do so.

In point of fact the whole argument was a mere verbal quibble. At the Council of Florence in 1439, Eastern and Western delegates agreed that "from the Son" and "through the Son" actually are equivalent to each other. In the meantime, however, largely because of the intransigence of Charlemagne, the debate over the use of *filioque* and the insertion by the West of a new and controversial formula into the sacrosanct Nicene Creed greatly exacerbated relations between the Latin and Greek churches.

Ever since 476, when Odoacer had deposed Romulus Augustulus, Constantinople had claimed sovereignty over the entire Roman Empire. And despite all the political upheavals which Europe had undergone since then, that claim never had been denied. Particularly since the appearance of iconoclasm, however, allegiance to Byzantium had seemed to the papacy more of a liability than an asset. A weak emperor would be unable to protect Italy, while a strong one might attempt to impose heresy on the West. By the end of the eighth century, Rome was looking for a way to terminate its legal obligations to the Empire.

But the popes could not simply proclaim their independ-

ence from Byzantium. That would have contradicted the
foundation of every Christian political theory since the
time of Constantine, for how could one be a Christian, let
alone a bishop and a patriarch, without being part of the
Christian empire? Besides, there was no legal way of doing
it. Then, in 797, a remarkable opportunity presented itself.
Irene deposed her son, Constantine VI, blinding and im-
prisoning him and seizing the throne in her own name.

This created absolute legal chaos. It was far from certain
even under Byzantine law that a woman could validly
reign—her own subjects were forced to call Irene "emper-
or," since the word "empress" literally did not exist in
Greek—and Frankish law certainly did not recognize
female monarchs. It was possible to argue, therefore, that
the throne was legally vacant. The coup also gave Charlemagne a personal motive for supporting papal rejection of
Byzantine rule. He held a grudge against Irene, not only
for being a woman and for having usurped the throne, but
also for having sabotaged the engagement of his daughter
Rotrude with the hapless Constantine.

All the elements were in place for the creation of a new
political order. What set them in motion was the kidnap-
ping and brutal assault of Pope Leo III by members of the
Roman nobility in the year 799. Leo, who barely escaped
being blinded by his captors, fled all the way to northern
Germany to ask Charlemagne to intervene.

The pope had been accused by his enemies of a variety of
crimes, including adultery and perjury. It was to resolve
these charges and to put an end to the unrest which they
had caused that the Frankish king came to Rome in 800.
Late in December he convened an assembly of Roman and
Frankish officials, and Leo cleared his reputation in the
Frankish style by swearing his innocence before them in a
series of oaths. Two days later, during Christmas mass in

St. Peter's, Leo freed himself and his successors from the last vestiges of Byzantine overlordship by crowning Charlemagne "Emperor of the Romans" and prostrating himself in front of him.

This was one of the great milestones of European history. But there was a serious problem with crowning Charlemagne emperor—in addition to the fact that it was a blatantly illegal and treasonous act—and that was that Charlemagne did not have an empire. And no amount of ecclesiastical ritual could turn the Frankish nation into one. His domain, like that of Alexander the Great, was not a political entity but a collection of peoples with very little in common, held together by the personal influence of a unique and absolutely irreplaceable warrior-king.

The church saw the Frankish kingdom as an empire because that was what it wanted to see. It had been searching for a new Constantine, and managed to convince itself that it had found one. Pope Leo made that quite clear when he decorated the Lateran Palace with an enormous painting showing Pope Sylvester and Constantine on one side and Charlemagne and himself on the other. But in reality Charlemagne's state was simply a tribal kingdom stretched to monstrous proportions, with a political structure which could not help but self-destruct.

All that united Frankish society was a network of personal allegiances, and these could be kept in effect only so long as they were rewarded. And they could be rewarded only if new conquests provided new land and plunder. If the Frankish state did not continue to expand it would collapse, and even before the death of Charlemagne it had expanded beyond the ability of the Frankish administrative system to hold it together. Within two generations it would disappear. Because he totally misunderstood the nature of Charlemagne's kingdom, Leo allowed himself to create a title to which no reality corresponded. And long after the ephemeral "empire" had vanished, that exquisitely desirable title remained: shoes which no one but Charlemagne could fill, but which many lesser men could not resist trying on. This was a dangerous mistake, and the papacy would suffer grievously for it.

But the greatest problem caused by the coronation of Charlemagne was that it destroyed the political unity of the Empire. And, in an age when the civil and the ecclesiastical realms were bound intimately together, a rupturing of political unity had a profound effect on religious unity. Because we look at things from a Western perspective, we have been taught to think of Charlemagne as having united Christendom. By his aggressive interference in doctrinal matters, however, and by his cooperation in the establishment of a separate Western empire, Charlemagne actually played a major role in helping to bring about what is known in the West as the Eastern Schism.

Chapter 7
DIVIDING THE UNIVERSAL CHURCH

CHRISTIANITY originated in the eastern portion of the Roman Empire, and it spread much more quickly and penetrated more deeply in the Greek-speaking East than in the Latin West. This was due in part, as we have seen, to the large number of *diaspora* Jews and "God-fearers" south and east of the Mediterranean, and also to the fact that Constantine, who took up residence in the East, ruthlessly imposed Christianity on the Greek-speaking world. The East was overwhelmingly Christian by the middle of the fourth century, at a time when the city of Rome and the Western provinces still were largely pagan.

As a result, most early Christian culture had Eastern roots. The first great Christian theologians lived in the East—men such as Ignatius of Antioch, Polycarp, Origen, Justin Martyr, Clement of Alexandria, and Irenaeus—and most church leaders even in the West spoke Greek rather than Latin until about the middle of the third century. The word "Christ" itself is derived from Greek.

While it acknowledged Rome's special status as transmitter of authentic apostolic teaching, therefore, it was only natural for the East—the oldest, richest, most cultured, and most populous part of Christendom—to think of itself as the center of the Christian world. And Constantinople, because it was the city from which the emperor ruled, saw itself as the Christian world's very heart.

This belief followed logically from the basic precepts of Byzantine political metaphysics, which agreed with Plato in holding that the visible, material world is merely the reflection of a higher and invisible reality. Just as God governs and maintains the celestial universe in ordered harmony, therefore, so the terrestrial world and everything in it, spiritual as well as material, should be subject to the Christian emperor, God's reflection and representative on earth.

The Byzantine Empire—which for Byzantines, who referred to themselves as *Rhomanoi,* was simply the original Roman Empire with a new and better capital—was theoretically coterminal with Christianity itself. When all the world had accepted baptism, then the emperor in Constantinople, as God's vicar, would rule over the whole earth. This almost mystical conception of the Empire, and of Constantinople's central place in it, was the ideological cornerstone of the Byzantine state. To suggest that there could be more than one Christian Empire would have been, for the Byzantines, as unthinkable as saying that there might be more than one universe or that God could rule over only a part of creation. It would have been a contradiction.

From the Byzantine point of view, therefore, the secession of the West from the Roman Empire was far more than an act of political rebellion. It was almost the equivalent of religious schism. Irene's successor to the Byzantine throne forbade a newly elected patriarch to send Rome the customary notification of his consecration, on the grounds that the pope, by crowning Charlemagne, had separated himself from the Catholic Church. Constantinople was beginning to see itself more and more clearly as the guardian of orthodoxy against a Roman Church tainted by heresy and schism.

The defection of the West came at a time when Constantinople already was reeling from a series of major disasters. By the year 800 the Byzantines had lost almost all their eastern and southern possessions—Armenia, Mesopotamia, Syria, the Holy Land, Egypt, and the entire North African coast—to the Muslims. Slavic tribes had occupied the Balkans and penetrated as far south as Greece, while the

Bulgars, distant relatives of the fearsome Huns, had become so powerful that within a decade they would besiege Constantinople itself.

This, in turn, gravely imperiled communication lines between Constantinople and the outside world. Muslim forces challenged Byzantine control of the Adriatic, and the Slavs periodically blocked overland travel through the Balkans or waylaid and robbed travelers. To send a message between Constantinople and Rome and receive a reply sometimes took a year or more—a fact which must be kept in mind if one wishes to understand the events leading up to the separation of the Eastern and Western churches. Already divided by language and by politics, now the two halves of Christendom often found themselves literally unable to speak with each other. It is not surprising that misunderstandings between them multiplied.

The first full-scale conflict came about as a by-product of the iconoclasm dispute. For although Irene was able to have iconoclasm condemned by Nicaea II in spite of the army's determined opposition, she did not succeed in ending the intensely emotional and frequently violent controversies to which Emperor Leo III's policies had led. Both sides had suffered persecution, tortures, and martyrdom; and some factions remained bitter enemies for years afterward. In 843 Empress Theodora (not to be confused with the Theodora who had married Justinian), acting as regent for her son, decided not to risk a new confrontation between iconoclasts and anti-iconoclasts by convening a synod to choose a new patriarch. Instead she simply appointed her own candidate, a monk named Ignatius.

For a Byzantine, Ignatius proved extraordinarily undiplomatic. He supported the most fanatical elements of the anti-iconoclastic party, some of whom had advocated open rebellion against previous emperors; and when several of his more moderate bishops protested, Ignatius suspended them. In 856 the regency of Theodora was overthrown and Michael III became emperor. When Ignatius, who remained loyal to the fallen empress, began making inflammatory statements and encouraging enemies of the new regime, his bishops persuaded him to resign rather than take a chance on calling the government's wrath down upon the church.

When the time came to select a replacement for Ignatius, bishops of both parties, in the interest of restoring harmony, decided not to choose one of their own number. Instead they elected a layman, Photius, who was ordained a priest and consecrated patriarch—as the bishops, again in a spirit of reconciliation, had proposed—by two of Ignatius's closest supporters and one of the bishops whom Ignatius had suspended but whom his fellow bishops had reinstated.

Photius was a remarkable man, reminiscent in some ways of Gregory the Great. He was a nephew of Tarasius, the patriarch who had presided at Nicaea II, and he enjoyed outstanding careers both in academic life and in civil administration before his election as patriarch. He had scarcely been consecrated, however, before some of the more extreme anti-iconoclasts began demanding that Ignatius be reinstated. This led to the convening of another synod, which, concerned that the clergy might split into pro-Ignatius and pro-Photius factions—precisely the kind of thing which the election of Photius had been designed to prevent—decided to eliminate any possibility of Ignatius's return. It declared that Ignatius never had validly held the patriarchate in the first place, since he had merely been appointed by Theodora and not elected by a synod.

That might have ended the controversy, had it not been for the intervention of Nicholas I, third and last of the popes traditionally called "Great," who objected to the fact that Photius still had been a layman when elected. Although both Tarasius and his successor, Nicephorus, also had been elected while laymen, and although the matter already had been fully adjudicated under Byzantine law, Nicholas sent deputies to Constantinople to investigate.

In 861, after conducting an independent inquiry which included an interview with Ignatius himself, the deputies completely ratified the decisions of the Byzantine synod. The patriarchate of Ignatius, they agreed, had been totally illegitimate; and Photius was indeed the valid patriarch. Ignatius declared that he would not contest their decision.

And yet two years later, when several unreconciled partisans of Ignatius came to Rome with a maliciously distorted version of Photius' accession, Nicholas chose to believe—or to pretend that he believed—their uncorroborated tales rather than the report of his own deputies. He excommunicated Photius on the grounds that Ignatius had never really resigned the patriarchate and that Photius had been consecrated by a suspended bishop, and he declared Ignatius to be the rightful patriarch. Then, just for good measure, he excommunicated the deputies. These actions would be extremely difficult to understand, had there not been a great deal more at stake than the legitimacy of a patriarchal election. Rome, as it happened, had several reasons of its own for preferring Ignatius to Photius.

One reason was that, since Rome had always firmly opposed iconoclasm, the extreme anti-iconoclasts in Constantinople tended to be staunch supporters of Roman authority. They formed, as it were, a kind of papal fifth column inside the Byzantine church; and by siding with Ignatius, who had favored these groups, Nicholas was also indirectly strengthening Rome's position in the East.

More important, however, was the fact that Nicholas

and Photius were engaged in a struggle for religious control of a sizable portion of eastern Europe.

Just as Gregory the Great had promoted the conversion of the Germanic pagans, so Photius was actively reaching out to the eastern tribes who had moved into the areas which the Germans had vacated. He sent missionaries to the Rus, who lived in the vicinity of modern Kiev, and to the Khazars, who inhabited the area north of where Volgograd now stands. It was Photius who sent Cyril and Methodius into what is now Czechoslovakia, where they utilized liturgical books written in a Salvic alphabet of Cyril's invention and created a Slavonic liturgy—and where their work eventually was sabotaged by Frankish missionaries who insisted that Latin, Greek, and Hebrew were the only proper languages for divine worship.

(Although Nicholas and several of his successors defended the use of vernacular liturgies, the Germanic hierarchy, which seemed to equate unity with uniformity, finally pressured Pope Stephen V (885-981) into enacting a Latin-only policy. This remained in force in the Roman church for almost eleven hundred years—part of the Frankish legacy to Christianity.)

These attempts to expand the influence of the Byzantine church inevitably brought Photius into conflict with Rome. For the Muslims' conquests in the East had profoundly changed the dynamic of ecclesiastical politics. Once there had been five patriarchs quarreling with and scheming against each other. Now, for all practical purposes, there were but two, one in Constantinople and one in Rome, who divided Christendom between them. Neither of the two, and neither of the secular powers with which they were so closely associated, could expand except at the expense of the other. This tension finally flared into open hostility in the Balkans—an area immediately adjacent to

Byzantium, but also an area to which the Roman Church had an ancient claim.

More than a century earlier, when the Lombards were despoiling Italy at will and Byzantium was doing virtually nothing to oppose them, Emperor Leo III imposed a remarkably ill-timed tax increase on the very Italians who were begging him in vain to protect them. This, plus Leo's advocacy of iconoclasm, led Pope Gregory II to stop paying imperial taxes at all. In retaliation, Leo had transferred Sicily, southern Italy, and Illyricum (roughly equivalent to present-day Yugoslavia) from the patriarchate of Rome to that of Constantinople. Rome had never acquiesced in this transfer, but had been powerless to reverse it.

Now Pope Nicholas saw an opportunity to gain at least a foothold for the papacy in Illyricum. He began negotiating with Boris, pagan king of the Bulgars—to the utter consternation of the Byzantines, who identified the papacy with Frankish interests and could not countenance the establishment of a Frankish-dominated state so close to their own frontier. It was at this point, while Constantinople was protesting his dealings with the Bulgarians, that Nicholas excommunicated Photius.

But Byzantine military pressure forced Boris to accept baptism from Constantinople, and in 864 Photius began sending Greek clergy to organize a Bulgarian church. Boris, however, was not a docile convert. He wanted a church under his own control, not one dominated by the Byzantines. When Photius refused to establish an independent patriarchate in Bulgaria, Boris reopened negotiations with Nicholas—who gladly sent him a contingent of Western clergy headed by two bishops. No sooner had the papal missionaries arrived than they began teaching the Bulgarians a version of the Nicene Creed which included *filioque*. Totally outraged, the Byzantines held a synod in 867, presided over by Emperor Michael, which excommunicated Nicholas for promoting heresy and called on the Western emperor, Louis II, to depose him.

Within a matter of months, however, Nicholas had died and Michael had been overthrown by Basil I, who, anxious to establish cordial relations with Rome, deposed Photius and recalled Ignatius. By the time news of Nicholas' excommunication reached Rome, Photius was no longer patriarch, Michael was no longer emperor, and Nicholas was no longer pope. It would have been an ideal time to reestablish harmony in the church, particularly since preparations were already underway for a general council in Constantinople. But Adrian II, the new pope, insisted on excommunicating Photius once again and also deposed all the bishops Photius had consecrated. Then he instructed his delegates to make certain that the council, which opened in 869, ratified his actions. And Constantinople IV, which is considered the eighth ecumenical council by Rome but is not recognized by the Byzantine churches, did indeed echo Adrian's anathemas.

But it was a hollow victory. Rome's heavy-handedness was deeply resented in the East; and after the death of Adrian, the "Photian Affair," as this tangled sequence of events sometimes is known, was quickly and amicably settled on Byzantium's terms.

Ignatius himself, who had never asked Rome to intervene on his behalf, proposed a conference to reunify the Byzantine church; and when he died in 877, Photius again became patriarch and was recognized as such by John VIII, Pope Adrian's successor. John also accepted the decrees of a Byzantine synod held in 879-880, during which the actions taken by Constantinople IV were annulled and both Eastern and Western delegates agreed that *filioque* should not be inserted into the Nicene Creed. By accepting these decrees, John either did or did not repudiate Constantinople IV itself—a question which was hotly debated in the twelfth century and still remains in some dispute.

Photius eventually canonized Ignatius, with whom he had never had any personal quarrel. And it apparently was Photius who was responsible for placing a mosiac of Ignatius in the Hagia Sophia, where it still can be seen.

While the evangelization of the Slavs made only fitful progress during the lifetime of Photius, the results of his initiative were destined to shift the attention of the Byzantine church away from the South and West and toward the North—the exact counterpart of what Gregory had done for the Roman Church. The followers of Cyril and Methodius, driven out of Czechoslovakia by the Frankish bishops, made Bulgaria the center of their Slavic mission. After the baptism of Vladimir of Kiev in 989, Bulgarians using copies of Cyril's liturgical books began the immense task of converting the eastern Slavs, and within fifty years a Byzantine-dominated hierarchy had been installed in Russia. The interference of Nicholas and Adrian in the internal affairs of the Byzantine patriarchate had accomplished little—except to greatly increase antipapal feeling and antagonize Rome's own supporters in the East.

Pope Leo III had adopted a policy of passive resistance when Charlemagne tried to pressure him into adding *filioque* to the Nicene Creed. He did not dare to defy the emperor directly. But he did prevent the introduction of *filioque* in Rome, and he placed in St. Peter's two silver shields inscribed with the text of the creed, one in Latin and one in Greek—and both conspicuously lacking *filioque*. "Why add the phrase," Leo asked, "when it is unnecessary and when it will tend to divide East and West?"

It was an excellent question. Many differences arose as time went on between the churches of Constantinople and

Rome. One used unleavened bread for the Eucharist, for example, while the other used leavened; one imposed celibacy on its clergy and the other did not. But the *filioque* dispute—not any fundamental difference in dogma, but simply the propriety of inserting the phrase into the Nicene Creed—was the only major theological issue in the controversy which produced the East-West schism. And even that issue might never have arisen had Rome not insisted on forcing Western usage on the East.

For the Byzantines had no objection to the West's use of *filioque* to express its own trinitarian theories. But they strenuously opposed its unilateral addition to the Nicene Creed, which since 325 had been the foundation stone of Christian orthodoxy and unity. They maintained that only a general council of the whole church could change what a previous council had decreed. Besides, they claimed, the Council of Ephesus had expressly forbidden any additions to the creed adopted at Nicaea.

Sometime after the year 1000, the Western emperor Henry II finally succeeded where Charlemagne had failed, and imposed the addition of *filioque* in Rome. And in 1009 Pope Sergius IV, along with the customary notification of his election, sent the Byzantine patriarch—who also was named Sergius—a copy of the creed which contained *filioque*. This was a direct and gratuitous provocation, and Patriarch Sergius responded by refusing to add the new pope's name to Constantinople's diptychs, the tablets which contained the names of all patriarchs and metropolitans in communion with the universal church. This was equivalent to declaring the pope excommunicated.

And yet friendly relations between East and West could easily have been restored. In 1024 Patriarch Eustathios offered to acknowledge the primacy of Rome, provided that the internal autonomy of the Byzantine patriarchate was respected. Pope John XIX initially agreed, but his advisors induced him to change his mind. Not long afterward an even better opportunity for reconciliation was provided by the appearance of an enemy who threatened both Constantinople and Rome.

Charlemagne had scarcely been buried before his domains fell victim to a new invasion from the North, an invasion all the more difficult to defend against because it moved by water. Along the entire coast of Europe and deep into the interior, raiders from Scandinavia raped, murdered, looted and burned with a merciless ferocity which left a permanent mark on the English language. "Berserk," derived from the Old Norse word for bearskin, originally was the name of a Viking warrior class.

In the chaos which followed Charlemagne's death, some of these men from the North, or Normans, took control of the territory between the mouths of the Seine and Loire rivers which is still known as Normandy. Other Normans preyed on Mediterranean shipping, occupied half of Ireland, and created the first Russian state. Still others drifted into Italy, and by the middle of the eleventh century they controlled large areas south of Rome.

This last development was looked upon at first with some favor by the papacy, since the Normans had been converted to Latin Catholicism, while much of southern Italy, still largely Greek-speaking, was under the political control of Byzantium. No one in Rome objected when the Normans suppressed Greek liturgical practices in the areas they conquered—although there were vociferous protests when the Byzantine patriarch, Michael Cerularius, reciprocated by forcing Latin churches in Constantinople to adopt the Greek liturgy.

When the Normans began to threaten papal lands to the north, however, Pope Leo IX suggested the creation of an

anti-Norman alliance. This proposal was agreed to by the
Eastern emperor, Constantine IX; and Patriarch Cerularius
sent Leo a letter offering to work toward the reunification
of the Greek and Latin churches. All conditions appeared to
be favorable for the resumption of normal relations between
East and West. But the delegation which Leo sent to Constantinople in 1054 to work out the details of reconciliation
turned out to be one of the most disastrous diplomatic missions in history. Constantinople and Rome, far from being
reunited, were driven ever further apart—primarily because
of the blundering of one man.

As head of his delegation Leo chose Cardinal Humbert
of Silva Candida, a noted theologian and polemicist who
would later play a leading role in promoting badly needed
reforms in the Latin church. But reformers, especially successful ones, tend to be intolerant, impetuous, and head-
strong—precisely the opposite of the qualities required of a
diplomat—and Humbert was no exception. Cerularius
already had demonstrated his hostility to Rome, most
notably by desecrating the Eucharist in the Latin churches
of Constantinople, and Humbert treated him as an enemy
from the very start.

At their very first meeting Humbert handed Cerularius a
letter which attacked his use of the title "ecumenical
patriarch" (which Byzantine patriarchs had been using for
five hundred years), denied that the bishop of Constantinople ranked second in honor and dignity to the bishop
of Rome (an issue which the Byzantines thought had been
settled at the first Council of Constantinople in 381), and
cast doubt on the worthiness of Michael's motives for entering religious life and on the legitimacy of his consecration as patriarch.

(The furor over the title "ecumenical patriarch" was
typical of the misunderstandings which had arisen between

the Greek and Latin churches. To the West it seemed to imply that Constantinople was claiming jurisdiction over the entire church; and Gregory the Great, who saw it as a denial of the primacy of Rome, had written a sharp note comparing Patriarch John IV to Anti-Christ for having used it. Actually the title simply reflected the fact that the Byzantines spoke of their empire in the same quasi-mystical way in which they thought of it. They called it *oekumene,* "the universe," and so it was only natural for them to refer to the bishop of the imperial capital as the imperial, or "ecumenical," patriarch—as the patriarch of Constantinople is known to this day.)

Cerularius, astounded by this deliberate affront, refused to meet with the delegation again, declaring that he could not believe that Leo IX had authorized the sending of such a letter. Humbert, nothing daunted, went on to publish a venemous diatribe against Greek liturgical practices and to vehemently attack the Byzantine rejection of *filioque* in a public debate. Finally Humbert, who was supposed to be negotiating a reconciliation, seems to have completely lost control of himself.

In one of the most bombastic ecclesiastical documents ever written, he excommunicated Patriarch Cerularius, Emperor Constantine, and all their followers; accused Byzantium of tolerating the buying and selling of church offices (at a time when the corruption of the Roman Church) was the scandal of Europe and less than ten years after John Gratian had openly purchased the papacy itself from Benedict IX); and made the incredible statement that the Byzantines were guilty of heresy for having taken *filioque* out of the Nicene Creed—when in fact it was the West which had added it.

Then, determined to deliver this inflammatory.message in the most offensive manner possible, Humbert marched into the most sacred place in the Byzantine world, the Hagia Sophia cathedral, and, just as services were about to begin, he dropped the document on the high altar and marched back out.

But the excommunications, which Humbert had issued on his own initiative, were of doubtful validity, since Pope Leo, who was totally unaware of what his representative was doing, was already dead when they were pronounced. And the inevitable retaliatory synod held in Constantinople contented itself with excommunicating Humbert and his companions, making no mention of Leo or of anyone else in Rome. Thus there was nothing to prevent a subsequent pope from repudiating Humbert's unauthorized and irresponsible actions and resuming the effort to reunite Christendom—nothing except the fact that several of Leo's successors were Humbert's close personal friends, and that Humbert's account of these events made it appear as though he had merely responded to intolerable Byzantine provocations.

And so Humbert's excommunications remained in force —until finally they were voided by Pope Paul VI in 1965.

The year 1054 is a landmark for church historians, just as 476 is for those who write secular history. And yet the events which occurred in both years were not recognized as turning points until long afterward. Just as no one in 476 realized that the Roman Empire had "fallen," so no one could have foreseen that the breach which was opened between the Eastern and Western churches in 1054, unlike all the separations which had preceded it, would never be healed.

Neither church had excommunicated the other, and neither ever would. But as more and more bishops were consecrated by patriarchs who were not in communion with Rome, eventually the entire Eastern episcopate was regarded by the West as having fallen into schism. Rome and Constantinople now had more separating than uniting them. Yet all need not have been lost, for the event which would make reconciliation truly impossible would not occur for another hundred and fifty years.

Chapter 8
MONASTICISM AND THE FEUDAL CHURCH

THE successors of Clovis faced enormous problems in trying to govern and defend a kingdom, let alone an empire, without a trained bureaucracy, without a workable mechanism for assessing and collecting taxes, without a standing army, and without a well-maintained communications network. These conditions made effective centralized administration of any large area physically impossible—and so a system of decentralized administration evolved.

Adapting ancient tribal customs to totally new circumstances, Frankish rulers granted their nobility conditional possession of huge tracts of land. The king retained actual ownership. So long as the nobles remained loyal, however, and so long as they provided the king with a designated number of soldiers and performed various other services when the need arose, they could do with the land and its inhabitants more or less whatever they wished.

But the nobles also found it difficult to administer large holdings. In addition, since smaller farms could be cultivated much more efficiently than great estates, it was far less costly for them to provide their fighting men with enough land to support themselves than it was to support them directly. Thus the original grant, or fief, was divided into smaller grants. As this process of division and subdivision was repeated, a hierarchy of conditional land tenure was established from the king down through the descending orders of nobility. At the bottom of this chain was the individual armored knight, who might control and be supported by a few square miles of land and a village of several hundred people.

This system, feudalism, kept the costs of running the Frankish kingdom so low that Charlemagne, like his predecessors, was able to meet them with the income from his own estates. And it provided at least a modicum of law and order in areas far removed from the king's personal control.

In one way or another, similar feudal hierarchies were established throughout Europe. It was feudalism which determined the political, social, and economic conditions under which the church would exist from the middle of the ninth century until almost the eve of the Reformation. And it was conflicts arising from the feudal system which brought about some of the most dramatic crises in the church's history.

Feudalism was essentially a network of man-to-man agreements between specific individuals. This meant that each agreement remained in force only during the lifetime of the parties who had contracted it. If, for example, a king or lord were to grant a fief to one of his subordinates, or vassals, then upon the death of that vassal the fief would revert back to the king or lord, who then could bestow it upon anyone he wished—collecting a sizable fee, or "relief," from the recipient—or else retain it himself. The fact that fiefs were continually coming up for renewal, as it were, gave tremendous power to those who were free to decide whom to grant them to.

This power became even more important after Charlemagne's kingdom, fragmented by the Frankish rulers' practice of dividing their lands among all of their sons and by the invasions of the Vikings, the Magyars, and the Saracens, disintegrated into a loose confederation of duchies. Now a king was little more than one lord among others, not necessarily richer or stronger than his own vassals. Under these conditions, kings who lost control of their land—kings with no fiefs to grant, and thus with few means of rewarding their friends and punishing their enemies—were quite likely to lose control of their kingdoms as well.

And when powerful nobles began to bequeath fiefs to

their sons, and to compel royal recognition of these bequests, this is precisely what happened. The nature of the
feudal bond itself remained unchanged, since each new
heir swore personal allegiance to his king and received his
fief from the king's hands. The difference was that,
although the king still granted these fiefs, he had lost the
power to decide who would receive them.

This change involved far more than the mere possession
of land. With trade routes blocked, the countryside in-
fested with bandits, and population centers isolated from
one another, the economy of Europe had practically
ground to a halt. Commerce and industry stagnated, and
land became virtually the only means of producing wealth.
As noble families acquired permanent possession of more
and more land, they also gained control of a large portion
of their country's productive power. This made them enormously wealthy. In time they threatened to grow rich and
powerful enough to challenge the crown itself.

Kings, on the other hand, began to realize that the
easiest way for them to enjoy the political and economic
benefits of decentralized administration and still retain
control of their fiefs was to grant those fiefs to men who
would have no sons. That meant giving them to the
church, particularly to bishops. This solution had a number
of advantages.

It was easier in some respects for bishops to be loyal
vassals than it was for laymen, since bishops (at least in
theory) had no interest in establishing their own family
dynasties. They usually had no motive for trying to overthrow the king, and no means at their disposal for doing it
if they had wanted to.

When one bishop died, his fiefs, in the absence of heirs,
would revert back to the king, who could then bestow them
again—and receive payment of "reliefs" from the new
bishop. While a see was vacant, revenues from its fiefs were

paid, according to feudal custom, directly to the king. And when it was occupied, they would be used for charitable purposes—or, at the very worst, to line a greedy bishop's pocket—and not to enrich the king's potential enemies.

At the same time, those who received episcopal fiefs assumed the same obligations as the holders of any other fief, including, in most cases, the duty of providing the king with soldiers in the event of war. And the king still could use these fiefs to reward his political allies—by arranging, let us say, to have younger sons of his loyal vassals elected to various bishoprics. But if the granting of episcopal fiefs was advantageous to kings, it led to a number of serious problems for the church.

Those who were appointed to bishoprics in payment of a political debt, for example, tended to be young noblemen far more interested in warfare, hunting, and other pleasures of the flesh than in their pastoral duties. (In fact, since many of these bishops, like other feudal lords, led their own troops in battle, kings often preferred that they be capable warriors.) This not only resulted in scandal, but, far more importantly, it led to gross neglect of such details of diocesan administration as the training and supervision of priests and the promotion of religious instruction.

Compounding these problems was the fact that prearranged appointments often had to be made when a suitable bishopric fell vacant, rather than when the designated successor was ready to assume the office. This on occasion led to the consecration as bishops of boys as young as twelve. Even worse, perhaps, was the practice of deliberately keeping vacant sees from being filled, sometimes for years, so that kings could continue to collect the revenues of their fiefs. This deprived the diocese of any spiritual leadership at all.

The customary payment of "relief," when applied to

episcopal fiefs, appeared tantamount to simony and sometimes led directly to it. While it may have been technically
true that it was merely the fief and not the bishopric itself
for which payment was being made, so long as the bishopric and the fief were inseparable it was difficult to distinguish payment for one from payment for the other. And
many bishops attempted to recover the cost of taking
possession of their fiefs by charging the priests under their
jurisdiction for various ecclesiastical appointments, thus
helping to spread the practice of simony down to the local
parish level.

Another inducement to simony was the fact that bishops
personally received the entire revenues from their fiefs and
then disposed of them as they saw fit, which made many
bishoprics extremely lucrative offices. Although a long-
standing church policy urged bishops to spend one quarter
of their revenues on their clergy, one quarter on church
property, one quarter on the poor, and only the remaining
quarter on themselves, not all bishops followed these
guidelines. And even if they did, one quarter of the revenues of a large see was a prize worth spending a great deal
to obtain.

Since the feudal system was by its very nature decentralized, feudalization of bishoprics tended to greatly
weaken Rome's control over the church. Many bishops
who, as feudal lords, had pledged their fealty to a king,
promising to aid his friends and oppose his foes, tended to
feel far more loyalty to the king than to the pope. Indeed,
men who felt differently had a hard time becoming bishops
in the first place, for no king could afford to allow men
who might oppose him to become great secular lords.

The whole complex tangle of problems caused by the
establishment of episcopal fiefs was summed up by the investiture of bishops—the act of giving them physical symbols of their fiefs—by secular authorities. This was no

more than the application to episcopal fiefs of a long established feudal custom. After a vassal pledged homage to his lord, he received some token of the fief which he was being granted—a clump of sod, perhaps, or a glove, or a sword. It was this physical act which legally transferred the fief from the lord to the vassal. A crosier and a ring frequently were used to represent ecclesiastical fiefs.

No one questioned the propriety of a secular lord's granting fiefs to a bishop. Under feudal law, in fact, there was no other way for the bishop to take possession of them. The problem arose, once again, from the fact that the bishop as spiritual leader and the bishop as feudal landholder became inseparable. Thus it was possible to construe the act of granting a bishop his fiefs as being equivalent to the conferring of episcopal rank upon him. And in some cases kings were able to exercise an effective veto over the appointment of bishops simply by refusing to bestow the appropriate fiefs on an appointee of whom they disapproved.

In time, the practice of "lay investiture," as it was called—the investiture of bishops by civil rulers—became symbolic of the general problem of secular control of the church. As such, it was bitterly attacked by ecclesiastical reformers. But episcopal fiefs represented only one form of ecclesiastical property.

Almost from the moment of its inception the church began receiving donations, at first to support charitable works and later to finance its own operating costs as well. Under the Christian emperors it was subsidized directly from the state treasury. As a result the church acquired enormous wealth, and the great majority of this wealth was in land.

One reason for this was the fact that land, as a highly productive resource, was frequently used to establish endowments. One who wished to found a church, for example, ordinarily provided it with land whose income was sufficient to cover the church's expenses. Land was received through bequests, and as gifts from emperors and kings. Since the church's holdings were not taxed, wealthy families frequently provided for their children by setting up the equivalent of tax-exempt foundations. They transferred all or part of their land to ecclesiastical institutions to be run by their descendants. And what the church acquired, it seldom gave back. Over the centuries, the combination of tax-exempt status and management by skillful administrators enabled these holdings to produce enough revenue to finance the purchase of still more land.

At the start of the early Middle Ages, the church was by far the largest landholder in every European country. Even in the days of Charles Martel, a hundred years before the coronation of Charlemagne, one-third of all the cultivated land in the Frankish kingdom—and thus something approaching that percentage of what we would call its gross national product—was under some form of church control. It was largely because of its possession of and dependence upon prodigious amounts of land, most of it held in fief from some feudal lord, that the church fell under the control of secular rulers, from its highest levels down to its very roots.

Feudalism even corrupted the monastic movement, the most enlightened and progressive institution in Christendom. For it was monks, more than anyone else, who preserved and promoted what was best not only in the Western church but in all of Europe. They completely dominated Christian intellectual life from the ninth through the twelfth centuries and provided most of the outstanding church leaders of the early Middle Ages. They also played a major role in converting and civilizing the northern barbarians; and, by establishing stable communities in areas where stabilizing influences were desperately needed, they helped to lay the foundations of medieval society. And yet none of these activities was part of, or even compatible with, the original monastic ideal.

Anthony of Egypt, who lived from the middle of the third century to the middle of the fourth, was the first Christian who is known to have withdrawn from society to lead a solitary ascetic life. For about a dozen years he lived in a graveyard outside his village; later he moved into the desert and made his home in an abandoned fortress. There he prayed and fasted, and acquired a reputation for holiness and miracle-working. And when Athanasius, the militantly anti-Arian bishop of Alexandria, wrote a somewhat imaginative but immensely popular account of his life, Anthony's example inspired literally thousands of imitators.

Part of the reason for this overwhelming response was the fact that Athanasius's book appeared around the year 357, or about twenty years after the death of Constantine. This was precisely the time when, due to the conversion of enormous numbers of pagans, Christianity was being transformed from a minority cult, only a generation or two removed from the persecutions of Diocletian, into the majority religion of the empire. Expansion of this speed and magnitude, and the elimination of persecution, inevitably led to a general lessening of religious fervor and the removal of one of Christianity's most compelling attractions—the opportunity for making heroic sacrifice. For those who sought to keep alive the ideals of a more demanding age, the asceticism of the desert offered a way to practice the Christian vocation in its most uncompromising form.

But not everyone who became an anchorite (from a Greek verb meaning "to withdraw") had purely spiritual motives. Bankrupts, malcontents, escaped slaves, criminals, and people who simply wished to drop out of organized society all joined the pious and the devout in their exodus to the wilderness. Most were illiterate and many knew little or nothing about theology—among anchorites, in fact, ignorance frequently was equated with virtue. About the only thing they all had in common was the fact that they did not support themselves.

And because they depended on alms to survive, many of them deliberately cultivated a reputation for bizarre behavior. Some became famous for the rigor of their fasts, or for scourging themselves, or for not washing or changing their clothes; some lived in tiny iron cages or in trees; some set records for staying awake or not moving. The most famous of all anchorites, Simon Stylites, lived thirty-seven years on a platform two yards square atop a sixty-foot column.

But while such excesses may have been admired, they were not officially encouraged—especially not by the episcopate. Bishops such as Basil of Caesarea vehemently attacked the anchorite movement and promoted in its place cenobitic ("common-life") monasticism, under which monks lived together under strict discipline, performed manual labor, and pledged obedience to a superior.

Cenobitism not only eliminated many of the eccentricities indulged in by the anchorites, it also brought those who practiced it much more firmly under episcopal control. In many Eastern dioceses, in fact, monks became virtually the bishop's private army, used first to intimidate pagans and Jews and later to silence theological enemies. Athanasius and Cyril of Alexandria, among others, used monks to spread religious slogans and to whip up mass hysteria against anyone who differed with their particular interpretation of orthodoxy; and some bishops brought them to church councils to terrorize their opponents. Monks were prominent among the rabble who assaulted minority bishops at the *Latrocinium,* and they played major roles in the iconoclasm and Monophysite controversies. At the same time cenobitism, with its insistence on productive manual labor, gave monks something which the anchorites, whatever may have been their claims to holiness, never had achieved: a way of life which was socially useful.

Athanasius was exiled five times from Alexandria because of his opposition to Arianism, and during his journeys to Rome, northern Italy, and Gaul he apparently introduced the monastic concept to Europe. Ambrose, Augustine, Martin of Tours, and John Cassian all put various forms of that concept into practice. But it was Benedict of Nursia, about the middle of the sixth century, who succeeded in translating the Eastern ideal of withdrawal from the world and devotion to prayer and penance into a type of cenobitic monasticism which was to become almost universal in the Western church.

No one but a saint or a lunatic could live alone forty or fifty years in the Egyptian desert. But Benedict's program, or Rule, did not demand heroic virtue. It proposed a way of life which was reasonable and practical for sixth-century Europeans, and it included nothing beyond the capacity of the average person. The Rule specified, for example, that each monk be given adequate clothing and sufficient food, including two warm meals and a pint of wine per day. Extreme fasting and penances were forbidden. This contrasted sharply with the practices of some monasteries of the day, such as those in Ireland, where dry bread was considered proper nourishment and physical penances and deprivations were almost brutally severe.

The monk's waking hours were to be devoted in roughly equal measure to community prayer, spiritual reading, and work—the phrase *Ora et Labora,* Pray and Work, succinctly expressed the Benedictine way of life. Fortunately for Western civilization, "work" was later interpreted to include the copying of manuscripts, thus allowing Benedictines to play an enormously important role in the preservation of ancient literature and culture.

Work, however, was to be performed not for its own sake but simply as a means of sharing in the total life of the community. Benedictine monasticism, like its Eastern predecessors, was to have no goal outside itself. The sole purpose of becoming a monk was to live like a monk, seeking an ever-closer union with God through an ordered life centered around meditation and prayer.

Benedict did not found a religious order: he simply created a Rule for the guidance of his own monastic community. His emphasis on moderation and on the importance of a well-organized daily routine, however, induced many other monasteries throughout Europe to adopt this Rule as their own. Because it was transmitted in this somewhat haphazard fashion, the Benedictine ideal was incarnated not in a large, centralized organization but in independent self-supporting and self-governing communities with little or no outside supervision. In time this would prove to be a near-fatal weakness.

Benedictine monks not only took the lead in converting northern Europe (Boniface and the other British missionaries who worked among the pagan Germanic tribes all were Benedictines); in a sense they systematically colonized it, penetrating almost every facet of early medieval life.

Since they represented an extremely large percentage of the literate population of every northern country, it was usually monks who wrote down and helped to codify tribal laws (which in turn meant that they often were called upon later to interpret them), handled royal correspondence, kept legal and financial records, and undertook diplomatic missions.

Many monastic communities made a practice of accepting young children whose parents wished to dedicate them to the religious life. And since monks were obliged to read the Bible and other spiritual works, these children had to be taught to read. Those who spoke only a vernacular language also had to be taught Latin. This lead to the creation of monastic schools, whose primary textbook was the Bible but where masterpieces of classical Roman literature also were used to teach the principles of Latin grammar and composition.

It was these schools which, despite their somewhat primitive beginnings, provided the foundation for the educational revival masterminded by Alcuin (himself a Benedictine monk) during the reign of Charlemagne. For hundreds of years, virtually every school in Europe was operated by monks.

But the primary business for all Benedictine monasteries was farming. At a time when agriculture in general was still suffering from the effects of centuries of neglect, Benedictines greatly increased the amount of land in productive use and farmed it with extraordinary efficiency, both because they utilized superior techniques and because they possessed a large, disciplined, and highly motivated labor force.

Benedictine monks cleared forests, drained swamps, and dug irrigation ditches; they worked systematically, persistently, and far more effectively than the slave labor with which many of the secular landholders still were trying to farm their estates. Certainly they were healthier and better fed than most of the peasants with whom they were in a sense competing. Monks also had few unproductive mouths to feed and were able to concentrate all their efforts on working their own land—unlike the peasants, who were obliged to spend up to a third of their time cultivating the fields of their feudal lord.

All of these factors made monastic agriculture a spectacularly profitable enterprise. And when the Cistercians, sometime in the twelfth century, invented the concept of lay brothers—who devoted nearly all their time to work, thus at least doubling the efficiency of the labor force— monasteries were able to farm on a truly awesome scale. None of this, obviously, could have been accomplished by anchorites.

And yet the Benedictine movement eventually became a victim of its own success. There was a basic conflict between the Benedictines' avowed spiritual ideals and many of the activities in which they were engaged; and the larger and more powerful their monasteries grew, the more troublesome this conflict became. As Benedictines came more and more into demand as government functionaries, missionaries, and teachers, for example, the more difficult it became to resist the temptation to pursue these activities for their own sake and to assign monks to work at them full-time. This led to an abandonment of the basic concept of withdrawal from the world; it was a betrayal of the monk's contemplative vocation.

At the same time, the very factors which made Benedictine monasteries ideally suited to the social and economic conditions of the early Middle Ages—their decentralization, adaptability to local circumstances, and talent for the efficient cultivation of land—left them particularly vulnerable to the worst abuses of the feudal system. For Benedictine abbots, as the managers of great estates, became feudal lords holding their lands as fiefs, a system which was subject to the same corruptive influences as was the system of episcopal fiefs. And the immense revenues produced by Benedictine estates, especially those of the larger monasteries, led to monastic fiefs being bought and sold, or exchanged for political favors, just as episcopal fiefs were.

Some monastic offices were sold to people who held them "in commendation," collecting the revenues without ever setting foot in the monastery. Even the Vatican made money by selling such offices. Young noblemen and children were appointed abbots, just as they were appointed bishops, with predictable effects on monastic discipline.

By the tenth century the church had fallen into what was probably the most widespread and profound corruption of its entire history. At the local level, many parishes were served by "proprietary churches," controlled by the persons who had founded them or by their descendants, who also appointed the priests and appropriated whatever share they wished of the revenues. Since this tended to impoverish the local clergy, it was another inducement to the practice of simony. Sometimes whole dioceses were run on this basis, with the bishops being appointed by and becoming the vassals of various noblemen. Bishops, monasteries, and even the papacy owned proprietary churches—an example of the church's feudalizing itself.

Practically the entire church, in fact, was being run for the profit of some secular ruler or other. And the only way to end the corruption, immorality, and venality brought about by ecclesiastical involvement with the feudal system was to remove the church, and particularly the bishoprics, from secular control.

Chapter 9
FROM CLUNY TO CANOSSA:
THE ELEVENTH CENTURY REFORM

BUILT into Benedict's rule were safeguards against every threat to monastic life which could be foreseen in the sixth century, and an abbot elected for life by the monks themselves was given complete discretion to handle any situation which the Rule did not cover. Since each community was independent and self-governing, the success of the entire Benedictine movement was totally dependent on these abbots' integrity.

This system proved remarkably effective for hundreds of years—so long as monks continued to elect capable abbots. As we have seen, however, the rise of feudalism and the steady increase of monastic wealth led secular rulers to appoint worldly and venal men as abbots, thus corrupting monasteries from the top down. This was a possibility which Benedict had not anticipated, and his Rule made no provision for it.

Thus there was little to prevent the abuses associated with feudalism from undermining the discipline of individual Benedictine communities, where abbots held almost dictatorial power inside monasteries and no mechanism existed for imposing reform from the outside. And the Benedictine movement, which had provided the chief impetus for church reform in the eighth century, eventually succumbed to the very forces which it once had taken the lead in opposing. And yet the Benedictine way of life had not lost its inner vitality. Someone merely had to remove the obstacles which were keeping it from functioning as its founder had intended.

There was no mystery about what this would require: individual monasteries needed some kind of outside supervision, and they had to be free from the control of secular rulers. But in an age when monasteries depended on landed endowments and almost all land was held in fief, no monastic community could create those conditions by itself. Some large landholder had to give a monastery land with no feudal strings attached. The papacy easily could have done this; many bishops could have as well. But the first step in what eventually became a thoroughgoing reform of the entire Western church was taken by a layman, Duke William of Aquitaine.

Just after the start of the tenth century, William donated land for the construction and support of a new monastery near Cluny, about sixty miles north of Lyons. The terms of this grant were unprecedented. Cluny was to be independent, not only of the duke himself, but of all temporal and spiritual authority except that of the pope. Its elections and other internal affairs were to be completely free from secular interference, and it was to adhere strictly to the original Benedictine Rule. Private property was abolished, silence imposed, and the eating of meat forbidden. Prayer, not teaching or missionary activity, was to be the primary occupation of all its monks.

Cluny was not founded as a center of reform, but it quickly became one. Like the anchorite movement six hundred years before, the Cluniac way of life had enormous appeal for those desiring to practice Christian virtues in the purest manner possible. Other monasteries began adopting Cluniac practices, and Cluny itself founded new communities. All of them shared Cluny's total freedom from secular and episcopal control.

But the Cluniac reform spread in a highly structured manner. Every new community and every monastery which accepted the reform vowed absolute obedience to the abbot of Cluny, who appointed all monastic superiors.

In this way the Cluniac monks established what was, in effect, the first religious order. This effectively counterbalanced the tendency of the feudal system to divide the church into a multitude of individual monasteries and bishoprics which could easily be brought under the influence of local rulers. (Eastern monasticism, which did not undergo this centralizing process, never developed religious orders.)

The Cluniac movement spread with amazing speed. Within two hundred years, well over a thousand communities had adopted its reforms. This phenomenon is difficult for even the most cynical commentator to explain in terms of material self-interest, since it required monks to voluntarily place themselves under stricter discipline and noblemen to voluntarily relinquish control of sizable amounts of valuable land. It seems, rather, to have been part of a genuine spiritual reawakening—one of several occasions on which, although the church appeared to be hopelessly corrupted, a reservoir of untapped spiritual dynamism was swelling just below the surface, waiting for some opportunity to express itself.

But no reform could achieve real success unless it reached the church's highest levels. For the forces which had subjected bishoprics throughout the rest of Christian Europe to secular control and exploitation had not spared the See of Rome. The papacy, having become the private possession of a few noble families, had entered the period of its most profound degradation.

This period can be considered to have begun in 904 when Cardinal Sergius, aided by the Marquis of Spoleto, Alberic I, seized the papal throne and had his predecessor strangled. He then took as his mistress an exceedingly ambitious teenage girl named Marozia, daughter of the Roman nobleman Theophylactus. According to the generally reliable *Liber Pontificalis,* Sergius fathered the child whom she later made pope.

Marozia then married Alberic, had another son, and settled down to the business of running the papacy. When Pope John X entered into an alliance with Hugh of Provence, King of the Lombards, Marozia had him deposed and murdered. (John was not a particularly unworthy pontiff by the standards of the day, although one of his more memorable actions had been to approve the consecration of a five-year-old boy as archbishop of Rheims.)

Marozia handpicked the next two popes. Then, in 931, she had her older son, who was about twenty years of age, elected as Pope John XI. Alberic, meanwhile, had been succeeded by his and Marozia's son, while Marozia herself had married Hugh of Provence, her third husband.

She now had achieved a position unique in history. One of her sons was pope; her husband, Hugh, was destined to become emperor (this was not difficult to arrange, since it was the pope who bestowed the imperial crown); and her other son, Alberic II, was in line to become emperor after Hugh. Marozia was well on her way to controlling both the papal and the imperial thrones, which would have made her one of the most powerful women who ever lived. Some historians, in fact, believe that it may have been Marozia's total domination of the papal court which gave rise to the medieval legend of "Popess Joan."

But Alberic was unwilling to wait. In 932 he seized control of Rome, expelled Hugh of Provence from the city, and imprisoned his mother in the dungeons of the Castel Sant'Angelo until her death. His half-brother, the pope, was placed under house arrest and died five years later.

Alberic held total power in Rome for the next twenty years. Somewhat surprisingly, perhaps, he proved a zealous promoter of church reform, particularly the Cluniac reform; but he kept the papacy itself under his complete control. He appointed the next five popes, all of whom were capable spiritual leaders—except the last one, his son (and Marozia's grandson), who is generally conceded to have been one of the worst men ever to occupy the pontifical throne.

John XII became pope when he was about eighteen years old, and his sins were those which might be expected of any arrogant, pleasure-loving adolescent suddenly given virtually unlimited power and money, plus complete freedom to indulge his every whim. If contemporary chroniclers can be believed, he met his end at the hands of an enraged husband who found him in bed with his wife. And yet John probably was no worse than many other rich young men whose families had obtained bishoprics for them. He may have been an exceptionally bad pope, but his case was really symptomatic of the evils afflicting the entire church. And after his death the successors of Charlemagne began to take the responsibility for reforming the papacy into their own hands.

The last east Frankish descendant of Charlemagne, Louis the Child, was succeeded by two German dukes and then in 936 by Otto I, Otto the Great, who laid the foundation for what came to be known as the Holy Roman Empire of the German nation. Otto I supervised the election of three popes (one of whom, John XIII, was a nephew of Marozia), and his son chose two more. All of them were vastly superior to the puppets selected by Marozia. But the Roman mob resented foreign interference in the selection of its bishop, and the nobility had come to look on papal elections almost as family affairs. As a result, four of these five popes were exiled or imprisoned by the mob, two were murdered, and at least three had to contend with antipopes supported by the nobility.

The next emperor, Otto III, was three years old when his father died. This allowed the nobility—particularly the Crescentii family, a branch of the House of Theophylactus—to regain control of Rome. In 984 the Crescentii overthrew John XIV, starved him to death, and installed antipope Boniface VII in his place. When Boniface died they enthroned John XV, whom they kept under virtual house arrest.

In 1012 the Crescentii were supplanted by the Tusculani, another branch of the House of Theophylactus. Benedict VIII, one of its members, was succeeded on the papal throne by his brother, a layman, who became John XIX. And John was succeeded by his thoroughly degenerate nephew, Benedict IX, who may have been the worst pope of all time, He is best remembered as the man who not only bought the papacy but sold it as well.

Benedict reigned only four years before the Romans, disgusted by his cruelty and depravity, defied his powerful relatives and drove him from the city. When he forced his way back, they expelled him again and elected an antipope, Sylvester III. The Tusculani restored their kinsman to the papal throne once more, but Benedict no longer wanted to be pope. In 1045 he abdicated in favor of his godfather, John Gratian, who became Pope Gregory VI. In return, Gratian promised Benedict a large sum of money—according to some accounts, the entire papal revenue from the English church for the rest of his life.

That might have been considered a small price to pay for Benedict's removal. But Benedict, even after being paid, did not have the good grace to leave. Rome now had three men claiming to be pope: Benedict, Gregory, and Sylvester III. The resulting paralysis of ecclesiastical administration, which would have been intolerable under any circumstances, occurred at a time when wise and firm leadership was desperately needed—precisely during the period when the dispute between the Eastern and Western churches was approaching its tragic climax.

Finally a delegation of Roman citizens asked the new German emperor, Henry III, to intervene. Henry had Gregory, Sylvester, and Benedict all deposed. Then he enthroned two German bishops, both of whom died soon after their installation (Benedict was suspected of murdering at least one of them). Finally Henry appointed his cousin, Bruno, whose consecration in 1049 as Leo IX can be considered the true beginning of what is usually referred to as the Gregorian reform.

Previous popes had loudly deplored such abuses as simony and clerical concubinage. Leo, who already had reformed several monasteries in his native Lorraine, attacked these practices like a man possessed. He spent five and a half years of his six-year pontificate traveling through Europe, holding synods and personally admonishing bishops and abbots. This not only provided a concrete example of how pastoral responsiblity should be exercised; it also demonstrated in dramatic fashion that the papacy, having emerged from a century and a half of isolation and political impotence, was ready to reassert its claims of jurisdiction over the entire church.

After Leo's death Emperor Henry appointed Victor II, who continued Leo's policies and enlarged their scope. But then Henry died, leaving as his heir a six-year-old child and temporarily depriving the reform movement of imperial support. The next pope, Stephen X, reigned only six months; and after his death the Tusculani, who were opposed to the whole idea of reform, attempted to place one of their sympathizers on the papal throne. If they had succeeded, everything Henry III and Leo IX had accomplished might have been lost.

At this crucial moment, a monk named Hildebrand took charge. With the support of Stephen X's brother, the Duke of Tuscany, he organized a meeting in Siena at which the cardinals who supported reform chose a Florentine bishop as Pope Nicholas II. Backed by the duke's military power Nicholas entered Rome and easily routed the Tusculani and their antipope. In that same year, 1059, Pope Nicholas issued an historic decree regulating the conduct of papal elections.

Events of the previous century had made it clear that when scoundrels became popes, they generally continued to behave like scoundrels. This meant that there could be no lasting reform of the papacy, and thus of the church as a whole, unless the papal throne were occupied by men of the very highest caliber. And the Cluniac movement had demonstrated, or so it seemed at the time, that the best way to obtain capable and dedicated leaders was to remove their selection from the hands both of secular rulers and of the lower clergy and entrust it to higher church authorities. It seemed reasonable to assume that the same logic should apply in the case of papal elections.

Nicholas therefore ordered that future popes should be elected exclusively by the college of cardinals, as they have been from his day to our own. This eliminated both the Roman nobility and the lower clergy from the election process. The emperor's traditional right to approve the pope-designate before his consecration was confirmed in theory, although it was subsequently ignored in practice.

It should be noted that this decree, the papacy's declaration of independence from secular control and a giant step toward eliminating the worst abuses to which it had fallen victim, was promulgated only fifteen years after the nefarious transaction between Benedict IX and John Gratian— an indication of how quickly the papacy was able to rehabilitate itself once Henry III freed it from the pernicious influence of the Roman nobility. Nicholas was succeeded by Alexander II, and then by Hildebrand.

"Hildebrand" can be literally translated as "Sword of Battle," and it was a name Gregory VII lived up to. He was convinced that reform should be promoted by applying to the church as a whole the same formula which had proved so successful for Cluny—absolute subordination to a central authority and complete freedom from secular influences—and he allowed nothing to interfere with his single-minded pursuit of that goal.

Even in Gregory's day, however, the weaknesses of Cluny's rigidly monolithic organization were becoming apparent. Less than fifteen years after his death the Cistercian order abandoned it completely in favor of a much more collegial system in which the internal affairs of each monastery were autonomous, while supreme power was vested in an annual assembly of all abbots. Had Gregory and his successors chosen to follow a Cisterican rather than a Cluniac model, the Roman church might have developed a much less authoritarian mentality.

As part of his campaign to bring the church more directly under papal control, Gregory required newly elected bishops to take an oath of obedience to Rome. He also greatly enhanced the status and responsibilities of papal legates, whom he dispatched throughout the Western church to ensure that his orders were carried out and to whom he gave the power to override decisions of bishops and to pronounce excommunications in the pope's name.

But true reform at the local level was impossible as long as corrupt and incompetent men were being appointed as bishops. This fact led Gregory into the traumatic "lay investiture" struggle, which began as an effort to improve the quality of bishops and lower clergy but evolved into a dispute over the relation between the spiritual and secular spheres and finally degenerated into a life-or-death struggle between the papacy and the Holy Roman Empire.

In February of 1075, Gregory issued a decree prohibiting the conferring of bishoprics by laymen. While this decree focused on the physical act of investing a bishop with the symbols of his authority, Gregory also was insisting that secular rulers had no right to participate in or to influence the selection of bishops. And in doing so he was attacking the foundation of every feudal kingdom in Europe.

We have seen that feudal monarchs could not keep themselves in power unless they maintained control of a large percentage of their land. This was one of the primary reasons why they had entrusted bishops with important administrative positions and the fiefs which went with them in the first place. In the circumstances of the eleventh century, any king or emperor who would have given up the power to select his bishops not only would have lost control of many of his most powerful vassals, he also would have deprived himself of the financial and military resources he needed to govern effectively. Land held in fief by bishops, to cite but one example, had provided more than half the troops in Otto the Great's army. Agreeing to Gregory's demands would have meant the end of kingdoms and empires as sovereign political units.

This consequence did not bother Gregory, however, for Gregory did not believe in the sovereignty of kingdoms and empires. He maintained that the power and jurisdiction of a pope are literally unlimited, and that the pope could depose emperors and release subjects from the obligation to obey their sovereigns. This amounted to universal theocracy, with the pope at its head.

In the practical realm, however, Gregory generally did not let these claims interfere with his primary objective, which was reforming the episcopate. The kings of France, England, and Spain, among others, continued to appoint and invest bishops just as they had done before the decree of 1075; but since Gregory approved of their choices, he did not strenuously protest. The crisis came in Germany. When Henry III's son began making appointments which the pope considered scandalous, Gregory threatened him with excommunication and deposition unless he stopped.

From Gregory's point of view, this action was simply one of the necessary steps in his campaign to restore the church's integrity by freeing it from the domination of secular rulers. Henry IV, on the other hand, who was doing no more than his predecessors had done, saw Gregory's threat as an encroachment upon essential and long-established imperial prerogatives. Both of them were right.

It should have been possible to reach some sort of accommodation. Gregory wanted bishops of high quality; Henry wanted men of his own choice. These desires were not irreconcilable. But the impetuous Henry destroyed any hope for compromise by having his bishops declare Gregory deposed. Gregory responded by excommunicating Henry and giving notice that he was coming to Germany in person to determine whether the emperor himself should be deposed. Henry hurried southward and intercepted the pope at the mountain fortress of Canossa. There, in one of the most memorable scenes in medieval history, he knelt for three days in the snow begging forgiveness.

Canossa often is described as a victory for the pope's spiritual power over the emperor's armed might. Actually it was nothing of the sort, for Gregory's edict of excommunication was not really a spiritual weapon but an act of political subversion. This is important to remember, for it helps to explain why conflicts between popes and secular rulers in the Middle Ages were fought with such bitter intensity.

Medieval popes' only practical means of imposing their will on a defiant emperor or king was to undermine the stability of his realm by encouraging his subjects to revolt. Since Christians were forbidden to associate with excommunicates, excommunication of an emperor had the effect of invalidating his vassals' oaths of allegiance to him. It amounted to official permission by the pope for jealous nobles or disgruntled royal relatives to seize the throne for themselves. Similarly, an interdict—the prohibition of masses, weddings, funerals, and all other liturgical activity in a country or region—was designed to incite unrest among the common people.

No ruler whose subjects remained solidly loyal to him had much to fear from excommunications or interdicts. Henry, however, who had put down a rebellion by his Saxon subjects only two years earlier and whose hold on the throne was still not secure, could not yet risk the effects of a papal invitation to overthrow him. It was this, and not any concern for his soul, which brought Henry to his knees in the midwinter snow.

But Canossa also demonstrated some of the weaknesses of the pope's weapons. They unleashed forces which could easily get out of control, and their effects often worked at cross purposes to long-range papal interests. Thus it happened that even after Gregory had revoked his edict of excommunication, the nobles of Saxony, encouraged by his actions against Henry, touched off a civil war by electing a rival German king. This was not at all what Gregory had intended. He did not want anarchy in Germany; he wanted an effective but subservient emperor. He was well aware that the nobility posed a far greater threat to church reform than the emperor did, and that simony and other ecclesiastical abuses had been far more prevalent during Henry's minority than they were after he came to power.

It was not to the ultimate advantage of Gregory or of his

successors to weaken the cohesiveness of the imperial government, and yet the weapons available to them were effective only to the extent that they did precisely that.

If there was a victor at Canossa, it was the emperor. By maneuvering Gregory into a position where he was forced to rescind his excommunication, Henry gained time to rally his forces in Germany and repress the Saxon uprising; then he drove Gregory out of Rome and into exile in southern Italy, where he died. And yet Henry's days of triumph were numbered. In 1106 he was killed while trying to put down a rebellion led by his namesake son.

Gregory's insistence that bishops—who unquestionably were civil rulers as well as religious leaders—should be subject to no authority except that of the church was perfectly consistent with his view of the papacy as possessing ultimate jurisdiction over both religious and secular affairs. As a practical matter, however, bishops could hardly expect to enjoy the privilege of holding enormously powerful and lucrative fiefs without shouldering the political obligations which went with them.

This fact led Pope Paschal II in the year 1111 to propose a radical solution. The church would give up all its fiefs in return for a pledge of free episcopal elections. Emperor Henry V accepted this arrangement, provided the German bishops would ratify it. But the bishops, appalled at the prospect of losing their sources of wealth, refused to do so.

The only remaining possibility was to admit that the episcopal office had both civil and religious aspects, and that the civil aspects fell under imperial jurisdiction. This was accomplished by the Concordat of Worms (1122), which stipulated that bishops were to receive the symbols of their religious authority from church officials and those of their temporal authority from the emperor—thus, in effect, repudiating Gregory's claim that the pope had sovereignty over both realms. In addition, episcopal elections were to be held in the emperor's presence, which in practice was tantamount to acknowledging his right to control the elections; and newly elected bishops were to swear allegiance to him.

This compromise settled the specific question of who should invest bishops. But the underlying conflict over the relation between the empire and the papacy, far from being resolved, was about to enter a new and much more vicious phase.

Gregory VII was not the first pope to claim ultimate jurisdiction over both religious and secular affairs—Leo I and Gregory I, in particular, had made similar claims—but it was he who began to turn the theory into fact. Gregory did not merely assert his right to sit in judgment over emperors and kings. He also exercised that right in the face of determined opposition, and in the process he established the battle lines across which popes and emperors would fight each other throughout the tumultuous twelfth and thirteenth centuries.

Christian emperors from Constantine to Henry III had felt no compunction about regulating church affairs, because they believed that the sacred and the secular were not two separate realities but simply two aspects of a single Christian society whose governance was their responsibility. This principle, in fact—the idea that there is no fundamental distinction between what we would call "church" and "state"—had been the foundation of European political theory for nearly eight hundred years. Thus the German emperors, as God's anointed representatives, were considered religious officials and had the right to wear clerical vestments, including a bishop's miter and crozier.

Gregory VII and his successors totally endorsed the concept of a unified Christian society in which there is no ulti-

mate separation between religious and civil authority.
They merely argued that, since society as a whole is
directed toward a supernatural destiny, it should be popes
and not emperors who rule over it. At the same time, however, Gregory also set in motion forces which helped to ensure that his dream of universal papal hegemony would
never be realized.

As part of his campaign against lay investiture, and as
a means of reducing secular interference in church affairs,
Gregory insisted that there is a radical distinction between
clergy and laity. This position was supported by some
highly imaginative arguments from scripture—such as the
Old Testament prohibition against yoking an ox and an
ass together, as well as the fact that Christ had distinguished between the "lambs" and the "sheep" which he
had entrusted to his apostles' care—as well as by an enormous mass of quotations from ancient documents and a
multitude of new ecclesiastical regulations. Every effort
was made to establish the principle that priests constitute a
distinct class, separate from and in some sense superior to
the laity, and thus that lay hands are unfit to bestow
clerical office.

But insisting that the ecclesiastical and the secular realms
are totally separate obviously was inconsistent with claiming papal jurisdiction over them both. As the church and
civil governments were more and more clearly distinguished from each other, they came to be seen as standing
in fundamental and irreconcilable opposition—as, indeed,
Christians always had considered them to be until the time
of Constantine. Already in the eleventh century the
medieval concept of a total Christian society was being
undermined.

Emphasizing the distinction between laity and clergy
also had the effect of fostering a distinction between the
laity and the church. This was reinforced by Rome's

refusal to allow its liturgy to be translated into the vernacular, despite the fact that Latin had not been the everyday language of common people since at least the time of
Charlemagne. Our word "patter," meaning a rapid, incomprehensible jargon, is derived from a slurred pronun-
ciation of "Pater Noster," the opening words of the
Lord's Prayer in Latin—a reminder of how meaningless
prayers and religious ceremonies eventually became to
many of the laity.

Yet another factor separating lay people from the life of
the church was the almost total absence of secular education in the West from the fall of Rome until well after the
rise of the medieval universities. This did not mean that all
laymen were illiterate (although the vast majority certainly
were), but it did mean that only clerics pursued higher
studies. As a result, there were virtually no lay theologians
in the West, and few lay philosophers, for perhaps a thousand years. In the East, on the other hand, where Greek remained the language of the people as well as of the church
and where secular education continued to thrive, the laity
were never excluded from Christian intellectual life.

As time went on, participation in ecclesiastical affairs
became the almost exclusive province of the clergy, just as
participation in the liturgy did, while the institutional
church became increasingly absorbed with clerical concerns and correspondingly less involved with the needs of
lay men and women. This process of estrangement may
have been the single most important reason why people in
centuries to come would seek satisfaction for their spiritual
needs outside the established church.

Another effect of the Gregorian reform program was to
widen the gulf between bishops and the lower clergy by
eliminating the last vestiges of participation by priests in
ecclesiastical government.

Gregory had insisted that secular rulers respect the ancient custom by which priests chose their own bishops in free elections. He and his successors, however, reserved to themselves the right to settle disputed elections. And eventually Rome began to circumvent the election process entirely and simply appoint bishops. This made the hierarchy, in effect, a self-perpetuating body, thus separating it even more from the lower clergy and laity.

At the same time, as more and more doctrinal, disciplinary, and liturgical decisions came to be made by the papacy, bishops, who once had been unchallenged leaders of quasi-independent local churches, slowly were turned into administrative functionaries whose primary responsibility was to carry out orders from Rome. This was a far cry from the traditional concept of bishops as the collective successors of the apostles. It also had the ironic effect of greatly reducing the status and power of what should have been the papacy's most valuable allies. Popes in the twelfth and thirteenth centuries had to fight their political battles without much assistance from local bishops, because by that time there were few bishops left with enough influence to be of much help.

Chapter 10
THE CHURCH MILITANT

SOMETIME before the turn of the eleventh century, Turkish tribesmen began moving westward from their homes in central Asia. In 1055, under the leadership of the Seljuk family, they seized control of the Arab caliphate of Bagdad; then they pushed south along the Mediterranean coast all the way to the borders of Egypt and west toward Constantinople. In 1071 they destroyed a Byzantine army at Manzikert in Armenia and seized about half of what remained of the already truncated Eastern Empire.

And the menace of Islam was only one of the threats Constantinople faced. At about the same time that the Seljuk Turks were moving toward Bagdad, Norman warriors were drifting into southern Italy. By 1071 one of their number, Robert Guiscard, was able to gain control of the entire southern half of the peninsula, thus putting a permanent end to Byzantine power there. But Robert had even larger ambitions. In 1085 he attempted to seize the Byzantine throne by launching a massive land and sea assault against Constantinople.

With the aid of ships provided by Venice, Byzantium was able to beat back this attack. As the price of its help, however, Venice demanded extensive trading privileges within the Byzantine Empire. This broke the monopoly Constantinople had enjoyed on the fabulously profitable trade with the Orient, thus cutting deeply into the Empire's tax revenues and reducing its military strength still more. It also whetted the Venetians' appetite for even greater profits. Meanwhile, Hungarians and a Russian tribe called Patzinaks were menacing the Balkans, while the Turks remained an ever-present threat on the eastern frontier.

These were the conditions which induced Emperor Alexius Comnenus in 1095 to ask the sovereigns of Europe, through Pope Urban II, for military assistance. What Alexius apparently had in mind was something like a squadron of Frankish heavy cavalry, or perhaps some Norman mercenaries to stiffen the backbone of his demoralized army. What he actually received was something entirely different, primarily because his appeal came at a time when Western Europe, after nearly seven centuries of stagnation, was entering an era of unprecedented wealth, energy, and exuberant optimism.

Of the many factors which contributed to this revival, perhaps the most important was the development, particularly on monastic estates, of improved agricultural methods such as crop rotation and land reclamation techniques. Labor-saving devices like the horse collar, heavier plows, and the water wheel also were introduced. As farm output rose above the subsistence level, it became possible to accumulate wealth and engage in trade.

By the twelfth century this prosperity was fueling a veritable orgy of church building in northern Europe, including construction of the first Gothic cathedrals (Chartres was begun in 1145, Notre Dame of Paris in 1163, and Amiens around 1200). It also subsidized the foundation of the first universities.

And as food production rose, population began to increase. Sometime in the ninth century, births began to outnumber deaths; and eventually it became necessary to increase the amount of land under cultivation. The Germans attempted to solve this problem by annexing Slavic territory to the east (a policy which proved so successful that they continued to follow it down to our own time), while the Flemish reclaimed huge areas from the North Sea. French and Spanish knights, meanwhile, were pushing the Arabs slowly but relentlessly out of Spain; and the Normans went so far as to conquer part of the North African coast.

Europe was no longer contracting under the hammer-blows of successive barbarian invasions. Now it was aggressively expanding, and the idea of sending an expedition to fight the Turks fit perfectly into the expansionist pattern. By providing an opportunity for Urban to assume the undisputed moral and political leadership of Europe and by offering at least the possibility of improving relations between the Roman and Byzantine churches, it also meshed with the objectives of papal diplomacy.

Thus it happened that Urban preached the famous sermon which lauched the First Crusade, and that the response to his call far surpassed everyone's expectations. Urban emphasized, of course, the obvious religious motive of recapturing the Holy Land for Christendom, and he made numerous references to atrocities allegedly perpetrated by the Turks upon their Christian subjects. (Most of these apparently were apocryphal. It is worth noting that the Palestinian Christians themselves were not clamoring for assistance.)

But Urban also bluntly pointed out to the assembled knights that their incessant warfare and random acts of violence had become intolerable and that there was insufficient land and food for them in their own country, while the Middle East, now in the possession of infidels, was theirs for the taking. France, in fact, had suffered a devastating famine that very year; and in some areas over-population was about to reach crisis proportions.

The legend of the Pied Piper is said to have originated in the fact that the citizens of medieval Hamelin, unable to feed their children, sent them off to fend for themselves as best they could across the eastern frontier. Urban and his peers, in a sense, were doing something quite similar. The early crusades offer one of the clearest instances on record of an older generation deliberately ridding itself of superfluous and troublesome youth by having them fight a foreign war. On the other hand the large number of young men, unable to find work, who were willing to trade their labor for a modest but secure living as lay brothers is what made possible the phenomenal growth of the Cistercian movement at precisely the same time.

So carried away was Urban's audience by his logic and eloquence that they immediately began making preparations to move *en masse* toward Palestine by the overland route. This was not what the Byzantines had asked for, and it was not at all what they wanted. Anna Comnena, the emperor's daughter and perhaps the most famous woman historian of all time, wrote that the imperial court was appalled to hear that the combined barbarian tribes of Europe were converging on Constantinople.

For the crusades, particularly the early ones, were far more than military expeditions. They were, rather, mass social movements, sometimes resembling large-scale migrations. The first Christian knight had scarcely left home before a mob of 20,000 men, women and children, under the leadership of an itinerant preacher named Peter the Hermit, were encamping around the walls of Constantinople on their way to seek land and wealth in the Middle East. Emperor Alexius quickly offered this unwelcome rabble free transport across the Bosphorus, where a Turkish army obligingly cut them to pieces. They were followed, not long afterward, by a similar band led by one Walter the Penniless.

The crusaders themselves saw their undertaking as something like an armed pilgrimage—they called it simply "the march to Jerusalem." And since the obligation of going on long pilgrimages frequently was prescribed as a penance for serious sins, it was quite natural for Urban to declare that for those who had made a proper confession, participation in the crusade would take the place of all other penances. This was the origin of the famous and controversial crusader indulgence.

Four Christian armies assembled in the fall of 1096 and moved separately toward a rendezvous in Constantinople. Then they fought their way across the mountains of Asia Minor and into Syria. Most of the roughly 30,000 soldiers were either Norman or French. Spain was preoccupied with its own war against Islam, England was recovering from the effects of the Norman Conquest, and Germany was effectively disqualified from participation by the fact that Emperor Henry IV was still feuding with the papacy.

Urban had declared that all territory liberated by the crusaders would be returned to Byzantine control. Emperor Alexius, taking no chances, had the leaders of the four armies repeat this pledge in a personal oath to him. And when the city of Nicaea was recaptured from the Turks, it was indeed restored to the Byzantines.

Before long, however, the crusader alliance began to fragment—a process which was greatly facilitated by the lack of a unified command. One contingent broke away from the main army to conquer and settle in a portion of Armenia. During the long and frustrating siege of Antioch, one of the Christian princes abandoned the struggle and headed back home with his troops. As chance would have it, he met Alexius coming the other way to join his European allies and convinced him that Antioch could never be taken, whereupon Alexius returned to Constantinople. This proved to be an extremely costly blunder, for it allowed the Europeans to argue that the emperor's withdrawal released them from the obligation of honoring their promises to him. When the crusader armies finally did take Antioch, therefore, slaughtering the entire Muslim population in the process, they treated it and everything they subsequently conquered as their own possession.

So rich a prize was Antioch that the entire crusade ground to a halt for seven months while the Christian princes wrangled over the division of its wealth. It was the rank and the file soldiers who finally forced their leaders to move on toward Jerusalem, which they entered in July of 1099, killing every Muslim man, woman and child in the city and many Jews as well. Similar massacres took place at Caesarea and Beirut.

Once the bloodlust of battle had cooled, however, the crusaders got along surprisingly well with the native population, whose culture they began to recognize as far superior in many ways to their own. Muslims were granted complete religious freedom, and no attempt was made to convert them by force. Christians loyal to the Byzantine church, on the other hand, frequently found themselves under the jurisdiction of Roman clergy, their own patriarchs and bishops having been deposed by the Latins.

Now that they had conquered the Holy Land—or, more precisely, now that they had established a chain of castles and fortified cities along the Mediterranean coast from north of Antioch to just south of Gaza—the crusaders faced the necessity of defending what they had seized. This meant, above all else, keeping enough men under arms to fend off Muslim attacks.

This was not easy, for most of the original crusaders either had perished in battle or else, having fulfilled their vow by liberating Jerusalem, wanted to return home. And the Christian population of Outremer (literally "Overseas"), as the medievals called their Middle Eastern enclave, produced far too few offspring to replace them.

There was no organized system for recruiting new settlers from Europe. The Crusader States, in fact, never became self-sufficient; and the shipowners of Venice, Genoa, and Pisa grew enormously wealthy by ferrying supplies across the Mediterranean to them. In the end, what made it impossible to maintain control of Outremer was the simple fact that its inhabitants were hopelessly outnumbered.

For a time, however, the defense of the Crusader States was made possible by the same circumstance which had permitted their conquest in the first place: dissensions and bitter rivalries among the Muslims—Shi'ites against Sunnites, Arabs against Turks, the caliphate of Egypt against the caliphate of Bagdad, and one ambitious local ruler against another. By adroitly manipulating these different factions, leaders of the four crusader kingdoms usually were able to prevent the Muslims from organizing large-scale assaults against them.

But sometimes they failed. In 1144 the crusader kingdom in Armenia was recaptured, leading Pope Eugenius III to commission the Cistercian monk and mystic Bernard of Clairvaux to preach a Second Crusade. And Bernard, who then was probably the most influential man in Europe, managed to raise an army roughly twice the size of the one which had answered Urban's call. He also persuaded Conrad III of Germany and Louis VII of France to lead it. (Although the number of men taking the crusader's vow had increased since Urban's time, their quality seems to have gone down. So many cutthroats and reprobates joined the Second Crusade that Bernard himself remarked that Europe would be as glad to be rid of them as Palestine would be to receive them.)

This enormous undertaking, however, accomplished next to nothing. Following the example of their predecessors, the two armies moved independently of each other.

Conrad, ignoring the advice of the Byzantines, led his
army into the trackless wastes of Anatolia, where it was
massacred by the Turks. Louis managed to reach Palestine, but was forced to retreat after a brief and strategically
senseless siege of Damascus. This left matters precisely
where they had been before the Second Crusade began,
and they might have remained that way had not one of the
Christian princes of Outremer foolishly broken the truce in
1187 by looting a caravan, an act of petty banditry which
was avenged many times over by a brilliant Muslim general
named Salah al-Din ibn Ayyub, or Saladin.

Luring the Christians into an ambush near the Sea of
Galilee, Saladin destroyed the military power of the
southern Crusader States in a single battle and then seized
its virtually undefended cities, including Jerusalem. This
led to the raising of a European army even larger than Bernard's and the declaration of a Third Crusade led by
Richard the Lion-Hearted of England, Philip Augustus of
France, and the nearly seventy-year-old Emperor Frederick Barbarossa of Germany.

But Frederick drowned in Asia Minor while trying to
swim the river Seleph, not far from Tarsus. This left
Philip, who for several years had been fighting to conquer Normandy from England, and Richard, who had
been fighting to retain it. These two kings managed to put
aside their mutual hostility long enough to capture the
coastal fortress of Acre, which became the unofficial capital of Outremer; but then Philip hurried home to conspire
with Richard's brother John, who was trying to seize the
English throne for himself.

Richard stayed on for another year. He was unable to
conquer Jerusalem, although he did obtain free access for
Christian pilgrims to that city and all the other holy places
of Palestine by negotiating a treaty with Saladin. But the

terms of this treaty did not satisfy Pope Innocent III, who in 1198 authorized the preaching of a Fourth Crusade, thereby launching one of the most disastrous fiascos with which the church has ever been associated.

Urban's crusade had been successful in large part because it had a single objective, transcending national and personal interests, behind which all Christians could unite —the liberation of the Holy Land. Like monasticism in earlier times, the First Crusade appealed to the imagination of Europe because it demanded heroic sacrifice for a noble cause. And yet, like monasticism, the crusading movement eventually became a victim of its own success, distracted further and further from its original purpose until the term "crusade" came to mean little more than a military action sanctioned by the papacy, and crusaders were spending more time killing other Christians than fighting infidels.

This process began during the Second Crusade when German and Scandinavian armies crossed into eastern Germany to attack the pagan Wends, and Pope Eugenius granted them the same indulgence Urban had reserved for those who risked their lives in Palestine. Later popes decided to award the indulgence to people who merely gave money to support the crusades (in theory, the money was supposed to purchase the services of a substitute soldier), thus opening the door to enormously destructive abuses.

English and Flemish troops made an impromptu detour on their way to the Second Crusade to capture Lisbon. And Roger II of Sicily, Robert Guiscard's nephew, took advantage of Constantinople's preoccupation with the Turkish menace by raiding Byzantium's colonies, thereby adding Corfu, Thebes, and Corinth to his Italian possessions.

This treacherous attack, the imposition of Roman liturgical practices on the people of southern Italy, the extreme distress which the Venetian trading concessions were causing Byzantine merchants, and a long series of other provocations stirred up intense anti-Latin feeling in Constantinople. And in May of 1182, or twenty years before the start of the Fourth Crusade, the Byzantine people rose up and massacred their city's Latin population. Three years later the Normans retaliated by capturing Thessalonika and slaughtering its inhabitants. It was out of this background that the tragedy of the Fourth Crusade unfolded.

The original plan was to travel to the Holy Land by sea and then to attack Egypt. The Venetians promised to provide ships in return for cash payment and one-half of everything the crusaders captured. When embarkation time approached, however, they demanded more money than the combined armies could raise.

But the merchants of Venice, who had grown accustomed to dealing in pounds of flesh long before Shakespeare's time, finally agreed to lower their price if the crusaders would do them the favor of capturing Zara, a city belonging to the Christian king of Hungary which was beginning to challenge their domination of the Adriatic. This was agreed to, despite Innocent III's express prohibition, and Zara was sacked and handed over to Venice.

The Fourth Crusade now was totally out of control; and the Venetians had little difficulty persuading its leaders to abandon their plans for the invasion of Egypt, with which Venice had lucrative trading agreements, and to attack the Christian city of Constantinople instead. In 1204 Constantine's "New Rome," perhaps the richest city in the world, fell for the first time in its almost nine-hundred-year history and was subjected to merciless pillage, rapine, and desecration.

A "Latin Empire of Constantinople" was established; and the Venetians, whose rapaciousness knew no bounds, claimed nearly half of Byzantium's territorial possessions and total control of Europe's trade with the Orient. They also deposed the Greek patriarch of Constantinople and engineered the consecration of one of their own number in his place.

Pope Innocent had not planned or encouraged these actions, but he moved quickly to turn them to Rome's advantage. What followed was nothing less than a deliberate and systematic attempt to destroy the Byzantine Church. Greek bishops and priests were required to swear obedience to the pope and to the new Latin patriarch; those who refused, as the majority did, were deposed and replaced by Latins. All new bishops were consecrated in the Roman rite. The intent of these moves, obviously, was to ensure that the existing generation of Byzantine clergy would be the last. When a group of Byzantines suggested that the Greeks might accept union with Rome voluntarily if the hated Venetian patriarch were replaced with a Greek, even one sympathetic to the papacy, and if the issues separating the two churches were discussed at a general council, Innocent rejected the proposal out of hand.

But part of the imperial court had escaped from the capital and established a government in exile at Nicaea. Gradually this group extended its influence, aided immeasurably by popular resentment against the persecution of the Byzantine church. When the Greeks recaptured Thessalonika, Pope Honorius III preached a crusade against them; but no one in Europe except the Venetians showed any interest in responding. When the army of Nicaea grew strong enough to march against Constantinople, the Latin emperor resorted to the bizarre expedient of asking the Turks to help him fight the Christian Greeks.

In 1261 Constantinople was retaken by Emperor Michael VIII Paleologus—assisted by armies from Genoa and

Pisa, who wished to break the Venetians' stranglehold on oriental trade. The Byzantine Empire was back in Greek hands; but it was an empire fragmented, exhausted, and permanently crippled. The Fourth Crusade, which had done nothing at all to diminish Turkish influence in the Middle East, succeeded in emasculating the one power which might have kept the Turks out of Europe. It also made reunion of Christendom impossible, for the Greeks never forgot or forgave Rome's campaign of extermination against their church.

And when the once-proud Byzantine Empire had been whittled down to little more than Constantinople itself and its suburbs, the Christian population of Byzantium would choose to let itself be engulfed by the Islamic tide rather than accept help from the West on the terms under which Rome was offering it.

Chapter 11
THE RISE AND FALL
OF THE LAWYER-POPES

MINDFUL of St. Paul's admonition that they should not air their grievances against one another in the presence of unbelievers, early Christians frequently submitted legal disputes to the judgment of bishops and elders rather than to civil courts. Decisions were based on the teachings of Scripture, precedents from similar cases, generally accepted legal principles, and, eventually, the writings of church Fathers.

Out of this practice arose a body of ecclesiastical law, with its own set of principles and procedures. And the church of Rome gradually made itself the acknowledged custodian of this law, particularly after Pope Gelasius I (492-496) began organizing and harmonizing the decrees of church councils and the papal "decretals," or written instructions on matters of ecclesiastical discipline. Bishops of other dioceses, especially in the West, grew accustomed to consulting Rome about legal questions, in large part because only Rome had the information to provide authoritative answers.

As the centuries passed, the church continued to generate decrees, rules, decretals, and laws. So when Gregory VII sent a small army of clerks to rummage through the libraries and archives of Italy for material to support his position on papal supremacy, they found a great deal more than Gregory had asked for. They unearthed nearly a thousand years' worth of what might be called the accumulated law of the church, although in such a disorganized and fragmented condition that no one could be certain precisely what that law was or what it meant.

About fifty years later, in the first half of the twelfth century, a monk named Gratian set off a legal revolution within the church by organizing, editing, and publishing this mass of material.

But Gratian did more than just edit. Employing a method developed at the University of Paris by Peter Abelard, Gratian grouped texts by different authors on each of some four thousand topics, and then tried to reconcile the apparent contradictions among those texts by applying consistent rules of interpretation—often showing, for example, that different sources were using the same words in different senses. Then he added his own commentary on each topic and drew a general conclusion.

Gratian, in short, transformed thousands of separate documents into a coherent body of legal knowledge. And he instituted the scientific study of canon law by lecturing on this body of knowledge at the University of Bologna. His work, although never granted official status by the church, was utilized to train generations of canonists, many of whom enjoyed brilliant careers at the papal court. Alexander III, who had taught at Bologna and had written a commentary on Gratian, became the first of the great lawyer-popes in 1159. And many of his successors, especially the more influential ones, came from similar backgrounds.

This influx of ambitious young lawyers into the Vatican's administrative structure gradually changed the character of the institutional church. It focused Rome's attention on legalistic issues and legislative remedies at the expense of theological and pastoral concerns. It also encouraged the enactment of still more church laws.

And as ecclesiastical legislation was extended into more and more fields, it overlapped areas already covered by civil law—such as the regulation of marriages and family relationships and the punishment of crimes like blasphemy, usury, witchcraft, and sexual misconduct. At the same time, civil law was undergoing a revival of its own, thanks both to the rediscovery of Justinian's *Corpus Iuris Civilis* —which became the foundation for the legal codes of most European countries—and to the rise of powerful and centralized national states, whose kings were attempting to strengthen their own authority by developing new theories of jurisprudence.

This simultaneous expansion of two competing legal systems, ecclesiastical and civil, inevitably led to jurisdictional disputes. The most troublesome of these involved the church's claim that all clerics—that is, anyone who had received at least minor orders—should be immune from punishment by the secular power for criminal offenses.

In the eyes of those responsible for maintaining public order, this argument was considerably weakened by the fact that church courts imposed far less severe punishment than their secular counterparts for the same offenses, so that known criminals sometimes entered minor orders to escape the penalties of secular law. In addition, clerical immunity was being claimed by an enormous number of people, most of whom had no real connection with the church's ministry. In England, for example, anyone who could memorize the first verse of the fifty-first psalm in Latin automatically qualified.

This issue was at the center of the clash between Henry II of England and his archbishop of Canterbury, Thomas á Becket. Henry, who established the basic principles of English common law and introduced the use of the jury system, was determined to raise the prestige of royal courts. His purpose was to induce litigants to bring their cases to trial in his courts rather than in the courts of local barons, thus weakening the power of the barons and— since one had to purchase a writ in order to bring suit before the king's justices—increasing his own revenues. (This was the exact counterpart of what popes were doing by insisting that any case in church law could be appealed directly to Rome at any stage of the litigation process. Here, of course, power and revenue were being drained away from bishops rather than from barons.)

It was with a mixture of exasperation and outrage, therefore, that the legal-minded King Henry discovered in 1163 that clerics had committed more than one hundred murders in England in the previous six years, not to mention armed robberies and other capital offenses, and that Becket was claiming that mere deprivation of clerical status was sufficient punishment for these miscreants if they were first-time offenders.

Henry refused to countenance such leniency for convicted felons, whatever their ecclesiastical status. He insisted that clerics found guilty by church courts be handed over to him for punishment, as had been the custom during his predecessor's reign. Becket first agreed to this and ordered his bishops to do likewise. Then he changed his mind, claiming, in the spirit of Gregory VII, that priests constitute a separate society not subject to the jurisdiction of kings. Henry was strongly supported by his barons, however, while Becket's intransigence alienated even his own bishops. Eventually he found himself standing virtually alone against the English church as well as the state, a predicament from which he was extricated only by martyrdom.

But the symbolic power of Becket's death was enormous, and Henry was obliged to allow himself to be stripped and publicly flogged as penance for his complicity in the archbishop's murder. He also was forced to acknowledge the principle of clerical immunity, which continued to be recognized in English law until 1827 and in some parts of the United States for a quarter of a century more.

Perhaps the most outstanding of the canonists trained at Bologna was the thirty-seven-year-old Innocent III, the quintessential lawyer-pope. Possessed of a quick, incisive mind and an extraordinary capacity for hard work, Innocent, who was elected in 1198, virtually showered the church with legislation—his offices issued an average of one legal document per day for the eighteen years of his pontificate—and he presided in person over the discussion of all important legal questions by his staff. He also took a number of steps to increase the centralization of legal authority in Rome at the expense of the bishops, whom he believed to possess juridical power only through participation in the power of the pope. It was Innocent's conviction that the papacy vicariously possesses the full legislative authority of Jesus Christ himself which led him to appropriate a title previously used by the Christian emperors and refer to himself as the Vicar of Christ, as subsequent popes down to our own day have continued to do.

The climax of Innocent's career was the Fourth Lateran Council of 1215, attended by more than a thousand archbishops, bishops, abbots, and heads of religious communities from all parts of the Western church. Lateran I (1123), the church's ninth ecumenical council and the first to be held in the West, had concerned itself primarily with defusing the investiture controversy by approving the Concordat of Worms. Lateran II and III (1139 and 1179) had put an official end to schisms caused by the election of antipopes. Innocent's council, however, was convened specifically to make and ratify laws; and this it did in abundance.

Lateran IV laid down rules for the administration and reception of the sacraments and obliged all Christians to confess and receive communion at least once a year. It defined the rights and powers of bishops, made laws regarding church property, and attempted to eliminate abuses connected with indulgences. It stipulated that church tithes must be paid before all other taxes, and prohibited the illegitimate sons of priests from inheriting their fathers' offices.

It even legislated for non-Christians, compelling Jews and Muslims to wear distinctive clothing and forbidding them to assume any position of authority over Christians. And it decreed that the patriarchate of Constantinople stood second in dignity to that of Rome, finally acknowledging what the Byzantines had been claiming since the First Council of Constantinople in 381.

In addition to his role as the supreme legislator of Western Christendom, Innocent exercised more direct influence over European politics than any pope before or since, intervening in the internal affairs of even the most powerful nations whenever he saw fit. Whole countries— England, Bulgaria, Portugal, and Aragon—became papal fiefs during his reign. But Innocent's interventions did not always have the consequences he had intended. Worse yet, he, like Charlemagne, established precedents which some of his successors attempted to imitate in vastly different circumstances, often with unpleasant results.

When the election of a new archbishop of Canterbury ended in controversy in 1205, Innocent simply dismissed both of the original candidates and appointed a man of his own choice—Stephen Langton, whose acquaintance he had made while Langton was teaching theology at Paris.

But King John, the brother and successor of Richard the Lionhearted, refused to acknowledge the validity of this extraordinary procedure. After two years of threats failed to change the king's mind, Innocent placed England under an interdict, which proved ineffective. Two years later he excommunicated John, also without result. Finally, in 1212, he declared John deposed and threatened to appoint a new king himself.

John might have been able to withstand this challenge as well, except that he, like Henry IV in 1077, was faced with a rebellion by his own subjects. Having managed to lose all of England's holdings in northern France, John had imposed drastic new taxes to finance another campaign on the continent. Even worse, he insisted on payment by the rich as well as by the poor. Outraged more by the king's efficient collection techniques than by the taxes themselves, his barons rose up in revolt.

But John, again like Henry IV, found a way to turn defeat into victory through surrender. He accepted all of Innocent's demands, and even granted him England itself as a fief. Then, when Stephen Langton began conspiring with the rebellious barons and encouraged them to force John to sign the Magna Carta in 1215, John, who had played his cards quite cleverly, appealed to the pope. Seeing Langton's actions as an affront to his own authority, Innocent had Lateran IV invalidate the Magna Carta on the grounds that the king, as a vassal of the pope, had no right to make such an agreement without his permission. Then he suspended Langton and forbade him to return to Canterbury, a prohibition which remained in force until Innocent's death.

Innocent's repudiation of the Magna Carta was echoed in 1261 when Pope Alexander IV invalidated the Provisions of Oxford, a somewhat similar document which Henry III, John's son and successor, had signed with his own barons. These interventions had little or no effect upon contemporary events in England. They did, however, tend to make the papacy appear to be opposed to English civil liberties, a reputation which would be exploited during the Reformation by proponents of a national English church.

In Germany, Innocent inherited a conflict between the papacy and the Hohenstaufen family which had been sim-

mering for years before his own election. Frederick Barbarossa, patriarch of the Hohenstaufens, had lit a slow fuse to
this dispute by arranging for his son and heir, Henry VI, to
marry Constance, daughter of Roger II of Sicily.

Since Roger had succeeded in uniting Sicily with the
Norman Kingdom of Naples, this meant that Henry and
Constance together would control not only the Empire,
which included northern Italy, but all of southern Italy as
well, thus completely surrounding and isolating the narrow
strip of Italian territory controlled by the papacy. It also
meant the elimination of Naples-Sicily as an independent
power which popes could use to counterbalance the influence of the German emperors.

In 1194 Henry, who already was king of Germany, king
of northern Italy, and Holy Roman Emperor, was
crowned king of Naples-Sicily. The church of Rome was
now encircled by the Hohenstaufens and appeared to be in
grave danger of falling under their political domination, a
threat which for the next three-quarters of a century it used
every possible means to remove.

Events at first seemed to favor the papacy. Henry died
unexpectedly at the age of thirty-two, leaving as his heir a
three-year-old boy named Frederick. Then Constance died
a year later. Realizing that orphaned royal heirs generally
did not live long, and hoping to preserve at least some of
her son's inheritance, she had renounced Frederick's right
to the German kingship, arranged to have him crowned
king of Naples-Sicily, and named Innocent III regent of
Sicily and Frederick's guardian. It speaks well of Innocent's integrity that he not only safeguarded Frederick's
inheritance but permitted him to rule in his own name
when he came of age. Some of his successors would never
have allowed the child to live.

His handling of the problem of imperial succession,

however, left much to be desired. In the confusion which had followed the death of Henry IV, two rival claimants had been crowned king of Germany—Otto of Saxony, a member of the Welf (or Guelf) family, and Philip of Swabia, one of the Hohenstaufens (also known as Ghibellines, a name derived from a Hohenstaufen castle called Weibelung). Innocent, after some hesitation, recognized Otto as the legitimate king and crowned him emperor.

No sooner had he done so, however, than Otto attacked southern Italy, which was still under papal jurisdiction. Innocent responded by excommunicating Otto and arranging for young Frederick to be elected king of Germany in his place. In return, Frederick promised not to allow Naples-Sicily and the Empire to be ruled by the same person, a promise which he failed to keep after his coronation as emperor in 1220. The ultimate result of Innocent's maneuver, therefore, was to expose the papacy to precisely the same danger of encirclement by Hohenstaufen power from which the death of Henry had just freed it.

Innocent's nephew, Pope Gregory IX, seems to have been determined from the very start of his pontificate to solve this problem by destroying Frederick, whose principal offense against the church was the fact that he controlled both northern and southern Italy. Only four days after his election in 1227, Gregory ordered the emperor to begin the long-postponed crusade which he had promised Innocent he would undertake. When Frederick finally did embark, and sickness forced him to return, Gregory excommunicated him. Six months later he excommunicated him again. Then, when Frederick was well on his way to the Holy Land, Gregory freed his southern Italian subjects from their oaths of allegiance and, incongruously, preached a crusade against the emperor while the emperor himself was on crusade.

Frederick, meanwhile, through personal negotiations with the Muslim leaders, obtained possession of Jerusalem, Bethlehem, and Nazareth without fighting a major battle, thus achieving singlehandedly what the combined armies of the Second and Third Crusades had failed to accomplish. When he returned to Italy, however, Gregory excommunicated him once again—and continued to do so at frequent intervals thereafter. Events were moving toward a dramatic climax, with the pope about to preside over a general council to condemn Frederick, and the emperor approaching the outskirts of Rome with his army to seize him, when Gregory died in 1241.

But his death led only to an escalation of the conflict. The next pope (not counting the seventeen-day pontificate of Urban III's nephew, Celestine IV) was Innocent IV, a lawyer-pope in the tradition of Alexander III, Innocent III, and Gregory IX. When Frederick refused to renounce imperial claims in northern Italy, Innocent excommunicated him once more—Frederick may well have been the most frequently excommunicated person in history—and moved from Rome to Lyons, where he could count on the protection of the French king. Then he convened a general council at Lyons in 1245, the primary business of which was to find Frederick guilty of heresy and perjury and order him deposed. Mindful, perhaps, of the example of Gregory IX, the council also passed a decree against the excessive use of excommunications.

Even after Frederick's death in 1250, the papal campaign against the Hohenstaufens continued. For the next eighteen years his descendants struggled to preserve their inheritance, while a succession of popes used every means at their disposal to deprive them both of Germany and of Naples-Sicily.

Innocent IV arranged for the election of a rival to Frederick's son Conrad, who had been crowned king of

Germany in 1237. When this proved insufficient to topple Conrad from his throne, Innocent excommunicated him. Just as a war between papal and imperial forces was about to begin in 1254, Conrad died. His reign was followed by a thirty-year interregnum which was marked, particularly in northern Italy, by vicious clashes between Guelfs and Ghibellines, as papal and imperial supporters came to be called.

But the same strategy did not work in southern Italy. Conrad's half-brother Manfred became regent of Naples-Sicily after Frederick's death, ruling first in Conrad's name and then in the name of Conradin, Conrad's son. And so firm was his grip on the kingdom that Innocent eventually was forced to recognize Conradin as the rightful heir.

When Manfred had himself crowned in 1258, however, and began reestablishing Hohenstaufen hegemony in southern Italy, Pope Urban IV persuaded Charles of Anjou, youngest brother of King Louis IX of France, to lead a crusade against him. Charles was crowned king of Naples-Sicily in St. Peter's in 1266; then he defeated and killed Manfred. And when young Conradin hurried south from Germany at the behest of the Sicilians to reclaim his kingdom, Charles, with considerable help from Urban's successor, Clement IV, took him prisoner.

But the bloodshed continued. Violent reprisals against Hohenstaufen sympathizers were carried out in many Italian cities. Conradin, at the age of sixteen, was beheaded. Manfred's three sons were cast into papal dungeons from which they never emerged. All told, no fewer than ten children and grandchildren of Frederick II met their deaths directly or indirectly at the hands of the papacy; and the Hohenstaufen family was totally annihilated.

This long and brutal struggle destroyed any possibility of recreating a true Christian empire like that of Charlemagne, and of establishing a centralized European government. It also helped to ensure that Germany and Italy would not become unified political entities for another six centuries. The papacy's entire anti-Hohenstaufen policy, in fact, had been motivated largely by a desire to prevent the unification of Italy—something which it would continue to oppose even after it finally took place in 1870.

Charles of Anjou turned out to be a solution worse than the original problem—as, for that matter, the basic strategy of using French power to thwart the Hohenstaufens would prove to be far worse than the original problem. Charles caused so much trouble in southern Italy that the papacy was forced to install a competent Holy Roman Emperor in 1273 to offset his influence. It chose Rudolf of Hapsburg, thus establishing a new imperial dynasty.

But Charles of Anjou had ambitions which went far beyond Italy. No sooner had he consolidated his power in Naples-Sicily than he began preparations to invade Byzantium. And Emperor Michael Paleologus, who had recaptured Constantinople from the Latins only a few years before, knew that his army was far too weak to withstand an attack from the West. This was the political background of the Second Council of Lyons in 1274. Michael, convinced that his only hope of forestalling the impending invasion lay in cultivating the good will of Pope Gregory X, agreed at this council to reestablish relations with Rome and acknowledge the primacy of the pope.

But Michael was unable to impose the settlement on his own subjects. Tortures, blindings, floggings, mutilations —all the excruciating torments which the Byzantine police apparatus was capable of inflicting were applied to recalcitrant monks and theologians, but popular hatred and fear of the Latin Church were simply too deeply ingrained to be overcome. In the end, Michael's efforts came to nothing. Pope Gregory died; and Martin IV, a Frenchman who owed his election to Charles of Anjou, nullified the decree of reunion, excommunicated the hapless Michael, and declared a crusade against him, thus giving a green light to Charles' invasion plans.

But Byzantium was saved—not for the first time—by diplomatic skullduggery. By concluding a treaty with King Peter of Aragon, Manfred's son-in-law, and discreetly pouring Byzantine gold into the right pockets, Emperor Michael was able to encourage a revolt which drove Charles out of Sicily.

Charles of Anjou, who not only failed to conquer Byzantium but lost half his kingdom in the attempt, died in 1285. Pope Martin died in the same year, having sabotaged everything which Gregory X had accomplished at Lyons. Michael Paleologus died in 1282 and was succeeded by his son Andronicus, who immediately repudiated his father's act of submission to Rome. Michael, considered a heretic by the people whom he had liberated from Latin rule and protected against invasion by the West, was buried in unconsecrated ground.

With Boniface VIII, the last pope of the thirteenth century, papal claims to ultimate authority over both spiritual and temporal affairs found their most exalted expression. And under his leadership the church collided with new political forces which it was tragically slow to comprehend. The most important of these forces was nationalism, particularly the evolution of feudal kingdoms into national states.

Boniface ran headlong into the power of these new national kingdoms in 1296, when Edward I of England and Philip IV of France began to impose new taxes on church property in violation of canon law. Boniface, who had studied both civil and canon law at Bologna, reacted in typical lawyer fashion. In a document entitled *Clericis laicos* (which opened with the gratuitous remark that lay people always have been hostile to the clergy), he excommunicated any king who imposed a tax on the clergy without his permission and any clergyman who paid such a tax. He was anticipating, perhaps, a long and dramatic contest of wills like those which had taken place a century earlier, ending in both kings' submission to his authority.

But times had changed. Neither king needed to confront Boniface. Edward merely ordered his judges to withhold the protection of civil law from clerics who refused to pay. Philip did not even bother to do that. He simply issued an edict forbidding the export of currency, knowing that the papacy could not survive without revenue from France.

The message was obvious: popes needed the support of kings at least as much as kings needed that of popes. And it was not long before Boniface issued a clarification to *Clericis laicos,* explaining that his prohibition was not intended to apply in cases of necessity and that kings could decide for themselves whether or not a state of necessity existed. This was as close as a good lawyer ever need come to unconditional surrender.

A much more serious conflict erupted in 1301, when Philip imprisoned a bishop for treason, a gross violation of clerical immunity. Boniface responded with the same weapons which had proved so effective for his predecessors. He issued thunderous manifestos. He threatened excommunications. He summoned the French bishops to Rome to coordinate their strategy against the king. But Philip had discovered a new weapon far more powerful than these.

Popes for centuries had used excommunications and interdicts to put pressure on kings by forcing their subjects to choose between loyalty to their sovereigns and loyalty to the church. Now, by making an unprecedented appeal to public opinion, Philip used precisely the same tactic against Boniface—and he shrewdly turned his quarrel with the pope into a quarrel between the pope and France.

Fraudulent documents were circulated which purported to show that Boniface was denying the authority of the king and threatening French independence. The first meeting of the Estates-General, France's parliament, was convened in 1302 specifically to disseminate these and other accusations. At the conclusion of this meeting, the French clergy sent an indignant letter to the pope, protesting what they believed to be his policies toward France.

While this outburst of nationalistic fervor was raging around him, Boniface, who was looking resolutely backward rather than forward, issued *Unam Sanctam,* the most sweeping and forceful exposition of papal claims to political power ever made. From a logical and legal point of view, *Unam Sanctam* was a masterpiece. Unfortunately for the pope, however, it bore no relation whatsoever to practical reality.

Four months after it was issued, a French court charged Boniface with blasphemy, heresy, simony, and murder (his predecessor, Celestine V, had died in Boniface's custody after having resigned as pope) and demanded that a general council be held to try him. To make certain that Boniface would not escape judgment, King Philip's chief advisor stormed the papal residence at Anagni, south of Rome, and took him prisoner. A few weeks later, Boniface died.

Anagni was Canossa in reverse, a dramatic symbol of how much the world had changed since the days of Gregory VII and Innocent III. It was, in its own way, as shocking as the murder of Thomas á Becket. But Philip did no public penance. He merely arranged to have a French bishop elected pope under the name of Clement V, and had him issue a solemn declaration that Philip's actions against Boniface had sprung from the highest religious motives.

Individual popes had been able to win great personal victories in the process of building a wall between the spiritual and the secular orders. But their triumphs provided no assistance to Boniface VIII and his successors as they struggled against the awesome power of the secular national state, an entity which those victories had done a great deal to bring into existence. And still the papacy was insisting that spiritual and secular powers were inseparable. This might have given a thoughtful and far-sighted observer pause. If ecclesiastical authority remained joined to secular authority, and the unity of secular authority was disintegrating into a multitude of national kingdoms, how could the unity of ecclesiastical authority be maintained?

Chapter 12
INQUISITORS, MENDICANTS,
AND THE REEMERGENCE OF THE LAITY

WHILE the early Middle Ages saw many dramatic political clashes, they were extraordinarily free from serious disputes over doctrine. There was, in fact, not a single major
heretical movement in the West from the fifth century until
the twelfth. This was due primarily to the fact that the barbarian invasions depopulated Europe's cities, making it almost impossible for large numbers of lay men and women
to communicate with each other.

Nearly a million people lived in Rome when it was captured by the Visigoths in 410, but a hundred and fifty years
later there were only a few thousand. Nîmes, one of the
chief cities of imperial Gaul, shrank so drastically that the
entire population was able to live for many years within the
walls of its Roman arena. Most communities simply vanished. As late as the year 1000 there were fewer than a
dozen important towns in Europe, none of which had
more than ten thousand inhabitants.

Under these conditions the church could easily control
the flow of ideas, because it monopolized the means
through which ideas could be transmitted. The few doctrinal aberrations which did appear in monastic writings
—some unorthodox theories about the Eucharist, for example—were suppressed before they reached more than a
handful of people.

And then, almost overnight, a spectacular revival of
commerce and trade began turning mere villages into major population centers. Merchants built warehouses. Arti-
sans opened shops. Weavers founded an immensely profitable textile industry. Serfs began fleeing into towns to
escape the drudgery and brutality of feudal bondage. Some

cities expanded so rapidly that they outgrew successive rings of fortifying walls almost as quickly as they could be built. This signaled the beginning of the end of the church's control over the channels of intellectual communication. Now that lay people were once more meeting and exchanging opinions, heterodox ideas could spread quickly by word of mouth. And one of these ideas was a heresy older than Christianity itself.

The theory that the universe was created by two opposing principles, one good and the other evil, has been traced at least as far back as the sixth century B.C. Persian prophet Zoroaster. Under the name Manicheanism, it circulated through the Roman Empire and exerted, as we have seen, a profound influence on Augustine. During the tenth century a priest named Bogomil popularized similar teachings in the Balkans, and soldiers returning from the Crusades carried them back to Western Europe. They spread quickly, particularly in the area surrounding the town of Albi in what is now southwestern France.

Manicheanism, or Albigensianism, was fundamentally anti-Christian on at least two counts: it was polytheistic, and it contradicted *Genesis* by holding that the material world is evil. And total renunciation of everything physical, even in theory, meant denial of Christ's true human nature and his resurrection, as well as rejection of a priesthood, the mass, the sacraments, and the very idea of an institutional church.

Since they believed that salvation consists of liberating the spiritual soul from imprisonment in an evil body and an evil world, Albigensians taught that one must avoid as far as possible all physical pleasures, practice celibacy and poverty, and abstain from meat and dairy products. Those who found it impossible or inconvenient to meet these stringent requirements could wait until death approached before being converted to strict Albigensian observance.

Although these ascetic practices were motivated by a totally unchristian theology, they coincided perfectly with
many of the most hallowed concepts of Christian spiritual-
ity. As a result, those who followed the Albigensian way of
life were generally held in great respect. Often they were referred to simply as "the good people."

To the church, however, the Albigensians posed a particularly thorny problem. Preaching and missionary activity failed to halt their growth. Finally, after the papal
legate Peter of Castlenau was murdered by an Albigensian
sympathizer in 1208, Pope Innocent III authorized a crusade against them.

The count of Toulouse, in whose territory the Albigensians were especially numerous, refused to take part in this
war against his own people. So did the king of France,
Philip Augustus. Then Innocent appealed to the barons of
northern France, who, under the leadership of Simon de
Montfort, eagerly marched south. This transformed the
Albigensian problem from a religious dispute into war
against an entire region of France.

The customary practices of crusader warfare were followed. Participants received papal indulgences. Since the
property of heretics was confiscable under church law, the
invading army was granted legal possession of whatever it
conquered. Inhabitants of captured cities, not all of
whom, obviously, were Albigensians, were routinely
slaughtered—fifteen thousand, according to contemporary
reports, at Beziers alone. These conditions ensured that the
south would continue to resist until it was totally crushed,
as eventually it was. Then it rebelled, and was crushed
again. And the butchery which took place after the fighting ended was worse than the war itself.

The territory of Languedoc and a large portion of Provence were devastated. One of the most vibrant cultures in
Europe was destroyed. Peter of Castelnau's death unques-

tionably had been avenged. But Albigensianism still lived. It became clear, somewhat belatedly, that military power alone could not extirpate religious beliefs. Some mechanism had to be found to confront the mind and heart of the individual heretic, not only in southern France but wherever heresy threatened.

It was for this reason that Pope Gregory IX began in 1231 to entrust the responsibility for identifying, interrogating, and reconciling heretics to special judges, independent of the local hierarchy and answerable only to Rome. This was the beginning of the medieval Inquisition. (The Spanish Inquisition, which was a separate institution, will be discussed later.) It was designed to be a more effective, more discriminating, and more humane way to fight heresy than the Albigensian crusade had been. And, judged by that rather gruesome standard, it was a success.

The Inquisition typically began its investigation by summoning every individual in a community over the age of fourteen (twelve for women) to appear before it. Each person was required to take an oath of orthodoxy and to report any suspicious behavior he or she had witnessed. This might include someone's failure to receive the sacraments with sufficient frequency, any eccentric behavior which could be construed as being part of a witchcraft ritual, or—since heretical groups frequently engaged in lay preaching, in violation of a long-standing church ban— possession of the scriptures or of prayer books. Since the accused were never told who had informed against them, this system provided a wonderful opportunity for anyone to obtain revenge against all his or her enemies, real or imagined. People who failed to testify were excommunicated, and if they still refused to appear they were themselves convicted of heresy *in absentia*.

Few of those accused of heresy, or even suspected of it, were able to establish their innocence, especially since they were not permitted to have witnesses testify on their behalf. Lawyers who offered to defend the accused were automatically considered accomplices to heresy.

Every effort was made to obtain confessions. Suspects could be imprisoned indefinitely, in solitary cells if the inquisitors so chose, and interrogated again and again until, out of fatigue or despair, they made some fatal slip. Torture theoretically could be applied only in conformity with a detailed set of guidelines. But Pope Alexander IV effectively nullified these restrictions, and most others as well, by granting inquisitors the power to absolve each other of all guilt for transgressions committed during the performance of their duties. By the end of the thirteenth century, torture had become a normal part of the interrogation process.

These procedures obviously differed greatly from those employed in criminal trials by any civilized society. In fact they are almost incomprehensible, unless one keeps in mind that the Inquisition did not consider itself to be a criminal tribunal. It saw its function, rather, as somewhat analogous to that of a confessor trying to reconcile reluctant penitents. Its purpose was to confront the heretic with his or her guilt, obtain a confession and an inner act of contrition, grant forgiveness, and impose a penance. For this reason the central event of the inquisitorial process was not a trial, as in criminal prosecutions, but a confession. Little would have been accomplished by proving conclusively that a man was a heretic if the man himself did not admit it. This helped to justify, in some minds at least, the use of torture.

In theory the Inquisition did not pass sentences: it imposed penances, which the defendant was obliged to agree to perform before hearing what they would be. Those who had confessed before being accused, or whose contact with heretics had been casual or inadvertent, might be sent on pilgrimages, fined, or scourged. A more onerous penance was the obligation of wearing a yellow cross on the outside of one's clothing, thus becoming a target for public insult and abuse and making it extremely difficult for one to find employment.

The penalty for heresy itself, established by Gregory IX, was imprisonment for life—although many received lesser sentences, particularly if they agreed to implicate others. Obstinate heretics (those who refused to admit their guilt or abandon their unorthodox opinions) and relapsed heretics (those who, having confessed, recanted or failed to fulfill the conditions of their penance) were handed over to secular authorities, again by order of Gregory IX, to be burned alive. The church, somewhat disingenuously, refused to pronounce the death penalty itself.

Since heretics could not be buried in consecrated ground, the bodies of those who had been convicted posthumously were dug up and burned. All property of those found guilty was confiscated and used to pay the Inquisition's operating costs. This naturally provided an extra incentive to continue producing confessions.

Not everyone supported these activities. The Inquisition represented yet another encroachment by Rome upon the authority of local bishops, who traditionally had been responsible for dealing with heresy within their own dioceses. A number of bishops simply refused to cooperate, for which they were reprimanded several times by Pope Innocent IV. The common people often opposed the Inquisition in more direct ways: several inquisitors were murdered, and a number of others physically assaulted. What finally brought the medieval Inquisition to an end, however, was that by the start of the fifteenth century it simply began to run out of suspects.

None of this, however, helped to solve the basic problem which confronted the church following the revival of European city life. Pope Gregory VII had taken great care to determine what role the clergy should play within the church, and he institutionalized that role with an enormous mass of legislation. But neither Gregory nor anyone else had seriously considered the question of what the laity's role should be. Whether deliberately or through some kind of incredible oversight, the great majority of Christian men and women were gradually excluded from active participation in the church's life.

And while a substantial part of the population was migrating to cities, the church still had the great majority of its money and manpower invested in the countryside—in papal, episcopal, and monastic estates and small rural parishes. These resources could not easily be shifted to meet other needs. Serfs could simply pack their belongings and walk to a nearby town, but monasteries could not. And the church's reliance on the system of benefices, through which clergymen were supported by the income from specific landed estates, made a large-scale urban apostolate difficult to support. As a result, the church was totally unprepared to meet the material and spiritual needs of the rapidly expanding cities.

But people are born with a capacity for spiritual activity and a need to engage in it. When they are not able to satisfy this need through approved means they will invariably find means of their own, some of which may be heterodox. It was precisely this irrepressible human need, in fact, which helped to make possible the rapid spread of Christianity in the first place. Thus it happened that in the twelfth century numerous groups of lay men and women, devoting themselves to the practice of simplicity, charity, and voluntary poverty, began more or less spontaneously to take over pastoral functions which the institutional church was unwilling or unable to perform.

The Humiliati, for example, who supported themselves by manual labor and wore plain woolen cloaks, took it upon themselves to nurse the sick, feed the indigent, and help the poor find work. A similar organization called the Waldenses, or Poor People of Lyons, preached to the poor and heard their confessions. In undertaking such activities, these groups and others like them violated a number of ecclesiastical laws, including the prohibition against preaching by the laity. Their insistence that the church renounce its wealth and worldly power aroused a great deal of hostility and suspicion among the hierarchy. And their desire to restore the spirit of primitive Christianity led them to attack some of the distinctions which had been established between laity and clergy.

While all of this was happening, the immorality of many of the lower clergy was becoming an intolerable scandal. One unintended effect of the Gregorian reform movement, in fact, had been to raise the standards by which lay people judged clerical behavior far more rapidly than the behavior itself could be changed. To many people, especially the poor, it began to seem that lay men and women like the Humiliati and the Waldenses were far more genuine witnesses to the gospel than the clergy were. This made some of them wonder why it was necessary even to have a clergy —or, for that matter, to have an institutional church at all. It was primarily because their teachings and their way of life raised such questions that the Humiliati and Waldenses were excommunicated by Pope Lucius III in 1184.

In 1181 or 1182, however, a man was born who would counteract much of these movements' popular appeal by the force of his own personal example. The son of a wealthy Italian textile merchant, he decided to take the gospel message at face value and model his life upon it. At about the age of twenty-four, he gave his not inconsiderable possessions to the poor and became an itinerant preacher. This man, Francis of Assisi, captured the imagination of Europe to a degree perhaps unequaled by anyone else before or since. It was said that he could talk with animals, whom he addressed as his brothers and sisters. He preached to flowers and to fish. Francis was, in fact, a living refutation of Albigensianism: it is possible that no other Christian ever loved God in and through nature as passionately as he did.

He and his followers preached to townspeople and tended the sick. They supported themselves by occasional day labor and by begging. They did not differ greatly, in outward appearances at least, from the Humiliati and the Waldenses; and had they appeared thirty years earlier they might easily have been included in Lucius III's excommunication decree.

Fortunately for the Franciscans, however, and for the church, the papal throne now was occupied by Innocent III. And Innocent, although remembered primarily for his political confrontations with the crowned heads of Europe, seems also to have been a perceptive and compassionate pastor. He already had received many of the Humiliati and Waldenses back into the church and permitted them to form religious communities. Now, realizing that some means had to be found to conduct an effective apostolate among the urban poor, he took a chance on the charismatic Francis by approving his followers' way of life and authorizing them to preach.

The same social conditions which produced the Franciscans also led to the establishment of other religious orders. The Augustinians, for example, performed various pastoral duties in the new settlements which had sprung up outside the walls of established cities. The Carmelites, originally an order of hermit-like monks, devoted themselves to similar work. Dominic de Guzman, the son of a Spanish nobleman, founded the Order of Preachers to provide the church with articulate, well-educated domestic missionaries who could fight Albigensianism at the grassroots level.

To appreciate the importance of the Dominicans' role, it must be kept in mind that there was no formal program for the training of priests—no seminaries and no specific educational standards—until after the Reformation. At a time when the papacy was centralizing many aspects of ecclesiastical life, the selection of candidates for ordination was still left entirely to each local bishop. In theory, those who aspired to the priesthood were at least supposed to demonstrate a basic understanding of church teachings and an ability to explain them to others. Even the most conscientious bishops, however, sometimes ordained candidates who were woefully unprepared simply because no one more qualified could be found.

Nothing facilitated the spread of unorthodox ideas more than the abysmal ignorance of a large portion of the lower clergy, who not only were unable to refute heresy but might not even know themselves what the orthodox teachings were. And as the educational level of the laity rose, particularly in cities and towns, this problem grew steadily worse.

Dominic, on the other hand, insisted from the start that his followers have first-rate educations and that every Dominican community have a professor in residence. Dominicans were sent to study at the best universities in Europe— Paris, Oxford, Bologna—and before long some of them were appointed professors of theology. So great was the

Dominicans' reputation for theological expertise that they, and later the Franciscans as well, were given responsibility for running the Inquisition. Thus it happened that while Thomas Aquinas was composing the *Summa Theologica,* some of his colleagues were supervising the torture of suspected Albigensians.

Since the Franciscans, Augustinians, Carmelites and Dominicans all took vows of poverty and begged for alms, they were referred to collectively as mendicant ("beggar") orders. But the early Franciscans differed from the other mendicants in several important respects.

They were unique, for example, in recruiting members primarily from the lower social classes and in admitting large numbers of laymen and illiterates, precisely the opposite of the kind of people who were becoming Dominicans. They were remarkable even among the mendicants for their almost obsessive devotion to what Francis referred to as Lady Poverty. And they grew at a prodigious rate—only twelve years after Francis' own conversion, they numbered in the thousands.

The Franciscans, in short, quickly became a mass movement riding the crest of a religious revival, analogous in some ways to early monasticism or the first crusades. This was precisely what was needed to counteract the appeal of the various heretical sects. But it was not long before changes were introduced, some of them at the suggestion of Rome.

The history of the early Franciscans in some ways recapitulated the history of the early church. Laymen were subordinated to the clergy, exhortations were reinforced by laws, and the practice of poverty and humility gradually was eroded.

The first companions of Francis had been simple, unschooled holy men somewhat like those who had followed

Anthony into the desert. As its popularity grew, however, the Franciscan movement began attracting people with university educations. Soon the Franciscans were following the lead of the Dominicans and sending their most promising members to study at Bologna and Paris. This decision produced some of the greatest intellectual figures of the thirteenth and fourteenth centuries—people like Bonaventure, Duns Scotus, William of Ockham, and Francis Bacon. But it also helped to transform the Franciscans from an essentially lay movement into a religious order dominated by priests.

Francis had appointed the lay brother Elias of Cortona to succeed him as head of the movement. But in 1239 Elias was deposed, primarily through the efforts of the more educated Franciscans; and three years later a new constitution excluded lay brothers from holding any office within the order. The right to preach, which Innocent III had granted to every Franciscan who had received the tonsure, soon was restricted to university graduates.

The first Franciscans had guided their lives by the personal example of Francis and by a simple Rule of his composition which consisted mainly of quotations from the gospels. In 1221, after the movement had grown too large for one man to supervise personally and some members had acquired legal training, a more formal document was drawn up. But this was superseded only two years later by a new Rule composed under the personal supervision of Cardinal Hugolino, who later became Pope Gregory IX. This, in effect, took control of the Franciscans out of their founder's hands. Those who wrote the new constitution did for the Franciscans something like what Benedict had done for monasticism: they translated an example which could be imitated only by saints into a way of life which tens of thousands could follow. But a great deal was lost in this translation, particularly with respect to the practice of poverty.

Francis and his earliest followers had owned nothing either individually or in common, in conformity with their interpretation of Christ's instructions to his disciples in *Matthew* 10:7-10. As the movement grew, however, this ideal became increasingly difficult to maintain. Not many people, particularly the more sophisticated and educated ones, were willing to depend for the rest of their lives on the day-to-day generosity of the public for their food. Besides, it was argued, begging took up valuable time which could be devoted to preaching or to prayer. And where were the thousands of Franciscans supposed to sleep?

Even during the lifetime of Francis, many of his followers had begun to claim that poverty pertains to the ownership of things, not to their use, and that it did not violate their vows to accept permanent possession of land and other goods and to enjoy the benefits of wealth, so long as donors retained legal title to the property and the money was administered by trustees. This split the movement into a faction which supported a more lenient interpretation of Franciscan poverty and another faction which opposed any changes.

Gregory IX supported the first group by declaring that the *Testament* of Francis, in which he had encouraged his followers to remain faithful to the ideal of evangelical poverty, had no legal validity. John of Parma, the order's fifth head, was forced to resign by Pope Alexander IV in 1257 because he had endorsed a somewhat more rigorous interpretation of the vow of poverty than that sanctioned by Alexander. And in 1283, Pope Martin IV transferred legal title of all Franciscan property to the Holy See and allowed the members to name their own trustees.

But the Franciscan Spirituals, as they were called,

claimed the right to live in a religious order which practiced
absolute poverty after the example of Francis and Christ.
If the church insisted upon changing the way of life which
their founder had established, then they demanded to be
allowed to withdraw from the order and live according to
the original Franciscan Rule.

Fifty years later, this is more or less what happened. In
the meantime, however, the Spirituals were subjected to
savage persecution. Many were imprisoned. Others were
declared rebels against the Franciscan Rule and subjected
to various physical punishments. Some were excommunicated. Over one hundred were burned as heretics. Part of
this persecution can be explained by the fact that the Spirituals' remarkable aversion to material possessions resembled in some ways the Albigensian belief that physical
things are intrinsically evil. And some of the Spirituals did
indeed associate with heretodox groups.

What finally sealed the fate of the Spirituals was their
totally unnecessary insistence that neither Jesus nor his
apostles had legal ownership of the goods which they had
used. When Pope John XXII, following the teachings of
the Dominicans, denied that this position was in harmony
with Scripture, a general assembly of Franciscans unani-
mously contradicted him. This was open defiance. And
John took his revenge: he terminated the Holy See's trusteeship of Franciscan property, which meant that the order
became legal owners of the lands and buildings which they
were using. This made the Franciscans identical to every
other order as far as poverty was concerned, a condition
which lasted for more than a century.

The result of all these changes was to transform the
Franciscans from an almost revolutionary movement into
one religious order among many others. And before long it

was becoming as lax as most of the others were. The church had succeeded in imposing its authority upon another spontaneous manifestation of religious enthusiasm. But it still had not solved the problem of developing an adequate role for the laity, and this may have been its single most important failure in the centuries which led up to the Reformation.

Chapter 13
AVIGNON AND ITS AFTERMATH

IN 1308, or five years after the arrest and subsequent death of Boniface III, Pope Clement V decided to establish his court in the town of Avignon, about sixty miles northwest of Marseilles. This began a sixty-eight year period which still is sometimes referred to, rather melodramatically, as the papacy's "Babylonian Captivity."

Avignon was not yet part of France, and in 1348 Pope Benedict XII purchased the entire town from the Queen of Naples. In theory, therefore, the Avignon popes were politically independent. But in actual fact Clement, the first of seven successive French popes, was almost totally subservient to King Philip IV of France. And Clement and his Avignon successors raised so many of their countrymen to the cardinalate—one hundred and thirteen out of the one hundred and thirty-four cardinals they created—that much of the church's administrative machinery passed into French hands.

In some respects this was beneficial, for it helped to free the church for a time from the avaricious grasp of the Italian nobility and permitted the creation of a much more efficient administrative system. Most of the long-term effects of the Avignon papacy, however, were catastrophic.

By abandoning the Eternal City, the papacy estranged itself from the most important source of its own prestige: its association in the public mind with the traditions of imperial Rome and with the apostles Peter and Paul. It became increasingly difficult for people to acknowledge as Peter's successor someone who was not actually functioning, or who appeared not to be functioning, as the bishop of Rome. And by identifying themselves with the interests of France, the Avignon popes drew down upon themselves the hostility of France's enemies. In England and Germany especially, people began to view the papacy less as the head of a supranational church than as the puppet of an alien state, somewhat as Americans might react today if the popes were to take up permanent residence in the Soviet Union. The English were particularly outraged to discover that Avignon was subsidizing French military operations against them during the Hundred Years' War.

Despite the aura of wickedness traditionally associated with Avignon, however, most of the popes who resided there were skillful and dedicated administrators, and none is known to have been particularly immoral. What did discredit them, more than anything else, was their insatiable thirst for money.

At a time when the ideal of evangelical poverty was capturing the imagination of Western Christendom, Clement and his successors insisted on maintaining the most opulent and extravagant court in Europe; and they constructed an enormous complex of palaces and fortifications at Avignon to house it. They also found themselves enmeshed in an interminable and ruinously expensive war in the Papal States, which were struggling for independence. Large amounts were spent in the pursuit of various diplomatic objectives, often in the form of loans which never were repaid.

Some of the Avignon popes further increased the financial drain by using church revenues to enrich their relatives. Other popes had set scandalous precedents—Boniface VIII, for example, who had diverted into his family's coffers half a million florins, or roughly two to three times the papacy's total annual income. But Clement V, the most notorious figure of the Avignon period, outdid all of his predecessors when it came to misappropriating funds.

Clement did not even bother to deposit church income in

the established banking houses: he had it sent directly to strongholds controlled by his family. No one knows how much Clement spent during his pontificate or what he spent it on, since he had the records of his expenditures destroyed; but in his will he distributed the equivalent of nearly four tons of pure gold. This was fifteen times the amount which remained in the papal treasury after Clement's death, and most of it went to his nephew. (His successor, John XXII, managed to recover some of this money by suing Clement's heirs.)

To meet these prodigious expenses, the Avignon popes imposed heavy taxes on the benefices upon which local clergy depended for support. The papacy already was collecting the entire first year's revenue ("annates") of all bishops, and in 1306 Clement V claimed annates from all minor benefices in Britain. John XXII extended this claim to benefices in other countries. Avignon also assumed responsibility for choosing a larger and larger percentage of bishops and abbots, since it had become customary for the pope to receive annual payments ("services") from those whom he had appointed to or confirmed in those offices. Finally, in 1363, Pope Urban V reserved to the papacy the right to appoint all bishops and all but the least important abbots, thus totally repudiating the concept of free episcopal and monastic elections which Gregory VII and the other reform popes had struggled so tenaciously to uphold. Responsibility for making these appointments, of which there were thousands every year, was entrusted to an enormous and incredibly venal bureaucracy.

Since this bureaucracy tended to appoint whoever was willing to pay the highest price, it awarded many benefices to people who never even bothered to visit the dioceses or monasteries which they were supposed to administer, especially when, as frequently happened, these were located in a foreign country. This naturally aroused a great deal of resentment. So many foreigners were appointed to benefices in England during the Avignon period that in 1351 Parliament denied the pope's right to exercise any control over English benefices at all. This was reinforced two years later by the Statute of Praemunire, which forbade appeals to the pope in any case involving an English benefice—another step in the gradual interposition of the English crown between the pope and the English church.

The papacy also collected "expectancies" from those who had been appointed to benefices which were not yet vacant, imposed tithes on clerical incomes, and demanded frequent subsidies for a variety of special purposes. Other important sources of papal revenue included the sale of exemptions from various ecclesiastical regulations and the fees associated with bringing suit in church courts. Ultimately, of course, the money to meet these obligations was obtained from the laity, through tithes and a multitude of other voluntary and involuntary contributions.

All of these mechanisms drained away resources which should have been used to finance pastoral activity at the diocesan and parish levels. And they further impoverished the lower clergy, many of whom already were forced to charge money for saying mass and administering the sacraments in order to avoid starvation. Delegates to the fifteenth ecumenical council, held in the French city of Vienne in 1311 and 1312, protested, without much effect, that holders of benefices should be allowed to keep at least enough of their income to support themselves. Many clergymen attempted to make ends meet by obtaining additional benefices, which further aggravated the problem of absentee bishops and pastors.

Clerics who fell behind in meeting these obligations, or who failed to pay the taxes already outstanding on benefices to which they were appointed, incurred automatic excommunication. In one three-year period during the Avignon papacy, at least one hundred and seventy-nine French and Spanish archbishops, bishops, and abbots were excommunicated for failing to pay their "services" on time. And hundreds of collectors scattered throughout Europe enforced the payment of papal taxes on the lower clergy.

Later popes eased these burdens by raising the minimum income on which annates and services could be charged, giving up the right to make appointments to many benefices, and legislating against absentee bishops and abbots. By the early part of the fifteenth century, after the insurrection in the Papal States had been suppressed, income from the church's own estates had replaced taxation as the main source of papal revenue.

But the financial excesses of Avignon, especially when contrasted with the evangelical poverty practiced by groups such as the Franciscan Spirituals, already had created a widespread impression that the state church had become a rapacious monster which exacted money from the poor in order to enrich an inner circle of high officials, that it had abandoned its commitment to the values taught by Jesus. This impression persisted long after the conditions which gave rise to it had changed, and it led some people to question the church's right to possess property at all.

Thus Marsilius of Padua, who was rector of the University of Paris during the pontificate of Clement V, wrote that any ecclesiastical wealth not being spent on the support of the clergy or on charity should be seized by secular authorities and used to promote the general welfare. And some fifty years later John Wycliff was teaching at Oxford that material possessions are divine gifts to which only those in the state of grace have a claim. From this he drew the conclusion that sinful church officials forfeited their right to own property. Both of these theories found a receptive audience among civil rulers, and they helped to pave the way for the wholesale expropriations of church property which took place during the Reformation. And even the slightest suggestion that the Avignon popes might be leading the church away from the teachings of the gospel raised serious questions about the nature and extent of papal authority.

These questions reached a crescendo in 1331, when Pope John XXII began to proclaim his belief that the saints do not yet possess the beatific vision (a direct, face-to-face contemplation of the divine essence) and that they will not possess it until after the Last Judgment. John, who was more knowledgeable about law than about theology, reasoned that since the beatific vision is a reward for the whole person, and the person is a composite of soul and body, the reward cannot take place until body and soul are reunited at the end of the world. This made perfect sense from a metaphysical viewpoint. But it contradicted a long-established popular belief, and it undermined the traditional practice of asking the saints to intercede with God on behalf of the living.

John's opinion was attacked by most leading theologians, and it was unequivocally repudiated by his successor. John himself retracted it on his deathbed. In the meantime, however, the controversy furnished potent ammunition for John's many enemies and particularly for the Franciscan Spirituals, with whom he had been fighting for more than a decade. And it greatly strengthened the position of those like Marsilius of Padua and William of Ockham who were arguing that supreme authority in the church should not be entrusted to any one person.

These developments were quickly exploited by the Holy Roman Emperor, Louis IV, whom John had excom-

municated and ordered to resign until the papacy had given
its approval to his election. Louis welcomed the dissident
Franciscan leaders to his court, where they joined him in
declaring John deposed for heresy. Since this conflict between the empire and Avignon was promoting the objectives of French diplomacy, France used every means at its
disposal to make certain that it continued as long as possible—just as, two hundred years later, France would prevent a resolution of the Lutheran crisis in Germany until it
was too late.

But France's gain was the papacy's loss. Once again the
new forces of nationalism proved stronger than the popes'
traditional weapons of excommunication and interdict,
and the German people did not waver in their support of
Louis. In 1338 the imperial electors declared that the candidate whom they chose automatically became emperor
with or without papal approval, a position which was
solemnly reaffirmed by the Golden Bull issued by Emperor
Charles IV in 1356. Germans, like Englishmen, were beginning to put loyalty to their national monarchy above loyalty to the universal church—particularly when that church
had its headquarters in France.

It was becoming increasingly clear that the political unity
of the Western church could not be maintained unless the
papacy returned to Rome. And in the latter part of the
fourteenth century this fact was driven home again and
again by two fearless and amazingly outspoken women.

Bridget of Sweden—mystic, reformer, prophetess, and
saint—devoted the last twenty years of her life to denouncing the Avignon regime in vitriolic terms. She did not
hesitate, for example, to declare that the soul of Pope Innocent VI had been "cast into hell." And she warned Pope
Urban V, who briefly took up residence in Rome, that if
he went back to Avignon he would die soon afterward: a

prophecy which was fulfilled less than three months after Urban returned there.

St. Catherine of Siena, perhaps the most remarkable woman of the entire medieval period, intervened even more directly. In an age when few women except royalty and abbesses of large religious orders exerted any influence whatsoever on public affairs, Catherine, an unmarried laywoman of humble birth, was entrusted by the city of Florence with arranging a truce between Avignon and the central Italian city-states. She took advantage of this mission, which proved unsuccessful, to castigate Pope Gregory XI to his face for neglecting his duties as bishop of Rome and spiritual head of Christendom.

Catherine's sharp tongue and Bridget's ominous prophecies helped Gregory find the courage to move the papal court back to Italy, despite the considerable obstacles placed in his way by the French crown and his own family. On January 17, 1377, Gregory and his entourage arrived in Rome, bringing the Avignon period to a close—and setting the stage for a tragedy of even greater magnitude.

Over a period of hundreds of years, much of the responsibility for ecclesiastical administration and discipline had been transferred from the local bishops to Rome. This, plus the explosive proliferation of papal taxes during the Avignon years, led to the creation of a gigantic bureaucracy, far too large for any one person to manage. As a result, medieval popes were forced to rely more and more heavily on their cardinals, not merely to give advice and carry out orders but to actually help run the church by taking over specific administrative functions. By the middle of the fourteenth century, the cardinals were taking active steps to consolidate and expand their powers. They were trying, in effect, to replace papal absolutism with a kind of government by committee.

Thus in 1352, during the election of a successor to Pope Clement VI, each of the cardinals agreed that, if elected, he would limit the number of cardinals to twenty, share his income with them, and give them the power to veto the appointment of new cardinals. This particular effort proved unsuccessful, since the new pope, Innocent VI, promptly declared the agreement contrary to church law and refused to honor it. But the cardinals kept trying, and their attempts helped to lay the groundwork for what amounted to a *coup d'etat*.

Pope Gregory XI died in 1378, less than two years after his triumphal entry into Rome. And since nearly three-quarters of Gregory's cardinals were French, it appeared quite possible that his successor might move the papal court back to Avignon. This was something which the people of Rome were determined to prevent. As preparations got underway to choose a new pope, street mobs clamored for the election of an Italian. Several cardinals were physically assaulted. A huge crowd, having helped themselves to the contents of the papal wine cellars, broke into the building in which the election was being held and threatened to burn it down. Even the commander of the troops guarding the cardinals advised them to elect an Italian, and quickly, if they valued their lives. In the midst of this uproar, the cardinals chose Archbishop Bartolomeo Prignano, a Neapolitan by birth and the last non-cardinal ever elected pope.

Almost immediately they regretted their choice. Prignano, who took the name Urban VI, exhibited such violent, paranoiac, and erratic behavior that many historians believe he must have been insane. He also made it clear that he intended to restore the papacy as an absolute monarchy, thus drastically reducing the cardinals' power, prestige, and wealth. Within six months of Urban's consecration as pope, the cardinals who had chosen him declared that his election had been invalid. Then they elected Robert of Geneva, who, as Pope Clement VII, took up residence along with the cardinals at Avignon.

The cardinals who deserted Urban may have sincerely believed that the conditions surrounding his election had prevented them from making a free choice. They may have denied the validity of his election as the only means available under canon law of removing supreme authority over the church from the hands of someone manifestly incompetent to exercise it. Perhaps they were trying to protect and enhance their own status as cardinals. Or they may have been motivated by some combination of these factors.

Whatever their reasons, the election of Clement threw the church into a state of total chaos. Urban excommunicated Clement, the cardinals who had elected Clement, and anyone who recognized the validity of Clement's pontificate. Then he appointed a whole new set of cardinals. Clement reciprocated the excommunications. And both men proceeded to collect papal taxes, grant or withhold indulgences and dispensations, and set up their own ecclesiastical courts.

This certainly was not the first time that more than one man had simultaneously claimed the papacy. Emperor Henry III, as we have seen, resolved a similar controversy in 1049 by summarily deposing all the claimants and having one of his own bishops elected pope. By the end of the fourteenth century, however, no single secular power was strong enough to take such a step. France naturally sided with the Avignon claimant, as did her dependencies and allies—Spain, Scotland, Naples, and Sicily. England and Germany, just as naturally, supported Avignon's rival, Urban. So did Scandinavia, and most of Italy.

There was ample room for disagreement, since the precise legal question at issue—the degree to which the threats of violence made against the cardinals who elected Urban had affected their freedom of choice—was impossible for anyone to answer with certainty. To this day the church has not taken an official position on the issue.

And since the administration of the church had become so centralized, with the papacy claiming the right to award nearly every benefice in Europe, the struggle was carried down to the diocesan and even the parish level. A cleric who supported one claimant was sure to be deposed by the other; if he supported neither he was likely to be deposed by both. Soon rival bishops were claiming the same sees, while pro-Rome and pro-Avignon priests were fighting for control of the same churches.

When Urban died in 1389, the Roman cardinals could easily have reunited the church by electing the Avignon claimant, Clement VII, to succeed him. Instead they chose one of their own number, Boniface IX. And when Clement died in 1394, the Avignon cardinals refused to accept Boniface as his successor. Thus the Western Schism, as this state of affairs came to be called, went on.

Eventually it became clear that since neither of the men who claimed to be pope would yield, and the two rival groups of cardinals showed every intention of perpetuating themselves indefinitely, a settlement would have to be imposed upon them. But this raised monumental legal and theological problems. How could such a thing be done? And who had the authority to do it? The answer was found in two theories which already had been circulating among canon law scholars for a century or more.

One of these theories held that the cardinals collectively possessed supreme jurisdiction over the papal office. The other theory, conciliarism, maintained that since the Holy Spirit is present in the church as a whole, a general council of the church is the highest doctrinal authority in Christendom and has the power to depose a pope who has fallen into heresy. Taken together, the two theories suggested a solution.

In 1409, or thirty-one years after the schism began, cardinals from both Rome and Avignon convened a general council in Pisa. Nearly five hundred bishops and abbots, the heads of most religious orders, seven hundred theologians, and most of the governments of Europe were represented. Taking care to observe all the appropriate formalities, the council summoned both papal claimants to appear before it, excommunicated and deposed them when they refused, and elected the cardinal of Milan to be pope in their place. And when he died less than a year later, cardinal Baldassare Cossa, who took the name John XXIII, was chosen to succeed him. But the men who occupied the papal thrones in Rome and Avignon refused to resign. So now there were three men claiming to be pope, and the confusion was worse than before.

It was Sigismund, King of Hungary and of Germany and soon to be Holy Roman Emperor, who finally brought the schism to an end by pressuring John XXIII into convening an ecumenical council in the town of Constance, about forty miles northeast of Zurich. John was confident that he could control the council's deliberations. Not only had he been accepted by most of the church, but he had appointed many of the bishops in attendance. And the Italians, who generally supported him, made up by far the largest block of delegates.

But the thousands of bishops, abbots, theologians, professors, and lower clergy who poured into Constance late in the fall of 1414 from the rest of Europe had other ideas. Determined to make the council as representative as possible of the entire Western church, they insisted that delegates not vote as individuals but that they be grouped into five "nations"—Italy, France, England, Germany, and Spain—and that each nation be given one vote. Once this rule had been adopted, John's partisans found themselves consistently in the minority.

And so when the nations of France, Germany, and England voted to force all three of the papal claimants to abdicate, John's only hope of retaining his position was to sabotage the council itself. This he attempted to do by sneaking out of Constance in disguise, taking refuge in Austria, and announcing that he had invalidated any actions which the council might take by revoking his approval of its convocation.

This forced the delegates at Constance to take a position on the momentous question of who possesses supreme authority over the church. They faced a simple and unavoidable choice.

They could accept the argument that the pope is the supreme head of the church and that a council's decrees are binding only if a pope ratifies them. In that case they might as well have ended their debates and gone home, which would have meant that the three-cornered schism would have continued—perhaps forever. Or they could stay and complete their work in spite of John's absence, which in effect would mean asserting that the council had received its authority not from the pope but directly from God. With the energetic encouragement of Sigismund they chose the second course, declaring, in a decree entitled *Sacrosancta,* that a general council is superior to the pope and to everyone else in questions of doctrine and in matters pertaining to church reform.

For two months John XXIII fled from one city to another, with Sigismund's forces in close pursuit. Finally he was taken prisoner and returned in chains to Constance, where he was stripped of his papal regalia by the council and deposed. Shortly afterward the Roman claimant, Gregory XII, abdicated. He took care first to formally recognize the assembly at Constance as an ecumenical council, thus asserting his own legitimacy and that of the other successors of Urban VI, even while relinquishing his claim to the papal throne. The Avignon claimant, Benedict XIII, steadfastly refused to abdicate unless he were allowed to name his own successor. Two years after Gregory's resignation, the council deposed him.

Now the delegates faced another crucial decision. Everyone agreed that the church was in desperate need of a thoroughgoing reform—"reform in head and in members," as *Sacrosancta* expressed it. But should the council enact all necessary legislation before electing a new pope? Or should pope and council undertake the work of reformation together?

Many delegates feared that any pope elected before the reforms were put into effect might block their implementation, particularly since a number of proposals on the councils's agenda would have drastically limited the exercise of papal authority. As later events were to show, this fear was not unfounded. But there were compelling arguments against further delay.

Not until a new pope was elected and universally accepted, for example, could the trauma brought about by the schism finally begin to heal. Many of the suggested reforms, such as curtailment of the pope's right to impose taxes and to appoint bishops, could not be accomplished without the renegotiation of international agreements and a total overhaul of the church's administrative structure. These were certain to be long and tedious tasks, and the council already had been in session for three years. Then there were the inherent difficulties involved in having an assembly containing thousands of people attempt to correct abuses in tens of thousands of individual monasteries and parishes.

Finally it was agreed that the delegates would pass a general reform program, elect a new pope, and give him the responsibility for implementing the program in detail. To make certain that the reforms would in fact be carried out, future popes would be required to convene general councils at stated intervals and report on the progress they had made. It was with this understanding that the council elected Odo Colonna as Pope Martin V, officially ending the schism. Then it adjourned, in April of 1418.

Much abuse has been heaped on the eight men who claimed the papacy between 1378 and 1415 for the damage each of them did to the church by continuing to insist that he and he alone was the rightful pope. The criticism, certainly, is justified. But there is no reason to assume that any of them doubted in his own mind that his claims were justified. And it is difficult to imagine that men such as Leo the Great, Gregory VII, or Innocent III would have acted much differently under similar circumstances.

At the same time the long agony of the Western Schism underscores in dramatic fashion the often-forgotten fact that no society, including the society which is the church, can flourish if its members—whoever they may be—insist on exercising the last full measure of their rights and privileges to the detriment of the welfare of the society as a whole.

Baldassare Cossa died in 1419, three and a half years after his deposition at Constance; and Cosimo de' Medici had his body interred in the baptistry of the cathedral of Florence. There his tomb still may be seen, its inscription a poignant reminder of the turmoil which accompanied the Western Schism: "Here lies Baldassare Cossa, who for a time was Pope John XXIII."

Chapter 14
REFORMATION EVE

POPE Martin V scrupulously followed the letter of the reform decrees passed at Constance, but he went no further than he had to observing their spirit. Constance, for example, had prohibited papal appointment of bishops for five years, or until the next ecumenical council was scheduled to begin. Martin dutifully waited five years, and then resumed the wholesale distribution of episcopal benefices.

He convened a general council in 1423, as Constance had stipulated. When this assembly began to pass decrees of which he disapproved, however, Martin first moved it from Pavia to Siena and then dissolved it. Eight years later, again in conformity with decrees passed at Constance, he convoked another council, this one to be held in Basel. But Martin died before this council began, leaving it to his successor. Eugene IV, to strike the decisive blow against conciliarism.

The Council of Basel began its deliberations in July of 1431. Five months later the newly elected Pope Eugene attempted to imitate Martin's example by ordering the council to adjourn. But the delegates at Basel were in a fighting mood. Not only did they refuse to disband, but they adopted an even stronger declaration of conciliar supremacy than the one approved at Constance.

This brought council and pope into direct confrontation. The basic issue, as far as most people were concerned, was whether or not the papacy should be allowed to block the reforms which Constance had initiated. Many church leaders, including the majority of Eugene's own cardinals, joined the assembly at Basel. Europe once more began to choose sides, and most of Europe sided with the council.

In December of 1433 Eugene accepted the inevitable

and formally acknowledged the legitimacy of the council, which now was in a position to enact a comprehensive program of church reform. It quickly became apparent, however, that none of the groups represented at Basel was willing to permit the curtailment of its own privileges. And so the delegates concentrated their attention on the one aspect of reform on which they all could agree: reduction of the power of the papacy. Among other things they totally abolished the payment of annates and most other forms of papal taxation, thus making popes dependent upon church councils for their financial support.

This was similar to the strategy which England's parliament was using at about the same time to impose its will upon the crown. If it had succeeded, the papacy might have evolved into a constitutional monarchy. But Eugene was able to stem the conciliarist tide and reassert his authority through a brilliant diplomatic maneuver.

Several times in the preceding centuries, Byzantine emperors had agreed to acknowledge papal supremacy in order to preserve their rapidly disintegrating empire. Michael VIII Paleologus, as we have seen, made a total submission at the Second Council of Lyons in 1274 in order to ward off an invasion by Charles of Anjou—although he was unable to terrorize his subjects into following his lead.

In 1369 John V Paleologus, seeking assistance against the Turks, traveled to Rome to formally recognize the authority of Pope Urban V. But John's entourage boycotted the official ceremony of celebration held at St. Peter's, after they discovered that Urban was planning to replace Byzantine church rituals with Roman ones. And the military assistance which Urban had promised never arrived.

By 1431 nearly the entire Byzantine Empire had fallen under Turkish control except Constantinople itself—an isolated, nearly bankrupt city-state awaiting the inevitable

Turkish assault. Emperor John VIII Paleologus, in a desperate attempt to obtain assistance from the West, opened negotiations with Pope Martin V, and, after Martin's death, with Eugene IV. And Eugene, who was seeking some way to bring the Council of Basel to heel, was extremely receptive to his pleas.

The council had accepted Byantium's offer to discuss the possibility of reuniting the Eastern and Western churches, but it had insisted that the negotiations take place either in Basel or in Avignon. Eugene, recognizing his opportunity, proposed that a council of unity be held in Italy; and he persuaded the Byzantines to agree—after Eugene had promised to pay the transportation and living expenses of all seven hundred people in their delegation. (When he found himself unable to make good on this pledge, Cosimo de' Medici helped to raise the necessary money.) This forced the Council of Basel either to accept Eugene's plan, thus giving a great boost to the prestige of the papacy, or else to put itself in the position of hindering church reunification.

Just as the establishment of conciliar supremacy had been made possible by the fragmentation of papal authority during the Western Schism, so it was by undermining the unity of the conciliarists that the papacy was able to regain what it had lost. At a tumultuous meeting on May 7, 1437, a majority of the council voted to remain in Basel and the minority simultaneously passed a resolution supporting Eugene, while leaders of both sides fought for control of the speakers' platform. This ignominious spectacle discredited the entire conciliar movement. Bishops and cardinals began to leave Basel in dismay, and secular governments started withdrawing their support. Four months later Eugene transferred the council to Ferrara, and later to Florence.

While the Byzantine leaders desperately needed military assistance against the Turks, they also needed a religious settlement which stood some chance of being accepted by their people. That meant in particular, no compromise on the *filioque* issue. Eugene, for his part, wanted a clear affirmation that the pope—and thus, by implication, not an ecumenical council—is the supreme head of the church. The decree *Laetentur coeli,* signed in July of 1439 after months of bitter wrangling, satisfied both sides.

Greeks and Latins solemnly agreed that the bishop of Rome possesses ultimate and complete authority over the entire church. They also agreed that the patriarch of Constantinople is indeed second in dignity to the pope, just as the Byzantines always had maintained. The *filioque* dispute was resolved by declaring that the Roman teaching that the Holy Spirit proceeds from the Father and from the Son and the Byzantine teaching that the Spirit proceeds from the Father through the Son actually are equivalent. The two formulations, in other words, are equally valid; and each church was justified in using whichever one it wished. Had the Roman church been willing to concede this point four centuries earlier, the Eastern Schism might never have occurred at all.

Laetentur coeli was a resounding victory for Pope Eugene in his battle against conciliarism. But popular feeling in Constantinople was solidly against the agreement, and the Byzantine delegates themselves repudiated it almost as soon as they returned home. To the Greeks, acknowledging that the pope had complete power over the church implied admitting that he had the right to change or abolish their traditional liturgy, something to which they could never agree.

Eugene remained true to his word, and did his best to organize a crusade to save Constantinople. But only Hungary and Poland agreed to send troops; and when these forces were routed at Varna, on Bulgaria's Black Sea coast, the last hope of large-scale Western help disappeared. With it vanished the last motivation of the Byzantines to seek reunion with the Roman church.

On May 29, 1453—two years after the birth of Christopher Columbus and thirty years before the birth of Martin Luther—troops of Sultan Mahomet II forced their way into the city through a gate which inadvertently had been left unguarded and engulfed the last remnants of the Roman Empire. But the last emperor of the East did not allow himself to be captured and pensioned off into obscurity like Romulus Augustulus. When it became clear that the battle for Constantinople had been lost, Constantine XI Paleologus cast aside his imperial insignia and charged into the onrushing Turks. His body was never found.

Byzantium's historic role as guardian of orthodox belief and benevolent overlord of the Balkans was taken over by Russia, which began to refer to itself as the "Third Rome." As a result, the Byzantine concept of theocratic empire continued to influence the course of European history for hundreds of years.

Like the men who claimed to be pope during the Western Schism, the delegates at Basel had insisted on the full exercise of what they perceived to be their rights and privileges, regardless of the effect of their actions on the welfare of the church as a whole. They also had created an impression that the very existence of ecumenical councils posed a threat to the papacy's traditional prerogatives. This made Eugene IV's successors extremely reluctant to convene another council, even though most of the reforms of which the church was in such desperate need could not be implemented without one. But then his successors were

not particularly interested in reform—until reform finally
was thrust upon them.

Nicholas V, elected after Eugene's death in 1447, set a
pattern which was followed for most of the next century by
wholeheartedly embracing the ideals of the Italian Renaissance. He rebuilt many of Rome's churches and palaces
and employed some of the leading artists of Europe, including Fra Angelico, to decorate them. He spent freely
from the papal treasury to acquire rare manuscripts and
have them copied. He founded the Vatican Library, which
by the time of his death had become the largest in Europe.
Humanist scholars, eager to revive the study of classical
literature, flocked to the papal court and were lavishly subsidized.

Nicholas declared on his deathbed that he had constructed grandiose buildings and encouraged literature and
the arts as a means of promoting religious devotion. This
claim, apparently, was quite sincere. And there was a certain logic to it—the logic, which can be traced all the
way back to Constantine, of utilizing colorful ceremonies,
richly decorated vestments, and awe-inspiring architecture
to symbolize the church's claim to be a more glorious and
exalted institution than any earthly kingdom.

But however well-intentioned Nicholas may have been,
his sponsorship of writers who glorified the values of pagan humanism had the effect of helping to popularize the
pre-Christian notion that people can lead virtuous lives
without supernatural assistance. And that notion tended to
make prayer, the sacraments, and the church itself appear
unnecessary.

More importantly, the example of Nicholas encouraged
the popes who followed him—even those whose personal
lives were considered above reproach by the standards of
the day—to devote most of their energy to erecting magni-

ficent buildings, patronizing the arts, and increasing their political and military power. The spiritual needs of the church, meanwhile, went virtually unnoticed.

Sixtus IV, for example, who became pope sixteen years after the death of Nicholas, concerned himself primarily with waging war and enriching his relatives. Six of his nephews and cousins were made cardinals, and one was given half a dozen bishoprics and several abbeys. Sixtus also involved himself in an attempt by his nephew to overthrow Lorenzo de'Medici, in the course of which Lorenzo's brother, Giuliano, was murdered during mass in the cathedral of Florence. To help finance his political and military ambitions, he doubled the number of purchasable church offices.

In 1492, eight years after the death of Sixtus, the Spanish cardinal Rodrigo Borgia ascended the papal throne as Alexander VI. And Alexander—who had been made a cardinal by his uncle, Pope Callixtus III; who had used bribery to secure his own election as pope; and who had fathered at least seven illegitimate children, one of whom he made a cardinal—summed up in his own dissipated life all the worst features of the Renaissance church.

By the end of the fifteenth century, the papacy had again become the private possession of a small number of noble families who exploited it for their own benefit. Of the ten popes who reigned from 1431 to 1513, eight were either uncles or nephews of other popes—and two of the next three were cousins. The basic reason why the church was unable to reform itself from the top down in the fifteenth and sixteenth centuries as it had in the eleventh century was that too many people at the top had a vested interest in keeping things as they were.

Popes and councils alike, for example, had been legislating for centuries against the buying and selling of

ecclesiastical offices, perhaps the single greatest evil afflicting the church. And yet the practice continued to flourish,
and the sale of offices became a major source of papal
revenue. Men would purchase bishoprics, on credit if
necessary, and then recover their costs and realize a profit
by exacting contributions from the clergy and laity of their
dioceses. This naturally resulted in the consecration of
many incompetent and profligate bishops. But it became
increasingly difficult for anyone to abolish the system, because the papacy and the curia came to depend more and
more heavily on the revenue which it produced.

Those bishops who attempted to root out local abuses
were frustrated by the fact that jurisdiction over many aspects of religious life in their dioceses had been taken out
of their hands. A large percentage of monasteries, for example, were accountable only to Rome; and both monks
and diocesan clergy often were able to block the efforts of
reform-minded bishops by filing suit in papal courts. Ecclesiastical authority had been centralized by the papacy in
the eleventh, twelfth, and thirteenth centuries in order to
facilitate the implementation of church reforms. In the fifteenth and sixteenth centuries, however, when the papacy
no longer was exercising effective control over the church,
that same centralization served to make the realization of
meaningful reform well-nigh impossible.

And the religious orders, which had spearheaded reform
efforts on a number of previous occasions, were now one
of the major forces supporting the status quo. By the fourteenth century, many religious communities had become
far too small to carry on any meaningful apostolic work.
In some cases, membership was only one-fifth of what it
had been three hundred years before. Part of this decrease
was caused by the Black Death, which struck Europe in the
second half of the fourteenth century and killed perhaps

one-third of its population. But there also was a deliberate attempt on the part of many communities to restrict their membership in order to increase each member's share of the common revenue. As the same amount of income was divided among fewer and fewer monks and nuns, of course, the allocation of the church's resources became increasingly inefficient.

Those who remained in the monasteries often did little or no manual work: they had become gentlemen farmers, with servants to look after their needs. Many purchased permission from Rome to live outside the confines of their communities or to cease wearing their monastic habits. It did not help matters that monasteries generally preferred that candidates for membership be of noble birth. Pope Benedict XII had complained in the first half of the fourteenth century that it was impossible to impose any restraints on the behavior of upper-class monks because of the political influence of their families—and the problem grew steadily worse as time went on.

Eventually even the mendicants, whose efforts were absolutely essential to the conduct of an effective urban ministry, acquired a reputation for idleness, worldliness, and dishonesty. It is indicative of how far the mendicants had strayed from their original ideals that the venal and nepotistic Sixtus IV, before his election as pope, had been head of the Franciscans.

Both the hierarchy and the existing religious orders, in short, generally were unwilling or unable to take the lead in renewing the spiritual life of the church. And so the impetus for reform had to come from another source, the same source which had given rise to the Benedictine movement in the sixth century and the Franciscan movement in the thirteenth: people's innate urge to satisfy the needs of their spiritual natures.

By the middle of the fifteenth century, many devout Christians were rejecting the sterile and superstitious ritualism into which popular religious practice had been allowed to degenerate. More specifically, they were turning toward the cultivation of an inner spiritual life and away from liturgical ceremonies, pilgrimages, and the veneration of relics. They were seeking knowledge of God not through the intricate abstractions of scholastic theology or through mystical raptures but by meditating on the New Testament and the life of Christ. As a result, they tended to ignore the distinction between clergy and laity and to downplay the importance of an intermediary between the believer and God.

This trend toward individual prayer and meditation based on the Scriptures was reinforced by the work of an international circle of scholars—such as Jean Colet in England and Jacques Lefevre d'Etaples in France—who began to apply the critical and editorial techniques of the Italian humanists to the classics of Christian literature, particularly the Pauline epistles. Best known and by far the most influential member of this circle was Desiderius Erasmus of Rotterdam, who was born eleven years after the publication of Gutenberg's first Bible and who devoted his life to promoting the cause of church reform through the printed word.

In addition to publishing inexpensive and readable editions of the writings of church Fathers, Erasmus flooded Europe with popular works of his own composition which castigated clerical immorality and greed and ridiculed the idea that salvation can be gained through external ritual and the purchase of indulgences rather than through inner spiritual perfection. He also prepared the first edition of the epistles and gospels ever printed in the original Greek, with his own translation—a far more accurate translation than the Vulgate, which had been the standard version since the time of St. Jerome—in parallel columns. It was this text which Luther and many of the other reformers used as the basis of their vernacular translations.

Erasmus quickly became by far the most widely read author in Europe. It has been estimated that during the 1530s, more than one million copies of works which he had written or edited were in circulation. In some years they represented twenty percent of all the books sold in Paris and London.

The audience which read his work had been brought into existence by the explosive proliferation of universities, thanks to which there were more educated lay people in Europe at the start of the sixteenth century than at any other time since the fall of Rome. And since these people knew Latin, they could participate in theological debates and in ecclesiastical affairs on more or less equal terms with the clergy.

It appeared, at least to the Christian humanists, that the printing press had made it possible to reform the church from below by appealing directly to large numbers of laity and lower clergy: that by disseminating the scriptures and other edifying works, and by attacking religious ignorance and superstition, they could promote a rebirth of genuine piety. And Erasmus was the man to whom everyone naturally looked to lead this campaign.

In Rome, meanwhile, nothing had changed. Pope Alexander VI was succeeded in 1503, after the month-long reign of Pius III, by Cardinal Giuliano della Rovere, one of the nephews of Sixtus IV, who facilitated his election through the generous distribution of bribes and took the name Julius II.

It was Julius who began construction of a new St. Peter's basilica to replace the structure erected by Constan-

tine more than a thousand years earlier, and who commissioned Michelangelo to paint the ceiling of the Sistine
chapel. It also was Julius, the quintessential warrior-pope,
who led the papacy into a dizzying series of military alliances, first with France and the Empire against Venice and
then with Venice and Spain against France and her Italian
allies. The high point of his pontificate came in 1512, when
one of his cardinals, after capturing the cities of Cremona
and Pavia, led the papal armies to a triumph over Milan.
In that same year, however, Julius was compelled to do
something which he would have much preferred not to do.

Ever since the debacle at Basel in 1437 and the subsequent reestablishment of papal supremacy, pressure had
been building for the convening of another ecumenical
council. At the conclave which elected Pope Paul II in
1464, every cardinal had solemnly sworn that, if elected, he
would convoke a council within three years. A similar
promise was made by each cardinal who participated in the
election of Julius. And yet both popes, fearful of encouraging a resurgence of conciliarism, had refused to
honor their pledges.

In 1511 a group of nine cardinals finally took matters
into their own hands by convening a council at Pisa which
was supported both by France and by the Empire. This
forced Julius to convoke a papally sanctioned council,
Lateran V, which opened in Rome in May of 1512. One
year later, with this council's work still in its initial stages,
Julius died.

At this fateful moment, in the middle of the last
ecumenical council before the Reformation, the exquisitely
hedonistic Giovanni de' Medici, son of Lorenzo the
Magnificent, was elected to succeed Julius. This ended
whatever minuscule hope there might have been for correcting the more flagrant abuses from which the church was

suffering before the unity of Western Christendom was destroyed. De' Medici, who became a cardinal at the age of thirteen but had not even been ordained a priest at the time of his election as pope, had no interest in making changes. It was he who uttered the infamous phrase, "God gave us the papacy; now let us enjoy it." And enjoy it he did, not only emptying the papal treasury but running it four hundred thousand ducats into debt.

And so Lateran V, which had been convened in the first place primarily to outmaneuver Julius's rebellious cardinals and to reassert papal authority, received no encouragement from the new pope to institute reforms. It discussed many of the issues which eventually were resolved by the Council of Trent, and many of the actual reforms adopted at Trent were proposed to it. But Lateran V contented itself with superficial measures, such as establishing for the first time a formal system for censoring books, and with repeating the customary prohibitions against simony and the holding of multiple benefices. It did not deal in any way with the underlying causes of the church's malaise. And the few reform proposals which Lateran V did adopt were being violated by the Medici pope, Leo X, even before it adjourned.

Chapter 15
REFORMATION, ACT ONE:
THE CHALLENGE

IN the year 1514, while the fifth Lateran Council was in the process of legislating still once more against the sale of ecclesiastical offices and the holding of multiple benefices, a transaction occurred which epitomized everything that Erasmus and the other humanist reformers were fighting against.

Albrecht of Brandenburg—who already, at the age of twenty-four, was bishop of Halberstadt, archbishop of Magdeburg, and superior of several wealthy abbeys—had outbid all rivals for the right to become archbishop of Mainz. He and his family were willing to pay more than anyone else for that particular office because it was worth more to them than to anyone else. Not only was Mainz an extremely wealthy see, but its archbishop was one of the seven electors of the Holy Roman Empire. And since Albrecht's older brother already was the Elector of Brandenburg, Albrecht's installation at Mainz gave his family two of the four votes needed to choose an emperor.

Albrecht bid fourteen thousand ducats for the archbishopric, in addition to which he had to pay ten thousand ducats for a papal dispensation from the law against holding multiple bishoprics and another ten thousand in various administrative costs. That made a total equivalent to about two hundred and seventy pounds of pure gold.

He borrowed this amount from the German banker Jacob Fugger, a specialist in ecclesiastical finance, who sent the money to Rome. And he agreed to repay the loan, plus interest, by giving Fugger one half of the proceeds of an indulgence to be preached in the archdioceses of Magdeburg and Mainz. The indulgence in question was the one which Pope Julius II had authorized to subsidize construction of the new St. Peter's basilica.

The practice of granting indulgences, which was to play such an important role in the early stages of the Reformation, seems to have evolved out of the custom of commuting penances—which in turn had its roots in the tendency of some confessors in the early Middle Ages, particularly the Irish, to impose penances of such incredible duration that people sometimes died before completing them. This was especially troublesome because until the eleventh century the church taught that a person's sins were not forgiven until the penance had been performed.

Gradually it became customary for confessors, after assigning arduous penances, to commute them to the recitation of prayers or the performance of various charitable works, such as giving alms to the poor. Then popes began claiming the right to reduce or cancel penances. Urban II did something of this sort in 1095, when he declared that participation in the First Crusade would take the place of all the penances which those who had confessed their sins ordinarily would have had to perform. And soon a relaxation of normal penances was being authorized for those who constructed or restored churches, supported hospitals or religious communities, or contributed to similar causes.

At this point, when penances were being reduced in exchange for monetary contributions, the practice began to take on the character of a commercial transaction. And although the church continued to insist, at least officially, that indulgences were efficacious only for those who had confessed and been absolved, this condition was not always emphasized by those who were collecting the money.

In 1476, or seven years before the birth of Martin Luther, Pope Sixtus IV added to the misunderstanding surrounding indulgences by declaring that they could be obtained by the living on behalf of the dead, in which case benefits from a treasury of merit which Christ and the saints had earned and which the church had been empowered to administer would be applied to their souls. This teaching seemed to imply that indulgences could be effective even without any act of contrition or repentance on the part of the recipient—since the deceased are, by definition, incapable of making such acts. And that, in turn, tended to reinforce the popular notion that an indulgence was a kind of automatic pardon which removed the effects of sin by its own power, independently of the inner disposition of the sinner.

At the start of the sixteenth century, many Christians undoubtedly believed that they could guarantee their own salvation or lessen the sufferings of a deceased relative by purchasing a piece of paper from someone like Johann Tetzel, the Dominican priest whom Jacob Fugger had commissioned to preach the St. Peter's indulgence.

Tetzel's sales pitch conflicted in several respects with what was later defined to be official Catholic doctrine, particularly with respect to the applicability of indulgences to the souls of the dead. Since Tetzel followed the handbook issued to indulgence preachers in his area, however, and since he already had preached indulgences on ten previous occasions, his extravagant claims must have reflected what many people believed the church's teaching to be.

And Luther, an Augustinian monk who was teaching biblical theology at the University of Wittenberg, found these claims to be totally opposed to the basic Christian belief that salvation depends upon an inner spiritual transformation.

(Luther himself never heard or saw Tetzel. Frederick the Wise, the Elector of Saxony, would not allow the indulgence into his territory because he feared it might cut into the revenue which he was collecting by exhibiting his prized collection of seventeen thousand relics. Luther's knowledge of Tetzel's activities came from reports by people who had traveled from Wittenberg to the nearby villages of Juterbog and Zerbst to hear Tetzel preach.)

It was not so much the sale of indulgences to which Luther objected as the very concept of indulgences. And to appreciate the logic of his objection, one must recall that he had just worked his way through a profound spiritual crisis which had forced him to come to grips with the most fundamental of all religious issues, the relationship between the individual person and God.

Oppressed by a profound, heart-wrenching terror at the thought of his own possible damnation, and despairing of his ability to live a holy enough life to earn salvation, Luther finally had found inner peace through the realization that, as St. Paul had emphasized so strongly, it is not through our own actions or merits that we are saved but through the infinite love and mercy of God, who justifies us in spite of our sins by virtue of our faith in Jesus.

Filled, then, with an overwhelming sense of joy and relief at the thought that Jesus already has paid the full measure of our salvation by his death, Luther came to look upon indulgences in somewhat the same way that Paul had viewed circumcision: as symbolic of a lack of faith that Christ's redemptive act was sufficient by itself to save us. It was in this spirit that he composed his Ninety-Five Theses, a list of objections to what Tetzel was teaching and to the whole theory of indulgences, plus objections to many of the same abuses which Erasmus and other reformers had attacked.

Luther denied, in particular, that the pope or any other human being can control the merits of Christ, bestowing them upon some people and withholding them from others. He denied that the pope can authorize the release of souls from purgatory. And if the pope does indeed have this power, Luther asked, why does he not free all of them from their torment out of pure Christian charity?

He sent a summary of these objections to his own bishop, asking him to delete anything which in his opinion conflicted with Catholic teaching. And he wrote to the bishop who had authorized Tetzel's preaching, Albrecht of Brandenburg, alerting him to the misconceptions which the people of Wittenberg had gained from listening to Tetzel —unaware that Albrecht had a considerable financial stake in the success of Tetzel's mission.

Luther's bishop wrote back that he could find no doctrinal fault with any of his criticisms and that he agreed with many of them. But Albrecht, fearful that the questions which Luther was raising might make it impossible for him to repay Jacob Fugger, reported him to Rome.

One year after composing the Ninety-Five Theses, Luther appeared before a tribunal presided over by the head of the Dominican order, Cardinal Cajetan, where he apologized for some of his more extreme statements about the papacy and agreed to stop criticizing indulgences. But he steadfastly refused to retract his teachings unless it were demonstrated to him that they contradicted scripture. And, anticipating excommunication, he raised a troublesome legal issue by announcing that he was appealing his case from whatever judgment the pope might make to the judgment of a general council.

Appeals of this kind had been specifically forbidden by Pope Pius II almost sixty years earlier. Enough uncertainty still remained about the relative competencies of popes and councils, however, that many of Luther's sympathizers refused to accept a verdict against him as definitive until it had been confirmed by a council, something which did not happen for over thirty more years.

Luther's fate was now in the hands of his secular ruler, Frederick the Wise, who was inclined to look with favor on his cause. Erasmus, among others, asked Frederick to make certain that he was given a fair hearing. But Luther's Augustinian superior already had been ordered to arrest him, and Cajetan was demanding that Frederick extradite him to Rome to stand trial. Under ordinary circumstances, Frederick would not have been able to resist these pressures for long.

What intervened to save Luther at this point was the impending election of a new Holy Roman Emperor.

Maximilian I, the reigning emperor, had been maneuvering for years to secure the succession of his grandson Charles. But Charles already had inherited Burgundy and the Netherlands from his father; and after the death of his mother's parents, Ferdinand of Aragon and Isabella of Castile, he had come into possession of Spain, Naples, Sicily, portions of North Africa, and Spain's colonies in the New World. He would automatically receive Austria, Hungary, and Bohemia when Maximilian died.

If he also were to be elected emperor, Charles would become by far the most powerful European sovereign since Charlemagne. More important, perhaps, as far as the papacy was concerned, his election would give him control over both northern and southern Italy, the same encirclement which Innocent III and his successors had fought so desperately to prevent.

Any European monarch could be elected emperor, and Francis I of France, Henry VIII of England, and Frederick the Wise all were campaigning for the crown. Rome would have preferred any of them to Charles; but its first choice was Frederick, the least powerful of the four. As a result, Pope Leo X did everything possible to conciliate Frederick, including legitimizing his two natural children. And even after the Hapsburg heir was elected, becoming Emperor Charles V, the papacy continued to cultivate Frederick's favor, hoping that he might counterbalance to some extent the influence of Charles within the Empire.

The effect of all this was to give Luther temporary immunity from ecclesiastical prosecution, a respite which he utilized to develop more completely the implications inherent in the Ninety-Five Theses. Meanwhile, thanks to the printing press, his ideas were being spread across Europe. By the time judicial proceedings finally were initiated against him, Luther had attracted enough support, particularly in Germany, to furnish him with some measure of protection.

Luther's primary concern was not to cleanse the church of corruption but to reform its theology, particularly by emphasizing each individual's absolute dependence upon God. And the foundation of this approach was his explanation of the process of justification, an issue which involves the interrelation of three of the most perplexing concepts of Christian theology: grace, free will, and the effects of original sin. It is extremely difficult even today, and it must have been much more difficult four and half centuries ago, to determine the extent to which the Lutheran and Catholic positions on this question represented differences of emphasis and the extent to which they were irreconcilably opposed.

It probably is safe to say that the differences between the Lutheran and Catholic positions, as they eventually were formalized, are so technical that not one Catholic or Lutheran in a hundred understands their full complexity. And it is also safe to say that it was not primarily because they had strong feelings on issues such as these that so many people responded to Luther's appeal. What they did feel, and what they responded to, was the fact that the Lutheran movement gave them a reassurance that their salvation did

not depend upon external rituals. It also gave them a sense
of being much more intimately related to God.

This was no accident. Anything which he could do to
tear down the barriers which for centuries had excluded lay
people from full participation in the life of the church,
Luther did.

He greatly simplified the mass, focusing attention on its
essential elements. He translated the liturgy into the vernacular and he promoted lay participation in divine worship rather than silent and passive observation of a ritual
performed by someone else. He encouraged the singing of
hymns, many of which he wrote himself. He emphasized
the importance of sermons, and made the preaching of the
gospel an essential part of the Eucharistic celebration. He
also denied any fundamental distinction between the clergy
and the laity and insisted that scripture is the only standard of Christian doctrine.

By emphasizing St. Paul's theory of the priesthood of all
believers and teaching that ordination does not confer any
special powers which lay people do not already possess,
Luther attacked two concepts which the Catholic Church
had taken almost for granted since at least the time of
Gregory VII: the existence of the clergy as a separate class
within the church and the distinction between the secular
and the religious realms.

And whereas Gregory and his successors had insisted
that the clergy remain celibate as a means of reinforcing
their separation from the laity—a regulation which the
church never had been able to enforce—Luther opposed
the whole idea of an unmarried clergy. This drew an immediate response from monks, mendicants, and secular
priests, perhaps half of whom had mistresses. Many of
these people, and many nuns as well, had never had a true
vocation to the religious life in the first place; and they

numbered heavily among Luther's first and most enthusiastic followers. At the same time, Luther denied that churchmen were exempt from the jurisdiction of civil law and requested the secular rulers of Germany's more than three hundred principalities to take the lead in implementing church reforms. Here again he found a ready audience: the first edition of his *Appeal to the Christian Nobility of the German Nation,* four thousand copies, sold out in less than a week.

It was during a series of debates with the theologian Johann Eck, held at Leipzig in June and July of 1519, that Luther first publicly denied the supreme authority not only of the papacy—which conciliarists had been refusing to accept for more than one hundred years and which many German bishops also opposed—but of general councils as well.

There is some evidence that Eck, in order to discredit Luther, maneuvered him into taking a more extreme position on this point than he otherwise might have done. Be that as it may, Luther went on to propose that ultimate doctrinal authority does not reside in any person or organization but in the Word of God as recorded in Scripture, which no declaration of pope or council can limit or override. This concept later was summarized in the phrase *Scriptura normans non normata,* or "Scripture is a standard which itself is not subject to any standard."

Luther's emphasis upon the Bible as the source and criterion of Christian belief was part of a widespread reaction against the tendency of many theologians, ever since the rediscovery of Aristotle's writings in the twelfth and thirteenth centuries, to rely more upon metaphysical theories and logical arguments than upon the teachings of Christ. This had the effect of shifting the focus of Christian thinking toward human reason and away from Scripture and from faith.

One example of this was the scholastic emphasis upon a natural law ethics based almost exclusively on human reason rather than on the words of Jesus, who taught a morality which transcends reason and perhaps even contradicts it. Many scholastic theologians tended to treat God himself not only as an object of reason but also as a being whose actions necessarily conform to human concepts of fairness and justice. This encouraged people to look upon God as a powerful but predictable cosmic lord with whom bargains could be struck and who could be put under some kind of obligation to do or not to do certain things by performing rituals or reciting prayers.

A hundred and fifty years before Luther's birth, William of Ockham had launched a devastating attack against this kind of thinking. The fact of God's absolute omnipotence, Ockham argued, means that there can be no necessary connection between causes and effects. God can make any event follow any other event—such as, for example, making a fire radiate cold rather than heat. Thus there is no ultimate reason for anything except God's unfathomable will, and no certainty of anything except through faith. There is nothing to prevent God from rewarding sinners and punishing the righteous, which implies that no one can earn divine favor through his or her own actions. In emphasizing the primacy of Scripture over reason, Luther, who freely acknowledged his debt to Ockham, was attempting to restore an omnipotent God and his revealed Word to their central place within Christianity.

Not only was this a necessary corrective to the metaphysical excesses of scholasticism, but it also helped to make Luther's teachings accessible to people with no interest in philosophical technicalities. Luther was saying that the essence of Christianity lies not in theological treatises but in the epistles and gospels, where even the most unsophisticated men and women can find it for themselves. And

Luther went on to reject, or at least to doubt, every religious doctrine for which he could not find clear and direct substantiation in the Bible. It was on these grounds that he denied the primacy of the pope and asserted that baptism and the Lord's Supper are the only two sacraments instituted by Christ. While acknowledging that the Eucharistic bread and wine truly are the body and blood of Jesus, he refused to accept the metaphysical concept of transubstantiation.

In addition, his insistence that there must be no intermediary between Scripture and the individual believer was incompatible with traditional interpretations of the church's teaching authority. Since people frequently disagree about what Scripture means, Luther's position amounted to an assertion of the absolute inviolability of the individual conscience, an idea whose implications were so revolutionary that even he finally repudiated them.

It should be emphasized that Luther himself felt that he was not departing from the Catholic faith but merely liberating that faith from the legalistic, ritualistic, and philosophical encrustations which, in his opinion, were suffocating its spirit. One also should remember that many of the points on which he did contradict the teaching of most Catholic theologians—such as the number of the sacraments—had not yet been officially defined.

It was in their emphasis upon reformulating doctrine that Luther and his followers differed most fundamentally from Erasmus, for whom the basic problem was not that the old theology was wrong but that there was too much of it. Erasmus was in some ways a more radical reformer than Luther. He insisted that it is not through knowledge of theology, Catholic or Lutheran, that a person gains salvation, but through the practice of Christian virtues. He was working for a different kind of reformation—the spiritual regeneration of individual people.

He had no fundamental objection to the Ninety-Five Theses. And, as the illegitimate son of a priest, he was more familiar with the evils caused by clerical concubinage than Luther was. He also agreed that there should be no intermediary between Scripture and the individual believer. Indeed, this was precisely why he opposed Luther's attempt to turn his own personal interpretation of Scripture into a new theological system, and why he was appalled by Luther's invitation to the German princes to impose his reforms upon the church.

As a scholar who had devoted his life to the editing of texts, Erasmus was more aware than most of his contemporaries of the degree to which theologians of both sides were basing their arguments on faulty translations and questionable interpretations of the Bible. In addition he realized, as had the minority bishops at the first Council of Nicaea, that Christian unity can be maintained only if as little as possible is dogmatically defined, with each person left free to believe whatever he or she wishes on doubtful points.

He kept insisting on something which both Catholic and Lutheran partisans, in the heat of their theological battles, tended to forget: that God has not revealed to us the answers to all questions, that the Christian faith does contain mysteries which have no logical resolution in this world. This was, unfortunately, a warning to which neither side paid much attention.

Eleven months after the end of the Leipzig debates, Pope Leo X published the bull *Exsurge Domine,* which listed forty-one propositions taken from Luther's writings and described some of them as heretical and others as scandalous. It is typical of the lack of concern with which Rome viewed the matter that Leo did not bother to indicate how many of the propositions were heretical, or which ones they were. There was, in fact, no authoritative declaration that any specific teaching of Luther contradicted Catholic doctrine until the Council of Trent—an omission which greatly hindered efforts to stop the spread of his ideas.

In January of 1521, Luther was officially excommunicated in the bull *Decet Romanum pontificem,* which Leo X issued from his hunting lodge outside Rome.

The normal procedure at this point would have been to summon Luther to appear before a general church council, which was precisely what Luther himself had been demanding for more than two years. Since the papacy still was reluctant to convene a council, however, the best that could be done was to have his case heard by the imperial Diet, or assembly, which was then in session in the German city of Worms, about forty miles south of Mainz.

In April of 1521, Luther appeared before the twenty-one-year-old Emperor Charles V and his court and was ordered to repudiate his teachings. This was the setting for Luther's famous declaration that his conscience was bound by the Word of God and that he would not, could not, recant. He was allowed to depart unmolested, after which the Diet passed the Edict of Worms, which declared him an outlaw. This meant that anyone could legally kill him on sight and that no secular ruler could offer him protection. To circumvent this ban, Frederick the Wise arranged for Luther to be kidnapped on his way back from Worms and hidden in the fortress of Wartburg for nearly a year.

It was during this period that Luther began his translation of the New Testament into German. (Contrary to popular belief, his translation was not the first. There already were fourteen different German versions of the Bible in print, although Luther's simple, direct, colloquial rendition quickly surpassed them all in popularity.) It also was during this period that a remarkable change in the leadership of the church occurred.

It was obvious to anyone, particularly after the collapse of the conciliar movement, that true reform of the church could not take place without vigorous leadership on the part of the papacy. But there could be no such leadership so long as the college of cardinals remained under the domination of a few noble families.

Working through their cardinals, families such as the Medici, the Orsini, and the Colonnas could exert a strong and usually pernicious influence over papal elections. And since the primary loyalty of most cardinals was not to the church but to their own families—which were constantly feuding with each other—each new pope had to contend with a powerful and firmly entrenched group of men at the highest levels of his administration who were more likely to oppose than to support him. The key to reforming the papacy, and thus the entire church, was to break the vicious circle whereby worldly popes appointed worldly cardinals who elected more worldly popes.

This finally came about in 1517, after a group of cardinals tried to murder Pope Leo X. Determined to put an end to these assassination attempts, which had been occurring with disturbing frequency ever since Gregory XI moved the papal court from Avignon back to Rome, Leo raised thirty-one men to the cardinalate in a single day. This greatly increased the size of the college of cardinals, and greatly reduced the influence of the Italian nobility over it. And when Leo died in December of 1521, these cardinals chose as his successor the Dutch theologian and diplomat Adrian Florensz, the last non-Italian pope before John Paul II.

Adrian, who retained his own name as pope, was in many ways the ideal person for the job. He had taught theology at the University of Louvain in Belgium, where Erasmus had attended his lectures. He had been chosen by Emperor Maximilian to be Charles V's tutor, and had served as viceroy of Spain before Charles had ascended that nation's throne. He was familiar with religious and political conditions in the Germanic countries. And he was a man of unimpeachable personal integrity who owed nothing to the established interests in Rome.

Deluged, when he took office, by ten thousand petitions for exemptions, privileges, promotions, and dispensations, Adrian refused all but one. He abrogated all the agreements which the papacy had made since the election of Rodrigo Borgia granting secular rulers the right to award benefices.

Even more remarkable was his approach to the crisis in Germany. Rather than simply appealing to authority and demanding unconditional submission, which had been the substance of the official Catholic response to Luther up to that point, Adrian sent a representative to the imperial Diet to make a public declaration that the Lutheran movement had been caused primarily by the sins of the Catholic clergy and that the evils from which the church was suffering had originated in the papacy itself.

It was one of the great tragedies of the Reformation era that Adrian died less than two years after his election. Had he been given more time, he might have been able to carry out the kind of reform advocated by Erasmus and the other Christian humanists. The church's response to Luther's challenges might have been more positive and assimilative, less defensive and repressive. And the unity of Christendom might have been preserved.

As it happened, however, Adrian was succeeded in 1523 by Giulio de' Medici, Leo X's cousin and the illegitimate son of the Giuliano de' Medici who had been murdered in the Florence cathedral. And by the time another reform-minded pope was elected, the opportunity had been lost.

Chapter 16
REFORMATION, ACT TWO:
THE ECHOES

IF the Lutheran movement had arisen during the reign of Constantine, or Justinian, or Charlemagne, it never would have been allowed to threaten the unity of the church. A general council would have been convened in the emperor's presence, and either the assembled bishops would have agreed on a doctrinal statement acceptable to the emperor or else he and his advisors would have drawn one up for them to ratify. This statement would have been promulgated by imperial edict and imposed, if necessary, by force. Those who refused to submit—be they bishops, cardinals, or pope—would have been exiled.

Had Luther been born even a century earlier, he and his followers might well have become the victims of a merciless crusade, like the one which Emperor Sigismund conducted for fifteen years against the followers of Jan Hus following Hus's execution at the Council of Constance.

Circumstances both inside and outside Germany, however, prevented Charles V from taking similar steps to resolve the Lutheran crisis.

No sooner had he been elected in 1519 than Charles was confronted with uprisings in Spain which took him six years to suppress. In 1521, the year Luther was excommunicated, Turkish armies under the command of Suleiman the Magnificent captured Belgrade and began moving up the Danube valley toward Vienna, which Charles, as archduke of Austria, was responsible for defending. The following year King Francis I, determined to break through the solid arc of Hapsburg possessions which now encircled France, began a war against the young emperor which continued, with some interruptions, for the remainder of Charles's life.

As the result of these and other problems which de-manded his immediate attention, Charles was absent from Germany during the nine most critical years of the Refor-mation—from the Diet of Worms in 1521 until the Diet of Augsburg in 1530.

Within the Empire itself Charles was more of a constitu-tional monarch than an absolute sovereign, the nominal ruler of a collection of mini-states and free cities which took advantage of every opportunity to reassert their tradi-tional rights and privileges and worked unceasingly to ex-pand them. This diffusion of authority made it extremely difficult to employ force against Lutheranism once it had gained the support of local German princes. Also working in Luther's favor was the fact that, whether he realized it or not, his writings harmonized perfectly with the desires and ambitions of many of the Empire's most powerful leaders.

His denial of the Roman church's authority suited the purposes of German nationalists, who resented every type of foreign influence over their internal affairs. His attacks on the St. Peter's indulgence and papal taxation, both of which were draining substantial amounts of money out of northern Europe, were welcomed by those who were con-cerned about the export of Germany's currency.

His appeal to the secular rulers of Germany to take the reform of the church into their own hands provided them not only with an excuse to expropriate ecclesiastical prop-erty, but also, in an age when religious unity was still con-sidered an essential prerequisite for political unity, with an opportunity to increase their independence from imperial rule.

Charles V, in opposing Luther, had to fight against the forces which were weakening the internal cohesion of the Empire, while Luther was riding their crest. This highly advantageous situation was seriously jeopardized, however, when many of those who called themselves followers of Luther began to challenge not only the emperor and the Roman church but every form of religious and secular authority.

As early as 1521, while Luther still was secluded in the Wartburg, a group of mystically-minded revolutionaries arrived in Wittenberg proclaiming that the world was about to end and demanding the execution of all priests. Two years later a spellbinding preacher named Thomas Müntzer, who had worked with Luther in Wittenberg and had assisted him during the Leipzig debates, attempted to form a communistic state not far from Eisleben, Luther's birthplace. Some of Müntzer's followers later turned the city of Münster into their version of heaven on earth, where women were subjected to compulsory polygamy and people who commited any of a long list of offenses were instantly executed. Excesses such as these, as Luther well knew, threatened to destroy everything he was trying to accomplish.

It always had been the nature of large-scale Christian reform movements, particularly those which drew their inspiration from direct communication with the Holy Spirit or from individual interpretation of Scripture, to tend toward revolutionary millenialism and thus to invite violent repression. We have seen that the charismatic enthusiasts in the early church frequently called down Roman persecution not only upon themselves but upon their fellow Christians as well.

Müntzer and the other radical German reformers—who, since they all opposed infant baptism for one reason or another, sometimes are referred to collectively as "Anabaptists"—presented a similar problem. And in 1524, when the peasants of Austria and southern and western

Germany rose in open rebellion with Müntzer as one of their leaders, Luther was in danger of being considered a rebel himself. Since the very existence of his movement and his own personal safety depended upon the good will of the German princes, this was something which he could not permit.

Although sympathetic to the peasants' demands, Luther had repeatedly warned them not to resort to violence. And when the uprising finally came he issued a brutal manifesto entitled "Against the Thieving and Murdering Peasant Hordes," which urged the nobility to slaughter as many of the insurgents as they possibly could. This they did. More than five thousand were killed at the battle of Frankenhausen alone—Müntzer among them—and similar massacres took place in other parts of Germany. One of the side-effects of this bloodbath was that the Anabaptists were eliminated as a serious challenge to Luther's leadership of the German Reformation. Another was that his reputation among the nobility as a spokesman of conservative reform was preserved.

As all large and socially acceptable religious movements inevitably must, Lutheranism had demonstrated that it posed no threat to the established economic and political order.

Shortly after the end of the Peasants' War, Philip of Hesse formally introduced the Lutheran liturgy into his territory and began to close monasteries and dismiss Catholic priests from their parishes. A number of other rulers and free cities did likewise. Prussia already had been lost to the Catholic church when the grand master of the Teutonic Knights converted to Lutheranism.

Scandinavia also was renouncing its allegiance to Catholicism, primarily because of the blundering of Giovannangelo Arciboldi, Pope Leo X's ambassador to the

Nordic countries. In 1518 the king of Denmark, Christian II, discovered that Arciboldi had been negotiating in Leo's name with Swedish nationalists who were preparing to rebel against Danish rule. This monumental indiscretion, which Christian construed as evidence of a papal conspiracy, induced him to import missionaries from Germany and to begin the conversion of Norway, Sweden, and Denmark to the Lutheran faith.

Germany, meanwhile, was dividing into Catholic and Lutheran states, according to the religious preferences of the individual rulers. At the imperial Diet held in Speyer in 1526, the enforcement of the Edict of Worms was suspended; and it was decided that for the time being each prince should act in accord with his own conscience. Three years later Charles V ordered the Diet to reverse this decision, a command against which the Lutheran members protested so vociferously that they, and later their coreligionists as well, became known as "Protestants."

In that same year the Turks failed in their attempt to capture Vienna, their farthest penetration into Europe, and retreated eastward. This allowed the emperor to devote greater attention to his subjects' religious problems. As a first step toward reestablishing unity he invited Catholic and Lutheran theologians to attend a Diet to be held in 1530 at Augsburg, a city which had already accepted the Reformation. Since Luther still could not travel freely within the Empire, the chief spokesman for the Lutheran cause at this assembly was Philipp Melanchthon, a humanist scholar who had been greatly influenced by the writings of Erasmus.

Melanchthon is best known today for having transformed the contents of Luther's somewhat bombastic religious pamphlets into a coherent theology. Less well known is the fact that he may have worked longer and harder than anyone else on either side to make reconciliation of the Catholic and the Lutheran positions possible. At the time of the Diet of Augsburg, and for some time thereafter, in fact, he still considered himself a loyal Catholic.

In preparation for the discussions at Augsburg, Melanchthon produced a summary of Lutheran beliefs which, he claimed, was compatible both with Scripture and with traditional Catholic teaching. Of the twenty-eight articles in this statement, which later became known as the Confession of Augsburg, a panel of Catholic theologians approved nine unconditionally and six more with reservations. Negotiations failed, however, to produce agreement on the remaining points.

Finally the Diet rejected the entire document and called for the restoration of Catholicism throughout the Empire, by force if necessary, within one year. This ultimatum led the Lutheran princes to form a military alliance called the Schmalkaldic League. Catholic princes already had taken similar steps. What Pope Leo X originally had dismissed as a "monkish quarrel" now was beginning to threaten the peace of Europe.

Meanwhile, while all eyes were focused on Germany, a religious movement which would prove far more influential in many ways than Luther's was taking shape in Switzerland. This movement, which often is referred to as the Reformed branch of Protestantism in order to distinguish it from the Evangelical branch inspired by Luther, began about a year after the publication of the Ninety-Five Theses when a humanistic-minded priest named Huldrych Zwingli was appointed to preach in the Minster, or cathedral, of Zurich.

Zwingli always insisted that he had developed his basic religious ideas independently of the other reformers—before anyone in his region of Switzerland, as he put it, had ever heard of Martin Luther. And although he agreed with Luther on a number of important issues, such as justification through faith alone, the number of the sacraments, and the sole and absolute doctrinal authority of individually interpreted Scripture, Zwingli went much further than Luther in attempting to restore the beliefs and practices of primitive Christianity. He rejected, for example, almost all religious art and ornamentation, the use of altars and organ music in churches, and most of the elaborate liturgical practices which had been developed during the Middle Ages.

A more basic difference concerned the manner in which Christ may be said to be present in the Eucharistic bread and wine. Luther, although he rejected the formula of transubstantiation, continued to maintain that the words "This is my body" must be taken in a literal sense. Zwingli, on the other hand, argued that since no physical body can be in two places at once, and since the physical body of Jesus is in heaven, "is" in this case must be interpreted to mean "signifies."

Zwingli also went much further than Luther in proposing that secular and religious power should be intimately combined, with the civil government carrying out the policies of the church and enforcing its excommunication decrees. This concept was an outgrowth of Zwingli's belief—in opposition to Augustine and Luther but in full agreement with Thomas Müntzer—that those predestined for salvation, the "elect," could be distinguished in this life from those whom God has chosen not to save, thus making it possible for them to organize their own political society. He was attempting to establish this kind of society in Zurich when he was killed in the course of a war with the Catholic cantons of Switzerland in 1531. And it was in Geneva, not Zurich, that his dream finally was realized.

John Calvin, who fled to Switzerland three years after

Zwingli's death to escape persecution in his native France, originally settled in Bern. It was there that he wrote *Institutes of the Christian Religion,* by far the most influential religious work of the early Protestant era. In the summer of 1536, however, he happened to pass through Geneva, which had just driven out its Catholic bishop, and was persuaded to help in establishing the Reformed church there.

The first step in turning Geneva into a theocracy of the pre-selected was to expel those whom God obviously had decided to damn rather than to save. Preeminent among these were Catholics, all of whom were exiled, and anyone who was excommunicated from the Reformed church for more than six months. The next step—since Calvin shared Augustine's belief that only by threat of punishment can depraved human nature be induced to refrain from evil— was to utilize the powers of civil government to enforce Calvin's conception of moral behavior and to root out unorthodox beliefs.

Calvin never held political office in Geneva, but his spirit completely dominated its everyday life. Calvinist pastors visited every home in the city at least once a year and reported any shortcomings they found to the civil magistrates. Offenses for which citizens actually were cited to appear before these magistrates included superstitious practices, dancing, criticism of Calvin or of the government, and laughing during a sermon. Adultery was punished by death. Most of those who opposed Calvin were exiled; the others were put to death. The most barbaric features of the Inquisition, such as torture and the ceremonial burning of the corpses of those posthumously convicted, were employed to preserve the purity of Calvinist theology. Michael Servetus, a renowned physician and anatomist whose theories on the Trinity had been condemned by the Catholic Inquisition in France, made the mistake of seeking asylum in Geneva, where he was seized by the Calvinist Inquisition and burned alive.

Calvin succeeded, for better or for worse, in creating a far more complete realization of what the medievals had considered an ideal society—one whose every aspect, including civil government, is directed by spiritual authority —than anyone else before or since.

This was welcomed with great enthusiasm by those who shared his views. Some six thousand Protestant refugees from all parts of Europe flocked to Calvin's utopia, increasing its population by nearly fifty percent. Thanks in large part to the presence of these refugees, Geneva soon became the center of an international movement. John Knox established a particularly militant form of Calvinism in Scotland, where a higher percentage of the population embraced the Reformed church than in any other country. Calvinism also made strong inroads in Hungary, Holland, Bohemia, and west-central Germany. It almost completely overshadowed Lutheranism in France.

Perhaps because the Evangelical movement had become so closely associated with the political fortunes and ambitions of individual German princes, the Reformed movement became the dominant form of Protestantism everywhere on the Continent except Germany and Scandinavia. But England followed neither Luther nor Calvin. It became Protestant, in fact, very much against the wishes of the man who separated it from Rome.

In 1492, or seven years after Luther's birth, King Henry VII concluded an alliance with Europe's newest major power, Spain. As part of this agreement, his six-year-old son and presumptive heir, Arthur, was betrothed to Princess Catherine, Ferdinand and Isabella's seven-year-old daughter. (Catherine was the sister of Charles V's mother, a fact which one day would assume extreme importance.) They were married nine years later.

Only four months after the wedding, however, the linchpin fell out of the Spanish alliance when Arthur died. Finally the diplomats agreed to resolve this crisis by having Catherine marry Prince Henry, Arthur's younger brother. Since canon law absolutely forbade marriage between a widow and her brother-in-law, a dispensation for this union had to be obtained from Pope Julius II. That requirement fulfilled, the marriage took place in June of 1509, less than a month before Henry's eighteenth birthday and his coronation as king.

Catherine gave birth to five children. All were stillborn or died in infancy, however, except one girl named Mary. And by 1526, after seventeen years of marriage, Henry had become preoccupied with two interrelated domestic problems.

The absence of a legitimate male heir, plus the fact that Henry's own family had seized the crown by force of arms forty years earlier, raised the possibility that his death might be followed by civil war. England never had been part of the Holy Roman Empire, and the provisions of the Salic Law which barred women from royal succession never had been formally incorporated into its legal system. But England also never had been ruled by a queen.

At the same time, Henry had become hopelessly enamored of a teenaged girl named Anne Boleyn. This in itself need not have caused any difficulty. Since the king already had seduced her older sister, however, and married her off to one of his courtiers when she ceased to amuse him, Anne refused to become his mistress unless he also would make her his wife. It seemed to Henry that the best way to solve both problems would be to rid himself of

Catherine and marry Anne, who had promised that she would give him a son.

Divorce in the modern sense of the word did not yet exist. What Henry wanted was an annulment, a declaration that he never really had been married to Catherine in the first place. (The fact that annulments at that time were called "divorces" in England gave rise to much subsequent confusion.) Henry argued that no true marriage could have existed because Catherine was his sister-in-law, which amounted to a denial that the dispensation issued by Julius II had been efficacious.

Two different lines of reasoning could have been employed to support this claim, because Henry's marriage to Catherine had violated not only canon law but also an identical provision of English civil law. Thus it was possible to argue either that the dispensation granted by Julius had been defective in some respect or else that, although it had been valid in itself, it had not removed the impediment created by English law. The latter position would have been in harmony with a long series of attempts by English kings, going back at least to the days of Edward I and Boniface VIII, to interpose the power of the crown between papal authority and English political affairs.

Henry wished to settle the matter within the framework of English law first and worry later about what Rome might say, which is more or less what eventually happened. But his chancellor and chief foreign policy advisor, Cardinal Wolsey, foolishly assured the king that he could obtain an annulment for him from Pope Clement VII. (In 1521 and again in 1523, Wolsey had campaigned for election as pope. If he had succeeded, or if Henry had succeeded in becoming Holy Roman Emperor, there might never have been a Reformation in England.) In actual fact

Wolsey could not possibly have made good on his promise, because Pope Clement, as the result of his clumsy intervention in the long series of wars between Charles V and Francis I, was totally at the mercy of Queen Catherine's nephew.

Clement had joined Charles V in opposing the attempt of Francis to recapture Milan, an attempt which ended in 1525 when an imperial army took the French king prisoner. No sooner had Francis regained his freedom, however, than he formed an alliance against Charles with Clement and several Italian city-states. This caused the emperor to send to Italy an army of mercenaries who not only defeated Pope Clement's troops but also, rampaging completely out of control, ransacked the city of Rome and held the pope captive in the Sant' Angelo fortress for seven months. No reasonable person could have expected Clement, under these circumstances, to agree to annul the marriage of Charles V's aunt.

And Clement did not agree. But he also did not refuse. Instead he staged a long and complex charade, hoping that, if he waited long enough, Henry might change his mind. As part of this charade he sent Cardinal Campeggio to England to adjudicate the matter, with secret instructions not to reach a decision. Campeggio delayed his arrival in England as long as he could; then, after making some preliminary inquiries, he announced that he was suspending proceedings in order to take a summer vacation. When Campeggio could stall no longer, Pope Clement transferred the case to Rome.

But Henry, whose position was growing more uncomfortable each day, was in no mood to play games. First he dismissed Wolsey and banished him to York, his own archbishopric, in which Wolsey had never before resided. Then he appointed a layman, Thomas More, as his new chancellor and set about dissolving his marriage in his own way.

In November of 1529 Parliament, under the king's direction, began a disciplinary reform of the English church, eliminating a multitude of highly unpopular abuses and establishing the precedent of parliamentary regulation of ecclesiastical affairs. Two and a half years later Henry coerced a national assembly of the English clergy into ratifying the Statute of Praemunire, which since the fourteenth century had prohibited appeals to any foreign power in cases over which royal courts claimed jurisdiction. This was equivalent to acknowledging that ultimate authority over the church in England was vested not in the pope but in the king.

By the end of 1532—more then six years after the issue first was raised—Pope Clement still had not announced a decision on the validity of Henry's marriage, and the king could wait no longer. Anne Boleyn already was pregnant, and if she gave birth to an illegitimate child all Henry's efforts would have been in vain. It was primarily for this reason that the new Archbishop of Canterbury, Thomas Cranmer, secretly married Henry and Anne in January of 1533. Four months later Cranmer ruled that Henry's marriage to Catherine had been invalid. The following month Anne was crowned queen. It took another nine months for Pope Clement to issue his own decision on Henry's first marriage, and by that time he was no longer able to influence the course of events.

Thomas Cromwell, who had replaced Thomas More as chancellor, now pushed through Parliament a great mass of legislation creating an independent English church and legalizing the administrative mechanisms through which Henry and his father had consolidated their power. Ironically, as it turned out, Cromwell's decision to have the royal prerogatives spelled out in great legal detail actually helped to increase Parliament's influence over the crown, since what it had enacted it also could repeal. This was to have important effects on English religious life during the reigns of Henry's children. Cromwell later organized the suppression of eight hundred monasteries, much of whose wealth was used to buy the loyalty of the nobility, and channeled into the royal treasury the church taxes which previously had been sent to Rome.

Parliament already had proclaimed England to be a sovereign nation, subject to no authority superior to that of its king. In 1534 it took the next logical step by passing the Act of Supremacy. Henry—who already was beginning to regret his marriage to Anne Boleyn, since the child she had been carrying turned out to be a daughter, Elizabeth, rather than the son he needed—now found himself the supreme head on earth of the English church.

Except for the legal formalities it involved, this was not entirely as radical a step as it might appear. Kings had been acting as effective heads of the church in England long before Henry's time, just as the kings of France had regulated ecclesiastical affairs in their realm. Similar developments had taken place in other lands. This was almost inevitable so long as religious and civil authority remained intimately related. The concept of a politically and religiously united Europe had given way to individual nation-states containing what were in fact, if not in name, national churches subject to royal control.

Henry, who was appalled by Luther's doctrinal innovations, tried to keep his church faithful to the basic tenets of traditional Catholic belief. He continued to uphold the seven Catholic sacraments and to oppose justification by faith alone, and in 1539 he decreed the death penalty for those who denied transubstantiation. He had, however, placed his nation's highest civil and religious offices in the hands of two men, Cranmer and Cromwell, who were far more sympathetic to Luther's ideas than Henry himself was.

While Henry VIII was severing England's ties to Rome, Charles V was struggling to keep religious dissension from tearing his empire apart.

For years Charles and many other political and religious leaders had been urging Pope Clement to convene an ecumenical council to resolve the issues Luther had raised. But Clement—who, like his predecessors, feared that a resurgence of conciliarism would undermine papal authority—steadfastly refused. Clement, in fact, had a special reason to feel threatened by such a council. Since his parents never married, he had been ineligible under canon law even to be ordained a priest, let alone consecrated pope; and he could not be certain that a council might not vote to depose him. (He had been created a lay cardinal by virtue of a dispensation from his cousin, Pope Leo X; then a document was issued declaring him legitimate and permitting his ordination.)

And Francis I, who not only encouraged the German Protestants at the same time that he was persecuting the French ones but even concluded a military alliance against Charles with the Schmalkaldic League, did everything he could to prevent the convocation of a council which might strengthen Germany by reconciling its Catholic and Lutheran princes. Francis also feared that a council might revoke the extensive powers over the internal affairs of the French church which he had been granted by Julius II and Leo X. The papacy itself, which only recently had gone to war against Charles, also dreaded the prospect of a reunited and revitalized empire.

Forced by circumstances, therefore, to take matters into

his own hands, Charles conducted a political holding action in Germany until a council could be held. Meanwhile he sponsored a series of colloquies at which he urged Catholics and Lutherans to settle their differences. And even at that late date, influential parties on both sides were anxious to work toward that end.

At Regensburg in 1541, only four years before the start of the Council of Trent, a Protestant delegation including Philipp Melanchthon met with a Catholic group which counted among its members Johann Eck and a papal legate, Cardinal Continari, and reached agreement on a number of basic issues. They were able, for example, to draw up a statement on justification acceptable to both sides. When it proved impossible to formulate a common technical definition of the Eucharist, the Lutherans proposed that both parties agree that Christ is truly present in the bread and wine without specifying the manner of that presence—a suggestion which reflected the spirit of Erasmus and which Charles V heartily endorsed.

There is evidence that, if an ecumenical council been held at that point, many Catholic cardinals and bishops would have been willing to agree to a married clergy and a number of other Protestant demands. One of these demands, reception of the Eucharist under the form of wine as well as of bread, already had been granted to the followers of Jan Hus more than a century before.

Ultimately, however, the colloquy of Regensburg and others like it were doomed to failure, because too few people on either side were willing to pay the price for success. Melanchthon's conciliatory attitude toward the Roman church, in fact—particularly his willingness to preserve many traditional Catholic customs and rituals because they were not opposed to Scripture—caused a split within the Lutheran movement whose effects are still being felt.

After the talks at Regensburg collapsed, attitudes hardened on both sides and compromise became impossible. Charles V undertook a series of military campaigns against the Schmalkaldic League and eventually suffered a crushing defeat at the hands of the Lutheran princes and their French allies. This guaranteed that Germany would remain a divided nation. In September of 1555, a decree issued at Augsburg gave each of the German princes the right to determine whether his territory would be Catholic or Lutheran, an event which marked the end of a unified Western Christendom.

This was precisely what Charles V had spent his entire adult life trying to prevent. And one month after the Peace of Augsburg was signed, having been unable to persuade the imperial electors to allow his son Philip to succeed him, he began to relinquish control of his territorial possessions —more territory than any European monarch ever had ruled before. Then Charles, who had failed completely at the one thing he had most wanted to accomplish, retired to a Spanish monastery and died there the following year.

His younger brother, Ferdinand, was given responsibility for governing the Holy Roman Empire and later was elected emperor. Philip received Spain and her colonies, Sicily, and the Netherlands. This division of authority made it possible to devote the full spiritual and material resources of Spain to the support of what became known as the Counter-Reformation.

Chapter 17
REFORMATION, ACT THREE:
THE RESPONSE

LUTHER had appealed his case to an ecumenical council as early as 1518, and five years later both the Lutheran and the Catholic princes of Germany had asked that a council be held somewhere in the Holy Roman Empire within a year. Emperor Charles V echoed their request at frequent intervals thereafter. Finally Pope Paul III, who had succeeded the weak and indecisive Clement VII, announced that a council would take place in 1536 at Mantua—a location which he later changed to Vincenza. When his representatives arrived in this city on the appointed day, however, they discovered that no one else had come.

This fiasco was followed by Charles V's attempt to resolve the religious conflict in Germany through personal negotiations. After this had failed, Charles recommended that a council be held at Trent, in the Italian portion of the Empire; and in 1542 Paul III asked the church's leaders to assemble there. Then war broke out once again between Charles and Francis I, delaying the start of the council until December of 1545—twenty-eight years after the publication of the Ninety-Five Theses.

It seemed unlikely at the time that anything of consequence could be accomplished at Trent. No preparatory work had been done. Not a single delegate appeared on the day on which the opening ceremony was to have been held. There were never more than seventy-two bishops in attendance during the first of the council's three convocations, and fifty-four, at most, during the second.

Delegates had scarcely settled down to productive work when Paul III ordered them to move to Bologna, a city which was under papal rather than imperial jurisdiction. Charles V and his bishops, however, protested that such a relocation would allow Paul to dominate the council, just as Julius II had dominated Lateran V, and keep it from enacting meaningful reforms. Since neither side would give way, the council was suspended until Paul III's successor agreed to transfer it back to Trent.

Then, less than a year after the council reconvened, the Schmalkaldic League's rebellion against Charles V forced it to adjourn once again. And ten more years went by before the start of its third and final convocation, which opened in January of 1562 and continued until December of 1563. The Council of Trent thus spanned eighteen years from beginning to end, even though its delegates were in session for only about four of those years.

All definitions distinguish or separate the things which they define from other things, but dogmatic definitions also separate those who accept them from those who do not. This was why Erasmus had argued against defining more articles of faith than are absolutely necessary.

But the delegates at Trent took the opposite approach. Since Catholicism was no longer the only Christian religion in Europe, they felt obliged to specify as clearly and precisely as possible what it means to be a Catholic, as opposed to simply being a Christian. As a result, they focused their attention on the comparatively few issues over which Catholics and Protestants differed rather than the far greater number on which they agreed.

For years Luther's Catholic opponents, rather than attempting to refute him on the basis of Scripture, had simply kept insisting that he and his followers were wrong because they contradicted church teachings. This proved to be a totally unpersuasive argument, since the teaching authority of the church was precisely the point under dispute. And since the two sides continued to argue from opposite presuppositions, they naturally found it impossible to agree.

Trent perpetuated this state of affairs by declaring, in its
very first doctrinal statement, that the traditions which have
been handed down from generation to generation since
apostolic times must be accorded a status equal to that of
Scripture. This was equivalent to saying that the church
itself speaks with the same authority as the Bible does.

This assertion was not new. It had been implicit, for example, in the decision of the Council of Nicaea to define
the consubstantiality of the Son with the Father as an arti-
cle of faith, over the protests of some bishops that this
terminology is not found in Scripture. By basing their
dogmatic definitions on tradition as well as on the Bible,
however, the delegates at Trent made it impossible for
Protestants to accept those definitions. This had the effect,
as Erasmus had foreseen, of driving Catholics and Protestants even further apart.

Trent went on to pass legislation touching almost every
aspect of Catholic life. The single most important thing
it did to promote reform, however, was to restore the
authority of the bishops. Privileges and exemptions which
had been accumulating for hundreds of years were abolished. Bishops, some of whom had control over less than
ten percent of the parishes in their dioceses, regained jurisdiction over monasteries, convents, religious orders, and
everyone engaged in any form of pastoral work. They were
given responsibility for appointing and supervising parish
priests and for educating candidates to the priesthood—the
first time in the history of the church that any formal
system had been established for the training of diocesan
clergy. Appeals to Rome against the decisions of local
bishops were sharply curtailed.

All of this marked an important step away from the kind
of monolithic church envisioned by Gregory VII and Innocent III and back toward the concept of local churches

headed by bishops wielding nearly absolute power. And it was primarily these bishops who accomplished the slow, painstaking task of reforming the church at the local level.

But while the Council of Trent was enhancing the status of bishops, it failed, like all previous councils, to give the laity any status at all. It refused to allow lay participation in ecclesiastical affairs or in the liturgy. It absolutely forbade the use of vernacular languages in liturgical rituals. It deliberately chose, in short, not to integrate lay men and women into the life of the church as Luther and Calvin had done. Catholics were expected to remain followers and spectators in a church completely dominated by the clergy, just as they had been in the centuries before the Renaissance. By and large they did so—or else they left the church. And the laity never again played as important a part in Catholic intellectual life as it had in the days of Erasmus and Thomas More.

Trent also refrained, at Rome's urgent behest, from interfering in any way with the papal bureaucracy. This meant trusting, against all the contrary evidence which had been accumulating for centuries, that the papacy could be relied upon to reform itself. To the amazement of almost everyone, however, the papacy actually did reform. Pius V, who was elected three years after the Council of Trent ended, became the first pope in more than two hundred and fifty years to be declared a saint—and only the second since Gregory VII, who died in 1085. Sixtus V, the most famous of the Counter-Reformation popes, completely restructured the papal Curia and imposed rigid standards of behavior on bishops and cardinals alike.

By the time Sixtus died in 1590, Catholicism had reorganized its administration, clarified its doctrine, corrected many of the abuses from which it had been suffering (conspicuous among those which escaped correction was papal nepotism), and solidified its position in the countries which had remained faithful to it. It was even beginning to win back some of what it had lost.

The Council of Trent may have exerted a greater influence over Catholic belief and behavior than any other single event—in large part because, although there had been nineteen ecumenical councils in the twelve hundred and twenty years between 325 and 1545, an average of about one every sixty-four years, there was not another one after Trent for more than three centuries.

Trent's doctrinal formulas, written in the tumultuous and emotion-charged atmosphere of the Reformation, remained the definitive statement of what the Catholic religion is and what it means down to our own time. And the staunchly conservative disciplinary decrees which it adopted to deal with conditions in the mid-sixteenth century remained in force for so long that Catholics began to regard some of them as being integral parts of their faith.

At the same time, as more and more people in northern Europe abandoned the Roman church, what might be called Catholicism's center of gravity shifted back toward the Mediterranean. It was primarily the Latin nations, and Spain in particular, which determined the direction in which post-Reformation Catholicism evolved. This was unfortunate in many respects, because Catholicism in Spain had become doctrinaire and repressive to a degree unequaled anywhere else.

Some of this was a legacy from Spanish Christians' centuries-long struggle to reconquer their land from the Muslims. But King Ferdinand deliberately turned religious intolerance into an instrument of national policy when, five years before Martin Luther's birth, he persuaded Pope Sixtus IV to revive the Inquisition in Spain. Almost as soon as this tribunal came into existence, Ferdinand began using it to impose upon his subjects a reign of such unbridled and indiscriminate terror that even Sixtus IV protested—without effect—against its excesses.

What made the Spanish Inquisition particularly fearsome was the fact that it was almost totally autonomous, answerable to no one except the crown. This was demonstrated quite clearly in 1559, when the Inquisition arrested one of the most powerful Spanish churchmen, the archbishop of Toledo, and kept him imprisoned without trial for seventeen years despite vigorous protests from Rome.

Almost everyone in Spain, no matter how orthodox, lived in fear of the Inquisition's dungeons. Even Teresa of Avila and Ignatius Loyola underwent investigation as suspected heretics, and Loyola was imprisoned twice. The Inquisition issued its own list of forbidden books, and included on it many works which Rome had approved. Spanish Catholicism became almost a church within the church, suppressing original orthodox ideas more severely than Rome was suppressing heretical ones. It was also a church at least as closely controlled by the Spanish crown as the church in England was by Henry VIII.

By the middle of the sixteenth century, Spain was the one solid bastion of Catholic orthodoxy in a continent swarming with heterodox ideas. It also had the largest and best-disciplined army in Europe and a treasury swollen with prodigious shipments of bullion from its American colonies. Spain became, as it were, the impregnable fortress from which the Catholic Counter-Reformation was launched and financed. At times, in fact, Spain seemed almost to be running the church.

Spanish monarchs often succeeded in securing the election of popes who subscribed to their own narrow interpretation of orthodoxy and who were willing to support their interests against those of other nations. In 1590 King Philip

II went so far as to announce that only seven of the cardinals eligible to become pope were acceptable to him. One of the seven became Pope Gregory XIV, who obligingly sent a papal army to attack Philip's archenemy, Henry IV of France. When Portugal rebelled against its rule in 1640, Spain was able to keep the Vatican from confirming the appointments of any new Portuguese bishops—until there was only one bishop left in the entire country.

Spain also gave birth to the Society of Jesus, founded in 1534 by Ignatius Loyola.

The Jesuits, as Loyola's followers came to be called, resembled in some respects a religious commando battalion. Recruits were carefully screened and subjected to a long period of probation. Those who were accepted underwent several years of spiritual formation and thorough training in philosophy, theology, and the humanities. Authority was rigidly centralized. There was only one elected official in the entire order; he held office for life and had the power to appoint and remove all subordinate officials. Members took, in addition to the standard vows of poverty, chastity, and obedience to their spiritual superiors, a special vow of obedience to the pope. And their obedience was expected to be absolute—like that of a staff in an old man's hand, as Loyola expressed it.

Jesuits dispensed with many practices which had been observed by religious orders since the time of St. Benedict. They did not wear a distinctive habit. They were not obliged to fast, to follow any particular diet, to perform specific penances, or to recite daily prayers in common. Rather than shunning the world like monks, Jesuits, most of whom were themselves members of the upper class, mingled easily with the rich and the powerful. Many gained fame as mathematicians, astronomers, physicists, linguists, dramatists, poets, and historians. They considered themselves, and generally were considered to be, an intellectual elite.

Within a hundred years of their founding, Jesuits were operating fifty-six seminaries and well over four hundred secondary schools. It was primarily their reputation among Catholics and non-Catholics alike as the most skillful teachers in Europe which allowed the Jesuits to promote Catholicism so effectively.

From the time Luther first began attacking indulgences, the fate of the Reformation had rested in the hands of local princes and noblemen. When the Peace of Augsburg decreed that the religion of each state in the Holy Roman Empire was to be determined by that state's prince, it was merely giving legal status to a principle which already prevailed in practice. Under these conditions it was possible to change the religious affiliation of an entire district by influencing a handful of important men—or by influencing their children, the leaders of the next generation. This strategy, which the Jesuits put into effect even before the Council of Trent began and which their missionaries still employ, paid spectacular dividends. Particularly in Austria, southern Germany, and Poland, Jesuit teachers helped to halt and then to roll back the advance of Protestantism by recapturing the hearts and minds of the educated upper class.

Jesuits also participated directly in formulating the diplomatic and military tactics of the Counter-Reformation through their positions as confessors and spiritual advisors to Europe's most powerful Catholic sovereigns, including those of France, Spain, Bavaria, Portugal, Poland, and the Holy Roman Empire. They played a major role, in fact, in preserving the Empire as a Catholic power.

Charles V's brother Ferdinand had been succeeded as

Holy Roman Emperor by his son Maximilian, who insisted on calling himself a Christian rather than a Catholic and who was so sympathetic to Lutheranism that his uncle Charles tried to prevent his election as emperor. And Maximilian was succeeded by his son Rudolph, who tolerated Protestantism in Austria and Bohemia and, like his father, refused the Catholic last sacraments. For a time it seemed that the Empire itself might come under Protestant control.

But neither Rudolph nor his brother Matthias, who succeeded him, had children. And Matthias chose as his heir the archduke Ferdinand, who had been educated by the Jesuits. In 1599 Ferdinand signaled an end to the era of toleration by closing all Protestant churches in a large portion of Austria. So aggressively pro-Catholic were his policies, in fact, that ultimately they caused the religious future of central Europe to be decided not in the classroom and the pulpit—where Catholics appeared to be gaining the upper hand—but on the battlefield.

Disorder broke out first in Bohemia, where Emperor Matthias had arranged to have Ferdinand elected as king over the strenuous objections of the Lutherans, Calvinists, and Hussites who represented a substantial part of that country's population. To dramatize their opposition, a group of noblemen threw several of the emperor's officials out of a sixty-foot high window—the famous "defenestration" of Prague. A year later, in 1619, the Bohemian electors deposed Ferdinand and chose the Calvinist Elector of the Palatinate, Frederick V, to be king in his place.

By this time, however, Ferdinand had succeeded Matthias as emperor. Assisted by Duke Maximilian of Bavaria, who had attended the Jesuit university at Ingolstadt and whose militancy in support of the Catholic cause exceeded his own, Ferdinand crushed the Bohemian army in

November of 1620 at the Battle of White Mountain, near Prague. Bohemia lost its nominal independence and became a hereditary possession of the Hapsburgs. All Protestant religions were outlawed. And Jesuits were brought in to educate the children of Bohemian nobility. The hapless Frederick lost not only the crown of Bohemia but also the Palatinate and his status as an imperial elector, both of which were awarded to Maximilian. This gave Catholics a permanent majority in subsequent imperial elections.

Emperor Ferdinand now appeared to be in a position of overpowering strength, particularly since the Lutherans and the Calvinists, who considered each other's theologies to be almost as pernicious as that of Catholicism, found it difficult to cooperate. Conditions seemed ideal for some kind of reconciliation, provided that the emperor offered reasonable terms. But Ferdinand did not offer terms.

After the Peace of Augsburg had been signed in 1555, Charles V had added a stipulation that any Catholic priest, monk, or bishop who converted to Protestantism after that date would have to resign his benefices—that is, he could not claim for his own use the money and property which had been provided to support him in the Catholic ministry. This unilateral "ecclesiastical reservation" had been widely ignored. Now, however, Ferdinand, without consulting the imperial Diet, decreed that all property which had been alienated from the Catholic Church during the preceding seventy-seven years must be returned. He also ordered that all Lutherans living in principalities ruled by Catholics and all non-Lutheran Protestants living anywhere in the Empire be exiled. Almost a hundred monasteries, many valuable estates, and innumerable parish churches were restored to the Catholic Church by this act—and thousands of people were forcibly uprooted from their homes.

Nothing could have been more effective in uniting all German Protestants against Ferdinand and encouraging them to support King Gustavus Adolphus of Sweden, who in 1630 invaded Germany. Gustavus also received considerable financial assistance from the French chief minister, Cardinal Richelieu, who was determined to continue France's longstanding policy of encouraging religious dissension in Germany in order to weaken the Hapsburgs. And when the seemingly invincible Gustavus was killed in 1632, after having defeated Catholic armies throughout the length and breadth of Germany, Richelieu entered the war directly. He allied France to Sweden and the German Lutheran princes against Catholic Spain and the Empire.

Richelieu's intervention helped to prolong the fighting, which already had caused more death and destruction than anything Europe had seen since the barbarian invasions, for thirteen more agonizing years. Eventually his armies tipped the balance of power in favor of the Protestant side, while Pope Urban VIII, who also wished to escape the threat of Hapsburg domination, looked benignly on.

Peace negotiations finally began in 1643, although it took five years to agree on terms. So complex had been the alliances and so convoluted the motives of the participants in this Thirty Years War, or series of wars, that at one point a conference had to be held to determine why the various nations had been fighting in the first place.

The Peace of Westphalia, signed in 1648, ended the era of armed conflict between Catholics and Protestants. It legalized all expropriations of Catholic property which had occurred before 1624. And it realized Richelieu's fondest desire by destroying the Holy Roman Empire as a political unit. Each of the more than three hundred ministates in the Empire was made independent, with the power to declare war and make peace without the emperor's consent. This prevented Germany from becoming a unified nation for another two hundred years and allowed France to dominate Europe for the same length of time.

Calvinists, who had not received legal recognition in the Peace of Augsburg, were given the same rights as Lutherans. Imperial princes still were permitted to determine the official religion of their states, but now the private practice of minority religions would be tolerated. This meant that an individual ruler no longer could change the religious affiliation of his subjects, which drastically reduced the effectiveness of Jesuit proselytizing techniques. After 1648 there were no more large-scale shifts of allegiance from one religion to another, and very little additional territory was won back to Catholicism. Westphalia, to all intents and purposes, brought the Catholic Counter-Reformation on the continent to a close.

In England, meanwhile, a combination of circumstances had prevented the Counter-Reformation from ever really getting under way.

Henry VIII, who before his separation from Queen Catherine had composed an anti-Lutheran treatise in defense of the seven Catholic sacraments, made certain that the Church of England did not depart during his lifetime from traditional Catholic doctrines (except, of course, that of papal supremacy) and that it retained a basically Catholic form of worship.

After his death in 1547, however, the crown passed to his and Jane Seymour's nine-year-old son, Edward VI; and the actual government of the country was entrusted to a council of regency dominated by men who had been strongly influenced by Lutheran and Calvinist ideas. Chief among these men was Thomas Cranmer, who even before his consecration as archbishop of Canterbury in 1533 had secretly taken a Lutheran wife and who was primarily

responsible for issuing the *Book of Common Prayer* and
the *Forty-Two Articles,* a succinct summary of Anglican
beliefs.

But the sickly boy-king Edward reigned only six years.
And he was succeeded by his half-sister Mary, the daughter
of Henry and Catherine, who throughout Edward's reign
had defied Cranmer and the royal council by having the
Catholic mass celebrated in her private chapel and who
was determined to restore the Roman faith.

By this time nineteen years had passed since Henry
VIII's break with Rome. Almost everyone in England
except Mary had grown accustomed to the idea of an
independent Anglican church. Even the man she chose as
her lord chancellor, Bishop Stephen Gardiner, had enthusiastically hailed Henry VIII as his spiritual overlord.
But Mary Tudor, who was, under English law, supreme
head on earth of the English church, was able to persuade
Parliament to repeal the religious laws of Edward VI and
Henry VIII and even to acknowledge papal jurisdiction in
England—after she and Pope Julius III, demonstrating
considerably more statesmanship than Ferdinand II was to
display in Germany, had agreed not to require restitution
of church property which had been confiscated during
Henry's reign.

There is no way of knowing how much progress Mary
might have been able to make in reconciling England to
Catholicism if she had continued to follow a policy of
moderation and if she had not insisted on marrying
Charles V's son, Philip II of Spain, with whom she had
somehow or other fallen deeply in love.

Such a marriage fit perfectly with Charles V's diplomatic
strategy, since it involved an alliance between England and
Spain which would close the last gap in the Hapsburg encirclement of France. It was bitterly opposed by the

English, however, who did not wish to ally themselves with a country whose economic and military interests were in conflict with their own. In addition, English Protestants —which is to say most of the people in the country—feared that Philip might unleash the Inquisition against them.

But Mary insisted on going ahead with the marriage, which took place in 1554 against the recommendation of her own advisors and of Parliament. It turned out to be an unmitigated disaster for everyone concerned.

Philip, whose first wife had died in childbirth when he was eighteen, had not the slightest bit of affection for the middle-aged Tudor queen. Once he discovered that Parliament would not make him king of England he left the country, taking with him the last hope of producing a Catholic heir to the throne. But Mary remained totally loyal to Philip, so loyal that she committed England to fight with Spain in a war against France and as a consequence lost Calais, England's last continental possession.

The greatest tragedy of the Spanish marriage, however, was that it turned Mary's subjects against her. She had been accepted wholeheartedly by the English people as their legitimate queen despite her commitment to the Catholic faith, and an attempt to depose her after Edward's death in favor of the Protestant Lady Jane Grey had quickly collapsed for lack of public support. Only a year later, however, after Mary's engagement to Philip was announced, a major Protestant uprising broke out. It was after this uprising that the persecutions began.

In the remaining four years of Mary's reign, some three hundred people were burned for heresy. Among them was Thomas Cranmer, who first recanted Protestantism and then, when he finally was led to the stake, made the magnificent gesture of thrusting into the flames the hand which had signed the recantation.

What made these executions so senseless, and thus made
Queen Mary all the more unpopular, was the fact that
most of the victims were uneducated people who had simply accepted what their priests and bishops had been telling
them for more than two decades—just as the officials who
arrested, tortured, and burned them had done. Members
of the upper class, many of whom had been instrumental
in establishing the Protestant religion and who might have
been able to swing the tide of public opinion back toward
Catholicism, escaped persecution by fleeing the country. A
number of them settled in Geneva and in northern Germany, and after Elizabeth succeeded Mary in 1558 they
returned to England more firmly committed to Protestantism than when they had left.

Elizabeth, who was concerned far more with unity than
with doctrinal purity, attempted to construct a national
church in which Lutherans, Calvinists, and Catholics all
could feel more or less at home. It was primarily because of
her desire to steer a middle course that the Anglican church
retained so many Catholic beliefs and ceremonies—and
she would have preferred it to retain a good many more.
But all through her reign Elizabeth had to deal with the
Calvinist or "Puritan" wing of the Anglican church and
with Parliaments which were a great deal more anti-Catholic than she was, and on some issues she found it necessary to compromise.

Elizabeth herself seems not to have cared what people's
inner religious convictions were, so long as they conformed
outwardly to Parliament's laws. She saw to it that the
Catholic nobility were exempted from the obligation of
swearing under the Act of Uniformity, which would have
meant denying the authority of the pope. Catholics were
permitted to excuse themselves from attending Protestant
services by paying a small fine. Private celebration of the
Catholic mass, although theoretically illegal, usually was

permitted in practice. This awkward but tolerable arrangement continued for twelve years, until in 1570 Pope Pius V suddenly decided to excommunicate Elizabeth.

Like the royal excommunications of the Middle Ages, this was far more of a political than a religious act. It amounted to a public declaration that the Catholic Church did not consider Elizabeth to be the legitimate ruler of England. Pius issued it only two months after an uprising in the north of England had been suppressed, and apparently he intended it to encourage similar rebellions. His successor, Gregory XIII, went several steps further by declaring that it would not be a sin to kill Elizabeth and by attempting to stir up a revolt in Ireland against her.

This talk of assassination and revolution was taken very seriously in England, particularly after the slaughter of thousands of French Protestants on St. Bartholomew's Day in 1572 and the murder of William of Orange, the Calvinist leader of Holland's revolt against Spain, by an agent of Philip II in 1584.

And yet Pius and Gregory had been tragically misled by inaccurate reports of conditions in England and by their own wishful thinking. It simply was not true that the great majority of the English population, or even a substantial part of it, wished to rise up against Elizabeth, who already in her own lifetime was one of the best-loved public figures in English history. The fact is that, as a general rule, most people in the sixteenth century neither had nor were expected to have any more of an opinion about religious matters than about who their secular ruler should be. They almost always followed the lead of the upper classes in such matters—and the loyalty of most of the English upper class had been purchased through grants of the monastic lands which Thomas Cromwell had confiscated for the crown.

Most of the Catholic clergy and hierarchy, to whom the

common people might have looked for guidance, already had given up the fight. Only one bishop, John Fisher of Rochester, had refused to take an oath acknowledging Henry VIII as head of the English church. And Fisher had been decapitated.

The very factor which had made the spectacular Catholic gains in central and eastern Europe possible—the willingness of the overwhelming majority of people to accept whatever religious orientation was adopted by their leaders—had the opposite effect in England. But Rome kept trying to encourage rebellion among people who did not wish to rebel, and in particular to depose Elizabeth in favor of Mary Stuart, the Catholic granddaughter of Henry VIII's sister Margaret. Mary, who also was Queen of Scotland and widow of King Francis II of France, was recognized by everyone as having a more valid claim than anyone else to succeed Elizabeth. Those who held that Henry's marriage to Anne Boleyn had been invalid considered her to be the lawful queen of England already.

None of the schemes for replacing Elizabeth with Mary could succeed, however, without the assistance of a large foreign army, preferably that of Spain; and Philip II frequently was urged by Rome to invade England on Mary's behalf. But Philip had no intention of conquering England and then handing it over to the French king's sister-in-law. It was only after Mary's execution for treason in 1578, when he was free to press his own claim to the English throne (based on his marriage to Mary Tudor), that he sent his Armada against Elizabeth. And the many lives which were lost in the intervening years as the result of plots and conspiracies to further Mary Stuart's cause were sacrificed to no real purpose.

Pius V's edict of excommunication was the turning-point in Elizabeth's treatment of her Catholic subjects, just as the Spanish marriage had transformed relations between Mary Tudor and the Protestants.

It was after 1570, and particularly after the defeat of the Spanish Armada, that the most severe anti-Catholic penal laws were enacted. Elizabeth eventually executed about as many people as Mary Tudor had—although Elizabeth reigned almost ten times as long. Many of these victims were priests, who automatically were assumed to be traitors or spies and some of whom, particularly among the Jesuits who were smuggled into the country, were in fact working to overthrow the Protestant government.

Elizabeth's excommunication also made it appear as though being a loyal Catholic was incompatible with being a loyal English citizen. This was a grievous mistake, for it created the impression among English Protestants that Catholics constituted a dangerous and politically subversive element in their midst. So long did this impression last that the Elizabethan-era laws which barred Catholics from participation in English public affairs were not totally repealed until 1829.

Chapter 18
REFORMATION TO REVOLUTION:
THE CHURCH IN FRANCE

FOR three hundred years after Jesus died, most of his followers considered their church to be totally separate and distinct from the secular state. But Constantine and the emperors who followed him believed that they possessed jurisdiction over religious as well as civil affairs. They intervened freely in the church's government and in the formulation of its doctrine, and the rulers of every country in Europe continued to follow their example wherever and whenever they were able to do so.

This was particularly true in France, where Clovis, a secular ruler, had almost single-handedly brought his entire nation into the church. He and his successors had donated enormous amounts of money and huge tracts of land to support that church. They had chosen most of the bishops who administered it. And they, like their Roman predecessors, had not hesitated to assume responsibility for regulating its affairs.

The efforts of popes like Gregory VII and Innocent III to remove ecclesiastical administration from laymen's hands, therefore, frequently were perceived in France as unwarranted attacks upon the monarchy's long-established privileges. Most of these privileges, including the right of the crown to appoint all bishops and abbots, were confirmed in a concordat which was signed by King Francis I and Pope Leo X in 1516, the year before Luther's Ninety-Five Theses, and which remained in effect until the monarchy was overthrown in 1790.

This concordat worked to Leo X's immediate advantage by muting French demands that he convene an ecumenical council to reform the church—something which Leo, as we have seen, had compelling reasons for not wishing to do. But it also ensured that most French men and women would continue to feel more loyalty to the church of France than to the church of Rome. And it helped to make France the only major European country in which the monarchy did not associate itself with either the Protestant or the Catholic reform movement.

French kings were not tempted to abandon Catholicism and seize control of the church's property, like Henry VIII and some of the German princes, because the church and its property already were under their control. But this same desire to maintain the status quo also kept them from promulgating the Council of Trent's disciplinary decrees, as a result of which the Catholic Church in France remained essentially unreformed until the Revolution.

And as time went on, many of those who found themselves unable to accept Catholicism as it existed in France began to abandon organized religion altogether—particularly after the French Protestant movement, which they might otherwise have joined, was first neutralized and then systematically destroyed.

Calvin had declared that resistance against civil rulers, even for motives of self-defense, could be justified only if it were led by a prince of royal blood. Lacking such a prince, French Calvinists—also known as "Huguenots," a word whose origins are now obscure—had been patiently enduring persecution for some two decades by the time King Henry II died in 1559.

In that year, however, Antoine de Bourbon, the king of Navarre and a direct descendent of King Louis IX of France, announced his conversion to Calvinism. Antoine's brother Louis, the Duke of Conde, did the same. So did Gaspard de Coligny, nephew of the Catholic Duke of Montmorency. This encouraged the Huguenots, who already represented seven to ten percent of the population of France and in some areas constituted a majority, to begin taking up arms. Soon a vicious struggle erupted between the Protestant and Catholic nobility, and in particular between the families of Bourbon and Guise.

Between these two groups stood Queen Mother Catherine de Medici, who attempted to follow a policy of religious toleration. Her motives were not entirely altruistic. Catherine, a widow with three small children, was surrounded by powerful noble families who were eager to increase their own power at the monarchy's expense. One way to deal with this situation was to play off the nobles against one another, and this was precisely what she attempted to do. Since the Catholic Guises represented the most immediate threat to her and her children, Catherine sought to strengthen the position of their Huguenot enemies in order to protect herself. She also could see that toleration, at least for the time being, was politically necessary.

Unlike their counterparts in England and Spain, who had been reduced to a position of political subservience, the noble families of France still were powerful enough to oppose the monarchy with military force. This allowed the Huguenot nobility to protect their coreligionists just as the Lutheran nobility had done in Germany.

The Guises, and the other nobles who refused to compromise with Calvinism, argued that religious uniformity was a necessary precondition to civil peace. This had been the conventional wisdom since Constantine's time, but it simply did not apply to cases where a religious minority was able to defend itself. To plunge a nation into protracted civil war in order to preserve the peace obviously made no sense, and the only alternative was a political rather than a military solution. Those who advocated this approach were known as *politiques,* and for a time Catherine joined their ranks.

This was not toleration on principle, merely toleration as a necessary expedient in circumstances where unity could not be imposed by force. By distinguishing the interests of France from the interests of either Catholicism or Protestantism, however, Catherine and the *politiques,* regardless of their motivations, were taking the first uncertain steps toward the creation of a truly secular state.

But this policy was sabotaged in March of 1562, when soldiers of the Duke of Guise slaughtered a group of Huguenots and touched off the conflict which Catherine had been trying to prevent. During the next twenty-seven years France endured eight "Wars of Religion," interspersed with political assassinations and a number of civilian massacres.

By August of 1570, three wars already had been fought. England, the Netherlands, Spain, several German states, and the papacy all had intervened. Antoine de Bourbon and the Duke of Montmorency had fallen in battle, the Dukes of Guise and Conde had been murdered, and thousands of soldiers and civilians had been killed. But the Huguenots, even though their armies had been defeated several times in the field, still were able to defend their fortified towns.

The resulting stalemate led Catherine, who had been supporting the Catholic side, to make another attempt at compromise. A treaty favorable to the Huguenots was signed. Their commander-in-chief, Gaspard de Coligny, was given a seat in the royal council and became an advisor to King Charles IX. And Catherine's daughter Marguerite was betrothed to Henry of Navarre, Antoine de Bourbon's seventeen-year-old son.

These arrangements were intended to promote unity by

allowing Huguenots to participate in the formulation of
national policy. But Catherine soon began to resent the
fact that her son Charles was falling more and more under
Coligny's influence. And when Coligny induced Charles to
support the Dutch rebellion against Spain, with whom
Catherine had formed an alliance in 1559 by marrying
one of her daughters to Philip II, she ordered Coligny's
assassination.

But the attempt failed. And the following day, terrified
that Coligny's supporters would seek revenge, Catherine,
her sons, and the Guise family decided to strike first by
murdering the Huguenot leaders who had come to Paris
to celebrate the wedding of Henry of Navarre and
Marguerite. Just after midnight on August 24, 1572, the
feast of St. Bartholomew, soldiers under the command of
the late Duke of Guise's son began slaughtering every
Huguenot they could lay their hands on. Before long the
citizens of Paris joined in, and eventually the massacre
spread to the provinces. No one knows for certain how
many thousands died. Pope Gregory XIII was told that the
Huguenots had been killed during an attempt to overthrow
Charles IX, and on basis of this misinformation a com-
memorative medal was issued to celebrate the event.

Henry of Guise and Henry of Navarre succeeded their
fathers as leaders of the Catholic and Huguenot factions
and fought five separate wars over a period of seventeen
years, the antagonism between them growing more and
more intense as it gradually became apparent that none of
Catherine's sons would leave a male heir. This made Henry
of Navarre, by virtue of his descent from Louis IX, first in
line to inherit the French throne. But Henry of Guise, who
also was descended from Louis IX, had an excellent chance
to become king himself if he could eliminate Navarre.

The beginning of the end of this long conflict came in

December of 1588, when Henry III, brother of Charles IX and the last of the Valois kings, had Henry of Guise assassinated. Seven months later the king himself was murdered by a Dominican priest. This helped to clear the way for Henry of Navarre, who, after converting to Catholicism, was recognized as King Henry IV in 1589.

Three years later Henry issued the Edict of Nantes, which granted freedom of conscience and civil liberty to Catholics and Protestants alike and permitted Calvinist religious services in certain specified areas of France. Huguenots, who were understandably concerned about their safety in a land where religious hatred had burned so fiercely for so long, were given permission to garrison one hundred fortified towns as refuges to which they could flee if persecution should break out again.

But Henry was assassinated in 1610, and the government of France passed into the hands of men who were determined to destroy every political institution capable of resisting the power of the central state—including the private armies of the nobility and the Huguenot "state within the state."

Prominent among these men was Cardinal Richelieu, who ruled France for eighteen years during the reign of Louis XIII, Henry IV's son, and who set his country firmly upon the path to royal absolutism. Richelieu personally directed the siege of La Rochelle, the chief Huguenot stronghold. And in 1629 he arranged to have Louis XIII issue the Edict of Alais, which deprived the Huguenots of all civil rights and ordered their fortifications destroyed. Finally, in 1685, Louis XIV revoked the Edict of Nantes and made the practice of Calvinism illegal—whereupon a quarter of a million Protestants chose to leave the country rather than convert.

Louis XIV also provoked a long and bitter quarrel with

Pope Innocent XI by attempting to extend the privileges contained in the Concordat of 1516 to several French provinces which had been claiming exemption from them. This dispute was reminiscent in many ways of the great church-state conflicts of the Middle Ages, with Louis threatening to call a general council and Innocent threatening to excommunicate him. And the French clergy responded by rallying to the defense of the monarchy just as their medieval predecessors had done.

In March of 1682 a national convocation of French bishops and priests issued a declaration which not only supported Louis against Innocent but also denied that the church possesses any authority over kings in the exercise of their secular power, repeated the pronouncements of the Council of Constance on the superiority of general councils to the pope, and asserted that the papacy was obliged to respect the ancient customs and traditions of the French church.

This declaration, the culmination of centuries of resistance to the papacy's efforts to assert its authority in France, reinforced the French church's sense of estrangement from Rome and identified its interests even more closely with those of the crown. All of this made the position of French Catholicism most difficult when the Revolution began.

Another complicating factor was the attitude which Rome had taken toward the Enlightenment, an intellectual movement which held that the most reliable guide to knowledge is not authority or faith but the natural ability of each human mind to reach true conclusions by following valid methods of reasoning.

The Enlightenment was analogous in some respects to the concept of individual interpretation of Scripture. It implied a rejection of all authority except that of reason itself, just as Protestantism had rejected all authority except that of faith. This was revolutionary in the extreme, because authority was the foundation upon which almost every social, political, and religious institution in Europe had been built.

The writers and scholars who initiated the Enlightenment—men like Descartes, Kepler, Harvey, Bacon, Newton, and Boyle—were not antireligious. Some of them believed so strongly that the truths of reason could never conflict with those of faith that they attempted to construct philosophical and theological systems which did not depend upon the presuppositions of any particular religion and thus could be accepted by people of all faiths, just as the theorems of geometry were.

This presented Catholicism with an opportunity similar to the one which it had faced when Aristotle's major works became available in the Middle Ages. It could not have accepted the Enlightenment's attacks upon tradition and authority without undermining the arguments it had used to justify itself during the Reformation. But it had long taught that the same proposition cannot be true in philosophy and false in theology, which was quite similar to what many thinkers of the early Enlightenment held. If someone had been able to reconcile the Enlightenment with the Catholic faith in somewhat the same way that Thomas Aquinas had reconciled Aristotelianism with it, the church might have taken a position of leadership in the seventeenth-century scientific revolution rather than alienating itself from it.

One reason why this did not happen was that the defensive attitude adopted by the Council of Trent made the church considerably less receptive to innovations than it had been in Aquinas's day. Another was that Catholicism, having devoted most of its energy for more than a hundred years to anti-Protestant polemics and intramural squabbles between religious orders, simply did not possess the intellectual resources needed to accomplish such a synthesis. Already in 1633 the church had taken a decisive step in defining its attitude toward the Enlightenment by condemning Galileo for insisting that the earth moves around the sun.

No one objected to the use of heliocentrism as a hypothesis in the interpretation of astronomical observations. Since it appeared to contradict several passages in Scripture, however, and since its truth had not been conclusively proved, Galileo was forbidden to teach it as an established fact or to hold that geocentrism is definitely false. It is because he allegedly disobeyed this command that Galileo was placed under house arrest by the Inquisition for the remaining seven years of his life.

The underlying issue in this case was whether the church should limit speculation about theories, particularly those which have not yet been established as facts, which might tend to weaken people's religious faith. The church, continuing to maintain that it has jurisdiction over everything which might affect its members' spiritual welfare, contended that it should. And since this was precisely what the Enlightenment refused to concede, Galileo's condemnation was interpreted both inside and outside the church as a condemnation of the Enlightenment.

Unable to assimilate the Enlightenment, or suppress it, or meet it on its own terms, Catholicism simply retreated deeper and deeper into intellectual isolation—a retreat which, ironically, helped to ensure that the Enlightenment's goal of separating reason from faith would be realized. Much of Europe's intelligentsia became first indifferent to religion and then actively hostile to it. And the church, which had been responsible for virtually every scientific, cultural, and economic advance of the medieval period, came to be associated in many people's minds with ignorance and intolerance.

In spite of all this, however, and in spite of the vitriolic attacks of men like Rousseau and Voltaire, an overwhelmingly high percentage of the French population in the second half of the eighteenth century still considered themselves Catholic. And when the Estates-General which Louis XVI convened to authorize an increase in taxes turned itself into a National Assembly and began passing laws, it had no intention of attacking the church. It merely wished to carry out the ecclesiastical reforms which everyone agreed were necessary at the same time that it was reforming the rest of French society.

Part of this was accomplished in August of 1789, when the clergy, along with the nobles, voluntarily relinquished their political and social privileges. This abolished feudalism in France almost overnight. And it also abolished many of the financial supports, such as the right to levy tithes, upon which the Catholic Church had long depended.

Three months later the Assembly passed the "Declaration of the Rights of Man," a summary of Enlightenment political beliefs which proclaimed, among other things, complete freedom of speech and of religion and civil equality for adherents of all faiths. This document, which quickly acquired a symbolic significance for French men and women similar to that which the Declaration of Independence has for Americans, was denounced by Pope Pius VI as contrary to revelation. In February of 1790 the Assembly declared the annulment of all religious vows on the grounds that they abridged the inalienable freedoms spelled out in the Declaration, whereupon thousands of monks and nuns abandoned their communities.

Meanwhile, in order to meet the threat of national bankruptcy which had compelled Louis XVI to assemble the Estates-General in the first place, the government decided to follow the suggestion of Bishop Talleyrand and confiscate the property of the Catholic Church, by far the wealthiest single institution in France. In return it promised to pay salaries to the Catholic clergy and to support the church's schools, hospitals, and other charitable works. The state, in other words, would provide out of the public treasury the annual income which the endowments of land and money which it had expropriated originally were intended to supply. This system was quite similar to the one which Emperor Joseph II had put into effect in Austria less than ten years before, and it met with very little opposition. Almost everyone agreed that redistribution of the church's assets was desperately needed.

On the eve of the Revolution, one historian has estimated, the income of some bishops was thirteen hundred times that of parish priests. The church owned ten percent of all the land in France, and in some areas more than sixty percent, most of which belonged to monastic orders. Not only was this greatly hindering the nation's economic development, but it also meant that a high percentage of the church's assets were unavailable to support the secular clergy or to meet pastoral and charitable needs which had arisen since those monasteries were founded.

The fact that the National Assembly was guaranteeing the parish priests of France a secure income for the first time in history was one reason why many of the lower clergy numbered among the Revolution's most enthusiastic supporters.

But this support eroded quickly after the enactment in July of 1790 of a "Civil Constitution of the Clergy" to regulate the nonspiritual aspects of French Catholicism—which in the opinion of the government included almost everything except doctrine. This measure, which the government considered an integral part of its attempt to reconstruct French society upon a just and rational basis, was not necessarily antireligious in content. It attempted to increase the administrative efficiency of the church, which some members of the Assembly already were coming to look upon as an agency of the state, and to introduce democratic principles into it.

Each of the *departements* into which the Assembly had recently divided France was to contain one and only one diocese, which meant the elimination of more than one-third of the country's bishoprics. There would be one parish for every six thousand people. Bishops and parish priests would be elected by all citizens, Catholic and non-Catholic alike. Since the clergy were now to be paid by the state, they were forbidden to collect money for the performance of their official duties or to move from their assigned posts without government permission.

Many of these reforms were considered even by churchmen to be long overdue. The most important thing about the Civil Constitution as far as the church was concerned, however, was not any of its specific provisions but the fact that it had beem imposed unilaterally. This, the church believed, amounted to a denial of its right to manage its own internal affairs independently of the state. And that was an issue on which the National Assembly felt it could not compromise, since the existence of any political society independent of the state would contradict the principle that the popular will is sovereign over everything except individual consciences, the principle upon which the entire Revolution and the legitimacy of the Assembly itself were founded.

Rather than negotiating, therefore, the Assembly attempted to obtain compliance by requiring all bishops and priests—who had now become, in effect, civil servants—to take an oath supporting the Civil Constitution as a condition of retaining their offices. This forced the Catholic clergy to choose between denying their church's right to exist as a self-governing entity and denying the authority of the National Assembly, which meant opposing the Revolution which most of them had supported until then. Louis XVI urged them to comply. Pius VI waited until after the deadline for making a decision had passed and then denounced both the Civil Constitution and the oath.

In the end only seven French bishops took the oath, Talleyrand among them, while the remaining one hundred and fifty-three refused. About half of the lower clergy also refused, although priests in some areas, particularly the region surrounding Paris, gave it overwhelming acceptance.

Two parallel church organizations immediately sprang into existence, one composed of juring clergy—those who had taken the oath—and the other of nonjurors. Both organizations had devoted followers in almost every parish, which created bitter dissension throughout France at a time when the leaders of the Revolution were trying desperately to impose unity. Finally, in November of 1791, tens of thousands of nonjuring priests, accused of disloyalty to the Revolution, were exiled.

Most of the nonjuring bishops, all of whom were noblemen, already had fled the country. Many of them joined other aristocratic refugees in plotting counter-revolution, while Pius VI attempted to put together an alliance of the great European powers to overthrow the revolutionary government and free Louis XVI from its control. All of this naturally tended to reinforce the image of the Catholic Church as an ally of despotism and an enemy of freedom in the eyes of those who supported the Revolution. In France as in England—although for totally different reasons—Catholics were put into a position where loyalty to their church appeared to be incompatible with loyalty to their country.

The Civil Constitution and the events to which it gave rise not only were the turning points in the relations between the Revolution and the church; they also were more responsible than anything else for dividing France into pro-Catholic and anti-Catholic factions, a division which persists to this day.

Even the patriotism of the juring priests and bishops, most of whom were known to be staunchly loyal to the crown, became suspect after Louis XVI was executed in January of 1793. With Austria, Prussia, Holland, Spain, and Great Britain all waging war against France, agents were dispatched to the provinces to eliminate anyone who might hinder the war effort or give encouragement to the Revolution's enemies. By definition this included royalist sympathizers, which all priests, both jurors and nonjurors, were presumed to be.

It was during this period, while the Reign of Terror was underway in the major cities, that a determined effort was made to exterminate all sources of authority except the state and to destroy Christianity in France. All religious ceremonies, Catholic and Protestant, were forbidden. Priests were hunted down and ordered to renounce their offices and marry; those who refused, and those who aided them, were condemned to death. Churches were closed, and use of the Christian calendar discontinued.

Having declared Christianity abolished, the Revolution attempted to replace it with a "natural religion" based entirely on reason. Several varieties were developed. For a time the Enlightenment itself was made into a kind of religion, and temples were provided for the worship of Reason. Robespierre, the guiding genius of the Reign of

Terror, attempted to cultivate belief in a somewhat nebulous "Supreme Being."

But all of these efforts were frustrated by the simple fact that "natural religion"—a religion, that is, which denies the existence of any truth not accessible to reason—is a contradiction in terms. All of these various manifestations really were nothing more than the philosophical ideas of the Enlightenment, dressed up in ceremonies so bizarre that before long Catholicism began to look positively "rational" in comparison. Reason alone proved insufficient to satisfy the spiritual needs of the people of France, just as it has proved insufficient for the needs of every other people; and after Robespierre's fall from power in July of 1794 the dechristianizing campaign quickly lost momentum.

Meanwhile the armies of the Revolution, to everyone's surprise, had pushed back the invading allied forces and had taken the offensive themselves. In February of 1798 a French army entered Rome and captured Pius VI, who was transported to France and died there eighteen months later. The papacy itself, completely at its enemies' mercy, appeared to be on the verge of extinction.

Less than three months after the death of Pius VI, however, Napoleon Bonaparte engineered a *coup d'etat* and put a totally different religious policy into effect.

During his campaigns in Italy Napoleon had received several direct orders from Paris to march on Rome and destroy the papacy. He had ignored all of them—not because he had any reverence for that institution himself but because he knew that the Italian people did. And he could not afford to increase the number of enemies with which his already outnumbered army might have to deal. By sparing the church, an act which cost him nothing, he made himself so popular among the Italians that he was able to leave their territory virtually ungarrisoned and devote his full attention to crushing the Austrians.

Napoleon saw the situation in France in similar terms. Because he was not an ideologue, he was not bothered at all by the fact that most of the French population had demonstrated an unflinching loyalty to the Catholic Church. He merely wished to turn this to his own advantage by making certain that the church would remain loyal to him. And he needed to stop the fratricidal struggle which was still going on between followers of the juring and nonjuring Catholic clergy so that he could mobilize the nation's total resources against the allied coalition which still threatened France.

He attacked these problems with the same energy and decisiveness he displayed on the battlefield. Within eighteen months he had not only eliminated the sources of religious dissension in France but also had turned religion, and the Catholic religion in particular, into one of the most potent forces supporting his regime. His chief instrument for accomplishing this was the concordat which he signed in July of 1801 with the newly elected Pope Pius VII.

The advantages Napoleon derived from entering into this agreement were fairly obvious. He was promoting unity among his subjects, establishing himself as the savior of Catholicism in France, and securing diplomatic recognition for the legitimacy of his government. He also had devised a method for ensuring the submission of the French Church to his will in spite of the fact that the concordat guaranteed its independence.

It was much less clear at the time what Pius had to gain from negotiating with Napoleon, particularly since such negotiations seemed to imply acceptance of the literally revolutionary concept that people can establish a legitimate government by overthrowing their anointed king—a

concept which threatened to undermine the authority of
every sovereign in Europe, including that of the pope
himself. The very idea of a concordat on any terms was
vehemently opposed by Louis XVI's brother, who was
now recognized by most of Europe as the lawful king of
France; by the royalist aristocracy who had emigrated during the Revolution; by many of Pius's own cardinals; and
by the allied governments which were still fighting an extremely costly war in order to restore the Bourbons to the
French throne.

Pius, on the other hand, was convinced that his primary
concern must be the welfare of the Catholics in France,
regardless of who their secular ruler might be, and that
normalizing relations between the church and the French
government would make it easier for them to recover from
the traumas of the Revolution. He also realized that a concordat would reinforce the papacy's claim to be an independent political force whose opinions and support still
counted for something in world affairs—a claim which
most of the governments of Europe had not been willing to
acknowledge since the Peace of Westphalia had been
signed more than a century and a half before.

The Concordat of 1801, which continued to define the
legal status of French Catholicism for more than one hundred years, stipulated that the state would pay the salaries
of the Catholic clergy and that the church would take no
steps to recover the property which had been confiscated
during the Revolution. Both juring and nonjuring bishops
would resign, and the pope would depose those who refused. Napoleon would then nominate new bishops, whom
Pius would consecrate. There would be no state religion,
but the practice of Catholicism and of all other faiths
would be completely unrestricted—except for such regulations as might be necessary to maintain public order.

In April of 1802 the French legislature ratified this agreement along with the so-called "Organic Articles," which according to Napoleon contained nothing more than the regulatory measures which the concordat authorized him to enact. In fact the Organic Articles effectively undercut many of the rights which the concordat was intended to protect, such as the right of the pope to communicate freely with French Catholics and the right of the French church to hold synods without government permission. In this way Napoleon was able to implement a number of provisions to which Pius had refused to agree when the concordat was being negotiated.

The unilateral adoption of these Organic Articles was denounced vociferously in Rome. When Napoleon requested the pope to come to Paris in December of 1804 to attend his coronation as emperor, however, Pius did not refuse, even though he was aware that his presence would be interpreted as a sign that he and the church acknowledged French sovereignty over the territory which had been annexed to form Napoleon's empire. But Pius did refuse to close the harbors of the Papal States to British shipping; and this refusal led to his being arrested and kept under confinement in France for more than five years.

But the tide of history was beginning to turn. Napoleon met defeat in Russia and in Spain; and in January of 1814, as the victorious allied armies neared Paris, the pope finally was set free. The following May, the same month in which Bonaparte began his exile on Elba, Pius returned in triumph to Rome.

The era of revolution had come to an end. And the era of reaction was about to begin.

Chapter 19
THE TRIUMPH OF PAPALISM

EVEN before Napoleon's final defeat at Waterloo in 1815, the papacy, which had appeared to be on the verge of extinction only a few years earlier, had begun to emerge from the chaos of the French Revolution stronger and more confident than it had been in generations—largely because the Revolution had weakened many of the political forces which previously had opposed it.

The Revolution, for example, had destroyed the complex web of political alliances which for hundreds of years had been encouraging the development of quasi-independent national churches in countries like France and Spain. The Revolution made it possible for the Vatican to extend its influence for the first time into the foreign missions over which the governments of Spain and Portugal always had maintained total and exclusive control.

The Revolution and its aftermath had reduced the ability of secular governments to interfere in papal elections, making possible the installation of a long series of popes who were, on the whole, far more highly qualified than those of any other period since the end of the Counter-Reformation two hundred and fifty years before.

And, perhaps most important, the Revolution had greatly eroded the position of the bishops, Rome's traditional rivals for power within the church. Napoleon himself had contributed to this erosion by abolishing the Germanic prince-bishoprics—particularly those of Mainz, Trier, Cologne, and Salzburg, whose incumbents had been the most vocal opponents of papal primacy and infallibility before the revolution—and by forcing all the bishops of France to submit their resignations to Pope Pius VII.

It was during this post-revolutionary period, when large

numbers of people were turning away from skepticism and back to religion and the bishops were rapidly losing their independence, that popes began to reach over the heads of the bishops, so to speak, and establish a direct relationship with the laity and the lower clergy—who came to regard them for the first time as leaders and teachers to whom they could look for spiritual guidance. This enabled Rome to exert a greater degree of control over the church's internal affairs during the nineteenth century than it ever had enjoyed before.

The papacy also benefited from the support of those who wished to restore, so far as was possible, the conditions which had existed before the Revolution. Some of these people had a personal stake in preserving the established order. Others were appalled by the bloodshed and destruction which the Revolution's egalitarian rhetoric had unleashed in France. Still others believed that the existence of monarchical government and a hierarchy of social classes had been divinely ordained, and that any attempt to abolish them constituted an act of rebellion against God.

All of them agreed, however, on the necessity of cultivating reverence for authority and tradition—which meant, among other things, encouraging respect for religion. And the religion which benefited from this more than any other was Catholicism, the religion which emphasized authority and tradition most strongly. Just as the Catholic Church had been denounced by Voltaire and Rousseau as the personification of everything in the old order which was oppressive and bad, so it seemed to many conservatives in the early nineteenth century to represent more effectively than any other institution those elements in the old order which had been good. Within a few years after Waterloo, most of the major nations of Europe had signed new concordats or other formal agreements with

Rome. The Congress of Vienna, which was pledged to safeguard the traditional rights of monarchs, was forced by the logic of its own position to return the Papal States to the Vatican's control.

Many European governments restored Catholicism to something approaching the privileged position which it had occupied before the revolution and gave it large financial subsidies. In France, Catholic clergy were given control of most primary and secondary schools. King Ferdinand VII of Spain revived the Inquisition.

The effect of all this was to draw the Catholic Church, which had just been freed by the Revolution from the control of absolutist monarchies, back into a close alliance with the forces of repression and reaction. Some Catholics, however, particularly in France, believed that the church should follow the opposite course. Among those who held this position was Felicite de Lamennais, a diocesan priest.

Lamennais was convinced that dependence on civil government had always proved harmful to religion, and that the various national churches and their hierarchies must subordinate themselves to the authority of a strong and independent papacy if they wished to escape secular domination. This position was similar in many respects to that of Gregory VII, Innocent III, and the other great medieval popes; and by advocating it Lamennais became one of the principal founders of modern ultramontanism ("beyond-the-Alps-ism"), or the glorification of papal authority over that of the national hierarchies.

But Lamennais went beyond anything which Gregory VII or Innocent III could have accepted. The best way for Catholics to ensure their own freedom in post-revolutionary France, he believed, was not to seek special privileges from the government but to support total freedom for all religions.

This implied accepting the separation of church and state. And Lamennais followed this implication to its logical conclusion by attacking the Concordat of 1801 and insisting that the French government should neither nominate bishops, as the concordat authorized it to do, or pay salaries to the clergy. He also wanted Rome to take the lead in promoting the principles of political equality, freedom of expression, and democratic government, because he believed that these provided the conditions most conducive to Catholicism's growth. When he encountered opposition from the bishops of France, all of whom had been chosen by the state under the terms of the 1801 concordat, Lamennais, somewhat naively, appealed to Pope Gregory XVI for support.

Pope Pius VII, by coming to terms with Napoleon, had tacitly acknowledged the inescapable fact that many of the changes brought about by the French Revolution had to be accepted as irreversible facts. But Gregory, who had been elected only a year earlier with the support of Klemens von Metternich, the fiercely reactionary Austrian foreign minister, had several excellent reasons for not following this example.

Since he himself was the head of one of the most repressive governments in Europe—that of the Papal States, where he still was engaged in putting down a rebellion against his rule—Gregory hardly could have been expected to do anything which might encourage the spread of democratic ideas. Memories of the French Revolution and its frenzied attempts to destroy the church still were fresh in his mind. The government of Austria, whose favor Gregory was obliged to cultivate because he needed the support of its .army in order to regain control of the Papal States, demanded that Lamennais's ideas be condemned as politically subversive.

For all of these reasons, plus his own belief that the theory of democratic government rests on the assumption that authority is founded on human reason rather than on the will of God, Gregory in August of 1831 issued the encyclical *Mirari vos,* which denounced separation of church and state, denied the right of rebellion against tyrannical monarchies, and utterly condemned freedom of worship and freedom of the press as contrary to long-established Catholic teaching. And Lamennais, despite having made an act of submission to Gregory, was subjected to such intense and prolonged harassment by his own bishops that finally he left the church.

In June of 1846, however, when the fifty-four-year-old Giovanni Mastai-Feretti was elected to succeed Gregory, it looked as though Catholicism might assimilate rather than oppose the new political ideas, and that Lamennais's fondest hopes might be realized after all.

Mastai, who took the name Pius IX, was by no means a progressive thinker. But he was perceptive enough to realize that Gregory XVI's policy of using foreign troops to terrorize the Papal States into submission was making the church increasingly dependent upon the goodwill of secular rulers—which was precisely what the pope's sovereignty over that territory was intended to prevent. Shortly after his election he declared an amnesty for political prisoners, and in the months which followed he repealed some of the more outrageous laws which had been imposed since the death of Pius VII and promulgated a constitution which gave the Papal States a measure of self-government for the first time in history.

These concessions, modest though they might seem by contemporary standards, made Pius one of the most popular and respected public figures in Europe, hailed by Catholics and non-Catholics alike as the pope who would reconcile freedom with religion. This was particularly true in Italy itself, where his name frequently was invoked by those who were agitating on behalf of the *risorgimento*, the campaign to create a unified and democratic national state. Ultimately, however, it was the attempt to create this state which sabotaged the auspicious beginning of Pius IX's reign and caused him to resume Gregory XVI's quixotic crusade against the modern world.

The turning point came in 1848, when portions of northern Italy revolted against Austrian rule and King Charles Albert of Piedmont-Sardinia intervened on the rebels' behalf. The newly-established legislature of the Papal States, rallying to the cause of Italian nationalism, voted to enter the conflict on Piedmont-Sardinia's side. And when this action was vetoed by Pius, who felt that he could not allow the country whose sovereign he was to wage war against what was then Europe's leading Catholic power, riots broke out all through the papal dominions including the city of Rome itself. Pellegrino Rossi, the pope's prime minister, was assassinated.

Nine days later Pius fled Rome in disguise and appealed to the major powers of Europe for help, whereupon Louis Napoleon, the recently-elected president of France, sent an army to recapture the Papal States and escort the pope back to Rome.

But Pius now was even more dependent upon foreign military power than Gregory had been. All that kept the armies of the *risorgimento* from seizing the Papal States were the French troops garrisoned there; and before long Camillo Cavour, the prime minister of Piedmont-Sardinia, gave Nice and Savoy to France in exchange for the removal of those troops. By 1861 the papacy had lost all its territorial possessions except the city of Rome and its environs, which Louis Napoleon had pledged to defend on behalf of the pope in order to appease Catholic opinion in France. This enabled Pius to reign for ten more years over what little remained of his kingdom.

This entire sequence of events—the murder of Rossi, the expulsion of Pius from Rome, and the assault by Italian armies upon a virtually undefended state whose origins predated Charlemagne—served only to increase Pius IX's already enormous prestige. Many Catholics came to look upon him as a living martyr, a way of thinking which Pius himself did everything possible to encourage.

Pius IX made himself into an international celebrity, the first pope in history to become one. His name was constantly in the newspapers, often in conjunction with statements in which he characterized himself as the victim of anti-religious aggression. He made it a point to receive large numbers of pilgrims and tourists, many of whom left Rome profoundly impressed, sometimes in spite of themselves, with the grandeur of the papal office and with the pope's own affability and charm. Pius summoned bishops and priests from around the world to personal audiences, which he frequently used to win grassroots support for his policies.

It was during the pontificate of Pius IX that there came into existence what might be called the cult of the reigning pope. In the case of Pius himself, this cult exceeded mere respect or veneration and sometimes verged on literal idolatry—as when one bishop described him in a sermon as an incarnation of Jesus Christ. Pius reigned thirty-two years, longer than any other pope in history; and the influence which he exerted was comparable to that of Leo the Great or Hildebrand.

His influence, however, was not entirely beneficial. Pius tended—understandably, perhaps, in view of the fact that he lived for sixteen years in a literal state of siege—to impart a siege mentality to the entire church.

This tendency received a powerful impetus in September of 1864, when France and Italy signed an agreement stipulating that the French troops who still were guarding Rome would be removed within two years, thus clearing the way for Italian annexation of the city. (As it turned out, this provision was not put into effect until 1870.) Within three months after this agreement was announced, Pius, as though to compensate for the impending loss of his temporal power, issued a highly controversial document entitled "A Syllabus Containing the Most Important Errors of Our Time Which Have Been Condemned by Our Holy Father Pius IX in Allocutions, at Consistories, and in Encyclicals and Other Apostolic Letters."

This *Syllabus of Errors,* as the document soon became known, must rank among the most confusing and maladroit compositions ever issued by the Vatican. It was not an exposition of doctrine, but simply a list of eighty excerpts from various declarations which Pius had issued during the preceding fifteen years, each one paraphrasing a philosophical or political position which Catholics were forbidden to hold. Its intent, therefore, was to assert the opposite of what it contained. All the excerpts were quoted out of context, and as a result many of them were understood in a much different sense than Pius had intended.

The most notable example of this misunderstanding was a section of the *Syllabus* which condemned the proposition that the pope should reconcile himself with progress, liberalism, and modern civilization. This played directly into the hands of those who had been arguing that Catholicism is incompatible with democracy and with modern science.

There is no telling how much harm the church might have suffered had it not been for Felix Dupanloup, the bishop of Orleans, who quickly put together a commentary which placed the excerpts of the *Syllabus* back into their original contexts and attempted to interpret them in a sense which would minimize their negative impact. Thus he pointed out that the statement about progress and modern civilization had been taken from a statement condemning the antireligious policies of the government of Piedmont, and that the words "progress" and "civilization" had been used in that statement in an ironic sense to refer to the suppression of monasteries and the restriction of religious education.

Despite Dupanloup's work, however, it was obvious that the *Syllabus* had been intended as an all-out attack not only upon such concepts as freedom of worship, political self-determination, and the separation of church and state, but also upon the entire direction in which the nineteenth-century world was moving.

But the *Syllabus* did nothing to diminish the esteem in which the overwhelming majority of Catholics held Pius, who in many ways was the ideal pope for his time. He symbolized the order, certainty, and stability for which many people were looking in the middle of the nineteenth century; and, paradoxical as it may seem today, the more authoritarian he became, the more his popularity increased. Even a number of non-Catholics preferred Pius IX's brand of papal absolutism and the incessant barrage of anathemas which he issued to the disedifying spectacle presented by some of the state-controlled Protestant churches. Such was the case in England, for example, where ultimate responsibility for resolving doctrinal questions was vested in Parliament, and where bishops, who sat in the House of Lords, often were chosen on the basis of their loyalty to whichever political party had won the most recent election.

During the same week in which the *Syllabus* was issued, Pius informed Vatican officials that he intended to convene an ecumenical council. It was clear to everyone that he expected this assembly to formally recognize his total and complete authority over the entire church and to declare him to be infallible.

All major decisions at this first Council of the Vatican —and most of the minor ones as well—were made in advance by Pius himself. By the time the bishops were formally notified that a council was going to be held, he and his assistants had been planning its agenda and determining the rules which would govern it for two and a half years. This was a radical departure from traditional practice: Vatican I was the first ecumenical council in history at which the delegates did not adopt their own rules and decide for themselves what subjects would and would not be discussed. Pius even reserved to himself the sole right to approve the consideration of topics which were not already on the agenda.

Another innovation was the establishment by Pius of six preparatory committees to draw up doctrinal statements which would be submitted to the bishops for approval. This work was closely supervised by members of the papal Curia, and no bishops outside of the Vatican were invited to participate.

After the council finally got underway in December of 1869, and it became apparent that a substantial minority of the delegates opposed the infallibility declaration, Pius changed the council's rules so that ten bishops, out of a total of about seven hundred, could sponsor a motion to shut off debate. Another change enabled doctrinal statements to be approved by a simple majority—a flagrant violation of the traditional principle that dogmatic definitions should express the overwhelming consensus of the entire church. These heavy-handed tactics had almost no effect on the final outcome, since more than three-quarters of the delegates already were prepared to vote for infallibility. They did, however, hinder a full and impartial discussion of some important points which the minority bishops were trying to make.

Many bishops who accepted infallibility as a fact were concerned that a formal declaration of that belief would make the reconciliation of non-Catholics to the church much more difficult—which has turned out, in fact, to be the case. Others insisted that the council must specify the precise conditions which must be met before a papal declaration can be considered infallible.

Perhaps the most important theological problem concerning the concept of papal infallibility, and one upon which the minority continually tried to focus attention, concerned the relation between the infallibility of the pope and that of the church as a whole. But Pius rendered full consideration of this issue impossible when, in order to speed up debate, he permitted the specific question of papal infallibility—which originally had been included in a document which discussed the entire church—to be voted on as a separate topic.

After two months of debate, the definition of papal infallibility was approved in July of 1870 by a vote of four hundred and thirty-three to two. More than sixty bishops, who felt that they could not in conscience support the definition but did not wish to embarrass the church by opposing it, left Rome before the final vote was taken. A few days later Pius declared the council adjourned. Of the fifty-one doctrinal statements which the preparatory committees had drawn up, only six had been submitted for consideration and only two had been approved. The others were to be voted on when the delegates reconvened.

On September 1, however, the armies of France were annihilated by Prussia at Sedan. The last of the French troops garrisoned in Rome were withdrawn in order to reinforce Paris, and on September 20 an Italian army entered Rome. Vatican I never resumed its work. The crucial question of the relation between the authority of the bishops and that of the pope was left unanswered, and it would continue to remain unanswered for nearly a hundred years.

The incorporation of Rome into the Kingdom of Italy left Pius in possession of an area roughly corresponding to present-day Vatican City. This area was granted extra-territorial status by the Italian government, which also offered the church a substantial annual subsidy as compensation for the losses it had suffered when the Papal States were annexed. But Pius rejected the subsidy, and he refused to acknowledge the existence of the Italian state or to accept the validity of any of its actions. In order to maintain this diplomatic fiction he was obliged to refrain from entering Italian territory, which meant enduring a kind of voluntary house arrest until he died, still a "prisoner of the Vatican," in 1878.

His successor, Leo XIII, also remained within the Vatican's walls throughout his pontificate, as every subsequent pope continued to do until a concordat with Italy finally was signed in 1929. But Leo, far from abandoning the modern world, was convinced that the church desperately needed to come to grips with it. He also was aware that although Pius IX had condemned virtually every prevailing philosophical, theological, and political idea in Europe, he had not offered any practical alternatives.

It was primarily in order to provide an alternative to the various philosophical theories of the late nineteenth century which were judged for one reason or another to be incompatible with Catholic teaching that Leo, in the encyclical *Aeterni Patris,* urged the revival and revitalization of Thomistic philosophy. And it was in order to prevent the church from losing the allegiance of most of the working class that he attempted to develop a Catholic alternative to socialism.

It had been obvious to most people for many years that the industrial revolution had brought into existence totally new kinds of social forces and relationships, and that it had created problems to which no satisfactory solutions had yet been found. Within the space of a few decades, literally millions of people had migrated into urban slums of unspeakable squalor. Whole families lived in a single room, without adequate ventilation or sanitary facilities. Those lucky enough to find work toiled up to fifteen hours a day, in return for which they were paid barely enough to keep themselves alive. And since those who could not find work frequently starved, there was always someone willing to work longer and harder for less money. Approximately one-half of the laboring force consisted of boys and girls under eighteen.

Socialists saw the root of these evils in the private ownership of the means of production. *Laissez-faire* theorists argued that the natural interplay of market forces must not be interfered with, and many of them declared it to be an immutable economic fact that wages always would remain at the bare subsistence level.

Leo, in the encyclical *Rerum Novarum,* attacked the basic premise of *laissez-faire* by insisting that the living conditions of the industrial working class are indeed a moral issue, and that the church has an obligation to concern itself with people's material well-being as well as with their spiritual welfare because the two are intimately related. And he went on to elaborate a comprehensive outline for the development of social policies consistent with the demands of Christian ethics—an outline which echoed many of the socialists' criticisms of capitalism but proposed radically different solutions.

Rerum Novarum was not a polemical diatribe, nor was it simply a statement of beliefs. It was a closely reasoned essay whose conclusions were logically deduced from an analysis of the Christian conception of human nature. Leo upheld the right to private property, but also the right of every worker to receive a "living wage." He condemned revolutionary violence, but defended the existence of labor unions. And he asserted that the state has a duty to prevent the exploitation and degradation of laborers, to regulate the conditions under which people work, and to encourage an equitable distribution of property. Some indication of how progressive these ideas were in Leo's time can be gained from the fact that even now, more than a century later, some people still refuse to accept them.

The most noteworthy thing about *Rerum Novarum,* however, was not any of the specific ideas it set forth but simply the fact that it attempted to analyze social problems from a Christian point of view. It insisted that these problems are matters of conscience, and that Christians have a moral obligation not to allow the lives of other human beings to be totally dominated by impersonal economic forces. Perhaps the most important practical result of this encyclical was to encourage the formation of Christian-oriented labor unions and political parties, which soon proved to be the most effective means of opposing socialism in the factory and at the ballot box—and not infrequently in the streets as well.

Through the influence of *Rerum Novarum* and his other encyclicals, Leo XIII may have played a more effective role as pastor and teacher to the entire world than any other pope. He also demonstrated a different kind of papal authority from that which Gregory XVI and Pius IX had attempted to exercise. Millions of people, inside the church and out, listened to Leo with respect not because he spoke infallibly but because they were convinced that what he was saying represented an accurate application of the gospel message to the conditions in which they lived.

Under Leo XIII's leadership, the Catholic Church appeared to be coming into contact for the first time with the realities of the post-Napoleonic world. But this impression was quickly dispelled by Leo's successor, Pius X—a man who was so obsessed with preserving the church from doctrinal contagion that he once refused to grant an audience to former president Theodore Roosevelt after he learned that Roosevelt had made plans to speak in one of the non-Catholic churches in Rome. Only two months after his election in 1903, Pius issued an encyclical in which he announced his determination to protect the Catholic clergy from "the snares of modern scientific thought."

What he was referring to was primarily the application of new techniques of criticism to the study of Scripture —techniques which revealed that the authors of the Bible, including those of the New Testament, did not record events with the same kind of literal accuracy as modern historians do. This implied that even the gospel narratives could not always be accepted at face value, which in turn suggested to some people that many of the church's dogmas might need to be revised in the light of a more accurate understanding of the evangelists' true meaning. Thus the French priest, Alfred Loissy, denied that Christ had intended to institute sacraments or even to found a church.

In July of 1907, a decree entitled *Lamentabili* condemned a collection of sixty-five propositions grouped together under the heading of "Modernism"—a most unfortunate choice of words, since it easily could be interpreted to mean that the church was opposed in principle to all modern ideas. What *Lamentabili* particularly objected to was the assertion, expressed or implied, that the very concept of religious dogma is incompatible with the discoveries of modern scholarship.

Two months later, in the encyclical *Pascendi,* Pius X ordered the establishment in each diocese of a committee to guard against the spread of Modernist ideas. And in 1910 he ordered every Catholic bishop, priest, seminary professor, and religious superior in the world to take an anti-Modernism oath. Loissy and several others were excommunicated, and many scholars were forced to make formal abjurations of their teachings.

But the worst aspect of this anti-Modernist crusade was that it set loose within the church hundreds of what can only be described as intellectual vigilantes. The most notorious of these was Monsignor Umberto Benigni, an official of the Vatican secretariat of state, who created a clandestine international organization dedicated to destroying the reputations of those whom it suspected of Modernist tendencies but whose guilt could not be proved. Members of this organization, the Sodalitium Pianum, operated secretely and communicated with one another in code. They used the columns of local Catholic publications to vilify writers, professors, and churchmen who deviated in any way from the Sodalitium's interpretation of orthodoxy. And they transmitted excerpts from articles and speeches by people of whom it ˙disapproved to Rome, where Benigni published them, along with defamatory commentaries, in his own newspaper.

The Sodalitium also channeled information to the Holy Office, the modern successor to the Inquisition, which kept detailed secret dossiers on everyone even remotely suspected of having Modernist sympathies. Since it was never completely clear what the term "Modernism" actually referred to, the Sodalitium and the Holy Office were able to intimidate almost every Catholic engaged in scholarly pursuits.

No one was burned alive by the Sodalitium, but its methods were in some respects even more vicious than those of the medieval Inquisition. Its victims, many of whom were not even aware that they were under suspicion, were dismissed from teaching posts, refused ecclesiastical promotions, and exposed to vicious and anonymous public calumnies. Since they had not been formally accused of anything, they found it impossible to clear their reputations. Even worse, perhaps, was the chilling effect which all of this had on Catholic intellectual life—especially in seminaries, where original research in philosophy, church history, and scripture practically ceased.

The existence and activities of the Sodalitium Pianum finally were brought to light during World War I, when the German army discovered some of its documents and a copy of its secret code in the Belgian city of Ghent. Pope Benedict XV, who succeeded Pius, ordered the group disbanded in 1921, bringing the worst features of this reign of terror to an end. But the inquisitorial mentality which Pius X had done so much to encourage lived on.

Among those who were accused of disloyalty during this period were Cardinal Piffl of Austria, Cardinal Mercier of Belgium, the archbishop of Paris, numerous bishops, and a young Italian priest named Angelo Roncalli. Alone of all these suspects, Roncalli eventually was allowed to see the contents of his Holy Office dossier—more than forty years later, after he had been elected pope.

And it was this pope, John XXIII, who almost single-handedly put an end to what was probably the most severe and widespread intellectual repression which the church ever has had to endure.

Chapter 20
BAPTIZING ALL NATIONS

IN the second decade of the fifteenth century, or about a hundred years before the publication of Luther's Ninety-Five Theses, Prince Henry the Navigator of Portugal began to encourage exploration of the west coast of Africa, an area almost totally unknown to the Europeans of his day. This set in motion a chain of events which helped to transform Christianity, which had not greatly expanded its area of influence since Charlemagne's time, into a truly universal faith.

By the time Prince Henry died in 1460, Portuguese ships had ventured as far south as present-day Sierra Leone. In 1488 Bartholomeu Dias became the first European to round the Cape of Good Hope, and ten years later Vasco da Gama reached India. Spain quickly followed Portugal's lead, and before the end of the fifteenth century had laid claim to an enormous empire in central and southern America. The fact that Portugal and Spain, the two leading colonial powers of the sixteenth and seventeenth centuries, also were the two countries least affected by the Reformation helped to give the Catholic Church a virtual monopoly in evangelizing the non-European world which lasted for several hundred years.

Both nations dispatched missionaries to newly discovered lands almost as soon as their existence became known. Columbus took Franciscans with him on his second voyage in 1493, and a bishop landed in the New World ten years before the first colonial governor. By 1521, the year in which Luther was excommunicated, Catholic bishoprics already had been established in what are now Morocco, Madeira, Zaire, the Dominican Republic, Puerto Rico, and Panama; and missions had been set up in Brazil, Argentina, Venezuela, Cuba, Mexico, India, and more than half a dozen African nations.

Alexander VI, the Borgia pope, granted exclusive rights to colonize the Americas to the Spanish government in 1493. (When the king of Portugal protested, he was given sovereignty over a portion of what is now Brazil.) Alexander also gave the Spanish crown the right of *patronato,* or total control over the church, in its American colonies. In return, Ferdinand and Isabella provided a bishopric for one of Alexander's illegitimate sons.

This agreement had the effect of isolating Latin American Catholics from the rest of the church from the time of Columbus until they achieved their independence in the nineteenth century. All communications between Rome and the American colonies had to be transmitted through the Royal Council of the Indies, which edited or suppressed the documents as it saw fit. Members of religious orders were prevented from maintaining direct contact with their European superiors. Latin American bishops, who were selected by the crown, were prohibited from making the periodic visits to Rome required by Canon Law.

The rules which governed the Catholic Church everywhere else in the world, in short, and the elaborate system of appeals and visitations which had been developed over hundreds of years to guard against abuses of authority, simply did not exist in the colonies. This gave the early Spanish conquerors a free hand to subject native Americans to conditions of such inhuman brutality that entire tribes were simply wiped out. Three hundred thousand Arawak Indians, for example, lived in the West Indies when Columbus landed; half a century later only five hundred remained.

But it was not long before some of the missionaries, particularly the Dominican Bartolome de Las Casas, began protesting against these outrages. And their descriptions of the barbarous cruelties inflicted upon natives in Latin America created such an uproar that in 1542 Emperor Charles V issued a series of laws which eliminated the worst abuses and eventually led to the development of Indian missionary settlements throughout Spain's American colonies.

These settlements, most of which were run by the Jesuits and the Franciscans, were communities in which Indians who had been baptized were kept isolated from the influence of Europeans and non-Christian natives. Their general purpose was to turn native Americans into reasonably close imitations of their Spanish conquerors. This meant, in particular, converting them to Catholicism (many had received only minimal instruction before baptism), replacing their native customs with European ones, and teaching them to live in an urban environment under Spanish rule. No Indians were compelled to accept baptism or to enter a mission, at least in theory; but once they did enter force was used, if necessary, to keep them there.

(Some of these communities served strategic as well as religious purposes by shielding vital Spanish interests from interference by foreign powers. Thus Spain encouraged development of the famous Franciscan missions in California as a means of protecting its shipping routes to the Philippines against the Russian settlers who were advancing down the Pacific coast.)

Indians were required to work for about three months of each year in mines, fields, or wherever else the Spanish needed them under a system of labor assessments which resembled the *corvée* of pre-revolutionary France. They also had to share in the work of the mission, most of which was domestic or agricultural in nature, and to attend religious instruction classes during which they memorized simple prayers and the rudiments of the Catholic faith.

Since one of the primary objectives of the whole mission

system was to "civilize" Indians—that is, to induce them to conform to European standards of behavior—missionaries usually tried to destroy native cultures rather than to adapt the Christian message to them. Another reason for this approach was that any attempt to fit Christian beliefs into the framework of native culture involved a risk of producing formulations which might be considered heterodox and thus attract the attention of the Inquisition, which the Spanish had brought with them to the New World. These measures had the effect of preventing the Latin American community from making a distinctive contribution to Catholic intellectual life until long after independence.

But while missionaries were eager to Christianize the natives, they were extremely reluctant to accept them into the priesthood. In 1578 King Philip II of Spain made official what already had become the accepted practice by forbidding the ordination anywhere in the Spanish empire of Indians, blacks (who had been imported to do much of the heavy labor in Latin America), or those of mixed blood. This edict was enforced by the Inquisition, which demanded that all candidates for the priesthood prove that there had been no Indian or African blood in their families for at least four generations. This kept the colonial churches totally dependent upon European priests, especially in positions of leadership. Thus more than eighty-five percent of the bishops in pre-revolutionary Latin America were born in Spain, and most of the remainder were descendants of the colonial Spanish aristocracy.

The missionaries of Spanish America brought more people into the church than were ever baptized in a comparable period of time before or since. They were instrumental in reducing mistreatment and exploitation of the natives, and they helped to domesticate huge areas of the New World. It was they, far more than the soldiers of the colonial garrisons, who held Spain's empire together.

And yet in the end the church played a major role in that empire's undoing. It was the attempt of the Spanish government to enforce anticlerical legislation in its colonies which touched off the Latin American revolutions of the nineteenth century, some of which actually were initiated and led by Catholic priests. This helped to establish a tradition of clerical participation in political uprisings which has continued in South and Central America to the present day.

In Africa and the Orient, meanwhile, a high percentage of missionaries were working in areas which were not under European control and from which they could be deported at any time. And Hindus, Buddhists, and followers of Confucius generally proved far less eager to become Christians than did adherents of pagan tribal cults, while conversions from Islam were extraordinarily rare.

Under these conditions the failure to train large numbers of native priests and to adapt Christianity to local cultures proved absolutely catastrophic, for most of the Asian and African missions simply collapsed when the European clergy were withdrawn or expelled. It is worth noting in this regard that opposition to an indigenous clergy seems to have grown more intense as time went on. Thus a Congolese was raised to the episcopacy in 1518, and an Indian and a Chinese about a hundred and fifty years later; but there was not another native-born Asian or African Catholic bishop until well into the twentieth century.

What may have done more than anything else to hinder evangelization in Asia, however, were dissension among the missionaries themselves and the absence of a centralized organization to coordinate their efforts.

In China, which had virtually sealed itself off from the outside world, Matteo Ricci and his fellow Jesuits achieved positions of remarkable influence by introducing the imperial court to the discoveries of European science and by correcting errors in the Chinese calendar. Their strategy was not so much to make individual converts as to Christianize Chinese society from the top down, and it appeared to be succeeding: thirty-five years after Ricci arrived in Peking, more than one hundred princes and several members of the imperial family, including the dowager empress, had been baptized.

The Jesuits did everything possible to make it easy for the Chinese to convert. They permitted native Christians to continue many of their traditional practices, such as rendering homage to their ancestors and to Confucius, and they employed Chinese rather than Latin in the liturgy. These concessions were approved by Pope Alexander VII, and they went unchallenged so long as the Jesuits retained exclusive control over the Chinese missions.

Almost as soon as Franciscans and Dominicans began arriving in 1632, however, complaints were lodged in Rome about the Jesuits' proselytizing techniques.

This touched off a bitter controversy which lasted more than a century and ended with the absolute prohibition of all the practices which Pope Alexander had allowed—a decision which made conversions in China immeasurably more difficult. It was during the course of this dispute that a delegate from Rome grievously offended the emperor, K'anghsi, transforming his benevolent attitude toward Catholicism into implacable hostility. In 1717 K'anghsi forbade all further missionary activity, and his successors initiated a series of persecutions which continued almost to the end of the eighteenth century and effectively destroyed the Chinese Catholic Church.

Jesuits in India followed the same strategy which Ricci had used in China, but they met with far less success. Roberto de Nobili, for example, adopted the dress and manners of a Brahmin holy man and gained a certain degree of acceptance among India's upper classes. But the existence of a rigid caste system made Christianization from the top down utterly impractical in India, and before long de Nobili's methods were denounced to Rome just as Ricci's had been—although in de Nobili's case it was one of his fellow Jesuits who initiated the complaint. Eventually it turned out that members of the lower castes, among whom the Franciscans concentrated their efforts, were much more receptive to Christianity than the Brahmins were.

But missionary efforts in India were seriously hampered by the fact that a large portion of the country was under Islamic control; by the wars which Portugal frequently waged against native princes; and, ultimately, by the conquest of much of the subcontinent by the English and Dutch. It has been estimated that between 1700 and 1800 the number of Catholics in India declined nearly forty percent.

Japan, which in the second half of the sixteenth century had disintegrated into quasi-independent feudal domains, appeared to offer more favorable conditions for evangelization than any other eastern nation. This was particularly true after Jesuit missionaries gained the favor of Oda Nobunaga, a warlord who by 1568, the year in which the Jesuits contacted him, already controlled most of central Japan. Nobunaga also was conducting a virtual war of extermination against Japan's Buddhist monks, whom he saw as his chief rivals for power; and it may have been in order to weaken the influence of the Buddhists that Nobunaga gave the Jesuits complete freedom to preach in his domains. Between 1570 and Nobunaga's death in 1582, the number of Christians in Japan increased five-fold to 150,000 persons.

By this time the Jesuits had established themselves as commercial intermediaries between China and Japan, circumventing the ban on direct contact between the two nations which China had imposed by routing their goods through the Portuguese colony of Macao. This allowed the Jesuits to control a large portion of Japan's foreign trade and gave them great influence over Japanese authorities for as long as Portugal monopolized European shipping in the Orient. One can only speculate about what might have been accomplished in Japan had the Jesuits been allowed to continue their work under these nearly ideal conditions.

In 1593, however, four Spanish Franciscans who had come to Japan as envoys from the governor of the Philippines decided to remain in the country and open a mission of their own, despite the fact that Spain, Portugal and the Vatican all had agreed that Japan should be entrusted solely to the Jesuits. Before long Dominicans, Augustinians, and more Franciscans followed.

This immediately sacrificed one of the principal advantages which the Jesuits had enjoyed—the unified front which they had been able to present against the Buddhist monks, who were constantly quarreling among themselves. The Franciscans also adopted a strategy diametrically opposed to that of the Jesuits by organizing huge rallies to win over the working class rather than trying to convert the leaders of Japanese society.

But the most important difficulty presented by the Franciscans was the simple fact that they were subjects of the king of Spain, a nation whose reputation for brutal and rapacious colonial administration was well known to the Japanese rulers. In 1596, when a dispute arose over the cargo of a European ship wrecked off the Japanese coast, a Spanish official not only threatened to invade the country but also made the incredibly stupid blunder of telling Hideyoshi, Nobunaga's successor, that Spain frequently used missionaries to prepare the way for military conquest.

In response, Hideyoshi had six Franciscans and seventeen of their converts crucified.

A few years later the appearance of Dutch and English ships in Japanese waters freed Japan from reliance on the goodwill of the Jesuits and of Portugal and permitted a full-scale attack on the missions, which by now were caring for more than four hundred thousand Christians. In 1614 all foreign clergy were expelled, and for the next forty years the government carried out a savage persecution which almost totally wiped out Christianity in Japan.

And while thousands of Japanese Christians were being put to death, the once flourishing missions of Africa were slowly disintegrating. Part of the reason was that Portugal, which had been granted total control over most of Africa by the papacy, insisted on maintaining a monopoly on proselytizing activity throughout this vast area even though it could not possibly supply enough missionaries to adequately staff it. Another factor was the rise of the slave trade, which saw some ten million men, women, and children shipped out of Africa into bondage and made the remaining natives understandably suspicious of all Europeans. In eastern Africa missionaries had to contend with the influence of Islam, against which they could make very little headway. By the end of the eighteenth century African Christianity had virtually died out, not so much from persecution as from the fact that the Catholic colonial powers had become unwilling or unable to sustain the missions upon which its existence depended.

By the second decade of the nineteenth century, in fact, or shortly before Pope Gregory XVI began reorganizing the missions and bringing them under papal control, there were fewer then three hundred active Catholic missionaries in the entire world. And except in Latin America and the Philippines, the church had very little to show for the pro-

digious amount of money and human suffering which had
been invested in the eastern and southern hemispheres. In
Africa, China and Japan, the entire undertaking had to be
started again almost from scratch.

In another corner of the world, however, a much smaller
investment had paid enormous dividends.

Christianity was introduced into what is now the United
States by Spanish Jesuits and Franciscans, who were operating Indian missions in present-day Arizona, New Mexico, Florida, Georgia, South Carolina, and Colorado
before the *Mayflower* landed.

In most of the British colonies of North America, however, Catholics formed a despised and infinitesimally small
minority—less than one percent of the population at the
time of the revolution. Except in the Quaker communities of Pennsylvania, and in Maryland, which had been
founded as a refuge for Catholics, they were subjected to
the same kinds of legal oppression which their coreligionists faced in England. Even in Pennsylvania—and for a
time in Maryland as well—they were not allowed to vote.

And Catholics remained second-class citizens, in a sense,
even after independence. For although the United States
had no specific state-supported church, a kind of nonsec-
tarian Protestantism had become its official religion in fact
if not in name. Even Benjamin Franklin proposed that
nondenominational, nondoctrinal religion be made part of
the general school curriculum; and his suggestion was put
into effect when the American system of public education
was established. The Bibles used in these schools, of course,
were the King James version.

All of this naturally tended to make those of other
faiths—Catholics and Jews in particular—feel not quite so
much at home in America as Protestants did. It also made
them anxious to avoid doing anything which might attract

too much attention to themselves. Thus several hundred Catholic laymen petitioned the Vatican in 1765 not to appoint an American bishop because doing so might arouse the suspicion and hostility of their Protestant countrymen. And when Rome finally did name a bishop for the diocese of Baltimore, which at that time included the entire United States, it chose a man with an unimpeachably American background.

John Carroll was descended from Lord Baltimore, the founder of the Maryland colony. His cousin, Charles, had signed the Declaration of Independence; and his brother Daniel had been a member of the Constitutional Convention. He himself, along with Benjamin Franklin and Samuel Chase, had undertaken a diplomatic mission for the Continental Congress. These credentials helped Carroll to dispel, at least for a time, the notion that Catholicism was opposed in some way to fundamental American values.

But they did not help to solve the most serious difficulties he faced, such as the fact that when he took office in 1790 the United States had only twenty-four priests, five of whom were ready for retirement, and the fact that there were no Catholic schools of any kind, few churches, and no religious orders. John Carroll not only had to administer the American Catholic Church; he had to create a large portion of it himself.

What made this possible was the immigration to the United States of numerous European priests and nuns who had been uprooted by the French Revolution. The first nuns arrived from Belgium in 1790, and the following year Sulpician priests who had been exiled from France established the first Catholic seminary in Baltimore. The first girls' school was founded by refugee Poor Clare sisters a few years after that. By the year 1818, fourteen of the fifty-two priests in the United States were French and another seven were Belgian. Only twelve of the fifty-two were native-born Americans.

Problems of a different sort arose when Carroll and his successors attempted to impose European-style administrative structures and practices upon an American church which had evolved under much different conditions from those which prevailed in Europe and which was not accustomed to the exercise of episcopal authority.

Chief among these problems was lay trusteeship, a system which American Catholics had borrowed from their Protestant neighbors under which all church property which had been acquired through the contributions of a specific congregation was considered as belonging to the entire group, with its administration being placed in the hands of elected trustees. What made this practice particularly objectionable from the viewpoint of the Catholic hierarchy was that these trustees often claimed the right to engage and dismiss the clergy who served their congregations, a right which frequently was recognized by state law.

The theory behind lay trusteeship—that whoever builds the church should appoint the clergy—was neither a Protestant nor an American invention. Its origins could be traced all the way back to Constantine, if not beyond; and it had provided the rationale both for the medieval proprietary church and for Spain's *patronato* over South America. But the practice violated many of the decrees of the Council of Trent and numerous provisions of Canon Law, and eventually it was stamped out by the imposition of ecclesiastical sanctions and by the far simpler but extremely effective expedient of having bishops demand that legal ownership of new church buildings be surrendered as a condition of their being consecrated.

And even after they had obtained undisputed control of the church's physical assets, the American hierarchy remained extremely reluctant to allow lay people to participate in any significant way in parish or diocesan financial affairs.

John Carroll died in 1815, and in that same year the end of the Napoleonic wars permitted resumption of unrestricted travel between Europe and America. Not long afterward the United States began to receive the first great influx of immigrants, many of whom were Catholic. And the atmosphere of religious toleration which Carroll's appointment had done so much to promote came to an abrupt and unpleasant end.

In 1824 approximately ten thousand foreigners landed; in 1832 fifty thousand; in 1842 more than one hundred thousand; in 1850 nearly four hundred thousand. This seemingly uncontrollable flood of aliens set off intensely xenophobic reactions among those Americans who took inordinate pride in the fact that their own ancestors had arrived somewhat earlier. It greatly intensified competition for jobs in the United States during a period in which massive financial panics were throwing much of the native-born labor force out of work. And it led to a great outpouring of anti-Catholic propaganda. Since it was not considered proper to attack people specifically because of their religious beliefs, most of this literature either accused Catholics of violating common standards of public decency or else intimated that they were politically disloyal.

In the first category were books such as the notorious *Maria Monk's Awful Disclosures of the Hotel Dieu Nunnery in Montreal* and its sequels, which described in lurid detail and with the aid of numerous illustrations various forms of sexual debauchery and other nefarious behavior allegedly engaged in by priests and nuns. These works enjoyed wide circulation as a kind of socially acceptable pornography; and they helped to place Catholics beyond the pale of civilized society in many people's eyes, thus making them easy targets for mob violence. (Similar charges against the Mormons at about the same time had a comparable effect.) Thus in 1834 the leaders of a mob .which had burned down a Catholic convent in Massachusetts were set free by a jury which apparently was convinced that the building had been used for the commission of blood-chilling crimes.

Accusations of disloyalty constituted a slightly more sophisticated and far more dangerous form of attack, since they played upon fears which had been lurking in the English Protestant psyche since Elizabethan times. One popular rumor of the 1830s maintained that the pope and the Emperor of Austria were plotting to seize control of the Mississippi Valley. The inventor Samuel Morse, among others, helped to spread the belief that the Catholic sovereigns of Europe were encouraging their subjects to migrate to America in order to help them seize control of the country—an allegation which caused increasing anxiety among the gullible as the rate of European immigration continued to accelerate.

Yet another source of friction was unleashed by the failure of Europe's potato crop, which drove a million and a half Irish to the United States between 1845 and 1855. The great majority of these people were uncompromisingly Catholic and wretchedly poor. Most of them knew no other trade than farming, but they could not afford to buy land and they could not compete with slave labor on the southern plantations. So they remained in the East, usually in the port at which they had landed, where they formed an enormous pool of unskilled labor which helped to drive wage rates down.

This tidal wave of indigent Catholics encouraged the rise of a militantly anti-immigrant and anti-Catholic group which, since its members refused to answer questions about its activities, frequently was referred to as the "Know-Nothings." In 1854 this group organized itself as the American Party, and it received one-quarter of all votes cast in the presidential election two years later. Riots between Catholics and non-Catholics broke out with increasing frequency—twenty-two people were killed during one such incident in Kentucky in 1855—and a serious crisis might have arisen had not the great national debate over slavery diverted public attention away from the issues of immigration and religion.

Even so, the basic question of whether and in what manner Catholics could be completely integrated into the social fabric of what still was a fundamentally Protestant country had not been resolved, only postponed.

By 1870 there were more than four and a half million Catholics in the United States, more than twenty-three times as many as there had been half a century before. This was a rate of increase more than five times as great as that of the general population. Well over half of the increase had been due to immigration, and nearly two-thirds of those immigrants had come from Ireland.

Immigrants, and Irish immigrants in particular, were even more strongly represented in the hierarchy than among the laity. Of the forty-five bishops at the Second Plenary Council of Baltimore in 1866, thirty-one were foreign-born and eleven were Irish. Eighteen years later, at the Third Plenary council, forty-seven out of seventy-two bishops were immigrants. Twenty had been born in Ireland, and fifteen of the twenty-five native-born American bishops were of Irish descent.

As a result of this extremely high representation of Irish and Irish-Americans, Catholicism in the United States began to adopt, more or less unconsciously, the doctrinal orientations, pastoral attitudes, and forms of piety found in Ireland—and therefore to pattern itself after one of the most theologically conservative and tradition-minded Catholic communities in Europe. And when immigration patterns began to change in the second half of the nineteenth century, Irish domination of the American church caused great resentment among Catholics of other nationalities.

During the 1880s, for example, five hundred and thirty thousand immigrants arrived from Germany and the Austro-Hungarian Empire, and slightly more than half that many from Ireland. In the following decade three hundred and forty thousand came from Germany and Austria-Hungary, three hundred and ninety thousand from Italy, one hundred and ninety thousand from Poland, and only forty thousand from Ireland. And the percentage of Italians and Slavs continued to increase until immigration was sharply curtailed during the 1920s.

This created numerous situations in which priests and their congregations were of different national backgrounds. Soon the newcomers, particularly the Germans, began demanding that priests be assigned to their parishes to whom they could confess in their native tongue and that their nationalities be given greater representation in the American hierarchy. Most of these demands were refused.

The treatment of national minorities in the American church became an international issue in 1890, when the directors of several European immigrant aid societies complained to Pope Leo XIII that ten million Catholic immigrants had abandoned their faith because American bishops had refused to provide for their needs.

What interested Europeans far more, however, was the fact that Catholicism in the United States had been able to grow so rapidly without benefit of preferential treatment or governmental subsidies at a time when Catholic Church membership in the Old World was declining. This seemed to many people, particularly in France, to indicate that Catholicism thrives best in an atmosphere of freedom and total equality—thus proving the truth of what Felicite de Lamennais had been silenced by the Vatican for arguing fifty years before. And in 1892, when Pope Leo XIII was attempting to persuade diehard French royalists to accept their country's republican constitution, Archbishop John Ireland of St. Paul made several speeches in Paris at Rome's request in which he credited the democratic freedoms guaranteed by the American constitution for much of the church's success in the United States.

It was in this manner that American theories of church-state relations became an issue in domestic European politics. For if complete religious toleration and separation of church and state had been good for Catholicism in the United States, why would they not be equally good in Italy, Spain, and everywhere else? And yet this seemed to imply a denial of Catholicism's claim to be the one true religion and to necessitate renunciation of the governmental support which the church had accepted and even demanded wherever possible since Constantine's time.

This kind of speculation prompted Leo XIII to issue *Longinqua Qceani,* the first papal letter ever addressed to the American church, in which he conceded that Catholicism in the United States had benefited from a lack of governmental interference but insisted that it would not be "lawful or expedient" for church and state to be separated everywhere. This position represented a considerable advance over the ideas of Gregory XVI and Pius IX, although it was capable of being interpreted—and was, in fact, interpreted by some American Protestants—to mean that Catholics might seek special favors for their religion if they ever became a majority in the United States.

Longinqua Oceani ought to have been the end of this dispute. In 1897, however, a book about the American Isaac Hecker, founder of the Paulist Fathers, appeared in France—a book whose preface, which had been written by a young French priest, contended that the Catholic Church could gain many more converts if it deemphasized those of its doctrines which non-Catholics found particularly objectionable and adapted itself more completely to the contemporary world.

A new controversy immediately broke out over the ideas expressed in this preface. Somehow or other these ideas began to be referred to collectively as "Americanism," although it is not certain that any American ever held them; and almost overnight a new heresy was born—a heresy which many people believed had orginated in the United States. This called forth a second letter from Leo XIII, *Testem Benevolentiae,* which was issued in 1899 over the anguished protests of Cardinal Gibbons, dean of the American hierarchy.

Once again, as with *Longinqua Oceani,* the letter itself was quite moderate in tone. Leo mentioned no names, and he made it clear that he was criticizing the ideas set forth in the preface to Hecker's biography, not America's system of government, or its way of life, or the patriotism of its people. In the United States, however, just as Gibbons and Ireland had feared, the condemnation of "Americanism" was understood by some non-Catholics to mean that one could not be a completely loyal Catholic and a completely loyal American—which was the very accusation which American Catholics since colonial times had been most anxious to disprove.

Even within the church, *Testem Benevolentiae* became a kind of sword hanging over the head of American Catholicism, especially after Pius X made reference to Americanism in his condemnation of Modernism. Like Modernism, "Americanism" was so vague a term that it might be applied to almost any progressive idea, particularly in the area of church-state relations; and after 1899 American bishops tended to become more cautious in doctrinal matters than they otherwise might have been for fear of provoking further condemnations.

Thus the darkness which descended over the church's intellectual life in the first half of the twentieth century was even more profound in the United States than in many other lands, and that darkness was not truly dispersed until the beginning of the Second Vatican Council in 1962.

CONCLUSION

EVEN the most dedicated enemy of religion would find a great deal to admire in the nineteen centuries of Christian history we have just reviewed—the courage of the church's missionaries, for example, the patient labor of its monks, the genius of its philosophers and theologians, the heights of perfection reached by its mystics and saints, and the sacrifices made by hundreds of thousands of anonymous men and women to feed the poor and nurse the sick.

It is an indisputable fact, whether one likes it or not, that the Christian Church has done more to advance learning, to reduce human misery, and to promote what we consider to be civilized behavior than any other institution on earth. As appallingly brutal as European history during the Christian era sometimes has been, one shudders to think what that history would have been like if there had been no church.

Even while we acknowledge the church's faults, which have been many, we also must keep in mind that the very moral standards which we use in making those judgments are, by and large, standards which the church itself has taught us. Had it not been for the church, we would not be who we are today. Having said all of this, however, we still must admit that there is much that is ugly and disgraceful in the history of the church, just as there is much that is ugly and disgraceful in every human heart.

Certainly the crimes of the inquisitors, the indulgence peddlers, the simonical cardinals, and the venal and politically ruthless popes do not by themselves invalidate the church's claim to be inspired by God, any more than the divine inspiration of the gospels would be disproved if someone were to discover that the evangelists had been

314

guilty of heinous sins. God was using thieves and adulterers to accomplish his designs long before Jesus was born, as even a casual reading of the Old Testament makes abundantly clear. But the fact that a number of unworthy men were entrusted with supreme power over the church does raise disturbing questions.

One way to approach these questions is to remember that although many people seem to expect popes to be saints, most of the qualities required of a pope are quite different from the qualities which one ordinarily finds in a saint. This was especially true in the Middle Ages, when popes assumed responsibility not only for administering one of the largest and most complex organizations in the world but also for protecting the rights of the church and of its members against infringement by Europe's most powerful secular lords.

It would be asking a great deal of any one person to function effectively as a major figure in international politics and to achieve personal sanctity as well, and what is remarkable is not that so many popes failed to do so but that any at all succeeded. It is worth noting that some men —Celestine V is an outstanding example—succeeded in becoming saints but failed miserably at being pope.

All of us have been taught that the kingdom of God is not of this world, but too few of us remember that the church is not the kingdom of God. We have observed the process by which the church became intimately involved in worldly affairs, and there is every reason to assume that this involvement will continue for as long as the church itself exits. This is merely one small part of the price which Christianity has had to pay for accepting Constantine's offer to become a wealthy and powerful institution.

Some bishops, cardinals, and popes, of course, went far beyond not leading holy lives; and several of them can only be described as degenerate scoundrels. This can be explained to some extent by the fact that up until shortly before the Renaissance the church provided virtually the only avenue to wealth and power for ambitious men who were not born into the nobility, and that for this reason it attracted not only the best elements of the society around it but the the worst elements as well.

One of the reasons why there are fewer reprobates in the hierarchy now than there were five hundred years ago is simply that more attractive opportunities have become available outside the church. Men like the Borgias and the descendents of Theophylactus, were they alive today, would not be popes but international financiers, corporate executives, or Mafia chieftains—if, indeed, they were not behind prison bars.

But the most terrible crimes which the church has witnessed were not the murders and adulteries which antireligious writers take such delight in dramatizing. None of these misdeeds, reprehensible as they were, begin to compare with the arrogance, the stubbornness, the pride, and the cynicism of those who allowed and sometimes even encouraged religious hatreds to spread among God's people, so that for hundreds of years Christianity has separated the followers of Jesus rather than uniting them.

Self-knowledge is the beginning of wisdom—of human wisdom, at least—and there can be no genuine self-knowledge without a recognition of one's own faults. In the present context this means being willing to admit that the entire church, from bottom to top, is, has been, and always will be a church of sinners as well as of saints. And this melancholy admission, if enough of us were only willing to make it, might prove to be the means of rescuing the church from the greatest of all the evils which have befallen it.

For the first and most important lesson which church history can teach us is humility. There is guilt enough in that history for all of us to share, and no member of any Christian denomination who seriously meditates on the tragic events by which the church has been victimized for so many centuries will be anxious to cast the first stone.

For this reason we may permit ourselves to hope that a better understanding of the history of our church will one day make it possible for all of the people of God to rejoin one another in the unity of Christ's forgiveness and love.

Index

Acacius (patriarch of Constantinople), 73-74
Act of Supremacy, 238
Act of Uniformity, 256
Adrian I (pope), 85, 88, 89
Adrian II (pope), 100, 101
Adrian IV (pope), 223-24
Aeterni Patris (Pope Leo XIII), 289
Aetius (Roman general), 60
Africa. *See* Missions, in Africa.
"Against the Thieving and Murdering Peasant Hordes" (Luther), 228
Alais, Edit of, 265
Alberic I (marquis of Spoleto), 124-25
Alberic II (marquis of Spoleto), 125-26
Albrecht (of Brandenburg, archbishop of Mainz), 210, 214
Alcuin of York, 86
Alexander II (pope), 130
Alexander VI (pope), 203, 207, 296
Alexander VII (pope), 300
Alexius Comnenus (Byzantine emperor), 140, 142-43
Albigensianism, 168-70, 175-77; crusade against, 169-70
Ambrose (bishop of Milan), 24, 33, 117
American Party, 309
Americanism, 312-13
Anabaptists, 227-28
Anchorites, 115-16
Andronicus Paleologus (Byzantine emperor), 163
Angelico, Fra, 202
Anglo-Saxons, evangelization of, 80

Anna Comnena, (Byzantine princess), 142
Anne (duke of Montmorency), 261, 263
Annates, 184, 186, 189
Anthony of Egypt, Saint, 115, 178
Antoine (de Bourbon, king of Navarre), 261, 263
Apostolic succession, 21-22, 25
Apostles' Creed, origin of, 51
Appeal to the Christian Nobility of the German Nation (Luther), 218
Arciboldi, Giovannangelo (papal legate), 228-29
Aristotelianism, 267
Arius and Arianism, 45-46, 50-54, 81, 82, 117
Arizona, missionary activity in, 304
Armenia, crusader kingdom of, 143, 145
Arthur (prince of England), 233-34
Athanasius (patriarch of Alexandria), 45, 52, 115-17
Attila, 60, 69
Augsburg: Confession of, 230; Diet of, 226, 229-30; Peace of, 241, 249, 251, 253
Augustine (bishop of Hippo), 57-59, 117, 168, 232
Augustinians, 175-76, 177
Augustus (Roman emperor), 46
Aurelian (Roman emperor), 43
Authority in the church, centralization of, 138, 189; aided by Inquisition, 172; under Gregory VII, 130; under Innocent III, 155; following French Revolution, 278-79; effects of, 138,

318

THE OFFICIAL MOVIE
NOVELIZATION

Also available from Titan Books

Alita: Battle Angel – Iron City (The Official Movie Prequel)

ALITA
BATTLE ANGEL

THE OFFICIAL MOVIE NOVELIZATION

BY PAT CADIGAN

BASED UPON THE GRAPHIC NOVEL ("MANGA") SERIES "GUNNM" BY YUKITO KISHIRO
SCREENPLAY BY JAMES CAMERON AND LAETA KALOGRIDIS

TITAN BOOKS

SF

Alita: Battle Angel – The Official Movie Novelization
Hardback edition ISBN: 9781785658389
E-book edition ISBN: 9781785658396

Published by
Titan Books
A division of Titan Publishing Group Ltd
144 Southwark Street
London
SE1 0UP

First edition: February 2019
1 3 5 7 9 10 8 6 4 2

A CIP catalogue record for this title is available from the British Library.

Printed and bound in the United States.

Did you enjoy this book?
We love to hear from our readers. Please email us at readerfeedback@titanemail.com
or write to us at Reader Feedback at the above address.
To receive advance information, news, competitions, and exclusive offers online,
please sign up for the Titan newsletter on our website
www.titanbooks.com

In Memory of:

Susan Casper
Georgina Hawtrey-Woore
Geri Jeter

Battle Angels live forever

And as always for The Original Chris Fowler,
whose kind, loving, generous heart
makes everything possible

CHAPTER 1

The floating city of Zalem was most beautiful at sunset, or so most people said. Or so most people *thought* most people said. In fact, Zalem was impressive at any hour of the day or night, hanging in mid-air like a good magician's best trick. It could have been some mythical realm—El Dorado maybe, or the Kingdom of Prester John, distant Thule or Camelot—except it wasn't lost. Everyone in Iron City could find it. All they had to do was look up and there it was: a perfect circle five miles across, wearing its skyline like a crown, ever present and ever out of reach.

Other than that, there were only three things the ground-level population knew for certain about the place: 1) the Factory in Iron City existed to support Zalem, sending food and manufactured goods up through long tubes that extended from it like graceful spiders' legs; 2) you couldn't get there from here—only supplies went up, *never* people; and 3) you never stood directly below the centre of Zalem unless you wanted to be crushed under the trash, junk and general refuse that suddenly and without warning rained down from the large, ragged hole in the underside of the disc.

This was just how the world worked, and no one now alive remembered anything different. A very long time ago there had been a War against an Enemy, and it had left the world in its current sorry state, where people on the ground had to scrounge around for whatever they could repair, revamp or remake, while Zalem sucked up anything worth having. No one had the time or inclination to wonder how people had lived before the War; the daily effort of survival kept them too busy for history.

Dr Dyson Ido, Cyber-Surgeon, MD, was one of the very few people in Iron City with a detailed knowledge of the past—the War, the Fall, and why Zalem was the only one of the original twelve floating cities to remain aloft. Right now, however, as the sun set on another long day of treating patients at the clinic, he wasn't thinking about history. He was picking his way through the sprawling pile of Zalem's refuse in search of anything salvageable, taking a circular path halfway between the centre and the edge.

The continual addition of new rubbish and regular scavenger activity meant the contents of the mound were always shifting; things buried deep in the centre were eventually pushed outwards and upwards. The area Ido was searching often yielded items that could be repaired or rebuilt, or sometimes just cleaned—Zalem's people were a wasteful bunch—while being far enough from ground zero to let him hunt without risk of being flattened by new arrivals. Assuming no one flushed a house down the chute, of course; so far no one had, or at least not all at once.

Ido spent the end of many days on the trash pile, using a hand-scanner to catch any stray electronic or biochemical signals from some bit of rechargeable tech. An observer with an especially sharp eye would have noted that although his long coat had seen a lot of wear, it had been nice once, too nice for Iron City. Then there was that old-fashioned hat—on anyone else it would have been a sad affectation, but it belonged on him, mostly because of his bearing. The way he carried himself suggested he was an educated man of some importance who'd taken a wrong turn off the open road and ended up in Iron City. But no observer would know he had once lived a life of privilege and gentility and, after losing everything, was now reduced to picking through the dregs and dross of a better world.

His previous existence felt as distant to him as the War nobody knew very much about any more. Nobody knew very much about him, either, except that he was a highly skilled cyber-surgeon who offered his services to Iron City's cyborgs at whatever price they could pay. For them, this was as miraculous as a floating city, only a hell of a lot more useful. They were grateful for his skills and he was grateful they never asked how he had come by them, or where he was from, or even how he'd got the small pale scar on his forehead. Everybody in Iron City had scars, as well as a past they didn't want to talk about.

Ido stooped to pick up a corroded metal hand, peering at it through his round spectacles. As he dropped the hand into the bag slung across the front of his body, he caught sight of a single glass eye nestled in the socket of a burned metal skull. The eye was perfect, without even a small crack. How had it escaped damage when the skull had been fried? Ido bent down to have a closer look and decided the eye didn't belong to this skull but had rolled into it by chance. All sorts of things happened by chance. If he hadn't come along at the right moment both the eye and skull might have sunk back down into Zalem's broken, unwanted crap, never to resurface. Or some nearby movement might have caused the eye to roll out of the skull as accidentally as it had rolled in and, unnoticed, would be mashed underfoot by an endless parade of scavengers.

Ido pushed himself to his feet and looked around, trying to decide whether he should continue while there was still enough daylight for him to see where he was going or quit while there was still enough night ahead for a few hours of sleep. Most of the other scavengers had given up and gone home, leaving only the desperate and the hardcore, the ones who were secretly hoping to find a real treasure. It was possible, for example, that a diamond ring had fallen off some Zalem aristocrat's hand into the trash by accident. Highly improbable, yes, but not *physically* impossible.

Selling it in Iron City for even half its worth—*that* was impossible.

Ido permitted himself a small chuckle and turned his thoughts back to the question of where to go next. Zalem had dumped a load about fifteen minutes ago; while there was no set schedule, there was usually at least twenty minutes between deliveries. *Usually*, however, didn't mean *always*. He was trying to decide whether to tempt fate in ten-minute increments—scavenge for five minutes, then stand back for another five. Normally he didn't take chances—he was the only doctor most of Iron City's cyborgs could afford and he took his duty of care seriously. That, however, was why he was weighing the risk. The centre hadn't already been picked over, which gave him a better chance of finding something usable, particularly servos. He needed more servos. He *always* needed more servos.

He was still deliberating when two things happened at once: his gaze fell on something half buried in the slope about three metres ahead of him, and he felt the scanner in his hand pulse ever so slightly. For a moment, he didn't dare move. If his eyes weren't playing wish-fulfilment tricks on him in the dying daylight, and if the scanner wasn't reacting to the last gasp of a dying circuit under his feet, he was looking at something worth more than a thousand diamond rings.

Keeping his eyes fixed on the shape, he moved towards it slowly, willing it to stay real and not turn into an illusion produced by a chance arrangement of junk. Then he was standing over it and, no, it wasn't a scrapyard mirage, it was a real thing that was really there, and he had found it by chance. But as any self-respecting, if outcast, scientist knew, chance favoured the prepared mind.

He knelt down and began gently excavating it from the trash, working as carefully as an archaeologist who had come across the find of the century. After a few minutes he sat back on his heels and stared at what he had uncovered. It was the face of a young girl: beautiful, angelic and completely impossible except in dreams of an especially pleasant, magical kind. He could tell he wasn't dreaming now by the sharp edges and lumps poking into his knees and lower legs, and the ache in his back.

This wasn't *her* face, either, not the one he wished so intensely to see again, but it could have been. She looked so utterly serene with her eyes closed and her mouth on the verge of a smile, as if she were dreaming of something wonderful. Only the rips in her skin—at the base of her neck, along the right side of her jaw, above her left eye—gave her away as synthetic.

Ido leaned forward and began clearing away the detritus below her neck. The work progressed more slowly because his hands were trembling now and he had to stop sometimes to steady himself. After what might have been a minute or an eternity, he had uncovered her cyber-core: upper chest, one shoulder, her metal spine and the ribs caging her perfect white heart, which shuddered with each slow beat.

Hesitantly he put the scanner to her temple and watched, mesmerised, as the waveform on the readout confirmed that a person was still present.

"You're alive," Ido said, unaware that he'd spoken aloud.

He couldn't let her lie there a moment longer. He manoeuvred his hands around the broken fragment of her form and lifted her out of the trash, holding her up in the fading daylight, wondering how anyone could discard her as if she were no more than a broken doll, and feeling something he had not felt since the birth of his daughter, and had thought he would never feel again when she'd died.

CHAPTER 2

Nurse Gerhad had swapped the surgical instruments on her cyber-arm for a normal hand in preparation for going home when she heard the basement entrance open and close. After a busy day treating patients and trading for parts, Ido had insisted on going out to see what he could find in the trash heap and hadn't minded when Gerhad said she was too tired to go with him. She wasn't as good at it as he was anyway, even when she wasn't tired, because of her personal feelings. The mere idea of picking through the discards of some unattainable and supposedly better world made her lose the will to live; actually doing it made her want to die.

Not that she'd ever known anything different. Her family had always lived in Iron City and most of them still did. One or two adventurous sorts had taken off in search of something better in parts unknown, and had never been heard of since. Gerhad didn't think this meant anything good. She had never considered doing anything like that herself; as far as she knew, the Badlands weren't hiring nurses, or anyone else for that matter. And even if they were, she doubted there were any other Dyson Idos out there. There sure weren't any others in Iron City, unless you counted the ice queen, and Gerhad most certainly did not.

Thinking of Ido's ex was something she preferred not to do, ever, and she wouldn't have, if it wasn't for what Ido had brought back. The way he'd come running up the stairs, Gerhad thought he had a bag full of servos. They needed more servos. They *always* needed more servos. But instead—

The cyber-core now locked into the stereotactic frame was the last thing she had expected him to bring back, right after a bag full of diamond rings. Well, if she'd found a discarded cyber-core showing the existence of a person, she'd have done the same. But she recognised the face; it was impossible, it could not be. And yet it was, big as life, and a heartbreak for sure. She wasn't certain how that would work since the doc's heart was already well and truly broken, but life could be very inventive.

After securing the cyber-core in the frame, he'd run back down to the basement for something. She'd known what he was after but she still caught her breath when he reappeared, carrying what looked like a child's body in his arms. In fact, it *was* a child's body, one that Ido had made. But the child had never used it and Ido had put it into storage, all those heartbroken years ago. Gerhad's feelings were mixed as she watched him lay it gently on the operating table next to the cyber-core in the frame.

It was beautiful, a work of art and an expression of profound love. She understood why Ido had packed it away unused, but she had also felt there was something inherently wrong about letting something so extraordinary go to waste. For a while, she'd hoped he might someday reach a place where he could let someone else benefit from his creation. But that would have meant he was healing, and healing was the one thing Ido would never, ever allow himself to do.

Ido had been jumping around the room, making preparations for surgery, shooing Gerhad away when she tried to do anything more than sterilise her own instruments. He was in the midst of recalibrating the micro-surgical robot arms when he suddenly turned to look at the slumbering cyber-core. After two hours of soaking up a pre-op infusion of brain nutrients, the cyber-core's eyes were now moving restlessly back and forth beneath the closed lids. Correction: *her* eyes, *her* closed lids; as the revival process went on, she looked more and more like the girl in the holo that Ido stared at countless times a day, every day.

Now he went over to the frame and reached out to touch her cheek. "What are you dreaming, little angel?" he asked with a tenderness Gerhad hadn't heard in a long time. He turned to her and she was shocked to see tears in his eyes.

Abruptly, he was jumping around again, setting up the micro-surgery workstation, running diagnostics, rechecking the robotic arms. He never said a word to her but he didn't have to. Gerhad was a registered nurse trained in cyber-surgery. She always knew what to do.

It wasn't the longest twenty-four hours Gerhad had ever spent in an OR but it was definitely the most intense. Ido had been a man in a fever, or a man possessed, working the micro-surgery arms and demanding she read data outputs from half a dozen different screens to him continuously, only because he didn't have six extra pairs of eyeballs to read them himself. She had no idea how he kept all the figures straight while he guided the micro-surgery instruments through all the tiny connections. He was just that brilliant—there were still times when she was awestruck by the breadth and depth of his intellect.

Like now, she thought as she watched the spidery surgical arms dancing in a delicate ballet choreographed by Ido. He didn't *have* to hover

over the instruments while they worked—he'd designed and built them himself and his surgical machines never malfunctioned unless you hit them with a hammer, and sometimes not even then. But it was more than his making sure nothing went wrong. The micro-surgery instruments carried out procedures that his own steady and practiced hands were simply too big to accomplish; as such, they were extensions of himself, and he had to witness every connection of every blood vessel, every muscle fibre, every nerve.

Ido turned to her, nodded almost imperceptibly. She fetched two bags from the fridge. One was filled with standard biological human blood, heart's-blood; the other, twice as large, contained iridescent celestial-blue cyber-blood. The term "blood" wasn't quite accurate, as the latter had a lot more to do in a cyborg body, using nano-machines instead of white or red blood cells. Having only one cyber arm, Gerhad didn't need as much as this girl would require for a Total Replacement body, even one smaller than an average mature adult.

Gerhad placed the bags in the transfusers and set the rate of flow for each; all Ido had to do was trigger them. He grunted his thanks and dismissed her by way of a head jerk, though only temporarily; he expected her to remain handy and alert until further notice. At one time, Gerhad wouldn't have tolerated grunts and head jerks from a doctor. She still wouldn't, except for Ido.

The day Gerhad met Dyson Ido, she had been lying in a bed in post-op, mourning for the career she had lost along with her arm. She'd known who he was—everyone at the hospital knew Dr Ido for his work with cyborg patients. Gerhad herself had referred people to his clinic.

When Ido had told her he could not only save her nursing career but enhance and improve it, she'd thought he was a hallucination generated by some rather iffy painkillers—not an unreasonable assumption. She was on staff at the hospital, and the Factory had been shorting their supply of meds. The pharmacy had become desperate enough to seek out alternative sources; as a result, in the last couple of weeks, people who came in with broken bones went out tripping balls, and migraine sufferers spent their nights going to raves and kissing everyone. Oddly enough, there wasn't a single complaint from anyone, but it was no solution.

The Factory had promised to make things right, but they'd taken their sweet-ass time about it. The Head Nurse told them there was nothing any of them could do except pray for rain and, *For God's sake, don't get hurt.*

Three hours later, her shift over, Gerhad walked out of the front door of the hospital just in time for an out-of-control gyro-lorry to sideswipe the front of the building, taking out all the windows, half a dozen newly installed hanging plants, a few No-Parking signs, and her left arm.

Somehow, she had remained conscious, although there were a few bad splices in her memory. One moment, she'd been stepping out on the sidewalk with the door of the hospital closing behind her; the next, she was lying on the ground amid broken glass, chunks of cement, clots of damp, dark dirt and torn-up flowers. She remembered knowing her arm was gone and, with it, her nursing career, such as it was.

Nursing wasn't always everything she'd hoped it would be—there was an awful lot of repeatedly patching up people who couldn't stop making the same mistakes, feet that hurt all the way up to her hips, and more vomit than she could ever have imagined. But there were good days, too, when she encountered someone who refused to be beaten down by circumstance, or at least weren't their own worst enemy. And there were the kids, the ones who had not yet begun to grow up too fast.

The pay was crap and sometimes it got crappier. They couldn't lay anyone off because they needed every warm body they had, so there were pay cuts. Always with the Factory's *sincere* apologies, played over the background noise of shipments travelling up to Zalem via the tube that arced right over the hospital from a nearby distribution annexe. Making ends meet required a lot of double shifts—not at overtime rates but at regular pay, sometimes less.

But being a nurse wasn't a *job*, it wasn't just a way to make a living while you looked for something better, it was a profession—a vocation. Nurses *wanted* to be nurses; it was the only thing Gerhad had ever wanted to be. Nursing had given her focus and discipline, which she discovered were crucial to surviving in a world that was shambolic and uninspiring at best and, at worst, pitiless and corrupt.

And now, thanks to a lorry driver who hadn't been qualified for a commercial vehicle heavier than half a ton, it was all gone. Compensation? She could whistle for it. The truck had been Factory-owned, and it hadn't been a kingpin like Vector behind the wheel, just some poor shlub who vanished without leaving a name. And that was the state of the nation, thank you and good night.

The next time she woke up, her upper body was locked into a stereotactic frame; Ido had her positioned so the nerves in her shoulder could most easily make the acquaintance of those in the cyber-arm. Ido was hovering over the robotic arms, his face set in an expression of intense concentration, as if Gerhad were the most important person in the world and he were performing the micro-surgery with his own hands.

She'd drifted in and out of consciousness, feeling no pain and seeing nothing psychedelic—later she found out he made his own medications, including anaesthesia—until she finally woke up completely and got her first good look at the work of art that was now part of her body.

"I don't know if I'm safe having an arm like this," she told him, admiring the designs etched into the metal. It made her think of an antique silver tea service. "I might get jacked the minute I step outside."

His smile had been knowing and even a little gleeful. "This town isn't full of geniuses but pretty much everybody knows better than to mess with my work."

She nodded, still admiring her arm. "I've treated more than a few patients who had parts they couldn't possibly afford. And now I'm one of them."

"Oh, there's no charge," he said, enjoying the look on her face. "Of course, there *is* something *you* can do for me that none of my other patients can."

That would have rung alarm bells except he didn't sound sleazy. "What?" she asked, more curious than wary.

"Work for me. I need a nurse and I can pay better than the hospital."

To her surprise, she'd said yes immediately. Then she'd waited for *that* moment, when he put his hand where it didn't belong and she had to break his nose or dislocate his shoulder, but it never came. She had accepted purely for the money, thinking she could build up a nest egg and if the job sucked, go back to the hospital. But before long, she decided it would be just plain stupid to give up an opportunity to work with a genuine, no-foolin' medical genius.

She had gone to work for Ido shortly after his heart had been well and truly broken, but other than that, she knew very little about him. He wasn't from around here, but you only had to talk to him to know that. He wasn't just bright, he was educated far beyond anything available at ground level, unless there was an ivory tower in some faraway land beyond the Factory's reach.

But Gerhad was certain Dyson Ido had not travelled from some far-off land to fetch up in the dead end of Iron City. No, he was from somewhere much closer, a place everybody in Iron City saw all the time but was more remote than the moon and just as unattainable.

Travel from ground level to Zalem was strictly forbidden, a law the Factory's Centurians enforced by lethal means. No heavier-than-air flight of any kind was permitted, for any reason; just flying a kite could get you killed. The Centurians weren't programmed to distinguish between machines and living creatures; as a result, whole generations of Iron City residents had lived and died without ever seeing a bird except in photos.

No one knew if Zalem's residents were equally restricted or whether the view from on high convinced them to stay where they were. Gerhad suspected it was the latter. Not that it made any difference—there was no way for anyone in the floating city to get to the surface.

Well, no way save one, and that was one hell of a long fall.

Gerhad didn't think many people could survive something like that. A parachute was out of the question—the Centurians would blast it into confetti and make mincemeat out of the person attached to it. The trash heap below would hardly provide a soft landing; at terminal velocity, a person was likely to pile-drive through several layers of accumulation, and the scrap metal would be like shrapnel.

You'd have to be some kind of batshit genius to figure out how to come out of that alive—and not just you but your wife and kid, too. And if the kid was kind of fragile, say, disabled—Gerhad had thought about it for years and she was still baffled.

Nonetheless, all three of them had survived. The girl had died a few years after that, in circumstances that were as brutal as they were pointless. Which, in Iron City, was unremarkable.

The real puzzler, though, was why Zalem had let someone so brilliant leave. Or had they? Gerhad wondered. They might grow the population a lot smarter up there but she doubted there was anyone who'd have made the doc seem dull by comparison. He was—she looked for a word other than *intense* and came up empty. Because that was what he was: intense. Everything he did for his patients mattered as much to him as it did to them, and she was sure he had always been this way. By all rights he should have gone crazy long ago but somehow he'd stayed sane. Or just sane enough.

Maybe Zalem *hadn't* let him go, Gerhad thought. Maybe leaving had been *his* idea. He certainly hadn't tripped and fallen over the edge by accident.

Ido turned to Gerhad, about to say something, and saw she had fallen asleep in the chair, head resting on her cyborg hand. He considered waking her, then decided not to. The embodying procedure was almost finished. He turned back to the girl on the table, to the white ceramic-and-titanium heart in her open chest. It was beating more quickly now, at a rate normal for a girl fast asleep and lost in her dreams.

She was alive.

CHAPTER 3

Waking was like drifting up from the depths of a warm, dark ocean. It was gradual, requiring no effort on her part, proceeding at its own rate. Time passed, or maybe it didn't, or it stopped and then started again. After a while—an hour or a week or a century—she opened her eyes.

The ceiling above her was blank except for a few cracks. There was nothing distinctive about it or even familiar—it could have been any ceiling anywhere. She was certain, however, that it wasn't the same ceiling she'd gone to sleep under. If there'd been a ceiling at all.

She yawned, enormously and deeply, her eyes squeezing shut as her lungs expanded to their limit. She had half a second to think her chest felt a little strange before she opened her eyes again and saw the hand she had reflexively covered her mouth with.

The hand wasn't hers. It wasn't even human.

Like that, she was awake; looking at the hand, turning it this way and that, wiggling the fingers. This wasn't *just* a hand. Someone had *envisioned* this hand, then brought it into existence, made it something that could move, that could touch and be touched.

And it was *beautiful*, decorated with designs of flowers and leaves and curlicues rendered in perfect, delicate lines. The metal inlay in the centre of her palm was etched with similar designs, only much smaller. She closed her hand slowly, then opened it again, watching the way all the sections worked; it had the same range of movement as a flesh-and-blood hand. Where there would have been pads at the base of each finger, she had small rounded sections, each one decorated with an exquisitely intricate sunburst. The metal shining in her finger joints was the same as that inlaid in her palm.

She even had fingerprints—but, oh, what fingerprints! The curved lines etched into the top two joints of each finger were a glorious riot of crashing waves that morphed into impossible flowers, clouds, arcs and spirals, dancing and swirling in a way that was exultant, even defiant.

On the back of her hand was a flower so complex she would have to study it at length to see all of its details. The thought that someone would give her something so beautiful was a surge of light and warmth inside her.

Her wrist was mechanical, its articulation and segments even more complex than her hand. Past that, more flowers blossomed in symmetry along her outer forearm, the lines delicate and perfect, some of them spilling onto her inner arm, right up to her mechanical elbow. The design resumed all the way up her bicep to a gold inlay etched with lines very much like her fingerprints. The segments that made up her shoulder were outlined in silver and gold. She'd never seen anything like this. If she had, she'd have wanted it immediately.

And her left arm?

She pulled it out from under the covers and was relieved to see that, yes, she had the set. She stretched her arms out so she could admire them both. With arms this beautiful, she might never wear long sleeves again.

The rest of her—what was that like?

Nervously she pulled the covers back. For a long moment she could only stare at herself in wonder. The whole body—*her* whole body—every bit of it, was a work of art. She stared at the—at *her*—creamy pinkish "skin" and the beautifully etched silver and gold inlays. How long had she been asleep?

And while she was at it, where had she woken up?

The bedroom was no place she knew, but she got the impression from the funny little figures on the shelves, the pictures on the walls and the stuffed bunny on her pillow that it belonged to a young girl. A *smart* young girl who loved to read—there were shelves and shelves of hardcopy books. But other things in the room didn't seem to belong—a shabby briefcase bundled with a stack of old file folders, for instance. Young girls didn't go for briefcases, not even smart young girls. A stuffed animal maybe—she picked up the bunny and ran a finger along its floppy ears. The fur was soft with comfort under her fingertips; she could practically feel the pattern of how the little-girl hands had petted and stroked it countless times. The bunny was old, too, just like pretty much everything else she could see. The very smart young girl who'd lived here must have been long gone by the time Alita had been tucked into her bed.

Who had brought her here and how had they done it without waking her? Because she had the strong feeling she had gone to sleep in a place far away. She couldn't remember where that had been, or what she had been doing there, or, now that she thought of it, anything at all.

But even if she didn't know where she was now, she was sure of one thing: it was safe. The place was old and a bit shabby, but it was intact. There was no visible damage from heavy munitions or explosives. Nor could she see any weapons stashed in convenient spots where they'd be easy to grab in an emergency, not even—she checked—under the bed.

She didn't wonder why that last thought had crossed her mind. It seemed only natural to think about safety after waking up in a strange place, not to mention in an unfamiliar body. Yes, the body was pretty, but was it useful? Was it able enough, fast enough, tough enough?

Her gaze fell on the full-length mirror across the room. She walked over to it on her unfamiliar but very beautiful legs and stood holding her arms slightly away from her body so she could see everything: the silver and gold inlays at her collarbone and the ornate but delicate artwork just below them and in the centre of her chest; the complexity of her segmented torso; the etched gold inlays at the tops of her thighs and the designs that curled along the front and sides of her legs above her complicated knees; the perfect symmetry of the fantasy flowers on her calves, mirror images of each other. She could actually imagine the work in progress, someone bending over each part in turn, working under a bright light, never looking up until it was perfect. The person in question was a dark blurry shadow with an impossibly steady hand and eyes that didn't see only surfaces— they saw all the way *through* the world, into its essence.

But the beauty she was admiring was a doll's beauty. The realisation brought her back down to earth with a thump. She was a toy girl, lacking the crucial anatomical features of a real person. There were pretty flowers along the line of collarbone, and gold and silver inlays just above the place on her chest where her breasts began, and more inlays below them. But her breasts were blank, featureless.

She pressed a finger to one of them, expecting it to be as hard as the rest of her, and was surprised to feel it give. Her body wasn't completely hard metal; there were some soft places.

Moving closer to the mirror, she touched her face. That was soft, too, but she was certain it was her own, not something that had come with the body. She looked down at herself and made a slow turn, looking over one shoulder and then the other. She was pretty in back, too; her behind also had some give, though it wasn't as soft as her breasts. But like her breasts, it wasn't real. She moved closer to the mirror, looking into her own eyes, but the toy girl in the mirror didn't seem to know anything more than she did. Some impulse made her tap the mirror with her fingers. She heard a quiet *tik*, metal on glass.

"Well, hell," she said, just to hear her own voice. It didn't sound strange to her. Whoever had given her this work-of-art doll body hadn't messed with anything above her neck. Or so she hoped.

As she turned away from the mirror, her gaze fell on some clothing folded up on a chair. She picked them up—a sweatshirt and some cargo pants.

Cargo pants were back in style? She must have been asleep for a *really* long time.

The door of her room wasn't locked, she discovered, and it was an immense relief to know she wasn't a prisoner. Of course, a young girl's room made a very unlikely prison cell, but as she didn't know where she was, she couldn't be sure of what was unlikely and what wasn't. Plus, cargo pants were back in style; all bets were off.

Careful to move soundlessly, she stepped into a short hallway, where she saw a flight of stairs. This was a private home. Did it come with her new body? If so, it didn't match; the place was clean but it was as old and shabby as the room where she'd awakened.

As she moved to the top of the stairs, she heard voices from below. Listening for a few seconds, she determined there was one woman and at least two men down there, although she couldn't make out the conversation. The voices didn't sound hostile, though. Time to see what she had landed in, she thought, and crept down the stairs, still moving silently, listening as the voices grew clearer.

When she got to the bottom, she found herself looking into a room that seemed to be some kind of clinic or laboratory. Was this place actually a hospital?

"Well, that's the best I can do for now," one of the men said. He was bending over something on a tray in front of him while a tall, dark-skinned woman in blue scrubs stood nearby; a nurse. "They don't make parts for this model any more."

The man moved back and she saw he'd been working on a piece of machinery that had obviously seen a lot of use. The metal was scratched and dented, with a few parts clearly taken from something else and adapted to fit. It looked heavy and clumsy and it was attached to the shoulder of a second man sitting in a chair beside the tray.

"I'm real grateful, Doc," the second man said, lifting the thing off the tray and testing its movements. "I'll be getting some overtime next week." He got to his feet and pulled up the top half of a greasy coverall, zipping it with his machine arm.

"Pay me when you can," said the first man in a kind voice.

The second man picked up a sack lying on the floor beside the chair. "Here, I got these for ya. My wife works out at Farm Twenty-two."

The woman chuckled. "Keep getting paid in fruit and we'll be pickin' these ourselves."

Just as she was thinking that she should look for a way out, the woman spotted her.

"Well, hello, sleepyhead." The woman smiled at her and she automatically smiled back. You couldn't assume someone was okay just because they smiled at you, but something told her this woman meant her no harm.

The man with the mechanical arm also smiled at her, but the doctor was startled. Maybe he'd thought she would still be asleep. He was pale with blond hair and round spectacles that gave him the appearance of a man who'd just been interrupted in the middle of reading something long and complicated. The woman—the nurse—ushered the man with the mechanical arm to a door across the room while she and the pale man stared at each other.

This was the man responsible for her beautiful work-of-art body, she realised. He had long fingers that seemed to move in a precise way even when they were just fidgeting with his lab coat and the small parts and tools in the pockets. Now that the surprise of her appearance had worn off, he was looking her over with the sharp, alert eyes of someone who knew so many things, far more than most people. She could also see he was a bit haggard, like he'd had a lot of long days and not enough sleep.

Unsure of what to do or say, she took a step forward and was briefly blinded by a shaft of sunlight coming in from a high window. The warmth felt good on her face.

"How do you feel?" the man asked her.

She sat down in the chair where the man with the heavy arm had been. "Okay."

Abruptly he reverted to his role as a doctor, grabbing a small flashlight so he could look into her eyes, then her mouth. He felt the area under her jawline and then the length of her neck, his long fingers expert and gentle.

"Any pain anywhere?" he asked, feeling her hands and bending each finger. "Numbness? Motor dysfunction?"

When he went into doctor mode, he went all the way, she thought. "Well, I'm a little… hungry."

He ushered her out of the laboratory or whatever it was and into a small kitchen. Seating her at the table, he reached into the bag his patient had given him and held out a round orange thing.

"Eat this," he said. "Get your sugar levels up."

She took it from him and examined it. The colour was pretty but she didn't think it looked terribly promising as food. A doctor wouldn't give her anything bad, she reasoned. She took a bite and immediately spat it out on the table.

"Taste receptors are working." Now he was an amused doctor. "You'll like that a lot better with the peel *off*." He took it from her and began removing the outer covering.

She watched him for a few moments, then decided it was as good a time as any to ask questions. "Um... I don't mean to be rude," she said, "but... am I supposed to know you?"

As if someone had flipped a switch, the doctor was gone and he was staring at her again, like he didn't know what to do. Finally, he said, "Actually, we've never met. I'm Doctor Dyson Ido." He nodded at the woman, who had just come in from the laboratory. "This is Nurse Gerhad." The woman's warm smile made her feel a bit less anxious about asking her next question.

"Okay, I don't quite know how to say this—" She took a steadying breath. "Do you happen to know who *I* am?"

The doctor and nurse looked at each other, taken aback by the question. Her heart sank a little.

"I was hoping you'd fill in that part. Since you're a Total Replacement cyborg, and most of your cyber body was destroyed, I can't find any records."

They looked at each other again, and this time she had the distinct impression Nurse Gerhad was displeased about something.

"But your very *human brain* was miraculously intact," Dr Ido went on after a moment. "Theoretically, you should remember something."

"Oh," she said. "Well, uh…" She thought for a moment. "It's pretty blank." They were looking at her expectantly. Her heart—or whatever she had as a Total Replacement cyborg—sank a little more. "It's completely blank, actually."

She didn't have to be a doctor herself to know that wasn't right at all. There should have been *something*, even if it was only a vague image: someone she knew or a place where she'd been, or a few words someone had spoken to her—whoever *that* was, or had been. All at once she felt like the world was becoming less solid, like she was about to fall through it into nothing.

"I don't even know my name!" Tears welled up in her eyes and spilled down her face.

"I know this is all very new and strange," the doctor said in the warm, kindly voice she was already growing to love. "But you're not alone— I'm here with you. I'm going to protect you and everything is going to be okay. And let's look on the bright side." The doctor dabbed at her face with a napkin as he handed her the thing he had finished peeling. "Your tear ducts are working."

She couldn't help smiling a little. That was just the sort of thing a very kind doctor would say. Although how she could know that but not her own name made no sense at all. She bit into the thing he'd given her. This time, there was an explosion of taste in her mouth; the feel of the pulp between her teeth and a flood of liquid that overflowed and ran down her chin was delightful. Suddenly she no longer felt like crying, about anything.

"This is *good*!" she said, looking from Ido to Gerhad and back again. "What do you call this?"

She saw the nurse give Ido a wry half-smile. "It's *your* fee, *you* tell her. And make sure she knows it's not money anywhere else in town."

CHAPTER 4

"YEEEOOOW!"

Ido ran out onto the porch, thinking the little cyborg had managed to put her foot through a loose board and then torn off a finger trying to free herself. But she was completely unhurt. Nothing wrong with her yelling function, he thought as she grabbed his arm and pointed at the sky. "What's *that*?"

Gerhad, who had followed more slowly, gave him a knowing smile that told him he'd be answering a whole lot of questions and he'd better get used to it. He pretended not to notice.

"That's Zalem," Ido told the cyborg girl. "It's the last of the great sky cities."

She turned back to look at it. "What holds it up—magic?"

Ido thought if her eyes got any wider, they might fall out. "No, something much stronger. *Engineering.*"

The girl ran down off the porch and into the street, where she stood gazing up at it and the low clouds sailing slowly underneath the disc, unaware of the two-wheeled gyro truck honking its horn madly as it bore down on her. Ido yanked her out of the way just in time. As the truck blew past, the driver made an angry gesture, yelling "*Pinche cabrón!*"

Ido was about to scold her, then thought better of it. She hadn't even known what an orange was, so of course she didn't know better than to play in traffic. "And down here," he said, turning her to face the direction in which the gyro-truck had gone, "this is Iron City, with all its charms."

The girl gaped as if it were an exotic wonderland filled with the promise of adventure and excitement rather than a sad, dirty town that Zalem used as a toilet.

That last thought was a bit dark even for him, Ido thought and blinked, trying to see Iron City's street life through the eyes of a girl who had never seen a city before. At the moment, however, she was looking at the sign on the front of the house: DR DYSON IDO CMD, CYBER-SURGEON. She could read, it seemed, yet she'd never seen an orange before; one more thing to add to the growing list of oddities.

"While I'm learning names," she said, touching his arm tentatively, "do you have one for me?"

It was out of his mouth before he could think better of it. "Alita. Alita is a nice name."

The girl beamed up at him as if he'd just given her the best present in the world. "I *like* it!" she declared, and he knew it would be no use suggesting anything else. "Let's keep it, at least until I can remember my real name. Thank you!" She threw her arms around him and gave him a hug that took his breath away.

Ido gazed down at the top of her head, which came to the centre of his breastbone, then looked to see how Gerhad was taking it, but she had already gone back inside. She'd heard him, though—Gerhad heard everything—and she'd make him answer for it later. As if he'd ever stopped answering for Alita.

Alita. He stroked her beautiful dark hair and held her tight. Of course, Alita—that face, those eyes. No other name would do. "Well, then, Alita, let's get you back inside for some tests. I need another brain scan now that you're conscious, and a full neuro-motor calibration and—"

She looked up at him with an eager smile. "No, let's take a walk! Can we? *Please?*" Without waiting for an answer, she started pulling him down the street.

Gerhad reappeared on the porch. "Go on. She looks pretty calibrated to me," she said, laughing a little. "Shoes! You should get shoes!"

As soon as she had a name, the floodgates opened and she deluged him with questions. What was engineering and why didn't anyone use it to make Iron City float? How big was Iron City? Had there always been so many people? Who'd named it Iron City and why? What was outside the city? Who lived there, and what did they do?

Ido gave her a potted history of the last three hundred years, including the War and the Fall, thinking she would be distracted while she digested new information. Fat chance—apparently he had forgotten what a bright fourteen-year-old girl was like. Well, it *had* been a while; he was out of practice. He decided to take her for a walk through the city so she could goggle at all the street life. He just had to make sure she didn't wander into traffic.

Alita trotted along beside him, her wide eyes taking in everything and everyone—the standard, un-enhanced humans; cyborgs of all kinds, from those with only one or two machine limbs like Gerhad to Total Replacements like herself; as well as the kids weaving among the crowds, some running barefoot, others on motorised rollerblades. Even the street signs fascinated her, including the ones she couldn't read. Ido made another mental note: she was fluent only in English.

As if she had somehow caught the flavour of what he'd been thinking, she turned to him and said, "Why so many languages?"

Ido smiled, telling himself to be patient. "After the big war I told you about—"

"The Fall," she put in, looking pleased with herself for remembering.

"Yes, after the Fall, Zalem was the only floating city left. Many survivors of the War and from the other fallen cities came here from all over the world. Now everybody down here works for Zalem—the Factory, the Farms, the Motorball games."

"Does anybody down here ever go up to Zalem?" she asked.

He shook his head. "Nobody from down here can *ever* go up. You can't get there from here—that's the rule, and it's never broken."

She looked surprised. "Why?"

Ido laughed a little. "We're going to have to put some kind of limit on how many times you can use the word 'why' in one hour." He waited for her to argue; when she didn't, he looked down and discovered that she was no longer beside him. He looked around frantically. If she had wandered into the street again—

No, she was safely on the sidewalk; her attention had been captured by a four-storey flatscreen on a building across the street. Then he saw what she was watching and all his good feelings fled.

Massive, heavily armoured cyborgs charged along a track at high speed, fighting each other and chasing a large motorised ball bouncing and tumbling erratically ahead of them. Alita was open-mouthed, enchanted by the sight of the cyborgs jumping and flipping through the air, delivering kicks and blows to each other, as if they were dancing some kind of brutal ballet on wheels at a hundred miles an hour.

Ido put a hand on her shoulder to usher her away from the screen and discovered that she would not be moved.

"What—what *is* that?" she asked finally. Her great big eyes were sparkling with excitement, as if she had seen something miraculous.

"Motorball," Ido said, letting his disapproval show. "It was created by the Factory so people can blow off steam. Everybody loves having heroes, someone to cheer for, idols to worship. So the Factory gave us Paladins. But it's nothing you need to be wasting your time watching."

They passed some kids in filter masks hawking cheap lube jobs. As soon as they saw her, they called out. "Hey, best-quality Teflon lube products! Fix you right up, only ten Cs!"

Ido put his arm around Alita protectively. "Never—*never*—get a street lube," he said firmly.

"Why not?" she asked.

He gave her a look. "You're over your quota, remember?"

She giggled and let him steer her up the street. But to his dismay, she kept looking back at the Motorball screen.

As sure as Alita was her name, falafel was *the* best food in the world, and oranges were second. Falafel was also the messiest. She licked hummus off her fingers while trying to keep the wrap from falling to pieces. Were all the best foods the messiest ones? She glanced surreptitiously at Ido to make sure he was too busy going through a bin labelled SERVOS to notice her wiping her hands on the seat of her cargo pants.

Ido had told her this was a marketplace, and it was *amazing*. There were so many people, doing all kinds of things. A lot of people were selling stuff, but there was also a guy with something called a double-necked guitar; his cyborg arm could play both necks at once, making wonderful music that made her want to dance instead of just walking.

But it was like Ido didn't even hear it. All he was interested in was those servo things. She didn't understand that at all. How could he not be excited in a place where so much was going on? People were selling all kinds of stuff—blankets, baskets, flowers (though none as pretty as the ones on her body), things to wear, things to play with, things for making other things, things that had uses she couldn't imagine.

And so many amazing items to look at—holos that tricked the eye, pictures made of shifting light, pictures that glowed *without* light. There were puzzles, games, dice with as many as twenty-one sides, although she wasn't sure how you were supposed to know which number was the right one.

She stopped in front of a rack of cages containing all sorts of birds. Some were little and flew around their enclosed spaces from one perch to another and sometimes to the bars, clutching them with their tiny feet like little prisoners.

"Please, can we buy some and let them out? Pleasepleaseplease?" she asked Ido.

"They wouldn't survive," Ido told her.

"But they should be allowed to fly free," she said.

"Anything that flies gets shot down by Zalem's defence system," Ido said. "There are no free birds in this city."

That was all wrong, Alita thought. *Someday, I'll find a way to free you,* she told the birds silently. *Someday.*

Now she moved on to the food area. So many wonderful smells! There were ingredients that sizzled in wide pans or bubbled in big pots, little meals in round bowls no bigger than her palm, and foods that came in big hunks on sticks. They even had foods that wrapped around each other or had other food stuffed into them, all served by smiling people who had replaced one hand with tongs or ladles or carving blades or even little torches.

But Ido had headed straight for a stall with nothing but machine parts, saying he always needed more servos—whatever those were. She was supposed to stay right by him and not wander off or even ask a lot of questions. Or any questions, for that matter. But how could he bring her here and expect her to do nothing when there was so much going on? She'd thought she was going to explode with frustration when he'd finally bought her the falafel.

Suddenly she realised she wasn't alone. A small dog of mixed pedigree was looking up at her hopefully and wagging his tail. She crouched down to pet him and he immediately began licking her face. Well, that solved the problem of how she was going to clean up.

"Here you go, buddy," she said, letting the dog have the rest of the mess in her hands. He was more than happy to finish it for her, licking every last trace from her fingers before he went back to washing her face. She enjoyed the feel of his warm tongue. Doggy kisses were great.

A gust of wind blew a sheet of paper against her ankle and she picked it up: WANTED FOR THE MURDERS OF SIX WOMEN. BOUNTY 10,000 CREDITS. There was no picture, only a black square labelled UNIDENTIFIED LARGE CYBORG.

That wasn't a whole lot to go on, she thought, frowning. Didn't anyone even know *how* large this unidentified cyborg was? He couldn't have been all that big if he'd got away with killing six women, otherwise someone would have seen him do it.

"What do you think, buddy?" she said to her new friend, showing the notice to him. "This sound like anybody you know?"

The dog sniffed the paper, smelled nothing delicious, and continued licking her face.

Hugo got out of bed that morning with no intention of doing anyone a good turn, much less saving a life. His usual schedule involved keeping his eyes and ears open for any opportunity to make some credits. He'd headed down to the market on his gyro, hoping to find some vendors with a pressing need for certain hard-to-find items and who were willing to pay for fast delivery of special orders, no questions asked, thank you and good night.

Finding the hard-to-find was, in fact, what Hugo was known for, and not just in the marketplace. He and his crew could have given up their marketplace customers and still made a good living. But the market was where he'd started out and where he'd built up his reputation. He wasn't going to forget where he came from—not yet, anyway. He glanced up at Zalem.

Bent low over the gyro's handlebars, he swerved through the crowds, occasionally taking a fast pass over the sidewalk to get around a truck or a slow-moving pedal-car. The gyro was built for speed but he spent a godawful amount of time stuck in traffic. He was going to have to take it out on the open road soon to blow out the cobwebs and keep the motor smooth.

At the moment, however, he was only thinking about meeting up with his crew, who would be hanging around in front of the CAFÉ café. Hugo had given the owner of this rather unimaginatively named establishment a break on some critical parts and now it was one of the few places in town where they could hang around without anyone complaining or trying to chase them off—well, as long as they didn't block the sidewalk or tie up tables during a rush. But that was only fair. Giving someone a cut rate on espresso-machine parts and then making it impossible for them to make a living was no way to do business. Tanji had argued that giving big discounts to cafés was no way to do business, either, but always having a place to hide out when it rained, or even when it didn't, had shut him up.

Tanji had absolutely *no* business sense; anything that wasn't just a straight money-for-goods deal always had to be spelled out for him; he was kind of a pain in the ass that way. But once he understood, he was good to go—and he'd go all the way, no second guessing or bailing at the last minute, which made him the kind of pain in the ass Hugo wanted in his crew. It was also why he was Hugo's closest friend.

Then he heard the sound no one ever wanted to hear, the metal clank and stomp of Centurians in the street ahead of him, and he forgot about everything else.

They were marching into the marketplace, which was never good. Centurian programming was specific and narrow to the point of stupidity. They existed to put a stop to illegal activity in one of two ways: bullets or missiles. Well, three ways if you counted the single warning Centurians gave to cease the proscribed activity under penalty of law. Unfortunately, their programming didn't allow for much time between the warning and the penalty. Worse, Centurians couldn't always tell the difference between cooperation and defiance.

But worst of all, they sometimes couldn't tell the difference between legal and illegal behaviour, especially in a place as chaotic as the market. There were always kids playing Motorball with jerry-rigged ramps and slopes. If a Centurian registered a kid doing a double somersault with a hot breakaway onto an overpass as an illegal flying machine, it would shoot the kid into hamburger and there wouldn't be a damn thing anyone could do about it. Unless they wanted to be hamburger, too.

The smart thing to do would have been to take off in the opposite direction and come back later; instead, Hugo followed them, albeit at a distance. They were definitely going to march right through the middle of the market, but why? Did the Factory actually *want* them to shoot the place up, or just make everyone crap their pants in terror?

Then he caught sight of the girl with the dog. She was crouched down directly in the path of the big metal bastards, looking at a flyer and patting the dog like she had no idea she was about to get trampled by three walking machine guns. And they *would* trample her and the dog both without missing a beat. Centurians weren't made to care about the safety of living creatures; they were executioners.

Before he even knew what he was going to do, Hugo shifted into high gear and zipped through the crowded street at a speed even Tanji would have said was whacko. And that silly girl was *still* petting that stupid dog! Was she crazy, or did she get dropped on her head too many times as a baby?

"Hey, you—girl with the dog! Watch out!" he yelled.

Somehow, despite all the noise, his warning got through to her. She stood up and looked at the clanking armoured gun platforms relentlessly advancing on her. But instead of running, she just stood there, gaping like she'd never seen a Centurian before. Rabbit in the headlights, thought Hugo, trying to go faster. The Centurian in the lead let out a warning siren. Anyone would run from that sound—anyone but *this* girl. This girl dropped into a crouch with her fists up, like she really thought she could fight Centurians and live to regret it. She wasn't just crazy, she was super-mega-*batshit*-crazy.

And so am I, Hugo thought as he launched himself off the gyro and tackled the girl. As they tumbled over and over on the street, Hugo closed his eyes, bracing himself for the feel of a Centurian foot crushing him into the pavement. But when he opened his eyes again, he and the girl were lying on the ground just out of the robots' path. The girl blinked at him in surprise. He had a second to think that she had the biggest eyes he'd ever seen before she pushed away from him and ran *towards* the danger he'd just saved her from.

To save the dog, he realised, the goddam dog. It was whimpering as the first Centurian passed over it. The girl dropped down in front of the second Centurian, grabbed the dog, and rolled away a heartbeat before the enormous foot came down on the spot where they'd been.

Hugo's jaw dropped. Had he just seen that? Had he *really* just seen that, or had he taken too many headshots playing Motorball?

Alita had no doubt she could reach the dog in time and get him out of the way. What she hadn't expected was the sudden picture show in her head. The images had flashed so quickly she couldn't really see what they were, although she had a very strong impression of weapons and combat. Whether these were flashes from one battle or several, she had no idea. The whole thing had been so fleeting she wasn't even sure if she were remembering a real event or a dream.

Then she was moving again, diving between immense mechanical legs with impossibly easy speed and fetching up on the other side of the street. She tucked and rolled into a sitting position, keeping her fists up, ready to defend herself.

"Outstanding!" said a voice beside her. She turned to see a boy sitting on her right staring at her with admiration. He was wearing a leather jacket and a bandanna over his dark hair, and he had the brightest, most wonderful dark eyes and the best smile she had ever seen. He leaned forward, looking past her at the retreating backs of the big stomping machines and yelled, "Hey, why don't you watch where you're goin'?"

Alita blinked at him, unsure of what to do or say. That bandanna was just about the best thing anyone could wear, she thought as he stood up and brushed himself off.

"Gotta admit, I *never* saw anybody play chicken with a Centurian before!" He offered her a hand to help her up and she took it. "Whoa, you're heavy!" he blurted as he tugged her to her feet, then looked embarrassed. "Sorry, I meant—" He broke off at the sight of her hand in his. "Oh! You're a cyborg!"

Suddenly self-conscious, she pulled away from him and hid both hands under her arms.

"I was just admiring your hand," he told her. "It's great. Let me see. Please?"

Still feeling self-conscious, she extended one hand. He looked at it closely, turning it over so he could see all the designs.

"It's really nice work. Did Doc Ido do it?"

She felt a surge of pleasure. "He built all of me, except my core."

"He sure did a great job," the guy said as she offered him her other hand to examine. She hoped he would take his time because she really liked his face, especially when he was looking at her.

"What *were* those things?" she asked.

It took him a second to realise what she was talking about. "You mean the Centurians? *Seriously?* Jeez, what planet are *you* from?"

She shrugged. "Ido found me in the scrapyard."

"The scrapyard?" Now his wonderful face was incredulous. "But that would mean—"

Before he could finish the sentence, however, Ido himself had materialised beside her, annoyed because she had wandered off and made him look for her. He'd been so busy finding servos, he had no idea what had just happened, she realised, which was a good thing.

"Hey, Doc," the guy said cheerfully. "I've got those driver-boards you were lookin' for."

Nodding at him, Ido put his arm around her shoulders in a way that felt both protective and possessive. "Alita is new here, and she's just learning about Iron City." He looked down at her, his face serious. "Centurians are Factory enforcers. You need to stay out of their way."

"Oh, so diving through their legs wouldn't be good?" said the guy, looking innocent.

Ido gave him a look. "Don't even joke about that."

The guy smiled at Alita and winked, and she felt a powerful surge of happiness run through her.

"Gotta go," the guy said to Ido. "I'll drop the boards off later. I need a rebuild on a quad servo." He paused and gave her a smile. "Maybe I'll see you around."

Alita watched as he ran to a machine lying half on, half off the sidewalk. There was a seat on it but only one wheel. He checked it over, then climbed on and fired it up. She stared after him, amazed at the way he could weave through the traffic on only one wheel.

"Who was that?" she asked Ido with a dreamy wistfulness.

"Hugo," Ido told her. "He's a hard worker, but…" He paused. "Well, it's a desperate city, Alita. Come on, let's go home."

She let Ido usher her in the other direction but she couldn't help turning around for one last look. To her delight, she caught a glimpse of him looking back at her. "Hugo," she sighed.

Ido sighed, too, but in an entirely different way.

CHAPTER 5

All day long the kids in the filter masks called out to passing cyborgs, shouting themselves hoarse about the miracles they could work for a mere ten credits. Shadows lengthened, the day waned, and the kids were still at it when the sun went down.

The city was a different kind of place after dark but the kids hung in, promising Iron City's cyborgs a glaze to amaze that would make them slick as a magic trick, sleek on every peak and smooth in every groove, they could slip, slide and electro-glide the night away. This was royal oil, grease of the gods, only ten credits for the lube of a lifetime.

The Total Replacement cyborg who decided to take them up on their offer may have been thinking he'd give them a break so they wouldn't have to go home with nothing to show for all those hours of pitching. Maybe they reminded him of himself at the same age—too young for the Factory, but money for rent and groceries had to come from somewhere.

Or maybe he'd been meaning to get around to a lube but there was always something else he had to do first, and now he was due, possibly a little overdue. And then—son of a gun—a couple of kids pop up with exactly what he needed at a bargain price. Only a fool would pass this up. Or he may have been thinking something entirely different and unrelated.

What he wouldn't have been thinking about was his personal safety. He'd always been a big guy and now that he was a TR, he was even bigger. Tall and heavyset—emphasis on heavy—for a moment, he wasn't sure the chair the kids were showing him to would take his weight, but it turned out to be stronger than it looked.

He certainly would have noticed the kids eyeing the custom designs carved into his chrome overlay. People always stared at his body art and he didn't mind. Every design had a special meaning. The spiral above his heart was for those he had pledged himself to for life, while the stars in the centre of his chest were his family. The waves crashing on his shoulders represented the power of love, a burden he was willing to bear and was, in fact, what he was hoping to find tonight. Broken chains ran up and down his arms, showing that he had already overcome things that had tried to hold him back.

The chair was partly blocking an alley and he meant to move it a few centimetres to the left so there would be only a solid building at his back—it wouldn't have been hard, the chair had wheels. But the kids were fussing and flitting around him so that he could barely keep track of them. They looked so alike in their filter masks, he wouldn't have been able to tell them apart if one hadn't been taller than the other. The taller one was in front of him saying they had the highest-quality lube in Iron City while the shorter one messed around with cans or something behind him. He was starting to wish he'd just kept walking.

"Make it fast, muchachos," he said, grimacing at the taller kid. "I got a date. I need smooth moves tonight, you know what I mean?"

"Don't worry," the kid said. "We're so fast—"

The world exploded in a blinding light. He felt his body stiffen all over, his arms and legs bent at hard, awkward angles. *This must be what it feels like to be struck by lightning,* he thought. Then the lightning let go of him and he went limp.

"—you won't know what hit you," finished the tall kid as they wheeled him into the alley.

It was a rough ride over cracked, uneven pavement; he bounced helplessly in the chair, unable to move even though the other kid had removed the paralyser from his spine. They'd taken him right out on the street—in public—someone must have seen what happened to him. Why wasn't someone yelling, trying to help him or at least saying they'd call the Centurians? How could a person be attacked in a public place and no one would do anything?

The chair came to an abrupt stop and they tipped him out onto the ground. He still couldn't move a muscle. When he heard the sound of power ratchets starting up, however, he managed to find his voice.

"You little *maricons*!" he yelled. *"Hijos de todo tu pinche madre!"* But he could barely hear himself over the power tools. But they could. He knew they could.

The noise cut out and he saw the kids lifting his arms away from him. Bright-blue cyber-blood poured from the severed ends. He could sense it seeping from his body and pooling on the ground around him.

They didn't bother with ratchets for his legs; they used a circular-saw blade that sent more cyber-blood spraying in all directions. Nasty little butchers! They cut him up like he was a steer and now they were handling his arms and legs like they were nothing, like he had never freed himself from chains that other people were too weak to break, like he had never stood up for his people, his family, himself.

The kids were packing them into the carriers on their gyro-wheels when suddenly the alley was filled with the brilliant glare of a Centurian's spotlight. Someone had called for help after all—he was saved!

"Help!" he shouted. "Help me, I'm getting jacked!"

"Move along," the Centurian ordered him in its expressionless, mechanical voice. The light went off and he heard the thing clanking away from the mouth of the alley.

"Come back!" Desperation took his voice up a full octave. "Come back and help me, you *pinche madre* piece of shit!"

The kids burst out laughing. "Forget it, this ain't no crime against production," said the short one. "The Centurians only care about the Factory, and the Factory don't care about *you*!"

He felt the kid kick him. The little bastard actually kicked him when he was down! If he ever found out who these *maricons* were he would tear them limb from limb, just with his hands.

"Leave him alone," said the other kid. "Come on, we gotta go!"

The cyborg watched as they took off on their gyros, leaving him armless and legless in a pool of cyber-blood, and still unable to move, even just to roll over.

"*Auxilio!*" he yelled. "Somebody help me, dammit!" He was probably going to lose his voice, too, before anyone came along.

He was right.

⁂

The gyro-cab rattling along the dark, deserted street was dented and scratched and very much in need of a new paint job. The driver was saving up for that, or trying to, but these were awfully lean times. Times were always lean in Iron City but the driver tried not to think about that.

He'd actually thought he'd get more night-time fares with a vicious killer roaming around looking for ladies to slice up, and he had, but not as many as he'd hoped. Women went out at night in packs of four or five or even six. He wouldn't have thought that would be much of a deterrent—it wasn't like half a dozen women could overpower a large homicidal cyborg and pin him to the street with their stiletto heels while they waited for the Centurians to show up and blast him to death. But the killer didn't take on groups; the killer liked to pick them off one at a time. With all the warnings, you'd have thought it would be impossible to find any woman alone on the street at night.

Sadly, not everyone could get a group together when they really needed to. Like this poor soul who was his current passenger—he'd spotted her standing on the Factory's front steps, and known immediately that she was contemplating the prospect of walking home all by herself in the dark. He stopped in front of her and told her to hop in.

She'd looked pained and said, "Well… uh… I don't…" Universal code for *I can't afford to.*

Instead of driving off in search of a couple of party animals too drunk to know the fare was padded, he said, "Get in. Special low rate for the danger zone. Don't know if you've heard but there's a killer running around."

She'd hesitated, then climbed in, thanking him in a way that wrenched his heart. What the hell—his mother had always said a good deed was never wasted. Although he still couldn't help thinking how good the fare would have been if he weren't such a soft touch. On the other hand, if he hadn't been a soft touch, he'd be driving around empty. So, what the hell.

The trip was quick at this time of night, and when he saw where she lived, he was doubly glad he'd picked her up. The block was deserted at this hour—Murder o'clock, one of the other cabbies called it. The woman gave him half of what he usually charged and tried to add a tip. He pushed it back at her along with a couple of credits. She looked startled. It was probably a long time since anyone had cut her a break for anything.

"Go on," he said, chuckling a little. "Just don't tell anybody or I'll never be able to make a living."

She gave a small laugh. "Your secret's safe with me. I'll take it to my grave."

Her words gave him a funny feeling and he wished she'd picked a different expression. He was probably over-tired, he thought, smiling at her. "Hey, a good deed is never wasted, right? Now get indoors fast, okay?"

She hurried off, and he waited until he saw her stop at what had to be her own front door before he drove away. It was just about time for the next wave of drunks to spill out of the Kansas Bar and that bunch *could* afford a padded fare. Not very nice of him, but what the hell—he'd done a good deed and even if it really wasn't wasted, it wouldn't do any harm to make up the loss.

❦

She couldn't help feeling relieved when the cab drove off. All the way home, she'd been worried: what if *he* turned out to be the killer? Or what if he started talking about how pretty she was and if she *really* wanted to thank him for giving her a break on the fare, etc., etc., etc. Instead, he *was* a nice guy. Or at the very least, a guy capable of being nice.

But dammit, where had she put her keys? Why hadn't she opted for a keypad, or even an implant in her forearm? She was going to put the money she'd saved tonight towards something better and flush that stupid key down the toilet—

Just as her fingers closed on the key in her purse, she heard something stir behind her, and though she knew it was absolutely the wrong thing to do, that she should just stick the stupid key in the stupid lock, rush inside, and slam the stupid door behind her, she couldn't stop her stupid self from turning around to look.

Something enormous and darker than the night rose up and threw itself over her. She opened her mouth but her scream didn't last even a second. Blood splashed across a nearby wall with a noise like a slap.

The sound of the elevator woke Alita. Curious, she got out of bed, tiptoed to the door, and opened it a tiny crack to see what was going on.

For a moment, she wasn't sure it was Ido because he looked so different. It wasn't so much the long leather trench coat and the black gloves, although she'd never seen him wear anything like them before. It was the expression on his face. There was no trace of kindliness or affection. He looked positively grim, like a man who saw the world as a terrible, dangerous place where only the worst could happen.

Stranger still, he had a wheeled suitcase that he was pushing ahead of himself. She drew back a little as he rolled it past her door, one of the wheels going *squeak-squeak-squeak*. It was a very strange suitcase; there was something about the size and shape that made her think of a toolbox rather than something to pack clothes in for travelling. He went down the hall to a door at the end, then paused to slip his coat off one arm, wincing as he did.

There was a nasty gash on his forearm and it was still oozing blood; heart's-blood. It must have hurt like hell. It was all she could do to keep from bursting out of her room and running to him to ask what happened. But even though he was grimacing in pain, his face was still cold and hard. This was not the Ido who had made this lovely body with all the flowers and the silver and gold inlays, not the Ido who named her Alita. She didn't know who this Ido was, and she hoped she never would.

Ido unlocked the door, wheeled the suitcase inside, then shut the door. The lock re-engaged with a hard metal click.

The next morning, she wondered if Ido would say where he'd gone the previous night, but he didn't even mention the bandage on his forearm. Not that there'd been much time for conversation—their first patient came to them in a box outside the front door, missing his arms and legs. Nurse Gerhad said it was as good a time as any for her to begin training as Ido's assistant. She was nervous at first, especially with the limbless cyborg. What if she screwed up, and as soon as he got off the operating table he fell apart? Or what if she dropped a bag of cyber-blood and it splashed all over the place—or worse, heart's-blood?

Gerhad assured her there was very little she could do that would cause anyone to fall apart, and transfusion bags were too tough to break open easily because everybody dropped them. It was all just a matter of becoming familiar with the instruments and the procedures. Once Alita was more experienced, Gerhad said, she'd know which instrument to hand Ido before he even asked for it. As for the patients, Gerhad told her most of them barely noticed there was anyone else in the room besides Ido. This certainly seemed true of the first patient, who was immensely talkative.

"So there's the damn jackers that ripped me to shreds standin' right there," he was saying as Ido tinkered with the arm socket in his shoulder. "I'm lyin' there yellin' and that *vale madre* Centurian wouldn't do a thing. Not a single thing. If it'd had fingers, it wouldn't have lifted one to help me."

"Torque coupling," Ido said, holding his hand out without looking away from what he was doing. "Jackers want your parts on the black market to supply the Motorball games," he added to the cyborg on the table.

"*My* parts? That's messed up," the cyborg replied.

As Alita handed Ido the torque coupling, her gaze fell on his forearm and her happy pride over giving him the right part faded. The bandage looked fresh but a little blood had seeped through it already. What had happened to him last night?

"You were lucky," Gerhad was saying to the cyborg on the table. "Another woman was murdered last night, right near where you got jacked."

The cyborg gave her an incredulous look. "Oh, yeah, this is me, lucky. You know, I heard he carves them up and puts them in little metal—"

Ido gave him a nudge and looked reproachfully at both him and Gerhad before nodding at her. "Alita, I don't want you out after dark. Is that understood?" he said, pushing both hands into his lower back as he straightened up from the table. "And if you do go out, don't wander too far from this neighbourhood."

Now Gerhad and even the cyborg were looking at her expectantly. "Okay," she said.

"Promise?" Ido said.

She was supposed to think he was being stern with her. She might have, if she hadn't seen that grim expression on his face last night. "Okay, I promise," she said.

He looked pleased as he turned back to the patient.

After Ido replaced the cyborg's arms and legs, he told Alita there wasn't much left for her to do, and she could go out if she wanted, but she had to remember her promise to be back before dark. Alita nodded, barely listening as she took off the surgical gown and gloves and dropped them in the USED bin. The market, she decided, was a good place to look for Hugo.

She bounced out the front door and onto the sidewalk. Something good was definitely going to happen today, she thought as she brushed past someone. As soon as she found Hugo—

"Hey, you—kid!"

Automatically, she stopped and turned around. A tall woman with long dark hair, icy blue eyes, and what looked like a purple jewel in her forehead stood on the sidewalk, staring at her like she was some kind of criminal. Alita was about to turn away but the woman was on her in two big strides. She grabbed Alita's wrist and started manipulating her hand, as if she were a doctor like Ido. Only, she was more like the Ido from last night, cold and grim and pitiless.

The woman looked up from her hand and glared at her with intense anger. Alita twisted out of her grasp and took a couple of steps back.

"What the hell is *your* problem?" she demanded.

The woman just went on glaring at her. Standing as straight as she could, Alita made a show of deliberately turning her back and walking away, mainly so the woman wouldn't see how creeped out she was. She could all but feel that icy gaze boring into her back, and she had to force herself not to run, afraid that if she did, the woman would chase her. After twenty steps, she sneaked a glance over her shoulder. The woman wasn't looking at her any more; she was staring at Ido's clinic.

No, not at the clinic—at Ido, who was standing at one of the second-floor windows and staring right back at her.

It was bound to happen, Ido thought as he watched Alita march away from Chiren. He just hadn't expected it to happen so soon, before he'd had a chance to tell Alita about his estranged wife. Or rather, warn her. Of course, that would have meant telling her everything, and he wasn't quite ready for that. He wanted Alita to be more acclimated, more at home in the body he'd given her before he told her whom he had really made it for.

Abruptly, Chiren turned and looked directly at him, as if she had not only sensed him watching from the window but caught the gist of his thoughts as well. He wouldn't have been surprised. There had been a time when he was sure she had known his mind better than he did, and that had been just one of many things he'd loved about her. But that had been a different time in a different world, before their own personal Fall. What they'd had was gone now, as if it had never existed.

The poster on the side of the building was enormous. Two people, one a TR cyborg, the other all-organic, both looking heroic and noble, stood shoulder to shoulder, eyes lifted up towards a bright future. Below their hopeful, optimistic faces were the words HARMONY, PRODUCTIVITY, SECURITY in bold letters as bright as the future that awaited them.

The message was more than slightly undercut by the splashes of paint as red as heart's-blood, an effect reinforced by the dripping letters that spelled out a different message: "The Factory does not own your soul."

Good to know, Alita thought. Then she turned the corner and found the kids skating on a makeshift course in the street, and she smiled for the first time since her encounter with the crazy woman. The kids had jerry-rigged a course with ramps and obstacles all around a plaza with a fountain in the middle. People were sitting at tables eating or drinking coffee and watching the kids swooping and spinning and skidding on motorised rollerblades as they chased a misshapen metal ball. Not as fancy as the real thing she'd seen on that big screen, and they didn't have armour, but they sure had the spirit.

Alita was wondering how to ask if she could get in on the game, or even if she should, when one of the players peeled off the track and skidded to a stop in front of her.

"Hey, Alita," Hugo said, taking off the bandanna covering his head and letting his hair fall free.

She beamed at him joyfully. "Hugo! This is Motorball, right?"

He beamed right back at her and she thought her heart would leap out of her chest and into the air. "Just a scrimmage. You want to join in?"

Her smile shrank a little as several kids rocketed past them. They might not be real Motorball players but they had a lot more experience than she did and they could leave her in the dust.

Hugo tugged at her arm. "Come on—*every* kid's gotta play Motorball!"

"Yeah," she said. Suddenly she had a yen to throw caution to the wind and jump into the game just to see what happened. "Why not?"

"Who's the girl?" Chiren asked.

As usual, she was overdone—fancy make-up, fancy hair, fancy dress, fancy fur jacket, fancy shoes, all vintage designs, possibly handmade by cyborgs who were paid extra for not sleeping or eating till the job was done. It was a desperate city full of desperate people, and Chiren was the most desperate of all.

She had a handkerchief pressed to her face, the way she always did when she was in this part of town. It wasn't remotely anything like an air filter; all it did was let everyone, especially him, know what she thought about everything around her. As they walked along the sidewalk together, Ido had an urge to yank it out of her hand and throw it into the street.

"She's my new assistant," he replied.

Chiren arched an eyebrow at him. "And you like her so much, you decided to give her our daughter's body. Needless to say, I was surprised, since you were supposed to have destroyed it years ago."

"I couldn't," Ido said. "I just—I couldn't."

"Clearly," Chiren said, not bothering to hide her scorn. She never had. "Did you tell your 'new assistant' whom you built that body for?"

"Our daughter is dead, Chiren," he said evenly. "You need to let it go."

Now she gave him an incredulous look. "Well, it's obviously not *me* that's clinging to something here."

He had no answer for that.

"You were the *best*," Chiren went on, "and now look at you. I suppose you think you're doing noble work, wasting your talent on the broken, mouldering masses while you angle for sainthood. Dyson Ido, patron saint of Iron City's rusted, wretched refuse. Don't you think it's about time to end your penance?" She stopped suddenly, her attention captured by a large screen over the taqueria. Ido had no desire to watch the screen, but he couldn't look away as a gang of Motorball Paladins crashed into each other at high speed. Motorball fans loved those pile-ups. One huge hulk in bright chrome armour emerged from the tangle, holding the fifty-pound ball high in the air with one hand.

The waiter who appeared on Ido's left was a wiry older man with a single cyber arm and a big smile for Ido. The man had come to the clinic with no feeling in the cyber arm from his elbow to his fingertips. Ido had fixed the botched job and upgraded the controllers for him.

"What are you having?" Ido asked Chiren.

Chiren wrinkled her nose with disgust. "Nothing."

As if he had to ask, Ido thought. *"Dos tacos y una cerveza,"* he told the waiter.

"Si, muy bien."

"Claymore regains possession!" shouted the announcer in Motorball ecstasy. "But Jashugan is coming up fast, looking for some payback at turn six!"

Back when they had first arrived in Iron City, Motorball had hooked both of them, and it had seemed like the city's one saving grace. Chiren had actually stopped talking about going back. That hadn't fooled him into thinking she'd finally come to terms with their situation and accepted reality. He knew it would be a very long time before that happened, if it ever did. He was well aware that she would still be awake for hours at night, trying to figure out some way to get their old life back, to regain paradise. It had never been any such thing, of course. But there was no point trying to remind her of just how short of paradise their old life had fallen, because she wouldn't hear him.

There were stretches of time when she was so engrossed in the work she did that she forgot to feel sorry for herself. Sometimes he thought she had even forgotten to be unhappy, although that may have been wishful thinking on his part. But it didn't matter now, not since it had all gone bad.

Chiren pointed at a juggernaut in black and gold on the screen who was now leading the pack. "He's one of mine."

As if that were a great accomplishment, Ido thought. It seemed to have slipped her mind that he also knew the Paladin in black and gold. He gave an irritated sigh. "What do you want, Chiren?"

To his surprise, she grabbed his hand and leaned forward, urgency large on her face. "I want us to be a team again," she said. "I've got a great new set-up. And equipment worthy of your skills." The hanky was no longer over her mouth because the hand holding it was stroking his arm from shoulder to elbow. "Work with me," she said, her invitation becoming a plea. "Together we can build Champions—the finest players the game has ever seen." She took his hands in hers. "And that can be our ticket home."

Ido pulled away from her. "When are you going to realise *there's no way back*?"

"*Vector* can make it happen," she said, almost snapping.

"I can't *believe* you trust Vector."

"He's got very high connections." There was a note of petulance in her voice. "He can get us back to Zalem."

Ido shook his head. "This is my home now."

Chiren's shoulders slumped, as if whatever was holding her up had started to give way. "Please. This is my shot. Help me. *Please.*"

She sounded so desperate his already-broken heart almost broke again. She had that effect on him. He wished that he could take her in his arms and tell her that everything was going to be all right because he would help her, take care of her, do anything she wanted, find a way or a work-around. But if he did, he would be as lost as she was. He pulled away from her.

"I can't help you build monsters," he said. "I *won't*. Your so-called 'champions' have a nasty habit of turning into killers. They wind up living on the street, junkies with big hydraulic arms and bad attitudes. Or have you forgotten?"

Chiren spotted a cockroach crawling on the table and used a napkin to crush it. "I'm going to get back to Zalem," she declared, standing up. "I'll claw my way back up with my bare hands if I have to."

Ido stared after her as she walked away. She didn't have to walk far— before she'd gone even half a block, an armoured limo pulled up at the kerb. She got into the back seat, and as it drove away Ido had a glimpse through an open window of the man sitting next to her. Vector didn't look at him as the window went up.

Ido felt a sudden, intense rush of pity for Chiren. Her histrionic desperation, pawing his arm—it had all been about Vector and for Vector, not him. The son of a bitch was stringing Chiren along, playing her for a fool, promising her things he couldn't possibly deliver even if he wanted to. This had just been his latest ploy: if Chiren could bring him the genius cyber-surgeon and get him to work on Vector's Motorball team, Zalem was a done deal. No place like home, baby.

Ido waited for his tacos and beer, then took them back to the clinic.

CHAPTER 6

Skating was a hell of a lot harder than she'd imagined, Alita thought as she wobbled along the street in the wheeled boots Hugo had loaned her. There was a lot more to the boots than just wheels—there were motors, drive wheels, gears, breakers, suspension, even shocks. It was like wearing cars on her feet. She couldn't get a sense of how they were supposed to work, even with Hugo telling her what to do and holding her hands to keep her steady.

"That's it. Keep doing exactly what you're doing," he said cheerfully. She nodded, but she had no idea what she was doing or how she was doing it. "I'm gonna let go now and you just keep going like you are, okay?"

But as soon as he stepped aside, her feet began rolling away from each other and no matter how hard she tried, she couldn't get them back together. Hugo was keeping pace with her but, maddeningly, he didn't take her hands again. Couldn't he see that she *didn't want* to do the splits?

"Try the remote," Hugo suggested.

Alita had forgotten all about the control button strapped to the palm of her hand. She tried it now, but her arms were flailing as she tried to keep her balance and she clutched it too hard. Her feet accelerated forward suddenly and she went down hard on her butt.

Hugo ran to her and she glowered up at him from under her brows. "You laugh, you *die*," she warned him.

He didn't laugh as he helped her up (still an effort for him, she noticed). "Next time, keep your weight a little lower and more forward," he suggested, walking her over to the edge of the makeshift Motorball track. Several other kids were skating around the course, which was laid out around the trestles of a long-unused highway overpass. "Hey, everybody," he said, waving at the other kids. "This is Alita."

The kids came over to say hello. Hugo introduced her to Tanji, a skinny guy with wiry muscles and a halo of thick, curly brown hair. Alita thought his hair was more fun than he was; he didn't smile much—or at all, really. Maybe he was having a bad day.

The other kids were lots friendlier. There was a tall guy named Risotto, a solid-looking kid named Dif, and a pretty girl named Koyomi, who told her not to mind Tanji. Koyomi wore her hair in long, thin braids gathered high on either side of her head. Alita envied the style and wondered if her own hair would grow that long so she could wear it the same way.

"You know," Hugo said, turning to her as everyone skated back to the track, "sometimes the best way to learn is just to go in."

Alita pressed the palm control, careful not to do it so hard this time, but the wheels still took off faster than she expected. Her arms pinwheeled as she fought to keep her balance, and for a moment she was sure she was going down again. But finally, she straightened out, bent her knees and leaned forward the way Hugo had told her to.

"Hey, I think I'm getting it!" she called to Hugo as she steadied herself. She squeezed the remote and the wheels took off with her just as she realised she had no idea how to turn or brake. She slammed into a concrete pillar, but instead of falling, she rebounded onto the track where she rolled around in crazy loops and zigzags as the other kids zoomed past her in a blur. Still trying to straighten herself out, she hit a kerb, flew forward and flattened an old street sign, before finally coming to rest on her back with her feet in the air, wheels still spinning madly.

"Uh, you can let go of the remote now," Hugo said.

Alita unclenched her fist. "Crap," she said in a small, humble voice.

Hugo helped her up and got her going again, this time on the track. He ran along beside her, reminding her to stay low and forward, then beckoned to the other kids. She felt nervous as they all rolled up around her but Hugo kept talking to her, yelling encouragement.

Koyomi zipped past her, carrying the ball. Alita had a second to wonder what she was supposed to do now before Koyomi whipped the ball directly at her. She amazed herself by catching it without losing her balance or careening out of control. Maybe I really *am* getting the hang of this, she thought. A moment later, something slammed into her. The ball flew out of her hands as she went down in a clumsy belly-flop.

Alita looked up, blinking in confusion. Koyomi was glaring angrily— not at her but at Tanji, who now had the ball. Tanji leaped up, performing a showy near-split in mid-air as he hurled the ball into the goal.

"Sorry, princess," Tanji said to her as he sailed past, skating backwards and laughing.

"Nice one, Tanji," Hugo said, disgusted. "Thanks for that. She's never played before."

Still showing off, Tanji did an effortless figure of eight on a jerry-rigged banked slope. "If she ain't ready to run with the hounds, get her off the track," he said, gliding away.

Hugo offered Alita his hand. She ignored it, getting back up on her feet by herself and watching Tanji do a lazy victory lap back to the starting line. Hugo was saying something to her, probably giving her more advice about staying low and forward, but his voice seemed to come from somewhere far away. Power was gathering inside her, telling her body exactly what to do as she moved to the starting position with all the other kids and dropped into a crouch.

The ball snapped into play and she clenched her fist for full throttle, blasting forward with everyone else, although she was barely aware of them. She only had eyes for Tanji as she pushed herself to go faster. The wheels under her threatened to go out of control but she wouldn't let them, shifting her body weight every time they tried to run away from her, pushing herself to go faster.

The ball zoomed past her, right into Tanji's hands. He looked smug as he turned towards the goal. Immediately, Alita saw how carrying the ball changed his balance and his speed; he wasn't quite as fast or as stable. She drove harder, refusing to lose her balance as she zoomed after him towards the goal.

Tanji looked surprised for half a second when she drew even with him, then tried to cover it with that smug expression. She was going to wipe every bit of smug off his face, Alita thought, looping around in front of him. He feinted left then went right, thinking he'd get around her. He brought up his arm, intending to elbow her in the face—just what she was hoping for. She took hold of his arm and twisted, spun around, then kicked him behind his knees. Tanji went down hard, skidded off the track with his arms and legs in an awkward tangle, and fetched up against a low wall. Alita scooped up the ball, took a flying leap and smashed it into the goal.

The loud *krang!* of the metal ball hitting the goal brought her out of the fury that had taken hold of her. Alita barely managed stay upright as she hit the track again and slowed to a wobbly stop while replaying the last minute in her memory, shocked. What the hell had she done?

Koyomi gave her a slap on the back, grinning like this was some kind of major accomplishment. Hugo had materialised on her other side looking impressed while poor Tanji was getting shakily to his feet, clutching his arm.

"I'm sorry, Tanji. I didn't mean—" Alita said as he glided past on one foot, unable to put his weight on the other.

He wouldn't even look at her and stopped in front of Hugo. "Your freak girlfriend's got some serious malfunctions," he said.

Hugo looked at him with a deeply worried expression. "I'm really sorry," he said, then suddenly burst out laughing, "that she humiliated you so severely!" He ruffled Tanji's hair.

"Yeah, *sure* you are." Tanji slapped at his hand and rolled away.

"Aw, come on, Tanji," Hugo called after him. "Who owns this city?"

Tanji swivelled around to face him and clapped his hands over his head. "We do!"

"Okay, see you tonight," Hugo said, resisting the urge to say he was glad Tanji's arm was better. "And she's not my girlfriend."

Tanji paused. "She's a Total Replacement cyborg. You know how we feel about those."

"She's just a kid," Hugo said, not laughing any more.

"Uh-huh."

"She's also from Zalem," Hugo told him.

"Whatever." Tanji skated off.

Alita heard them but she was too wrung out to pay close attention. It seemed to take everything she had just to get the borrowed wheels off her feet.

"You have some talent for this game," Hugo said, sitting down beside her.

Is that what they call it? she thought. *Brutalising a kid who's all flesh and blood with no cyborg parts is talent?* Guilt and confusion were bubbling around inside her; all she wanted to do was get away before she started crying like a baby or something equally stupid. "I gotta go home," she said. "Ido wants me in the house before dark."

"You wanna ride?" Hugo asked.

Suddenly she no longer felt like crying; in fact, she couldn't smile widely enough.

Hugo hadn't really believed she'd never ridden on a gyro before. But the way Alita was clutching his waist and laughing as the wind whipped her hair—she was definitely enjoying it far more than anybody else he'd ever given a ride to. It was like this was some kind of special treat. But then, from what she'd told him about herself, *everything* was a special treat.

"So you can't remember *anything*?" he asked her. "Not family, friends—not even favourite food?"

"No," she said. "Well, maybe oranges. But that's just since yesterday."

"Nope," he said. "Unacceptable."

"What do you mean?" she asked, baffled.

Hugo jumped a kerb and came to a stop in front of a market stall. This girl needed a *real* special treat. "Give me some chocolate," he said to the woman minding the stall, handing her a few credits. He passed the small brick to Alita. "Eat this. It'll change your life. Trust me."

Alita hesitated, holding the brick between finger and thumb and studying it closely like it was something from another world—which for her it was, he supposed, nodding encouragement at her. Still hesitant, she bit off a small part of one corner.

"Oh my God!" The way her face lit up, she was practically glowing with delight. She took another, much bigger bite, then another, making ecstatic noises between each until it was all gone. "That was *soooo great*!" she said finally, licking her fingertips. "Hey, Hugo—I have a favourite food!"

Hugo laughed, enjoying her reaction. The woman behind the stall was chuckling too, though she also looked a bit puzzled. As well she might, Hugo thought. No doubt this was the only time she'd come across a kid who had never tasted chocolate before. He felt pleased with himself for being the one who had introduced Alita to her new favourite food.

Hugo turned around to fire up the gyro, then paused when he spotted a familiar figure making his way towards them on the sidewalk. The night-time crowds didn't give him much trouble—people were only too happy to get out of his way.

"Check it out," he said, giving Alita a nudge. "Hunter-Warrior."

The cyborg had stopped to take a look at the people around him, a predator in search of his prey. He was all metal and proud of it, his cyborg body an idealised version of the male form, decorated with a profusion of carved designs that everyone was supposed to think were symbols of highly significant things. They might have been, for all Hugo knew—the guy spent as much on body art as he did on plastic surgery to keep himself looking handsome and dangerous. It should have been silly, and maybe on anyone else it would have been. On him, it never failed to intimidate.

"Who *is* that?" Alita said in a low voice.

"He's a bounty hunter. Named Zapan," Hugo told her. "Scanning for his mark. I wouldn't want to be *that* guy."

Zapan was coming towards them now. As he went past, Hugo saw that he'd upgraded his face with new cheekbones and a stronger chin. He had a few more fancy carvings on his back, too, but he was still carrying his trademark weapon.

"What's with the sword?" Alita asked.

"Guns and advanced AI are outlawed in Iron City, punishable by death. Those are things that challenge Zalem."

She looked so creeped out and unsettled that he wished he'd kept his mouth shut and not put such crappy stuff in her head, especially when she couldn't remember anything about her own life. Then it occurred to him how he might be able to make up for that and he started the gyro again.

Alita stared open-mouthed at the enormous ruin of a cathedral as Hugo brought the gyro to a stop. This must have been an incredibly important place since it was so big, she thought. The windows were all empty holes now and part of the roof had fallen in; what bits were left were home to some wind turbines turning lazily in the breeze. But there was still something about it that was—she searched for the right word and came up with—*majestic*.

It really is, she decided. *Like even though it's a wreck now, it's refusing to give in.*

She looked at Hugo, who had gone a bit solemn.

"It's a harsh world," he said. "The strong prey on the weak down here and the Factory doesn't care about anybody. Which is why you gotta stay focused on your dream."

"What's your dream, Hugo?" she asked.

"I'll show you." He motioned for her to follow him.

It didn't take very long to climb up the scarred face of the ruin—there were plenty of handholds and toeholds. Hugo led her all the way up to a platform attached to one of the towers. The sight of Iron City spread out below made Alita catch her breath.

"This is my secret place," Hugo said. "Best view in town."

"It's cool," Alita said, gazing at the lights dotting the darkening land below. "I like it."

"Uh uh, not *that* view down there," Hugo said and pointed upwards. "*This* one. Up *there*."

"Oh," she breathed, staring at the floating city. The structures near the edge were glowing a reddish gold, and here and there she saw lights shining like jewels. Or maybe stars.

"Especially this time of day," Hugo added. "The way the light is. It's the most beautiful thing in this whole ugly world."

Alita wished she could see the buildings better. The people in all those buildings glinting in the dying sunlight—what were they doing? Were they watching the sunset? Was it more beautiful from up there? Or did they have something better to look at?

"I wonder what it's like up there," Alita said wistfully.

"Better than this dump down here," Hugo said. "I mean, it's *gotta* be."

Alita wished he didn't sound so dispirited, that being here with her could make him as happy as she was to be with him in his special place.

Suddenly he touched her shoulder and said, "Listen!"

She heard a whooshing noise above her and looked up to see the long arc of a tube stretching upwards across the sky, all the way to the floating city.

"That's the sound of stuff going from the Factory up to Zalem. But the tubes are only for supply shipments, food and other things, not people." Hugo sighed; his longing radiated from him like heat. "Y'know, if I were as strong as you, I'd climb that tube to Zalem right now."

She blinked at him. "But they don't let anybody go up."

Hugo gave a short, humourless laugh. "That's what they *want* everyone to think. You gotta know the right people. I happen to be connected." He pointed at the skyscrapers sparkling as sunset turned into night. "You have to be willing to do what it takes—*whatever* it takes.

One day—and not too long from now—I'm going to be waving down at this garbage heap from right up there."

Alita couldn't take her eyes off his face. It was like he was glowing as the wind lifted his dark hair. The way he looked now—*he* was the most beautiful thing she had ever seen, not Zalem, and she wished she could tell him that.

"You're looking at me funny," Hugo said.

"No." She smiled. "I'm just… looking."

"You think I'm crazy," Hugo said, a bit accusingly.

"I don't," she told him. "I respect you for your dream."

Something fluttered around her. She put out her hand and a butterfly came to rest on her finger, its orange-and-black wings beating slowly and deliberately, almost like a heartbeat. A heart with wings. It let her study it for a few seconds before it lifted off again, flying a leisurely course down into the cathedral, where golden sunlight poured through the vacant windows onto a small area of grass that had grown up to make a wild meadow in miniature among the rubble and broken stones.

"I want to see what's up there so bad I can *taste* it," he went on. "And the funny thing is—" he turned from Zalem to her. "You've already seen it, but you can't remember."

"What do you mean?" she said, puzzled.

"Doc found you in the scrapyard. All that stuff is dumped from Zalem. So *you* must be from up there."

"Oh. Well. I guess… I dunno." She shrugged awkwardly, unsure what to say.

Hugo took her by the shoulders and looked earnestly into her face. "If you could only tell me what your eyes have seen."

"I wish I could," she said, thinking he had no idea how much she wished she could, if it would make him happy. "But to be honest, I have a feeling I couldn't have been anyone very important. Just an insignificant girl, thrown out with the rest of the garbage." She looked over at Zalem and, as if on cue, trash poured out of the torn bottom of the sky city.

They sat and watched as debris continued to fall.

CHAPTER 7

Ido caught Alita trying to sneak in undetected. He was at the top of the stairs leading from the basement, wearing an apron, which should have made him look silly with all the frills and ruffles, but it didn't, not even a little.

"I asked you to be home before dark," he told her sternly, marching her into the kitchen and sitting her down at the table.

"I'm sorry," she said. "I lost track of time."

Ido sighed. "I told you, don't trust anyone. People can do terrible things to each other here."

Her gaze fell on the bandage on his forearm. He'd changed it since she'd gone out but a little heart's-blood had seeped through. She looked up at him. "Are you okay?" she asked with a slight emphasis on "you".

"Yes, I'm fine," he snapped as he put a plate of food in front of her. "Eat this. You still need proper nourishment for your brain."

She hesitated, frowning at her dinner doubtfully. It smelled pretty good but it didn't look terribly exciting. She looked up at him again. "Do you have any chocolate?"

They stared at each other for a long moment, then they both burst out laughing. He was still chuckling a little while he expounded on corn, potatoes, green beans and chicken, which was actually fortified chicken product, and how each food would benefit her brain and central nervous system because even Total Replacement cyborgs did not live by the nanos in cyber-blood alone. It was all pretty good, but none of it was chocolate. Not even close.

Alita went to bed as soon as Ido told her to, making a big show of yawning and looking like she could barely keep her eyes open, but a show was all it was. She was wide awake when she heard the *squeak-squeak-squeak* in the hall, and she was ready. She fully intended to count to thirty before she followed him out of the house so there would be less chance of his catching her but she barely made it to twenty; losing him, she decided, would be worse.

Fortunately, the suitcase slowed him down. It wasn't very big but it was awkward on rough pavement. It was also heavier than she'd thought. He kept having to turn around and tip it onto two wheels so he could drag it over kerbs and broken sections of pavement. Following him on the street, she had to hang back so much there was a very real chance she'd lose him.

But there *was* a way she could put more distance between them and still stay close—and she had Hugo to thank for it. The building she scaled didn't have quite as many hand- and toe-holds as Hugo's cathedral, but it did have windowsills and pipes and it was only two storeys tall. She was able to keep pace with him, leaping the gaps between one rooftop and another with no trouble. Sometimes she could even move ahead of

him and wait to see which street he would choose, whether he would go left or right or straight on.

This was how she spotted the woman. All she could really see of her was a pair of very shapely legs and a few centimetres of very short skirt; the rest of her was hidden under a hooded jacket. At first Alita thought she was merely on her way home after a night out and hadn't been able to find a cab. But while the woman was walking at a good pace—her high heels clicked so loudly on the pavement, Alita knew where she was just by listening—she was in no hurry.

She also seemed to be taking a very roundabout way home; she saw that the woman walked along streets without making much progress in any one direction. Was she lost? If so, she didn't act lost. She didn't stop to peer at building numbers, she never stopped to look around or get her bearings. She just kept walking and walking and walking, the way people did when they knew exactly where they were going.

And so did Ido. Alita saw from her elevated vantage point that the route he took was somehow connected to the woman's. Sometimes he got to within a block of her and Alita knew he must have been able to hear those high heels going *tik-tik-tik* on the pavement. But he never got within sight of her—

Ido, she realised with cold horror, was *stalking* the woman in the hood.

No, he couldn't be. Not Ido. He *wouldn't*.

The woman entered a narrow passageway and went down a flight of cement stairs, pausing for a moment to look behind her. Ido wasn't there. He had gone down a different street and stopped on a corner. Alita held her breath. The woman came down the stairs barely a block up from Ido and was now walking straight towards him.

And Ido knew it.

He opened his case and took out some metal rods, one of which had a weird head on it—one side looked like a hammer, the other came to a deadly-looking rounded point. From her vantage point above and behind him, it was hard to see exactly what the thing was. Alita leaped to the next roof, which was a little bit lower. She tried to be silent but she made a small scraping sound when she landed.

She froze, holding her breath, waiting for Ido to call out, but he didn't. Finally, she crept over the low brick wall at the edge of the roof and peeked down at him. He was apparently too absorbed in putting that hammer weapon together, he didn't hear anything—except the *click-click-click* of that woman's high heels. He fitted the pieces together and flipped a switch. The thing came alive in his hands and Alita knew he was going to use it on the hooded woman. Feeling as if her heart had shattered into a million pieces, she leaped down two storeys and landed in front of him.

"No! Stop!" She grabbed the shaft of the hammer weapon with both hands.

Ido's jaw dropped. "Alita?! What—"

"I'm *not* going to let you kill her!" she shouted, trying to pull the hammer away from him. She turned to look at the woman but she was gone. There was no one on the street except her and Ido.

In the next moment, she heard a low, rumbling laugh echoing through the labyrinth of narrow alleys around them, the alleys the woman had been walking through. The shadows around them seemed to shift as one, moving towards them and swelling into a silhouette three metres tall.

Alita heard a long, nasty scraping sound on the street behind her and Ido. They turned to see a second cyborg, a gangly metal skeleton with a tuft of purple-and-white hair and a death's-head grin, holding a blade in one hand.

"A trap," Ido said, his voice absurdly matter-of-fact.

"Looking for me, Doctor?" said the eight-foot shadow. "Or should I say *Hunter-Warrior*?"

Alita gaped at Ido. Dr Ido, the cyber-surgeon who had laboured for days to embed her core in this work-of-art body, a Hunter-Warrior? There had to be some mistake—

"Oh, no!" said the skeleton, shuddering in fake terror. "Looks like he's got us now! I'm *so scared!*"

Ido stepped in front of Alita protectively. "Alita, don't move," he told her.

"Thanks for bringing a girl," said the skeleton, and he clanged his blade against his ribs, making sparks. "That's gonna save us time."

Ido and the skeleton charged each other. Alita stepped back, hearing the hammer roar. Blue flame burst from the back of the hammer's head as it slammed into the skeleton's forearm and tore it off. It clattered loudly on the street and the skeleton staggered backwards, laughing.

"Nice shot for a meatboy!" he jeered.

Ido swung at him again, but the skeleton side-stepped and the hammer took a chunk out of a concrete wall. The skeleton laughed and swiped at Ido's shoulder with his curved blade. To Alita's horror, the hammer cartwheeled out of Ido's hands as he staggered back, bleeding.

"Nooo!" Alita screamed.

Ido dived for the hammer but a shapely leg with a spike heel slammed down on the handle, and a long black blade appeared at his throat. The woman Alita had thought Ido was going to kill crouched over him, putting her carefully made-up face close to his.

"Did you come to rescue me?" she said. "That's so *sweet!*" She used the blade to flick his glasses away. "Say, you have nice eyes."

"*He's mine!*" yelled the skeleton, clutching his mangled arm. "You can have the *girl.*"

Alita took a step back and then another, moving farther down the alley behind her.

"I don't care, so long as I get his eyes," said the woman, touching the tip of her curved black blade to Ido's cheek.

The other two closed in on Ido, and the skeleton yanked him up by his hair.

Ido squeezed his eyes shut. "Alita, run!" he yelled.

Alita ran—

—flat out, hard and fast, her feet pounding the pavement as she made herself go faster, faster, *faster*, then launched herself into the air. There was a loud metal *clang!* as she slammed into the skeleton and sent him tumbling away from Ido. She stayed on him, her fists moving almost too fast to follow until there was only a pile of twisted metal junk on the street.

Ido stared at Alita and the wreckage she had created in disbelief. "My God," he breathed. "Alita...?"

The giant stepped all the way out of the shadows with a roar of anger. He had impossibly broad, muscular shoulders and thick arms that hung too low, a head the size of a barrel, and a body that looked like a tank that had been hammered into a shape that was supposed to be humanoid.

"*Rip that flea!*" he bellowed, pointing at Alita.

The other cyborg came to life, throwing off her hooded jacket, and Alita saw that her face and her shapely legs had been her only human features. From the waist up, her shiny black metal body was segmented like an insect. She extended her arms, showing off triple joints like those of a praying mantis and the nasty curved blades on the end of each one.

"You're so *beautiful*," she gushed at Alita. "I want to rip you open and see if you're ugly inside, like all the others."

Evil certainly could find its form in this city, Alita thought and then leaped at her.

Ido shook off the shocked incredulity that had frozen him in place. His little girl needed him—

Or did she?

As the insectoid's curved black blade sliced through the air, Alita jumped clear effortlessly as if she were levitating. She rebounded off one of the old causeway pillars and sprang back towards the cyborg. Ido dived for his hammer, started it up, drew back for a swing—

Only to find his hands empty. The eight-foot monster took the hammer in one hand and Ido by the neck with the other. It pinned him against a wall, turning his head, forcing him to look at Alita.

"Watch her die," the cyborg commanded him.

The insectoid's homicidal madness was in full bloom as she slashed at Alita with her nasty black blades. Alita evaded every swing, gradually moving nearer until she was close enough for a powerful kick that sent the insectoid flying backwards to slam into the wall behind her. But just before smashing into it, the insectoid twisted her body with a sudden frightening ease and hit the wall on her feet, upside down and unhurt. Grinning, she clung there for a second, then sprang at Alita.

Alita was already in motion. She met the insectoid in mid-air with a crash of metal, ramming her into the wall again. Moving with the fluid grace of a dancer, Alita turned her body, pointed her toes at the insectoid's skull, and drove it against the stone. The segmented body slid down to the ground, headless, blue cyber-blood gushing out of its ruined neck like a fountain. Alita somersaulted backwards and dropped into a crouch facing the eight-foot cyborg.

The monster dropped Ido and smiled at her, showing gleaming metal teeth like knives.

"Come here, little flea." He raised one massive hand and pressed his forefinger and thumb together: *Tick! Tick! Tick!* "Come here so I can pinch your head off."

Alita sprang at him, easily dodging his arm, which smashed into a concrete barrier hard enough to make his whole body shake. She came down behind him and immediately launched herself straight up to make her next move. But just as she rose past his head, he reached up and swatted her, sending her backwards into—

A sudden blinding flare of light.

Time stopped.

Alita found herself looking down at a stark black-and-white landscape, lifeless rock and dust under a black sky filled with unblinking stars. Time started again, but it moved at a crawl now as she drifted down towards the lifeless, dusty surface. Her body was different, much more heavily armoured. This was a body meant for danger, for combat, although she didn't know how she knew that, any more than she knew why the number 99 was printed on her shoulder. She only knew she was ready.

Her shadow was floating down in front of her. She pointed her toes and they met her shadow in a burst of ancient dust. Immediately, time shifted into normal speed and she was bounding over the dead landscape, charging towards a squad of enemy soldiers also in combat armour. She knew they were as ready as she was.

Alita exploded into action, becoming a lethal storm of blows and kicks, her movements not frenzied but disciplined, born of the martial art that she lived to follow and that now kept her alive. Each enemy soldier that advanced to kill her died at her hands instead; each death was another move forward. She had to keep moving forward, too fast and too deadly for anyone to stop her.

One after another, the enemy soldiers reached for her, lunged at her, then fell away from her as she took them out, twisting their bodies, tearing them apart. Fighting her way through them, she turned to look at the person fighting by her side with moves just as fast and deadly. The face looking back at her was one she saw every day, fierce and unafraid and unrelenting: Gelda, her squad leader.

There was a sudden brilliant flash overhead and everything went white. She heard Gelda yell, "Incoming!" The white faded out and Alita looked up to see warships soaring through the black sky, firing missiles and energy beams while the unblinking stars looked on in silence.

The enemy command centre was in sight. Alita gathered herself and leaped again. Gelda watched her trajectory with a warrior's pride.

"You're going to be the best!" Gelda called to her. "The best the world has ever seen—ours or theirs!"

She was flying through the void, saw the Earth hanging in the airless black before the blinding light flared again. The battle was gone and there was a stone wall rushing at her.

The memory of combat suffused her body with knowledge and expertise that let her move without thinking. She caught herself on the top of the wall instead of smashing into it and held on. They were at the causeway now, where the road curved out over empty space to meet connections from high ramps that no longer existed. Beyond it was a darkness unbroken even by the streetlights. Alita took a firmer grip on the wall, watching the monster cyborg advance on her. Behind him, Ido's gaze met hers; then he was running at the cyborg.

As the monster turned to knock him away, Alita bent her knees and aimed herself at the place where his arm met his shoulder, letting out a war cry that came from a place her body remembered even if her mind didn't. She rammed into the cyborg's shoulder feet first, adding a sharp twist just as she hit—another move her body remembered. There was a scream of metal, drowned out by the cyborg's bellow of anger and disbelief as his arm dropped to the ground, splashing cyber-blood on the pavement.

Alita tucked and rolled away, bouncing to her feet with the rocket hammer at the ready when he lunged for her.

"Who are you?" he roared.

In answer, she slammed the hammer into his chest.

There was the loud *crack!* of something enormous breaking apart, something that should have been invincible but had met a force that it could not stand against, a force that had shattered not just its material but the faith behind it. Alita watched as lines of breakage spread over the front of the cyborg's body and, for a moment, she thought the monster might actually fall to pieces in front of her. But he used his remaining arm to hold himself together as he staggered backwards. Ido was gaping like a man going into shock, but he was safe. Alita hefted the hammer and advanced on the cyborg, intending to finish him off.

"You'll pay for this, little flea," he rasped, backing away from her. "Grewishka does not forget! I'll be coming for you—*both* of you!"

Before she could draw back for another swing, he toppled backwards over the side of the causeway. Alita ran to the barrier and looked down but couldn't see anything in the darkness below.

"Alita, are you all right?" asked Ido, his voice high and fearful. "Alita?"

"Another second," she growled, looking down into the darkness. "Another second and he would have been mine."

She raised her head and suddenly felt cool night air blowing into her face. The frustration and disappointment of not being able to finish her enemy drained out of her, leaving her with the feel of bodily lightness that came after expending so much physical energy in an extremely forceful way. It wasn't so much a letdown as a return to a base level that, under battle conditions, didn't even exist.

"Alita? Can you *hear* me?"

She blinked up at Ido, at the blood trickling down his face—heart's-blood. "Oh my God, Ido!" she said, horrified that he was injured. "Are you all right?"

He stared down at her and she couldn't tell if he were mad or sad, scared or confused. Maybe after seeing what she had done with this body, he was sorry he'd put her in it, she thought; maybe he wished that when he'd found her core in the trash pile, he'd left it there.

Abruptly he turned away, pulling her with him.

The little killing machine that looked so much like his daughter walked quietly along the night-time streets beside him. There was no sign of aggression or belligerence, not even a little adolescent bad temper. Since Grewishka's long fall off the edge of the causeway, she had reverted to being only a young girl, worried that he was hurt, wanting nothing more than to go home.

Or more precisely, since about half a minute *after* Grewishka had fallen, when she'd glared down into the shadows and growled about how a second longer and he'd have been hers. As if *she* were the Warrior around here.

Which, he understood now, she was. He had seen it in her, and all the pretty flower designs and silver and gold inlays on her pretty body wouldn't, couldn't, change that. Perhaps he could try to keep it at bay, keep it dormant by being a good father and keeping her out of danger, something he had once again failed to do, and in an even more spectacular way than the first time.

When they got home, she insisted on bandaging his shoulder and he let her. She looked so contrite as she prepared the dressing and cleaned his wound. The fourteen-year-old girl trying to make up for disobeying him, for sneaking out, and putting herself in the middle of a bad situation—

Except if she hadn't, I'd be dead, he reminded himself unhappily. And now she was doing a superb job with his shoulder, using just enough paste to close the laceration smoothly, without lumps. He wondered if this was something she learned from Gerhad or whether it was actually battlefield first-aid that came with her Warrior nature.

But the night wasn't over yet—he still had to deliver the bounties to the Factory. While he didn't really want to take Alita with him in case something else happened that would flip her into full-on combat, he didn't want to leave her home alone, not after everything that had happened. She needed him to talk to, to be with her so she wouldn't have to think about it all by herself. And that was leaving aside the possibility of her sneaking out and following him again if he didn't. Or the possibility that friends of the two cyborgs they'd killed might come looking for payback. If some of them broke in—

He clamped down on the thought and shut it off. It wasn't very likely, given who he was to the Iron City cyborgs, but it wasn't totally out of the question.

He decided to take Alita with him to the Factory. Case closed. No agonising necessary.

He sneaked a sidelong glance at her as they headed for the Factory. She was still quiet, still looking contrite, like any other young teenage girl who had defied a parent and found herself in the middle of a situation far more serious than she'd imagined. And now she was probably wondering how much trouble she was in, how angry he was, how he was going to punish her, and would things ever be the same between them.

Are you sure about that? asked a tiny voice in his mind. *Seeing as how she saved your ass, could you be projecting? Is she really the only one here with something to apologise for? Yes, she thought* you *were the killer—but if she hadn't, Grewishka would have your head on a pike and the bug would be wearing your eyes as earrings.*

Alita—*this* Alita—had been in his life for a grand total of two days, not fourteen years. She wasn't really a young girl, not the way his daughter had been. His daughter had been defenceless, needing his protection. This Alita needed no protection. She might be worried about how angry he was with her, but maybe he should consider about how angry *she* was with *him*. Because he'd seen what happened when she got angry.

The killer in her was core-deep. It wasn't a bad habit she could break or a problem to handle with anger management classes; it was her nature. On the other hand, it wasn't a pure drive to kill. No matter how heated she was, she distinguished between friend and foe. But once she was in motion, she was set to go all the way. She didn't stop once the immediate danger was past.

Another second and he would have been mine.

Even just remembering the sound of her voice gave him a chill.

As they walked up the steps to the front door of the Factory, Ido felt Alita looking at him with a question on her face. When they reached the top, he hefted the sack he was carrying and turned to her.

"Listen," he said, and then his mind went blank. "Listen," he said again, taking out his Hunter-Warrior ID badge. "You—*we*—just killed two of the most notorious criminals in the city, and pissed off a third. Grewishka *will* come for us, even if friends of the other two don't."

Alita nodded. "I understand."

"Before the Fall, there were police to stop criminals and protect the innocent," said Ido. "Now the Factory pays people like me to do their dirty work and stop criminals." *And nobody protects the innocent*, he added silently. He raised his badge over his head. "Hunter-Warrior 17739."

"You're *really* a Hunter-Warrior?" Alita said, her voice quiet and tremulous.

"Can I trust you to stay right here, while I'm inside?" Ido asked her. "You don't move for any reason?"

"Yes," she said in a small voice.

"Good." He didn't really want to leave her outside, but he didn't want her to have any part of the bounty process, not even as a witness. He had no qualms about her safety—no one would start any trouble on the Factory's front steps unless they had a death wish.

The enormous front doors rumbled open. Ido started to go in, then turned back to her. "And *don't kill anybody*."

"I won't," she promised meekly.

Ido upended the sack, dumping the two heads out onto a metal plate so they could be scanned. A deckman slid into place on the other side of the counter. Exactly what deckmen were for was one of the Factory's great unanswered questions. As far as Ido could tell, their only role in the bounty process was to pop up and creep humans out, looking like trash-cans with their cartoon faces and machine voices.

"Bounty for the cyborg Nyssiana is twenty thousand credits," the deckman informed him. "Bounty for the cyborg Romo is fourteen thousand credits."

Ido had a strong urge to tell the deckman that, after all he'd gone through to deliver the heads, the Factory was getting a real bargain. And Romo would have been outraged to know that Nyssiana was worth more than he was.

Tough stuff, fella, Ido thought, watching a mechanical arm sweep the heads into a disposal chute. *She had better legs.*

He had a sudden mental image of the cyborgs' heads tumbling down the chute, falling and falling and falling until they landed on a trash pile where a sadder and even more downtrodden version of humans hunted for salvage while looking up at Iron City, believing it was a better place and wondering what it was like to live there.

His reverie broke as another mechanical arm dropped a sack of credit chips on the counter in front of him. He stuffed them into the pocket of his coat.

Alita was waiting exactly where he'd left her, despite the fact that it was now pouring and she could have taken shelter closer to the building. The killing machine that didn't know enough to come in out of the rain. What *was* he going to do with her?

"You should have told me who you really were," she said.

I could have said the same thing to you, he thought, and bit his tongue so he wouldn't say it aloud.

"Is this just something you do for the money?" she asked as they descended the stairs and headed for home.

"I take the money *for the clinic*," he said firmly, and a bit more defensively than he meant to. "Otherwise I'd have had to close up shop long ago. And there are other reasons I do this work, but I'd rather not talk about them."

"But you *have* to!" she insisted, grabbing his coat sleeve. The emotions of a fourteen-year-old girl were always so close to the surface, so ready to flare. "You're not who I thought you were—but something happened tonight, and *I'm* not who I thought I was!" She stopped, and took hold of both his hands with hers. Her pretty little hands, decorated with pretty little flowers and designs, had a grip too strong for him to pull free. "You know more about me than you're saying, I *know* you do. I need the truth."

He was helpless before her, more helpless than he would have been before the killing machine. After a bit, he heard himself say, "I had a daughter. Her name—her name was Alita…"

CHAPTER 8

Looking out over Iron City confirmed to Vector once again that the best thing about the view wasn't how, during the day, the horizon stretched without limit in all directions, or how, at night, it looked as if there were a fortune in glittering jewels spread out below him.

No, the best thing about it was that he *owned* it. It was his to enjoy, his to control, his to keep. It would always be his and his alone. It was like owning a chunk of the world. Or maybe all of it.

He heard a soft rustle of sheets on the bed behind him. Those were very expensive sheets. Not the legendary Egyptian cotton, but something even more exquisite, thanks to certain textile nanos, very special and very hard to obtain, which he also owned. The woman he shared his treasures with had said she loved the feel of those sheets. He knew Chiren loved the view as well, just by the expression on her face when he let her look at it.

Lately, though, he'd begun to think she no longer had the proper amount of appreciation for the finer things, or gratitude for the generosity of the man who deigned to share his prized possessions with her. It wasn't like she could find anything better lying around, just waiting for her to come along and pick it up.

Vector turned to look at her. Chiren was lying with her back to both him and the view. In one of her moods again. Time to remind her of what was important. He went to the bed and rolled her over, gently but firmly, so she was looking at him.

"I only want my players losing when I tell them to," he said, "and I don't want that left to chance. You promised me champions."

Her blue-eyed gaze was icy and intense. "And you promised me the best of everything. Get those military-grade servos I asked for. Or get your street rats to jack something decent for a change."

He chucked her under her beautiful chin, mainly to push her beautiful mouth shut. "You don't have a winning attitude," he said. His voice was soft but there was no mistaking the edge in it. "Now, how do we look for tomorrow's game?"

She gave him her put-upon look, like he was making her life harder than it had to be. Like she wasn't her own worst enemy. "Claymore's a complete rebuild. Zariki's not tracking in the high-gee turns."

"That so? You know the betting will be very high on Zariki." He leaned in close, wanting her to feel his breath on her face. "How soon you go to Zalem is determined by the quality of your work. And the size of my profits."

She lifted her face as if she were going to kiss him. "I'll be ready."

He didn't have to tell her she'd better be. He got up and left, pausing to opaque the window as he went.

When Vector left a room, it was, as far as he was concerned, empty. It certainly felt that way right now to Chiren. There had been a time in her life when she would have found his attitude totally unacceptable; she'd have done something about it, railed against it, taken a stand. But that time was long gone. Everything was empty now—this room, this building, this world. Her life.

She was about to close her eyes against the outer emptiness and retreat to the emptiness within when she heard some kind of funny scraping sound coming from the window. Vector's precious view; annoyed, she threw on a shirt and got up. If some of Vector's dirty little street rats had climbed up here again, she was going to drop-kick them off the ledge and see how they liked *that* trip.

She tapped the control to clear the window and almost screamed at the twisted, blood-drenched horror looking in at her. Reflexively, she jumped back; at the same moment, the glass shattered and the thing toppled forward into the room, red blood and bright-blue fluid splashing on Vector's expensive carpeting. This room was no longer empty.

Its breath came in raspy shudders as it rolled over and fixed its tortured gaze on her. "Help... me..." it begged.

"Grewishka!" She spat the name, almost gagging. It was hard to believe this bloody mess at her feet had ever been a Motorball star and a serious contender for Final Champion. "You're not the pampered star of the coliseum any more! Why should I waste any of my precious talent on *you*?"

Grewishka made a strangled gargling noise. "Look—*look* what she did to me! Ido's little cyber-bitch!"

All at once, the world tilted sideways and Chiren had to put a hand on the wall to steady herself. "What did you say?" she demanded. "*Who* did this?"

"A... li... ta," Grewishka said, getting the syllables out with a tremendous effort.

Alita. Chiren stared down at the cyborg, at the cracked and broken armour that barely kept his insides from spilling out, the empty socket in his shoulder where his arm had been. She had never seen a cyborg reduced to such a state, on the Motorball track, or anywhere else.

Alita.

As soon as Ido had secured Alita in the surgical frame, the doctor in him took over. He set a neural block to prevent her feeling any pain and removed her legs for scanning and diagnostics. The small cracks he found were right where he'd expected them to be. Otherwise, her pretty, flower-bedecked legs were sound. Now he was studying the solid-state organs in her thoracic cavity and checking the efficiency of circulation in both cyber- and heart's-blood in her upper body.

"I don't see any internal damage at all," he said. "Just those cracked bushings in your leg. You'll have to go easy on it until I get them replaced." For once there was something other than more servos at the top of his shopping list. Gerhad would faint.

He was running through a mental list of other parts he might upgrade or replace when he heard Alita say, "So this girl was your daughter? You built this body for her."

She was looking at the holo on the desk behind him. It was the last picture he'd taken of Alita. She was thin and frail, as she always had been throughout her too-short life. But she'd had a smile that could light up a room. She always looked so hopeful, like she was sure something good was just around the corner. That had been his fault.

"Yes," he said, "that was my daughter, Alita." Dr Dyson Ido, CMD, consummate professional, wavered slightly and had to take a steadying breath. "She was really looking forward to waking up with legs that worked—legs that would walk and run and take her anywhere she wanted to go."

In his peripheral vision, he saw tears welling up in Alita's eyes and he willed her not to cry. He wasn't sure Dr Ido could maintain control if she did, and she needed a doctor to close her chest cavity and reattach her legs, not a grieving father.

"You made her a pair of fast legs," said Alita.

"She never got to use them," Ido replied. He meant to leave it at that but he couldn't. "A patient of mine came to the clinic one night… looking for drugs. He was a Paladin, a star of the track—or he had been, before Motorball used him up and threw him away. The Game did that. It still does. A lot of Hunter-Warriors started out looking for glory on the track. The lucky ones end up looking for bounties on the street. The unlucky ones—"

In his mind's eye, he could see the crazed cyborg rampaging through the lab as clearly as if it had happened an hour ago. Once upon a time, this cyborg had been a man like any other, not perfect but reasonable, a man who had wanted something other than the Factory treadmill of producing goods for people living better lives in a better place. With no way to get up there, he'd tried to make the best of what Iron City had to offer, and like most things in Iron City, it had all gone bad on him.

"I was a Tuner for the First League," Ido went on, "and when I looked at him, all I saw was someone strong and healthy, ideal for cyborg enhancements. I gave him a body of obscene strength, and then I made him even stronger and bigger." For the cheers; because when the crowd had cheered for the Paladin Ido had made, he felt as if they were cheering for him, too, for his talent, his skills, his dedication to the Game. He hadn't been able to get enough of those cheers. Back then, he'd thought the adulation of Motorball fans was the most addictive high in the world.

He'd been sadly, terribly, horribly wrong.

"I turned him into a demon—*my* demon," Ido added, "and he came back to me."

Ido had barely recognised the creature running amok in his lab, ripping the doors off cabinets, yanking out drawers, sweeping equipment off shelves and tables in search of the drugs that made him feel invincible on the track. His right arm was gone below the elbow; his left was a mish-mash of cheap tech that had been swapped out for the better hardware he had sold to buy drugs.

Ido's first thought had been to talk him down from the frenzy of his need so he could get close enough to hit him with a sedative. But his scarred and battered demon had taken one look at him and known immediately with the sharp and unerring instincts all junkies develop that there was no help for him here, that Ido only wanted to stop him, and once that happened, the days of feeling invincible would be over for good. He had picked Ido up with his one hand and heaved him through a bank of equipment, destroying delicate machinery it would take months to rebuild. His demon had made him part of the destruction.

As Ido had struggled to get to his feet, wincing at the broken glass stuck in his hands and face, the cyborg finally gave up looking for the drugs his system craved. He turned away and blasted through the double doors into the hallway, where—

"Alita—" Ido's voice trembled a little. "Alita couldn't get out of the way fast enough."

The thin little girl in a cyber-chair, always hopeful, always anticipating something good, had picked the wrong moment to follow her father to his laboratory. Ido had had a momentary glimpse of her face, pale and frightened, before the demon turned his madness on her; she hadn't even had time to scream. But the last image of her face burned forever into

Ido's brain (he couldn't remember her smile without the holo), made him think it hadn't really been so quick for her, that the terror she'd felt had made the last second of her life seem like an eternity.

Not for the demon, though—he'd killed Alita without even slowing down. Ido reached the hallway just in time to see him burst out the door at the other end while Alita's wrecked wheelchair tumbled down the hallway behind him as if it were trying to catch up and remonstrate.

"Alita's mother, Chiren, couldn't deal with her death," Ido said after a pause. "Or maybe she just couldn't deal with me. Or both." He shrugged. "Probably both. She went away—she went with the winning team. But I couldn't go back to the Game. I went hunting instead."

Every good Hunter-Warrior needed a weapon—not just *a* weapon but the *right* one. He'd looked high and low for that weapon. When he hadn't found it, he'd gone home and made it himself. It was the first and only thing he had ever made for the purpose of taking life rather than saving it. As soon as he'd picked up the finished product, it had felt *right* in his hands, as if it were something he had been destined to build. And use.

"I needed to kill him," said Ido. "Or maybe I was hoping he would kill me."

But he hadn't, and somewhere deep down, Ido had known he wouldn't. He could remember every moment, every swing of every kill. Each time he had gone hunting, there had never been any doubt in his mind that he would be coming back with heads for bounties. Even tonight, when three monsters had had the drop on him, when he'd been dangling from Romo's grasp by his hair, on the verge of having his throat cut, he'd been sure that somehow he'd be going home with a bag of credits from the Factory.

"It brought me no peace," he said. Calm and steady; apparently the doctor in him decided that confession would be good for the soul. "There were other demons like him out there, and I felt somehow I was responsible for all of them. So I registered as a Hunter-Warrior. There was nothing noble about it."

"Did you ever find peace?" Alita asked.

He smiled. "I found you."

"But I'm not your daughter," she said, sounding apologetic. "I don't know *what* I am."

"I do." He hit the switch for PROJECT on one of the screens. Immediately a life-size translucent 3D graphic of Alita appeared, showing all her internal systems. "Have a look at your original cyber-core." He gestured at the graphic to highlight her head, neck and the structural column extending into her chest.

"Here's your brain," he said, pointing. "It's a normal healthy teenage girl brain—if there is such a thing." He chuckled, then lowered his hand to the chest area. "But this is your heart, part of your original core. It's powered by an antimatter micro-reactor."

"So I've got a strong heart, right?"

She didn't understand, of course. How could she? "You have a heart that could power all of Iron City—for *years*. And your skull—it's a precision-machined carbon-nanotube composite."

Her quizzical expression made him smile. "This is *Lost technology*," he told her. "Nobody's made this stuff since… *before the Fall*."

Alita blinked at him, then laughed. "Yeah, right. Like I'm three hundred years old!"

Ido waited for her to wind down, then said, "Sweetheart… you are."

Sweetheart… you are. You are.

Ido's words echoed in Alita's mind as she sat on her bed hugging her knees and gazing out of the window at the full moon beneath Zalem. The moon; she'd been there, fought there. Killed there.

What you saw was a flash from your previous life, Ido had told her. *You were someone very special, and* very *important.*

Her gaze fell on a stuffed animal and she picked it up. This had belonged to a different teenage girl, one who didn't have memories of fighting and killing on the moon or anywhere else. How could *she* be holding it in her hands?

Abruptly she got up and went to the full-length mirror.

Who was I? she had asked Ido.

Good question. All at once, she was moving with graceful strength, her body taking itself through a martial kata, moving fluidly from one striking position to another with a precision that felt reassuringly familiar.

In time, you'll remember, Ido had told her.

She threw her fist straight at the mirror, stopping the movement with her knuckles precisely one centimetre away from the glass. She had no idea how she knew it was a centimetre but she did.

Slowly, she lowered her arm. The girl in the mirror looked lost.

CHAPTER 9

"A *space* battle?" Hugo said, standing beside Alita as she looked over the makeshift Motorball track they'd set up in the drainage canal. The girl definitely wasn't from around here, just like Ido had said, but Hugo really didn't know what to make of what she'd told him. "You really think you were remembering the War? *The* War?"

Instead of answering, Alita skated away from him. At fifty metres, she turned, and came back at full speed. Hugo grabbed a bamboo pole and held it out in front of her at knee level. She jumped it easily and landed without a wobble. He shook his head. When she'd started out yesterday, she'd barely been able to stay upright. Then she'd kicked Tanji's ass, and it was like she'd been born on wheels.

"I mean, if you're really *that* old," Hugo continued, "and you have an organic brain—"

"Ido says my biological age is somewhere between fourteen and eighteen," Alita said, in an offhand way that made Hugo grin. Closer to fourteen than eighteen, he thought. "And somewhere along the way, time must have stopped somehow."

And then, as if she'd just told him something mundane like she thought it was going to rain (always a good bet in Iron City), she skated off again. Hugo watched her whip through the obstacle course he'd set up with trash barrels, kegs, boxes, and the wooden slam-dummies he and Tanji had cobbled together for serious practice. Tanji would probably kick his ass if he knew he was letting Alita use them, Hugo thought. But even at full speed, she swerved and dodged around all the obstacles without hitting even one.

"Wait a minute,' Hugo said when she skated up to him, catching her arm to keep her from rolling away. "You were in a space battle and then time stopped? How does *that* work?"

"Suspended animation," Alita said, shrugging. "Ido thinks I entered some kind of time field." As if that explained everything—although for Ido, it probably did. It was probably some kind of genius-scientist shorthand for complicated stuff regular people couldn't possibly understand, and Alita was simply going with it.

Before Hugo could say anything else, she zipped back through the obstacle course. This time, however, she made a point of *hitting* every single thing. Kegs flew, barrels shattered, dummies cracked and splintered, wood fragments went everywhere. Hugo wasn't sure what he was going to tell Tanji. Maybe he wouldn't have to tell him anything— one look at the wreckage and Tanji would know what had happened.

"This is all baby stuff for you," he said to Alita as she rolled up to him. "I think it's going to take more if you want to trigger any of those memories. You need a bigger challenge."

Alita nodded, her face thoughtful. After a moment, she looked down at her skates. "Okay, rip out my feet."

Hugo wasn't sure he'd heard her right. "Say again, Ali?"

"The pros have onboard wheels, not skates, right? It makes a big difference in how they move. They can manoeuvre faster. That's what I need to do. You've got some wheel-feet I can try, don't you?"

She had a point about the manoeuvring but Hugo couldn't help hesitating. "It'll be a big change for you," he said slowly. "But okay, I'll swap them out for you. Hop up on that—" He pointed at an empty barrel lying on its side. "—And I'll get my tools."

She was grinning like a little kid as she watched him remove the skates. They were pretty good skates, but she'd taken them to their limit. Hugo peeled her socks off and then stared. Her feet were as beautiful as the rest of her, perfectly shaped with flowery designs and silver and gold inlays. Ido's work was always recognisable by its sheer excellence, but he had really outdone himself. These weren't merely feet, they were works of art—or rather, part of a larger, even more beautiful work of art.

Hugo looked up at her. "Are you sure?" he asked. "I love your feet. They're pretty special—you wear them well."

"Lose 'em," Alita said, waving one hand in a careless, dismissive gesture. Hugo obeyed, removing them carefully, making sure he didn't tear any connections before he set each lovely foot on the ground by the barrel. He gazed at them for a moment, then realised to his horror he was mentally calculating how much he might get for them on the black market.

Alita's feet—*his friend's feet.*

He got busy attaching the wheel-feet to her legs, hoping she wouldn't pick up on any of his thoughts. Also hoping she would never find out he was the kind of person who thought about how much body parts would sell for. You didn't jack a friend, and you didn't screw with anything Doc Ido made. Those feet were so obviously the doc's work, even if he had been low enough to jack them, he wouldn't have been able to give them away.

There was a name for someone who knew the price of everything and the value of nothing, wasn't there?

Yeah, he thought; in Iron City, they called that "normal".

"You know, I've never seen anyone pick up the Game so fast," he said chattily, focusing on matching up the muscle and nerve links. The doc had made her legs so adaptable, they could probably make a couple of rocks operate as feet.

"I mean it, Ali," he added, double-checking the connections before he attached the other. "You've got the kind of talent it takes to go pro and make serious cash." She smiled at him, but he could tell she was getting restless; she wanted to see what she could do with wheel-feet. As soon as he was finished, she was off the barrel and rolling around as if she'd been on wheels all her life. The girl was unstoppable.

All at once, she was shoving a two-by-four into his hand and explaining how she wanted him to hit her with it. "Aim right at my head," she instructed him, "and don't hold back. Give it everything you've got. Okay?" Without waiting for him to answer, she glided off to set up some of the targets she had hit earlier, the few that were still usable. When she finished, she rolled farther up the track and took a moment to remind him via gestures how to swing the board at her head.

Hugo gave her a thumbs up. The girl sure had talent but she also had a control thing, which might be trouble for her down the line. Only a player with a mountain of talent could get away with bossing everyone around.

Never mind, he thought, watching her come at him full-throttle. By the time Alita hit the pros, her talent would probably be the size of an entire mountain range.

She was definitely faster on wheel-feet and more in control of every movement, changing her roll-stride and posture like a barefoot marathoner. Or like a barefoot marathoner ready for a fight. Using open-palm blows, she took out three of the four remaining wooden slam-man dummies—there'd be no setting those up again, Hugo thought, as they shattered into wood-chip confetti—and destroyed the last one with a perfect flying roundhouse kick.

Hugo frowned. When had she learned how to do *that*?

She landed and, without missing a beat, drove towards him, her legs pumping so powerfully he was afraid she would take him out along with the two-by-four. But he held his ground and when she reached him, he swung the board the way she wanted him to, as hard as he could. She raised her forearm almost casually to block it; the impact knocked it out of his hands.

Hugo wondered if she were going to make another circuit—there didn't seem to be much point since all the targets were down. Instead, she detoured to the nearest ramp, hit it without slowing down, and executed a long backwards flip, which, he realised belatedly, was aimed right at him.

The next thing he knew, he was lying on the ground with Alita straddling his chest, her face scant centimetres from his and one fist cocked for a blow she had thankfully held back.

"So." Hugo swallowed hard. "Did that shake anything loose for you? Did it work?"

Alita's face softened. She drew back and climbed off him. "No," she sighed. "So *frustrating*!"

Hugo raised himself up on his elbows and looked at the remains of the obstacle course. "Well, there's nothing left to break." *Except me*, he added silently.

But he was safe. She helped him up, pulling him to his feet as if he weighed nothing (which made him think of when they'd met), and rolled back to the barrel where her pretty feet were waiting for her. Practice was over for today. Hugo couldn't have been more relieved. As he started to disconnect the left wheel-foot, a sudden thought occurred to him.

"Hey, maybe it's gotta be the real thing. I mean, maybe only a real life-or-death situation can pop up a memory for you," Hugo said. "That's what happened before, right?"

Alita nodded, her big eyes turning thoughtful and distant while Hugo wished he'd kept his big, fat mouth shut. Because he knew damned well she was going to try it, do something crazy-dangerous, just for the sake of her memory, and he'd never be able to talk her out of it. In fact, she'd probably get mad at him for not trying hard enough to kill her.

On the other hand, he thought, looking at the wreckage of the practice track he'd set up earlier that day, *I'd be a fool to bet against her.*

CHAPTER 10

Grewishka's groans and screams were giving Chiren a headache. But then, Grewishka had been a headache even in his Motorball glory days. He'd been a major talent and a serious contender for First Champion, but he'd also been volatile, demanding, egotistical, intransigent, selfish and belligerent. It had been like wrangling a giant armoured two-year-old who had lethal weapons.

Now he was a waste of space and resources that Chiren thought should have been parted out and flushed away long ago. But somebody very important was watching his back for reasons Chiren wasn't privy to, but was obliged to accept. They were probably very good reasons to this very important person, but to her, they were absurd, like everything else in her life.

Fortunately, she was almost done with the painstaking procedure of disconnecting his cyber-core from the wreckage of his body. Grewishka had insisted that she not give him a neural block to cancel out any pain. The idea of him suffering through the operation without relief had given Chiren a sour, spiteful pleasure but it was very short-lived. Suffering seemed to be Grewishka's new passion—he did it with gusto, and he liked it entirely too much. Having to listen to Grewishka's screaming rage had become old pretty damned quickly.

Eventually, the robotic surgical arms disconnected the last of the most minute nerves and freed his core from the ruined body. It should also have put an end to any physical pain but Grewishka had not finished suffering. Hanging in the surgical frame, he looked like an oversized contorting metal worm attached to a giant human head. That was exactly what he was, Chiren thought—a human worm. But at least she could stop and take something for her headache now.

"I want to rip her in half!" Grewishka shrieked as Chiren shook two tablets out of a bottle. She paused, then added a third and swallowed them dry.

She turned around to find Vector had come in. Her head throbbed. Vector knew how she felt about him walking in on her when she was in the middle of a procedure. But it was all part of his possessiveness—he had to keep asserting ownership. He had to keep reminding her that the lab was his, the equipment was his, and she was his.

"Grewishka," Vector said, openly contemptuous. "How the mighty have fallen. You know, I had money on you in your Final Championship game. When you lost, I *lost*." He turned to Chiren. "So, are we stripping him for parts?"

Chiren hesitated, then decided that as long as Vector was here, she might as well show him. "I need you to look at something," she said as she hit PROJECT on one of the display screens and brought up a 3D graphic of Grewishka's skull. "See this?" She pointed at something small and disc-shaped at the base of his brain. "It's a telepresence chip. He's wired," she added in response to Vector's blank expression. "Someone in Zalem is riding him."

"So what?" Vector shrugged. "There are watchers behind eyes all over this town. You know that."

Chiren had never wanted to slap him as much as she did right then but she managed not to. "I'd just as soon remove it, while I'm rebuilding him."

"Why are you wasting your talent on this—this piece of burned-out street junk?" Vector gave a short, humourless laugh. "He's nothing to anyone."

"He's something to someone," Chiren said. "An important someone. It's a personal matter."

Vector drew himself up. Chiren was just a little too tall for him to loom over, but that didn't stop him from trying. "This is *business,* and personal matters have no place in business," he said in his best lecturing tone. "Stop wasting time. Grewishka's junk. Salvage what you can, scrap the rest."

Chiren turned back to Grewishka, intending to tell Vector to go assert his dominance over something else and let her finish her work, then stopped. Grewishka had gone quiet, which was a relief, but his face was calm and composed in a way she'd never seen and didn't like. His eyes were clear and strangely, disturbingly knowing as he looked past her.

"Tell me, Vector," Grewishka said in a polite tone that made the hairs on the back of Chiren's neck stand up. "Do you like your job?"

Chiren had never seen Vector so taken aback. If any of his employees had seen him this way, she thought, he'd have lost his authority over them. "Who—" He had to swallow. "Who is speaking?"

"You know very well who it is," the voice that wasn't Grewishka's replied. "And if you like your position, and all the comforts, privileges and perks that come with it—" His eyes swivelled briefly to Chiren, and she hated the way he looked at her even more. "If you don't want to lose those things, you will pay attention to Dr Chiren. Business is business, but *I* say what your business is. And if *I* say something

personal to *me* is *your business*, you'd do best to listen."

Vector's dark-brown skin took on a greyish quality and Chiren wondered if he were going to pass out. "Nova. I didn't realise you were—" Vector cleared his throat. "Please accept my apologies." All the arrogance had gone out of him; he sounded practically meek now. How the mighty had fallen indeed. "What is it you'd like us to do for you?"

Us? That sounded dangerously close to a willingness to share responsibility, something she'd been sure Vector was incapable of. It might have been a joke, but Vector wasn't capable of that, either.

"Grewishka is like my own son," the Watcher, Nova, said darkly. "Who did this to him?"

Vector turned pointedly to her. So much for *us*, Chiren thought, surreptitiously leaning on the desk to support herself. The thing speaking through Grewishka was making her feel nauseated.

"It was a cyborg girl—a little cyborg girl." It seemed important to Chiren that she add that detail. "These impact points—" She gestured at several different places on Grewishka's wrecked body. "To do this sort of damage would require an extraordinary amount of power. I can't fathom how that much power could be generated by such a small body."

The presence behind Grewishka's eyes gave a harsh, menacing laugh. "It was not the power of the *body* that did this. It was the *mind*. This *little cyber-girl*—" There was pure hatred in his voice. "She knows the fighting techniques of Panzer Kunst. She must be stopped. Rebuild Grewishka—make him better, stronger, more lethal. Have him bring her to me." Pause. "*Dead.*"

Grewishka's eyes lost their focus and his ugly features twisted into a grotesque mask of pain as the lower part of his core began writhing again.

"He's gone," Chiren said, almost limp with relief. She made to get back to work, thinking if Vector didn't know enough to leave, she'd tell him to get the hell out of her operating room. But, instead, he moved around in front of her.

"No, *not* gone—re-patched."

It was Vector's voice, but it wasn't. Chiren barely managed not to back away from him. The presence of the Watcher behind Vector's eyes was so much worse, so much more monstrous. She made herself stand up as straight and tall as she could and focused her gaze on the small area between his eyebrows, so Nova would think she was looking straight into his eyes without flinching.

"You're a very clever woman, Doctor, that's never been in doubt," Nova said silkily. "So I make you this offer: if and when you have pleased me, I will grant you your fondest wish—the destiny you seek."

And there it was: the one thing, the *only* thing she wanted to hear, and in so many words. *Finally.*

"Zalem," she said. "You'll send me to Zalem."

"I'm there right now," Nova said, with the easy, insouciant grandeur that was the hallmark of the powerful. "When I close my eyes down there and I open them up here, I'll step outside, go to the west viewing deck, and watch the sunset. Do you remember the sunsets here, Chiren? What it's like to see them when you're so high up that the rest of the world is already in darkness?"

Now Chiren did look directly into Nova's eyes, staring hard into the dark holes of his pupils, wanting the Watcher to feel the force of her gaze and the power of her presence. *I am here, I am real.*

"You may consider my services engaged," she said, promising everything.

Nova suddenly reached out and grabbed her by the back of her neck, bracing her so he could jam Vector's mouth over hers, thrusting Vector's tongue into her mouth in a deep, penetrating kiss that was as brutal as it was lascivious. It felt like a striking snake, vicious, uncaring, inhuman.

Finally, Nova drew back, grinning nastily. "Sealed with a *kiss*."

Disgusted, Chiren wiped the back of her hand over her bruised lips, knowing she would never be rid of the ugly taste. At the same moment, Vector's eyes fluttered and rolled back in his head. He dropped to his knees in front of her and would have toppled over sideways had she not caught his shoulders and held him up. Seeing the mix of shock and confusion on his face as he looked up at her, she could almost have pitied him. But not quite. *Welcome to my world, you bastard—this is what it's like for me every day of my life.*

"Now that you're yourself again," she said, lifting his chin to make him look at her, "would you mind telling me who—or what—I just made a deal with?"

"The Watcher behind the eyes," said Vector. He put his hands on her hips to steady himself as he got to his feet. "Pray to whatever god you believe in that we can deliver."

We. Was that a slip of the tongue, or did he really want her to think he was in this with her?

"The bigger and more powerful I make Grewishka," Chiren said, "the harder he'll be to control."

"Control?" Vector gave a short, humourless laugh. "He only needs to kill." He straightened his clothes, brushing imaginary lint off his jacket. "Get to work."

There—*that* was the Vector she knew and didn't love, Chiren thought, staring after him as he walked out and left the room empty.

Alita ran around and around the bounty kiosk, weaving in and out of the passers-by as she tried to see every screen and all the paper notices at once. Ido sighed. She had insisted on coming out with him, despite his telling her he didn't like her being out after dark, even with him. But there was no stopping her; she insisted on seeing the posted bounties for herself. If it had been up to her, she'd have dragged him to every kiosk in town.

She hadn't said what she was looking for, but he knew. After she'd made upwards of half a dozen orbits around the kiosk, he decided to put her out of her misery.

"You can forget about finding anything on Grewishka," Ido told her. "There's no bounty on him. Not tonight, not tomorrow, not next week, or in our lifetime. Or ever."

Alita's big eyes got bigger. "But you reported him to the Factory, didn't you? You told them about how he killed all those women with the other two, right?"

Ido nodded sadly, looking down at her. "Grewishka is under someone's protection. Someone important."

"Like who?" Alita demanded. "Who could be so important they'd have that kind of power?"

"Someone far beyond our reach, or the reach of anyone else in Iron City," replied Ido. "So for now, we should stay off the streets. If we lie low, we'll live longer." He put a hand on her shoulder, intending to steer her towards home, but she dug in her heels and wouldn't budge. When Alita *would not* be moved, she *could not* be moved.

"Now, Alita—" he started.

"No, listen to me, I've got a *great* idea," she said. "I want to become a Hunter-Warrior like you."

Ido winced. The way her big eyes were shining, she might have been talking about wanting to take ballet lessons. "*No*, absolutely *not*," he said, trying to be gentle but firm. "You can forget about it right now."

"But we can be a team!" she enthused. "We're *already* a team. We were a team when we—"

"You don't know anything about this," he said, trying to control his impatience. "It's dirty, dangerous work. It doesn't just scar you physically. Ending someone's life is a strike on your soul—"

Alita glared at him, her big eyes dark with anger. "Why are you always holding me back?"

Always? Ido blinked at her. Even in the midst of carnage and catastrophe, a teenage girl was a teenage girl was a teenage girl. *Why are you always holding me back from killing crazed cyborgs?* Of course, given the fact that she'd only been in his life for three days, her claim that he was always holding her back might not be so exaggerated.

"I can't allow it, and that's that," Ido said with all the parental finality he could muster and tried to usher her away from the kiosk again. But again Alita stayed put.

"And just how is that *your* decision to make?"

And here was the typical adolescent demand that parental authority stand and deliver justification for bossing the adolescent in question around. Someone brushed past Ido roughly, knocking him off balance. The same person bounced off Alita without moving her. She noticed; Ido saw her chin jut forward and lift belligerently. He knew this bit of physical superiority proved to Alita he had no business reining her in. He also knew to surreptitiously check his pockets in case the passing stranger had off-loaded some stolen chips or circuits they planned to recover later. The criminal element in Iron City was nothing if not resourceful, and that was only one of many things his little immovable girl didn't know.

"I said it's out of the question and I mean it," he told her. "Don't you remember the cracked bushings in your leg? Your body is not built to take that kind of physical stress—"

"Then make it *stronger*!" she said, as if that were the simplest thing in the world and the solution to everything. "When I'm fighting, I don't just *remember* who I was, I can *feel* who I was. Even if just for a moment."

Ido felt himself sag. "Alita, if that's the only way you can remember anything, then you're better off leaving it all forgotten." He took both her pretty hands in his and turned them palm-up. "I don't want blood on these hands, too."

Alita yanked away from him, practically shaking with rage and frustration. As Ido reached for her again, she turned and ran.

"Alita!" he called, but she had disappeared into the night.

Hugo was hanging out in front of the CAFÉ café with Tanji and the rest of his crew, talking about the upcoming Game, when his cell vibrated on his wrist. When he saw it was Alita, he grinned; Tanji gave him a sour, knowing look. The poor guy was still smarting from the spanking Alita had given him. Perhaps because Hugo hadn't stopped laughing about it. He moved away slightly to answer.

"Where are you?" Alita asked.

"I'm about to head over to the arena for tonight's game," he said, smiling at the sound of her voice, which made Tanji even more sour-faced.

"Can you pick me up?"

His smile got bigger and he hopped on his gyro. "Say where and I'm there."

CHAPTER 11

"...and he just wants me to be his *perfect little girl*," Alita fumed as she followed Hugo through a narrow access tunnel that led to the Motorball track.

Ever since Hugo had picked her up, she'd been venting her frustration with Ido. She'd had no idea how much she had built up in such a short period of time. Now, however, she was finally winding down. Hugo had said she'd have other, better things to think about tonight, and the distant muffled roar of thousands of people cheering and screaming seemed to promise exactly that. Her heart beat faster in anticipation.

Hugo handed her a laminated tag on a lanyard like the one he was wearing around his neck. "Here, put this on," he told her. "It gets us in anywhere."

Alita obeyed, feeling a rush of pleasure at hearing him say *us*.

"So you gonna live by his rules or yours?" Hugo added.

The question took her completely by surprise, partly because she hadn't really been sure he'd been listening to everything she said. "Whose rules do *you* live by?" she asked, honestly curious.

"Nobody's."

The sheer defiant independence of his answer made Alita catch her breath in admiration. *Nobody's.* That one little word contained a whole world of freedom. *Nobody* could force him to do anything. *Nobody* could hold him back. *Nobody* could touch him—except her, because she had a pass like his that would get them in anywhere, and together they were *us*.

She was still marvelling about it when they came up to a tough-looking guy wearing a black t-shirt that said SECURITY on the front in big, danger-yellow letters. Alita watched how Hugo flashed his pass at the man and flashed hers the exact same way, so the SECURITY guy would know where they could get in—anywhere—and whose rules they lived by—*nobody's*.

"I have a small crew," Hugo was saying, "and we only deal in high-end parts." He had to raise his voice to make himself heard over the crowd noise, which was getting louder and louder. "Low overhead, high profit—it's the only way."

Alita nodded, trotting happily along beside him. Low overhead, high profit, and nobody's rules—it was the only way. Easy to remember, too.

The tunnel sloped upwards and then opened out into the enormous, brightly lit stadium where a game was already in progress. There had to be tens of thousands of people, all screaming for their favourite players while an announcer who sounded as if he were in the throes of delirium called the action.

Alita turned around and around, trying to see everything at once. Hugo caught her hand and led her away from the tunnel to a passageway beside the track, which was bordered by a low concrete barrier topped with ten-foot-high plastic shields. Scratches and marks high up on the plastic showed where players had hit hard.

"It takes time to build a name for yourself in this business," Hugo said, yelling now. "Like me, for example—I built a reputation for getting the real hard-to-find stuff. Now people know if there's something they're having trouble getting hold of, I'm the guy to call." Alita could hear the pride in his voice and she felt proud, too. Low overhead, high profit, hard-to-find stuff, and nobody's rules; she'd never learn things like this from Ido.

Hugo stopped and pointed at a knot of heavily armoured cyborg Paladins far up the track, approaching at high speed. As they screamed past, a player in red-and-black armour with knife-like blades running the length of both arms suddenly leaped up and delivered a powerful spin-kick to a player covered in shiny chrome like the knights Alita had seen in one of the books in her bedroom. The shiny chrome Paladin skidded across the track and crashed into the barrier directly in front of her. Alita jerked back, startled but thrilled. A second later, a third player in bright crimson flew over both of them, landing safely out of reach. That Paladin was a woman, Alita realised, watching her zoom away. Women were Paladins! She'd already known that, but actually seeing a fully armoured woman on wheels made her heart soar. *Hello, sister!*

She felt Hugo's lips close to her ear: "Welcome to Motorball."

Alita smiled, thinking it was more like, *Welcome home.*

<hr>

"And *what* a *combination*!" the announcer raved over fifteen thousand screaming fans. "A double-spin kick from Ajakutty sends Claymore into the boards while Crimson Wind leaves them both eating her dust—*and here comes Jashugan!*"

Hugo grinned as the giant screens switched briefly to Jashugan's bodycam to give the crowd a Paladin's-eye view of the track. The stadium crowd was a blur as Jashugan skated into and then out of a steeply banked turn; there was a slight, rhythmic side-to-side motion as he pushed himself to go faster, followed by a brief shot of the Motorball in his possession before the point of view returned to track-side.

Alita had her face pressed to the plastic shield, her big eyes fixed on the action. Hugo couldn't help laughing a little. The last time he'd seen that look on a girl's face, she'd been falling in love. But this girl—well, he'd already figured she wasn't like anyone else he'd ever known, especially when it came to her talent for Motorball. She was absolutely smitten with the game now.

Hugo was about to suggest they move along when something massive flew through the air above them, high enough to clear the shields but close enough for them to feel a breeze in their hair, and landed on a Paladin right in front of them. Damn, Hugo thought, the girl was some kind of action magnet. Things happened around her.

"...and Kinuba hops the pit wall and lands right on number seven, Takie, who goes down hard!" the announcer rhapsodised. "You gotta know *that* one's not in the playbook!"

Kinuba—*that* figured. Hugo watched the one-time champion—not Final, but Kinuba acted like he was—raise his arms to acknowledge the crowd while skating backwards at a hundred miles an hour. Kinuba was a good player and definitely a contender for Final Champion, but the one thing he did better than anyone else was show off.

Hugo nudged Alita and pointed at the giant screen where Ajakutty had just roared out of a banked turn and was now coming up fast on Kinuba, pumping his arms as if he were cutting through the air with the blades. Ajakutty wasn't superstar material—not yet, at least—and he had a smaller following than most of the Paladins. Hugo had never been that interested in the guy himself, but if he made Kinuba eat track, it would be a big boost for Ajakutty and one hell of a comedown for Kinuba—

something Hugo would definitely enjoy seeing. From the way the fans were screaming as Ajakutty gained on Kinuba, a lot of them felt the same.

Just as Ajakutty got within metres of him, Kinuba swivelled around to skate backwards and pointed a finger at the other Paladin.

What the hell was that supposed to be, Hugo wondered. Ajakutty looked as taken aback by the gesture. A second later, Kinuba's finger flew out from his hand towards Ajakutty, trailing a long writhing metal coil.

Ajakutty reared back, trying to slow down and get out of range, but he was going too fast. The bullwhip sliced through his armour, chopping his legs out from under him, then cutting through them again below the knees. Ajakutty went down in a spray of bright-blue cyber-blood mixed with a small amount of red heart's-blood. Hugo felt like gagging. Up on the big screen, one of the crowd cams caught a few fans actually fainting. Well, it wasn't a *real* party until somebody passed out.

The steely whip whistled viciously, like it was slicing through the air itself as Kinuba's finger snapped back into place on his hand. Ajakutty's feet rolled on for a few metres and then, as if finally realising there was no point in going on without the rest of him, toppled over. The crowd reached a new level of frenzy.

"…the Champion Kinuba went through Ajakutty like a red-hot blade through a butter-ball with that newly acquired grind-cutter. And that was only one, folks, the man's got four more!" sang the announcer, transported by such innovative violence. "Somebody tell me, *is that even legal*?"

The passageway was starting to get crowded as pit crews ran to meet their Paladins or to fetch parts for quick repair. "C'mon," Hugo said, pulling Alita away from the barrier. "I know all the pit crews and Tuners. I'll introduce you around. If you're gonna play Motorball, you gotta know these guys. They can save your career, even your life. For *real*."

Hugo towed Alita farther along the pit lane while she kept straining to look back, until they came to another SECURITY guy. Mel was big and scary-looking and he usually had only one facial expression—stone-cold killer—but he actually raised his eyebrows when he saw Alita. Hugo grinned at him but only received his stone-cold killer face. Good old Mel.

Hugo gave Alita a quick explanation of how the pits were organised and how each team had service bays facing onto the pit lane. Paladins always had the right of way on the pit lanes, so you move aside when you see one coming towards you.

Alita's big eyes got even bigger as she took in all the furious activity. She made Hugo stop briefly so she could watch Ajakutty's and Claymore's respective crews swarming over them. The din of power tools and hydraulics actually drowned out most of the crowd noise. She seemed enthralled by how quickly the crews could swap out parts and even whole limbs.

"So, who's the best player?" she asked.

"Well, the best player *ever* was Grewishka," Hugo said and was surprised by her reaction. She seemed startled when there was no reason why she should have been; she didn't know anything about Motorball, so she couldn't have heard of him. Unless Ido had told her something, and, given the doc's feelings about the game, that didn't seem too likely.

"Grewishka had a pretty wild story," Hugo said. "He spent his whole childhood underground—like, actually under the streets, in the sewers and stuff. Somebody found him—don't ask me who or how, nobody knows. But they gave him all the best training and they built him up to be Final Champion, the best Paladin ever."

"But that's not how it went," Alita said, sounding thoughtful.

Hugo paused, remembering. He'd wanted to feel sorry for Grewishka, but he'd never been able to find any sympathy for someone who'd been given everything he needed to succeed—money, a place to live, training, opportunities—and blown it all. "Grewishka burned out and went bad. Got himself banned from the Game. They even scrapped his number."

He pulled Alita to one side so she wouldn't get trampled by Jashugan's pit crew as they ran to meet him. A moment later, the Paladin himself rolled past going the other way while his crew buzzed around him with scanners and other gadgets, checking him for damage.

"Wow," Alita breathed, staring after Jashugan with an expression of utter hero-worship that didn't make Hugo feel at all jealous. Besides, he couldn't really blame her. He'd seen Jashugan up close thousands of times and he still found the guy impressive.

"Right now, I'd say that guy—Jashugan—has the best chance of becoming First Champion," Hugo said. "You know, he runs some of my parts. A lot of my parts, in fact." He couldn't tell if she were impressed or not, but then, it was hard to impress anyone when Jashugan was in the vicinity.

Hugo and Alita followed Jashugan and his crew to their service bay and watched as they strapped him into a maintenance frame so the techies could open him up. The Paladin seemed completely at rest under their ministrations. They removed his helmet to reveal a face composed and calm, with grey eyes fixed on some faraway place or thing that only he could see. Everyone said the best Paladins, the real contenders, were those who could find a still place among the chaos of the game, instead of letting themselves be seduced by the high life, with the booze and drugs and all the other pleasures until they woke up one day with no nerves, no reflexes and no pit crew because they'd moved on to someone without permanent damage.

"What's a Final Champion?" Alita asked.

"It's the highest, biggest, best honour a Motorball Paladin can get," said Hugo. "Every few years, when there are enough really good players to make it worth it, they have these play-offs. Last one standing is Final

Champion, and they get to go to Zalem."

Hugo decided they should move on before Alita got too entranced. He took her past several other service bays, introducing her to the various techies, Tuners, and bosses who waved, called out or high-fived him as they went. Now she did look impressed, and he realised that he very much wanted to impress her, wanted her to think he was important around here and not just some dumb guy who hung out at the Motorball track pretending to be special.

He was about to remind Alita about his reputation for getting hard-to-find stuff when he saw she was staring at something with a weird look on her face. He followed her gaze to a tall, dark-haired woman in one of the bays just ahead of them. She had a fancy-looking servo in one hand and was giving somebody hell on her head-set.

"Twenty-two needs to pit *right now*!" she said angrily. "Unless you really *like* losing? Is that what you really like—losing? No? Then get him in here *now*!"

Then she looked up and saw Hugo and Alita. To his surprise, her expression mirrored Alita's. It was almost like Chiren recognised her, but Hugo knew that couldn't be right. Abruptly, she turned away to talk to the expensively dressed dark-skinned man who was overseeing all the activity from a seat behind the service bay. Or maybe it was a throne.

"The guy over there? That's Vector," Hugo told Alita. "He pretty much runs Motorball. Everybody's supposed to think it's run by the Factory Commission, but it's really Vector calling the shots—who skates, who doesn't, which teams play which, and when, and who's a serious contender and who's washed up. Me and my crew, we do a lot of business with him and the teams he owns personally, getting all the best parts for his new Tuner."

"Chiren," Alita said, nodding. "I know her."

Hugo's jaw dropped. For once, he couldn't think of a single thing to say.

"Hey," she said, her big eyes twinkling with amusement at his reaction, "you're not the only one around here who's *connected*, you know."

Damn, he thought as they continued along the pit lane. How the hell was he supposed to impress her now?

Chiren watched the two of them move on, then turned back to what she was doing. On a nearby screen, Kinuba emerged from another messy pile-up intact and relatively unscathed, except for a few scorch marks on his armour. He was holding the Motorball high over his head, and the crowd's screams were especially loud because another Paladin's detached, smoking hand was still stuck in the finger-holes. God, the guy just never stopped showing off.

Vector gave her a tap on the shoulder that wasn't quite hard enough to be a physical blow and shoved a palm-sized display under her nose. "Look at this," he ordered her. "It's Kinuba. He's too strong with that new weapon and it's screwing up the odds. Bets are in the toilet."

As if that were *her* problem, she thought, annoyed. Betting was his turf, tech was hers. "Well, did you talk to him?"

"Of course I talked to him," he said, almost snapping at her. Almost; he made a point of never losing his cool unless he was behind closed doors. "The prick refused to take a fall, even for a twelve-game guarantee."

"Those grind-cutters *are* pretty remarkable," Chiren replied. "I'd like to have something like that for our, uh, other project."

An approving smile spread slowly across Vector's face. He really hadn't thought of that himself, Chiren realised, hiding her amazement. Vector, the big boss, in charge of everything, Mr Big. It made her wonder how he'd managed to stay on top for as long as he had.

Oh, right—he had her.

Vector grabbed a pit boss by the arm as he was going past and pointed at the kid with the big-eyed girl. "Hey, what's the name of that kid who runs the parts crew? You know, the one that gets all the hard-to-find stuff?"

The boss looked. "That's Hugo. Don't know who he's got with him but she's cute."

"Yeah, real cute," Vector said, smiling as he sat down again. "Thanks."

That magic time of the evening arrived, the golden hour when a portion of the crowd were no longer satisfied with watching violence and had to cut loose themselves. Several times Hugo pulled Alita off the pit lane so she wouldn't get caught up in any fistfights or run over by crazed fans trying to climb onto the track. But not because he was afraid she'd get hurt—he doubted even a cranked-up giant had much of a chance against her.

"So how do you like the Game?" he asked her.

Her answering grin was practically feral. Alita had heard the call of the wild and she couldn't wait to answer. "I *like* it," she said.

Before Hugo could say anything else, Tanji appeared beside him with the rest of the crew. "Call came in from a VIP," he told Hugo. "We gotta go."

That only meant one thing and it wasn't *Let's go out for a beer.* "Sorry, Alita," Hugo said. "Can you get home okay?"

"Yeah. Sure." The girl was trying not to look too disappointed, but those eyes said it all. She'd never be able to hide her feelings, Hugo thought, which wasn't a good thing in Iron City.

Behind him, Tanji made an impatient throat-clearing noise to let Hugo know he was keeping them waiting, which meant he was keeping the VIP waiting, and that was no way to do business. Still, Hugo hesitated; he had to think of something or those big sad eyes were going to be in his head all night.

"Hey, can you go out tomorrow?" he asked her. "I want to show you a place me and Tanji know." He glanced at Tanji with a smile, as if Tanji weren't trying to blow up his head with a death-ray glare. "It's out in the Badlands. I think it might even help with your memory."

Alita's face lit up and Hugo felt everything in the world glow. "I'd appreciate that. Thanks." She caught his arm as he started to leave and added, "For *everything*."

For a moment her radiant smile had him rooted to the spot, and he wished he could stay just a little bit longer. But he'd pushed it to the limit with Tanji, and now even the rest of the crew were antsy. Hugo hopped the rail between the pit lane and the front row of seats to join the crew already following Tanji to the access tunnel. But he couldn't resist taking one quick look back.

Alita had her face pressed up against one of the shields again. In profile, she looked oddly serious, like she thought Motorball might be the answer to all the questions in her mind.

CHAPTER 12

There were three main kinds of drinking establishments in Iron City: joints, dives and hell-holes. The Kansas Bar was definitely behind door number three. But it wasn't just *any* hell-hole—it was a Hunter-Warrior hell-hole.

The owner had long ago resigned himself to the fact that bounty hunters had made his place their turf; this meant, among other things, they called the shots as to who could drink with them. Usually these were either attractive companions who were partial to the company of Hunter-Warriors without insisting on commitment, breakfast or being remembered from one night to the next, or Paladins, mainly because a lot of Hunter-Warriors had been Paladins themselves. Only a few of them were like Dyson Ido, who was welcome everywhere.

In general, the Kansas Bar's core clientele preferred to drink with winners, like Paladins who had won at least half a dozen games in a year. The number wasn't an absolute cut-off but it served as a guide. Having winners on the premises raised everyone's property values; losers were ejected as quickly as possible before they stank up the joint with failure.

Kinuba had earned his way into the Kansas Bar many times over. He was not only a champion, but a Hunter-Warrior favourite. There were a lot of advantages to being a Hunter-Warrior favourite. For one thing, he couldn't remember the last time he'd bought his own drinks; in the Kansas Bar, that was really saying something. The Hunter-Warriors who drank there could afford to be generous but they weren't charitable. If one of them bought you a drink, you deserved it.

And for another thing, he could walk out with the three best-looking ladies and nobody would shoot him in the face. Well, not unless he tried poaching a lady from someone who already had her attention, and Kinuba had never been *that* drunk or crazy. Kinuba had *standards*, dammit. Sadly, not everyone did.

That was the way of the world, though, and he knew he shouldn't have been surprised whenever he met someone without standards. But somehow he always was, mostly because the slimeballs would show up in places where they shouldn't be.

Like that son of a bitch, Vector. He ran the whole damned Motorball Game *and* had a whole stable of Paladins playing on teams he owned. The guy had to have money falling out of every hole in his body, out of his friggin' *pores* even, and still he didn't think he was rich enough. Vector had actually asked him to take a dive just so he could get better odds.

Kinuba had thought it was a bad joke at first. When he'd realised his mistake, he'd had a strong urge to use the grind-cutters on Vector and then skate around the track with his head on a pike. His pit crew had actually strapped him down, telling him he wouldn't live long enough to make it around the track once, and neither would they. The pit boss told him to channel his anger into winning and, as stupid as that sounded, it had worked. He'd won three straight games since Vector had come to him with his slimy offer, and each win was sweeter than the last. The next one would be sweeter still. He was going to keep on winning—he didn't need Vector to give him a twelve-game guarantee; he could get those twelve games all on his own. He'd win all of those, too, and each time he did, Vector could go home to his fancy Factory penthouse and cry himself to sleep. While Kinuba celebrated with the prettiest ladies on the premises.

Tonight he needed three—two just to hold him up on either side while he carried the third over his shoulder. Fortunately, these ladies were pretty *and* strong; they were doing pretty well at keeping him upright. Of course, he was in his street body now, not his game body. The street body was nowhere near as heavy, although he still had his grind-cutter hand. That stayed on twenty-four seven so he'd always know where it was. And he wouldn't have to disappoint any pretty ladies who asked him to demonstrate how it worked.

As they staggered out of the Kansas Bar into the street, Kinuba decided that the real problem wasn't all the booze he'd poured down his throat. It was the third lady over his shoulder who was throwing his balance off. He should have taken four ladies—a lady on each shoulder would have stabilised him.

But it wasn't too late. They were still right in front of the bar; he could just go back inside. Maybe he could avoid any misunderstandings if he made it clear to number four that she was strictly for ballast.

He was still thinking it over when something hit the ground in front of him with a crash and the pavement burst into flames.

"What the hell?" he roared as the ladies screamed and ran, even the one over his shoulder. Well, that was ladies for you—fire scared the spit out of them unless they were Paladins, so they'd have been no help to him anyway. Kinuba staggered around in a small circle, looking for some part of the street that wasn't on fire. When this happened on the track, it was usually because some idiot didn't know how to secure their fuel line.

But he wasn't on the track and he wasn't an idiot—drunk as a punk in a trunk, but not stupid enough to roll with his fuel line exposed.

But he wasn't rolling, he was on the street and he wasn't carrying a fuel supply. Kinuba tried to think. He was—he was—

He was in deep shit, he realised as a net dropped over his head and shoulders. Two gyro riders circled him, wrapping the net around him. Their faces were covered by goggles and bandannas, making them look like cyborg bugs on wheels. *Little* cyborg bugs—these were *kids.*

"You little bastards, I'll kill you!" he yelled and gave the net a hard yank. Said little bastards went flying off their gyros. Not into the flames— those were already dying down—but they'd get a good case of road rash.

Unfortunately, the movement threw him even more off balance. He swayed and staggered, flailing his arms as he tried to fling the net off and stay upright. Then the ground rushed up on his left and he met it with a crash of metal loud enough momentarily to drown out his slurred curses.

Didn't *anyone* hear that? he wondered as he struggled to get himself up on his hands and knees. It must have sounded like a truck crashing into a building. That kind of noise should have had every Centurian in town heading straight for this very spot. What the hell was wrong with them? Why wasn't there ever a Centurian around when you really needed one?

As Kinuba pushed himself up to his knees, he caught sight of two more cyborg-bug gyro riders holding what looked like spears. He had a second to think how unfair it was for a champion like him to be so well and truly screwed before lightning struck him in the back of the neck.

Every nerve in his body exploded with pain. His arms and legs stiffened and flailed, his torso jerked and twisted, as if every part of him were trying to rip itself free. All five grind-cutters flew out from his hand to twist and turn wildly on the pavement, as if they were trying to escape. He tried to call them back, but his mind was too full of pain and lightning that went on and on and on, until he lay on the ground, breathless and dizzy and unable to feel anything below his neck.

"You bastards," he panted, staring up at the black sky. Somewhere behind him, he heard the sound of a truck pulling up. "You bastard jackers, you're dead!" he told them. "Do you hear me? You're all dead!"

He was still cursing them as they hooked him up to a cable. It dragged him backwards along the street, up a short ramp and into the back of the truck; the grind-cutters trailed after him for a few seconds before he heard them snap back into his hand. Three more little cyborg-bug bastards strapped him down.

"Who owns this city?" yelled one of them suddenly.

"We do!" the rest of them replied and shut the door.

They ignored his promises of long, painful deaths for all of them as the truck lurched forward and accelerated. Little bastards couldn't even drive a truck right, Kinuba thought. He was going to kill them all *twice*.

Separating a cyber-core from a Total Replacement cyborg body was a painstaking procedure for a cyber-surgeon; for the average jacker, however, it was just a big pain. Doing it in a hurry was hard, and the job wasn't made any easier when the person being disconnected wouldn't stop bitching about it.

Putting them to sleep, or even sedating them, would have made everything easier but it never worked. Jacking sent their adrenaline into overdrive and they just wouldn't *shut the hell up*.

A lot of jackers started out kind of squeamish. They didn't want to jack a whole cyborg body. But, really, who did? Times being what they were—i.e., desperate—even the most well-intentioned would eventually find themselves backed into a corner. If your pockets were empty enough and your cupboard was bare enough, you'd do whatever you had to do.

One jacking was usually enough to give even the most tender-hearted first-timer a massive case of compassion fatigue. The way the person in the cyber-core yelled and hollered, anyone would have thought they were getting killed instead of jacked, when nothing could have been further from the truth. Total Replacement cyborgs were set up so their cores could survive for days without a body. They'd go into standby mode, which was sort of like a coma, until the Factory Prefects picked them up. Jackers weren't savages—they *always* called the Prefects to let them know there was a cyber-core lying around loose. The Prefects put the cores on life support until they could get a new body. And, yeah, it wasn't exactly anyone's idea of fun, but it wasn't murder. It wasn't even painful.

Besides, it wasn't like most of these Total Replacement cyborgs couldn't afford another body. Like Kinuba, for example—he was a Motorball champion and he was loaded from tonight's win. What he saved just from everyone always buying him drinks was probably enough for top-of-the-line hardware. So what if he missed a few games? He'd come back with a TR body a hundred times better than the old one. So the jackers were actually doing him a favour.

Not that *he'd* ever see it that way, of course. Even after he got all tooled up in a better body, he'd still piss and moan about big, bad jackers stripping him for parts. Kinuba had been almost too drunk to walk but it had taken four of these so-called big, bad jackers just to get him off his feet and another three to strap him down in the truck after he was paralysed.

Rich people were such big babies, and Kinuba was one of the biggest. All rough and tough on the Motorball track, but get him out on the street and he was practically crying for his mommy.

The still-masked jackers were hard at work when headlights appeared at the other end of the alley. The car rolled slowly towards them, lighting up the open back of the truck. They all stopped, waiting for a sign that would tell them whether to bail or stay. Their goggles glowed with reflected light.

The car came to a stop and two men got out. They were silhouettes in the headlights but their outlines were familiar. One was tall and neat in a bespoke suit, the other had the enhanced build and ready posture of a professional bodyguard.

One jacker straightened up and motioned for the others to keep working. He jumped down from the van and went to meet the men, raising his goggles and pulling down the bandanna covering the lower half of his face.

"Nice work, Hugo," said Vector. His tone was approving, even warm, but his expression as he watched what was going on in the van was more sneer than smile. "My compliments to your crew."

"Thank you, sir. I'll pass that on." Hugo winced, thinking he sounded like some Factory suck-up hoping to make employee of the month.

Vector seemed to find his answer amusing. His bodyguard passed him a thick package, which he handed to Hugo. Credit chips; from the weight, it felt like enough for everyone with a little bonus on top. Hugo felt awkward as he stuffed the chips in his jacket pocket and covered it by pretending he had to check on how his crew was progressing with Kinuba's chop.

"Hey." Tanji detached himself from the crew and crouched at the open door. "When you gonna tell your little hardbody you jack cyborgs for a living?"

"I'm not," Hugo growled at him. "And neither are you, if you know what's good for you."

Tanji shook his head. "What I know is, hardbodies are only good for one thing. And so do you; you're the one who told me that." He jerked his head at the bulge in Hugo's jacket. "And while I'm at it, where's *my* cut?"

Kinuba's cursing suddenly became louder. The crew had finished separating his cyber-core from his body and it took three of them to heave him out the back of the van. Kinuba roared with anger as his core hit the street and rolled. Hugo automatically pulled down his goggles and replaced his bandanna. The last thing he needed was a pissed-off Paladin coming after him for payback in a new, improved body.

"Get the body over to Chiren right now," Vector ordered. "Use the service gate."

Hugo frowned. Vector wasn't masked so he probably didn't think it mattered if he used Chiren's name. At least he hadn't used Hugo's. And Vector was so powerful, he probably figured he didn't really have to care that Kinuba could identify him. Still, Kinuba was pretty popular, enough that Motorball fans might not take it too well when they found out Vector was behind his jacking.

Unless Vector was going to pay Kinuba off to keep his mouth shut. Vector could afford it. The pay-off was Vector's speciality. Kinuba would probably give him a lot of grief but eventually Vector would find a number he liked. And Kinuba still wouldn't have to use any of it to buy his own drinks. Hugo was pretty sure that was how Vector would play this.

He realised Vector was staring at him expectantly. He nodded at Kinuba's cyber-core. "What about him?"

"Don't worry, I'll have my people tip off the Prefects," Vector replied. "He'll be fine, they'll pick him up and take care of him. Now will you get the hell out of here already?"

I don't believe you, Hugo thought, looking into Vector's face. But that was stupid—Vector wouldn't lie to him, not to *him*. Not about *this*. Vector hadn't got to where he was now by lying to people he did business with and double-crossing them. When you lived outside the law, your word had to be your bond. Everybody knew that.

It still didn't smell right to Hugo, but there was nothing he could do. It wasn't like he could take his jacked merchandise elsewhere.

He slammed the van door shut and banged on it twice. "Let's go," he yelled. The van sped off and he followed on his gyro.

As soon as they were gone, Vector strolled over to what was left of Kinuba and crouched down to make sure Kinuba got a good look at his face.

"Vector, you *prick*!" Kinuba snarled. "I should have known you were behind this."

"No," Vector said with a small laugh, "what you *should* have known, my friend, is that no one—*no one*—is greater than the Game."

He reached for something beyond Kinuba's range of vision, then held it up for him to see. It was nothing special, a plain old arc-cutting torch, the kind used by every pit crew in the Game.

For a couple of seconds, Vector let himself enjoy the expression on Kinuba's face as it dawned on him what was going to happen next.

Then he turned the torch on and showed him.

CHAPTER 13

Passage into and out of Iron City was strictly regulated. Nobody came or went without being accounted for. It was a matter of keeping track of numbers—so many in, so many out—and detecting the presence of hazardous or illegal materials. This didn't require much processing power, which made it ideal for Centurians. The single determination they had to make was a mere yes or no, and only yes required them to do anything: open fire.

Centurians didn't engage in conversations, so the law-abiding had only a minimal delay, while those attempting to smuggle in banned goods could not argue or make excuses, allowing contraband to be confiscated promptly. There was no bureaucracy, no justice system so badly backed up with pending actions that the Factory had to waste resources providing free food, clothing and shelter to criminals when the same things could be sold to people in Iron City at a profit. The savings in time and money were substantial.

Plus, the Factory handled all data so no one ever had to fill out forms. In fact, no one in Iron City had any idea what paperwork was.

Iron City itself had come into existence not long after the arduous era of bureaucracy characterised by forms and paperwork.

While the Factory hadn't really set out to make life simple and uncomplicated for people at ground level, it had just worked out that way. Of course, while most of them weren't idiots, none of them understood the nature of their existence well enough to be as appreciative as they could have been. But that wasn't the Factory's problem. People could complain to the weather for all the good it would do them; they had no direct access to the Factory except in the persons of deckmen or Prefects. Or Centurians.

The only thing left over from the tail end of a less efficient, more complicated era was the Hydrowall and the Victory Gate. These were actually a single thing in two parts, originally built as a war memorial. The Victory Gate had been made to commemorate Zalem's remaining aloft after all the other sky cities had fallen. The Hydrowall was a sort of fountain, but much fancier and more ambitious than the old-fashioned devices that dribbled and spat water into the air.

The designer had intended for people to walk through a tunnel of continuously running water that would lead them to the giant, shiny metal Victory Gate, which was supposed to elicit feelings of pride and contentment. Unfortunately, assumptions of victory had been slightly premature. The gate had been badly damaged in the final attack, during the War that no one knew very much about any more. The Factory had restored it and made it into something useful, an actual gate that allowed people to enter and leave under supervision.

The Hydrowall was left as it was. People liked it, and the white noise of rushing water kept people calm while they waited in line to be approved for either entry or egress without any additional action on the Factory's part. Very handy.

Hugo had definitely been right about the Hydrowall, Alita thought. It really was amazing, and the noise was kind of pleasant and soothing. But after you'd been stuck in a long line waiting to get out of Iron City, it wasn't so much amazing as it was boring. And noisy.

Although she couldn't say she really minded sitting next to Hugo in the front seat while he drove.

In the backseat, Koyomi seemed to have dozed off while Tanji was wide awake and as sour-faced as ever. He was still mad at Alita for what she'd done to him playing Motorball. Well, he should have expected payback. Anyway, the boy sure could hold a grudge.

Alita shifted position, while trying not to appear impatient or restless. It really was great being with Hugo and she was so happy they were going to spend the whole day together. But they weren't even inching forward—it was more like millimetring. At this rate, it might take them half the day just to get out of the gate. She'd really been hoping they'd be doing something a lot more fun with their time than waiting in a queue for Centurians to decide not to shoot them.

"Oh, look," Tanji said. "It's the iron fist of Iron City. Everybody tremble before your masters."

Hugo shushed him as a Centurian plodded towards them. Alita could feel him tense up, which made her tense, too. He'd said there wouldn't be any problem and she'd been sure he was telling the truth, so why was he nervous? She had been surprised when he picked her up in the van; she'd thought they'd be going on gyro-wheels. And the van was big— *really* big. Where had Hugo got it, she wondered, and why would he ever need anything so enormous?

But she'd kept all her questions to herself, figuring she could ask him about it later. But what if the Centurian thought it was strange that they had such a big truck for only four people? What if it decided they must be up to something illegal? Would it confiscate the truck and then shoot them? Or would it shoot them first?

By the time the Centurian reached them, Alita barely dared to breathe. It stuck its brutal machine head through Hugo's window and scanned them.

A hundred years later, it pulled its head back. "MOVE ALONG," it ordered them in an expressionless, mechanical voice and stomped away to investigate the vehicle behind them.

Alita felt everyone relax a little as Hugo shifted the van into drive. But it wasn't until they were in the shadowy tunnel of the Hydrowall with water thundering on either side that everyone really calmed down.

"They always make me nervous," Hugo said, giving her a smile. "Even though getting out is really pretty easy. They don't give a crap what people do in the Badlands."

Hugo steered the van up an entrance ramp and onto the open highway, where unlike Iron City, the traffic was non-existent.

"Welcome to the land of the free," Hugo said cheerfully.

"'Land of the free'—that's a good one," said Tanji. But his tone wasn't so much sarcastic as it was wistful.

❦

Alita couldn't help goggling at the acres and acres of cultivated land on either side of the highway. It stretched for as far as she could see in all directions and there were no people anywhere, only an occasional spidery machine raising clouds of dirt and dust as it harvested crops or planted more in long furrows in the soil. The dust clouds made her think of the impact of her boots on the lunar surface.

"So," she said, turning away from the passenger side window she'd been leaning over for almost half an hour. "Who started the War anyway?"

Tanji did a sort of double take, so surprised he forgot to look disgusted, but Koyomi took the question in her stride.

"I don't think anyone remembers what the fight was about, or even who won," she told Alita. "But Factory schools don't teach you *squat*."

"'Cause they don't want us knowing anything," Hugo added.

Alita frowned. This didn't sound quite right. Someone had to remember everything. Although Hugo was probably right about the Factory not wanting people to know much. If the Factory would protect a murderer like Grewishka, there was no telling what else they were hiding, or how far they'd go to keep their secrets.

For the next hour, they talked about the War on and off. Cultivated land had given way to fields of tall grass and weeds. Here and there along the roadside were remnants of things Koyomi said were "guard rails". Alita thought they must not have been very good guards—all that was left of them were stubs of damaged concrete, some with bits of wire sticking out of the side. Had the guards covered them, Alita wondered? And what did they do with the rails? The road and the land were more or less even, without any sharp drops.

Koyomi told her about how the road they were on had been part of a system that started at the shore of the eastern sea and spread out over the land like an enormous spider web, all the way to the western ocean.

"If there *is* a western ocean," Tanji put in. "Personally, I don't think there is."

"Oh, here we go," Koyomi said, rolling her eyes.

"Why don't you think there's a western ocean?" Alita asked Tanji.

"Because there's land and there's water—one of each. The land's in one place and the water's in the other. The so-called 'western ocean'"—Tanji made air quotes—"is just the other side of the eastern ocean."

Alita frowned, remembering how the Earth had looked in her memory of battle. "That's not how it works."

Tanji gave a short laugh as Koyomi launched into a lecture about continents and oceans, speaking so quickly that Alita had trouble keeping up with her.

"Don't mind them," Hugo said to her as Tanji began to argue. "Tanji only says that stuff because he knows it makes her crazy. The schools in Iron City suck but I never heard anything *that* stupid."

Alita thought again of the Earth as she had seen it. "I hope not."

The fields began to alternate with wooded areas before finally giving way to them altogether. The air took on an aroma that Alita could only describe as *greeny.*

"Everything out here is wild and overgrown," Koyomi said when she remarked on it. "No one takes care of these places, although the Factory sends people out every so often to take samples and readings."

"What for?" Alita asked.

"So they can measure how contaminated the soil and the trees and plants are," Koyomi said. "They can't reclaim the land till all the poisons have broken down. It's because of the War. Nobody lives out here—"

"That's not true," Tanji said. "A few people do. But they aren't anyone you'd want to meet. They lived off the land, hunted and planted crops, and now they're all deformed and mutated. Biological warfare ruined the world."

"The *whole* world?" Alita asked, appalled.

Tanji and Koyomi nodded in unison. "You think people would stay in

Iron City if there was anywhere else to go?" Tanji asked.

"Truth," Koyomi assured Alita.

They had been driving for almost two hours when Hugo turned off the highway and onto a narrow dirt road that took them deeper into the forest.

"It's gonna get bumpy," Hugo told Alita unnecessarily as the truck bounced and swayed.

"It's easier on gyros," said Tanji. "But somebody seems to think we might find something big that's worth bringing back."

"You never know," Koyomi said with a slightly sassy tone in her voice.

"Oh, here we go," Tanji said and rolled his eyes as Koyomi winked at Alita. "But then, what can you expect from someone who believes there's a western ocean? Someday they'll announce the Earth is flat and her head'll blow up."

"If the Earth were flat, you'd have already tripped and fallen over the edge," Koyomi said, sassier now.

"This is it," Hugo announced, bringing the truck to a stop and killing the motor. "This is as far as we can drive. Gotta walk the rest of the way."

They all got out and Alita stretched, glad to be out of the confines of the truck. She heard a cry and looked up to see a hawk circling above the trees.

"It's *free* out here," she said with a happy sigh.

"Yeah," Hugo said.

"It can be dangerous, too," said Tanji. Alita saw he had something in his sleeve like a metal rod; it had slipped down so he was holding the end in his hand. "Stay alert."

Koyomi rolled her eyes as Hugo motioned for them to follow him into the woods.

"All we know for sure," Hugo said as they made their way up a steep incline in the rainforest, "is the Enemy launched one last attack with every ship they had and it caused all the sky cities to fall in one night. All except Zalem."

For the last hour, conversation had been made a bit more difficult by the sheer effort of getting through the densely overgrown forest. Well, it was more difficult for Hugo, Koyomi and Tanji. Alita tried to be considerate, but she was dying to know what they knew, even if it wasn't very much. She wanted to compare it to what Ido had told her. He seemed to have left out or glossed over some things.

"Who was this Enemy anyway?" Alita asked as she held a clutch of branches back for Koyomi.

"The *Urm*," Tanji said in a spooky voice, as if he were saying *the bogeyman*.

"United Republics of Mars," Koyomi said, giving Tanji a look. She paused to catch her breath. "You know—U-R-M, Urm."

"Yeah, I get it," Alita said. Why hadn't Ido mentioned Urm, she wondered. He had to know about them.

"On the last night of the War," Hugo continued, grabbing at branches to pull himself the last few feet up to the top of the slope, "they say the earth shook and the sky itself caught fire. They *say*." He glanced over his shoulder to smile at Alita. "But the next morning, the sun rose and Zalem was still there, still flying." Standing at the top of the incline, he pointed. "What I want to show you is just up ahead."

Alita took giant climbing steps, like when she went upstairs three at a time, and made it to the top beside Hugo. And then she caught her breath sharply, staring at the sight laid out before her.

The lake was at least half a mile across, fed by a turbulent waterfall on the right-hand edge. But it wasn't a naturally occurring lake—it was actually a crater that had been gouged out of the earth by an unbelievably massive object. The land had reclaimed itself; overgrowth and weather erosion had hidden or smoothed over a lot of the old scars, though some of the blasted and broken rock was still visible.

But it was the unbelievably massive object itself that dominated the scene. The spacecraft sat partially submerged in the centre of the lake, its hull badly damaged. Chunks had been blown out, showing a skeletal framework within. Now it was succumbing to Nature's final insults of rust and corrosion. But it hadn't fallen completely into ruin—here and there Alita saw a few shiny spots.

"This ship is from the Battle of Zalem, the last battle," Hugo told her. "I thought if you saw something actually from the War, maybe it would help trigger your memory. And it would be safer than—well, you know, the other way."

Alita barely heard him; she was already making her way down the slope towards the lake.

Hugo showed Alita how part of the ship was close enough to the shore that they could walk on it all the way out to the main part of the wreck. Before he could show her the best route, though, she was halfway to the centre, more sure-footed than any of them on the wet metal.

"Salvagers have picked plenty off the bones over the years," Hugo said when he finally caught up with her. "Mostly metal." He pointed at the numerous small gaps and holes. "But because it's all Urm tech, they left most of it alone. People don't wanna mess with stuff when they don't know what'll happen."

"This is really an Urm ship?" Alita asked, wide-eyed.

Tanji gave a sarcastic laugh. "Pretty hard to sell crap when nobody knows if it's gonna blow up in their faces or—"

Alita shushed him. In her peripheral vision, she saw him roll his eyes and make a face at Hugo, but she didn't care. She could hear something, or rather, she could *almost* hear something—it faded in and out at the very edge of audible. It was special and rare and so much more important than how condescending Tanji looked right now.

But it was no good. No matter how hard she tried, the sound eluded her.

Alita looked the wreck over carefully, measuring with her eyes, trying to estimate its true dimensions. "We need to get to the command deck," she said after a bit and pointed at the section in the middle of the lake. "It's forward. There."

"How does she know?" Koyomi asked just as Tanji said, "What does she mean, *we*?"

Alita saw Hugo motion for both of them to be quiet, and she smiled to herself. She moved farther along the hull, all the way to the point at which it sank below the water.

"Aw, can't get there because it's underwater," Tanji said. "What a shame. Oh well. So what should we do next? I vote no to swimming."

Still smiling, Alita stepped off the hull, plunging feet first into the dark water. She dropped in slow motion, though not as slowly as she had on the moon. Ribbony aquatic plants below her leaned back, rippling, disturbed by the water she had displaced.

Alita looked down at her pointed toes. As she touched bottom, swirls of mud blossomed and swirled around her feet. She took a moment to orient herself in the murky water. Looking up, she could just make out the edge of the hull and a vague shadow that was probably Hugo looking for her.

Don't worry, Hugo—I'll be back.

She lowered her gaze. The part of the spacecraft that was underwater was festooned with patches of moss, mostly green, but some with gold overtones, others with bits of red. Or maybe that was rust.

Alita took a few long, slogging steps, stirring up more muddy clouds, until she reached the hull. The spacecraft was stuck deeply into the earth—getting it out wouldn't be easy. That was probably why the Factory hadn't already dug it out for their own purposes. And like Hugo had said, nobody wanted to fool with something when they didn't know if it would blow up in their face. Which meant the Factory didn't have a clue either. Good to know, she thought, as she put her hand on the hull just above an irregular green patch of moss.

The sound she hadn't quite been able to hear jumped into her hand and ran all through her like an electric current. It was talking to her, telling her it had been waiting such a long time for her to find it and there was so much to tell her.

Keeping her hand on the hull, Alita began plodding towards the command centre, every step raising billows of mud from the soft lake bottom. Not quite like on the moon—there was no one to fight here and this place was anything but lifeless. Still, she had a feeling of déjà-vu. Maybe that was the ship.

Hugo looked from the time on his wrist cell to the spot where Alita had vanished into the water and back again, aware he'd done almost nothing else for so long that the sun had moved and the shadows had begun to stretch. The girl was practically invincible on land, but there was nothing about her that suggested she could breathe underwater.

"How long do you think she can hold her breath?" Hugo asked Koyomi and Tanji.

Koyomi was pacing back and forth looking worried. Tanji only shrugged, looking bored.

Hugo looked at the time again. If anything happened to Alita, Ido would kill him. But that wasn't really what he was so worried about.

The sound-sensation led her into a place of complete darkness but she kept moving, trusting the feeling under her hand. After a while, the sound-sensation changed and somehow she knew she had to swim upward. Barely a minute later, she broke the surface somewhere inside the spacecraft. The call was much clearer now but everything was still pitch black.

Alita felt around until she found a surface that seemed solid and stable enough to take her weight. The moment she boosted herself up out of the water, her surroundings lit up with a soft violet glow. She was in some kind of antechamber. Pushing her wet hair back from her face, she stood up; the surface remained stable under her without buckling or moving. She looked around until she spotted an open doorway and moved towards it.

The light grew brighter as she went, still trailing one hand along a curved, rust-covered wall. She was curious but at the same time oddly comfortable. This strange place didn't *feel* like a strange place, but she had no idea why.

As she stepped through the doorway, the hum that had been calling to her intensified into a deep, choral thrumming. This was the flight control room, which meant the skeletal remains in the half-dozen seats had been the flight crew. Their uniforms had rotted away and their bones were covered with various kinds of moulds that flourished in the tropical humidity.

The crew had been mostly biological with only a few cyborg enhancements, rather than TRs like herself. Alita found that a bit surprising—she'd have thought everyone on a warship would be a Total Replacement cyborg as a matter of course. Maybe there hadn't been time to give them new bodies, she thought as she stood over the lead pilot's chair. The eye sockets in the skull lying on the rotted cushion had been enlarged to accommodate sight enhancements. Whatever they had been, however, were gone. With one finger, she rolled the skull over; a neat, egg-shaped hole at the back of the skull showed where something had been added to the visual cortex. It, too, was missing. Had someone come in and helped themselves to some tech they later discovered they couldn't understand? Or had the crew somehow destroyed all of it themselves when they'd realised they weren't going to make it?

Alita let go of the skull; it rolled back to its original position, staring up at her with its too-big eye sockets. *Have we met?* she asked it silently. *Were you in the black sky above me on the moon?*

The thrumming wanted her to keep moving. But to where, she wondered, looking around. There was no other open doorway. The purplish light grew a little brighter and she spotted a large, sealed metal blast door.

With a last glance at the flight crew, she went to the door and felt the thrumming intensify even more. While she stood in front of it, wondering what to do, she saw her hand move of its own accord and slide open a cover plate at chest height, revealing a thick handle. Maybe it was the humming that guided her hand, Alita thought as she twisted the handle a hundred and eighty degrees. A motor somewhere in the door came to life with a long, drawn-out noise that went from rumble to whine, as if it were dragging itself out of standby to activation.

Rusty metal made shrill complaints as the door slid open to her left. This was it, she thought as a brighter, purple glow spilled out and flowed over her. Whatever was calling her was right here.

As soon as she stepped inside, however, her eager anticipation turned to bafflement. Most of the space was taken up by an enormous mirrored sphere, leaving very little room for anything else, including herself. The sphere was actually too big for the room—the top passed through the ceiling and the bottom penetrated the floor. Weird, but also incredibly beautiful. The surface sparkled with flashes of purple light as some kind of energy danced on it. Or within it?

After a second or two, she realised the light was sparkling in rhythm with the thrumming. So were her nerves—every part of her, in fact, was vibrating in time with whatever was inside that sphere. Careful but unafraid, she pressed her hand to the surface. Light danced around her hand and sent long flickering threads out from each point of contact. It tingled in a lovely way, as if it welcomed her touch, but she could get no sense of what the sphere was made of, whether it was cloth or plastic or metal or even if it might be alive.

Alita closed her eyes and immediately had a sense of the sparkling brightness flowing around her and through her. After a moment, she reached out and put her other hand on the wall. Her eyes were still closed but she felt the keypad take form under her fingers, which knew what to do. They danced over the keys in a precise, perfect pattern that felt sensible, agreeable, irrevocably correct.

Because sense memory stays in the core and moves with it from body to body. Thus there is no need to relearn motions from one incarnation to the next. The cyborg embodies an answer and a challenge to what was once referred to as "The Hard Problem". Consciousness is, in fact, always embodied in the cyber-core and easily adapts to inhabit any corporeal—

Oh, not now, *professor. I've got my hands full with—*

The words evaporated from Alita's mind as she opened her eyes. At the same moment, the sphere flickered, then collapsed in on itself.

She jumped, startled but unafraid as she looked around. The part of the room that had been contained in the sphere was shiny, polished, completely untouched by damp, rust, or corrosion. It was as if no time had passed here at all, she marvelled.

No, not *as if*—it *was* the case that no time had passed here. Was this the same kind of time field Ido said she had entered when time had stopped for her? The difference between the parts of the room that had been outside the wall and the parts that had been inside was dramatic—the rust and dirt ended sharply at a curved line of demarcation.

Urm technology. She wished with all her heart that Ido could have been there with her so he could see it, too. Except she was pretty sure he'd have tried to stop her from going inside in the first place. Still, she wished he could have seen it all, especially the thing in the centre of the room, the thing that had been calling and calling and calling until it had finally brought her here.

The cyborg body hanging on the rack was a work of art, but not in the same way as the body Ido had given her. That body had come directly out of Ido's heart, a labour of love and now a memorial to the daughter he had lost. But as lovely and loving a gift as it was, it would always be a body meant for someone else, for Ido's perfect little girl.

This body in front of her was a magnificent instrument: strong, steadfast, resolute, made to withstand, to defend and protect. It wasn't pretty with flowers and leaves. Its beauty was fierce and powerful.

Its perfect fluid lines were androgynous; it could adapt as male or female or non-binary. This alone was tech far ahead of anything in Iron City.

Alita moved closer and reached out to touch it.

A blue-white arc of energy leaped from the body to her fingers, not a shock but a connection, a link. In the next moment, she heard the body exhale long and slow, and somehow understood it was acknowledging they were now bonded. It had waited patiently for such a long time and at last she had come. Now they would belong to each other for as long as they both existed.

Hugo had insisted they all go back to wait on the shore so Koyomi could pace without risk of falling into the water. Now, as the sun was getting lower in the sky, Hugo was becoming less certain that Alita was all right. She had just jumped into the water, taking it for granted that she wouldn't drown. How could she possibly know that? He didn't think she'd ever been in water before. Hell, he didn't even know if she'd been out in the rain. What if she shorted out? Or mud got inside and gummed up her works. Or—

Tanji suddenly elbowed him hard in the ribs and pointed. Hugo jumped up from the rock he'd been sitting on with Tanji and stared openmouthed as Alita walked out of the lake, carrying what looked like a headless body in her arms.

"That can*not* be good," Tanji said to Koyomi. She ignored him and ran to meet Alita with Hugo. After a moment, Tanji followed, although he was certain anything that came out of a wrecked Urm spaceship had to be bad, especially if it looked like a headless corpse.

"You heard me: no. I won't do it," Ido said without taking his eyes off the complicated figures on the screen in front of him. "Should I spell it out for you? N-O. No. So you might as well forget it."

"But you *have* to!" Alita insisted with the desperation that a fourteen-year-old is especially adept at. "This would help us fight Grewishka and anyone else that comes after us!"

Ido looked over his shoulder at the cyborg body on the operating table. Alita had been fluttering around it like a butterfly since she'd brought it in. Now she had the right arm raised and was flexing it at the elbow, checking the range of motion. It didn't take a cyber-surgeon to sense the power contained in the body. He turned back to the screen before Alita caught him looking.

"This body has the strength I need," Alita declared. "Also the speed, the flexibility and the endurance. And I'm *connected* to it—it's *mine*. We're bonded for life. This could be who I am, who I've always been."

Ido sighed and swivelled around in his chair to face her. "Alita, you've been given a chance to start over with a clean slate," he said heavily. "Do you know how many people get that chance? Almost none. None that I've ever heard of, certainly."

"I don't want to start over when I can't remember how I started out in the first place," she said. "And the slate can't be all *that* clean if I could wake up an Urm warship. You got any thoughts on why that would happen?"

Ido got up, intending to leave the room, but Alita swung a gurney in front of him to block his way.

"I *knew* that ship." She looked into his eyes as if she were trying to hold him there by sheer force of will. "I've been in ships like that before, haven't I? *Haven't I?*"

Ido leaned on the gurney, suddenly overwhelmed by fatigue. He felt as if every day of his life had been a little heavier than the one before it, and now he was barely able to stand up under the accumulated weight.

"Whatever you *were*," he said, "it's not who you are *now*."

Alita moved back to the cyborg body on the table. The body was breathing slowly and deeply. She laid both her hands on it. Ido had a sudden absurd mental image of her making it levitate like a magician. *Presenting the flying cyborg body of Iron City. Like the flying city of Zalem, but in humanoid form.*

He wished he'd been there with her in the Urm spacecraft when she had reached out her hand, just so he could have pulled it away or even knocked her down before the arc of connecting energy could jump from it to her. He wasn't sure what would have happened if the body had sent out a connecting arc of energy and there'd been nothing to receive it. Probably it would have just hung there and gone on waiting, taking shallow little breaths, unbonded, permanently out of action.

Or maybe the arc would have found her. It might have gone right to her, homed in on her, and she'd be even angrier at him.

"Alita," Ido started.

"This is an Urm warrior body," she said, talking over him, "and I activated it when I touched it. Which must mean *I'm* a warrior. And *you knew*. You've *always* known."

Ido dropped his gaze to the floor. Why couldn't Hugo have taken her anywhere else? Fourteen-year-old girls were supposed to come home from a day out with a bouquet of wild flowers or a handful of shiny stones, not a lethal cyborg body.

A loud crash of metal made him jump. Alita had smashed both fists down on the edge of the table, leaving deep dents. Those weren't going to buff out.

"It's a Berserker," he heard himself say. "A Berserker is a humanoid weapon system created by the Urm Technarchy. Your cortex was designed to interface with this type of body." Ido moved to her and touched her

temple gently. "Your identity code activated it."

Alita's face lit up as if this were the best thing she'd ever heard.

"The instinctive fighting technique you use is called Panzer Kunst," he continued. "It's a lost combat art specifically for machine bodies, and used almost exclusively by Berserkers. This is why you're drawn to conflict without hesitation and without fear. It's how you were trained."

She was flexing her hands as she listened. Ido wasn't sure if she knew she was doing it or if it was a training reflex.

"You're not just a Berserker, Alita," Ido told her, wishing he could shut himself up. "You're an *Urm* Berserker—the most advanced cyborg weapon ever created."

This bit of information seemed to startle her a little. Perhaps finding out she was someone else's weapon would give her reason for pause.

"And *that*," he added, "is why I will *never* unite you with that body."

They stood facing each other in the lab for some unmeasured amount of time. He tried to will her to understand he had made this decision because no human being should be weaponised and made into a killing machine, especially not a fourteen-year-old girl. Even if she was, in fact, over three hundred years old.

Alita set her jaw. "Fine."

Ido's heart sank as she whirled around and fled into the night.

CHAPTER 14

The enormous Factory doors rumbled open the same way they had the first time Alita had come here with Ido. That night, he'd been mad at her. He'd made her stay outside while he went in, despite the fact that if it hadn't been for her, he wouldn't have been able to collect any bounties. In fact, if it hadn't been for her, he wouldn't have been able to do *anything*—he'd have been a splattered mess on the street with three homicidal cyborgs picking over his bones. With one of them making earrings out of his eyeballs.

But did he appreciate it? Hell, no! She'd saved his life and he'd showed his gratitude by forcing her to live a lie, to be someone she wasn't, refusing to let her discover her identity.

Well, tonight *she* was absolutely furious with *him*, and she was taking charge of her life—*her* life. She was calling the shots now, and if Ido tried to make her be his perfect little flower-covered darling, she'd tell him whose rules she lived by: *nobody's*.

Alita strode between the gargantuan doors. (If they tried to close on her, she would shatter them with *one blow* from her open hand.) Her footsteps echoed in the cavernous entry hall; she liked the sound.

Centurians were lined up along the walls on either side of her, and she could sense they were tracking her as she went. Ready to open fire if she did something against the rules. Alita gave them a sidelong glower. *You know whose rules I live by?* Nobody's. *What are you gonna do about it, you walking junk-piles?*

She stared hard at the platform ahead of her. Maybe she'd find out there was a rule against what she wanted to do. Well, too bad—if the Centurians even *tried* to get in her way, she was going to send them all to walking-junk-pile heaven. Her footsteps were even louder when she reached the platform and stomped up the few steps to the counter. She rested her elbows on it, pretending it wasn't just a little too high for her to do so easily. A couple of seconds went by. What the hell, she thought, was the night shift asleep on the job? There wasn't even a switch or a button to press for service, just a trashcan behind the counter.

Abruptly the trashcan spun around, and Alita found herself looking at a weird cartoony cat face. "State your business," the trashcan ordered her in a voice that was somehow both cartoony and mechanical. The Factory used *trashcans* for receptionists? Was this place for real?

"I'm here to register as a Hunter-Warrior," she told it. "Any questions?"

"Name?" asked the trashcan.

❧⸙❧

She came out and found Hugo sitting right where she'd left him, at the top of the steps. Just like she'd done with Ido, she remembered, and then pushed the memory away; it wasn't the same at all, not even slightly.

"Well? How did it go?" he asked. "Did they give you any crap?"

Alita scowled for a second, then broke into a broad, triumphant grin as

she held up her new ID badge. She let Hugo take a close look at her photo and ID number before she put it away.

"Congratulations," Hugo said. "You're an official Hunter-Warrior. But man, is the doc gonna be pissed. He's gonna lose it bad."

Just like that, she was scowling again. "He can be pissed and lose it all he wants," she said. "Whose rules do I live by?" She gave him a look, one eyebrow raised, then she stumped down the steps and Hugo followed.

In Hugo's experience, Hunter-Warriors came in two varieties: a) big; and b) big and drunk. The two who came staggering out of the Kansas Bar were definitely the latter. They stumbled around in a small circle, which made Hugo think uncomfortably of Kinuba, before they finally zigzagged up the street, barely managing to keep each other upright. Hugo hoped that might make Alita think twice about her current life plans, but no such luck. She reached for the door handle like she was a Kansas Bar regular.

"Hold up a minute!" Hugo caught her arm. "Are you sure about this? This is a bounty-hunter joint—"

Alita shoved her new ID in his face. "What do you think this is, a shopping list? Besides, everybody in there must *hate* Grewishka. I just know it!"

Hugo felt something brush his leg and looked down. The little stray dog Alita had saved from the Centurians in the marketplace was dancing around their feet, tongue lolling and tail wagging in doggy delight.

"Hey, I know you!" Alita stopped to pet him and scratch behind his ears while he licked her face. Hugo shook his head slightly. Ali was about to go into the toughest Hunter-Warrior bar in town, but first she had to let a dog wash her face. Could the night get any more surreal?

When the stray had been thoroughly petted and scratched, Alita stood up. "Okay, just watch my back in there," she said and went inside. Hugo was about to follow when the dog cut in front of him.

"Oh, boy. She was talking to *me*," he told the dog, and then wondered if that was true.

The fun was already in full swing, Hugo saw. They entered just as Zapan slammed another hunter down onto a table, which collapsed into splinters. Somehow Zapan still managed to look like he was posing, in case someone was taking pictures or making a video.

"Dammit, Zapan," yelled the barkeep, his sweaty round face red and irate. "You know the rules: you gotta break something, break each other—*not* my furniture!"

Zapan turned to look at the man. Behind him, the hunter he'd just body-slammed got to his feet. Without looking at him, Zapan drove his elbow into the guy's face; he dropped like a stone.

"And we're done," Zapan announced cheerfully. He was posing in the centre of the room like he was waiting for applause, Hugo thought. The guy was a hell of a hunter but entirely too in love with himself. He wondered why Zapan hunted at all, given the enormous risk of getting hit in the face; plastic surgery wasn't cheap. Zapan could obviously afford it, though. It looked like he'd upgraded his cheekbones *again* in the last couple of days.

Abruptly, he realised that Zapan's gaze had fallen on Alita. The hunter dusted himself off and ran a hand through the narrow strip of hair on the top of his head, and swaggered over to her. He actually thought he was oozing charm when, in fact, he was just oozing. Hugo leaned against a column, waiting to see how this portion of the Zapan Show would play out.

"And what brings such a pretty lady like yourself to this fine establishment?" Zapan smarmed. "Did you come to see some real live Hunter-Warriors up close and in the flesh? Close enough that you can actually touch them?" He offered her his arm. "Go ahead, feel free. And freely."

Instead Alita showed him her ID badge. Zapan stared at it incredulously for a couple of seconds, then snatched it out of her grasp and held it up high, laughing. "You guys ain't gonna believe this," he said, "but Cupcake here? She's a *bounty-hunter*!"

The whole room, including the barkeep, stared at him in silence. A young girl claiming to be a Hunter-Warrior was something none of them had ever seen before. Hugo could feel in his bones that this was going to end badly; he just didn't know how badly or who would get the worst of it.

Zapan turned back to Alita and bent down, putting his hands on his knees as if he were talking to a child. "So you took that cute little behind of yours down to the Factory and told a deckman what you wanted. Say, did you get the one that looks like a kitty-cat or the sad clown?"

"I thought it was a trashcan," Alita murmured.

Zapan didn't hear her. "And now you've got your very own official ID, which means *you're* just like *us*!"

Hugo's glower deepened as he gave his right arm a little shake. The compact paralyser bolt he kept up his sleeve for emergencies slid down into his cupped hand. *Give me a reason*, he told Zapan silently as the Hunter-Warrior made a big deal of presenting Alita to the room, talking in the exaggerated voice of a game-show host. *Just* one *reason*.

"Allow me to introduce some of your professional colleagues!" Zapan was saying as he made an expansive gesture at a very wide, very grim-faced Asian man sitting alone at a table. He was completely organic, dressed like a Samurai, and busy emptying the bottle in front of him shot by shot, his dark eyes and scarred face inviting the rest of the world to go to hell.

"Here we have Master Clive Lee, he of the White-Hot Palm!" Zapan enthused. "With over two hundred confirmed kills—"

"Two hundred and seven," Master Clive Lee said in a low, dangerous voice.

"Two hundred *and seven*! I stand *corrected*!" Zapan made a deep, apologetic bow and turned Alita towards a different table.

"Over here, we have the one and only McTeague, Dogmaster Supreme, with his infamous yet notorious Hellhounds!"

McTeague was grizzled and even more fierce-looking, not a Total Replacement cyborg but definitely more metal than flesh. The dogs lying on the floor around him were about half and half; they were the size of mastiffs, and they all got to their feet with a warning growl as soon as Zapan took a step in their direction.

Zapan immediately moved back, putting his hands up. "McTeague's only problem is having enough left of his prey so he can collect the bounty." He laughed as if this were hilarious.

Hugo had forgotten about the little stray organic dog until it ran over to the Hellhounds and started bouncing around like it wanted to play. Horrified, Hugo closed his eyes, not wanting to see what came next. But instead of the ghastly sounds of a canine massacre, he heard slurping noises. He opened his eyes; one of the Hellhounds was running its enormous tongue all over the little stray while the dog wriggled in ecstasy.

Then McTeague reached down, picked the little guy up, and put him on his lap. "Who wants to be a Hellhound?" McTeague asked him, his gravelly voice full of tenderness. *"You* wanna be a Hellhound, dontcha? Yeah, you do."

Hugo blinked, wondering if he were about to wake up.

Zapan seemed to be just as nonplussed at the sight of McTeague ruffling the stray's fur affectionately. He turned Alita around to face him. "And of course, there's *me!*" He struck a pose that was supposed to be heroic. "I am Zapan, the ultimate Hunter-Warrior, chosen as the keeper of—" He drew his sword with a sweeping gesture. "—the Damascus Blade!"

Zapan whipped the sword through the air in a series of complex patterns before holding the cutting edge up in front of Alita at eye level, so she could marvel at the full effect of its otherworldly iridescence. Despite everything, Hugo couldn't help being impressed himself. The blade looked like a supernatural blend of diamonds and steel.

"Honed to a monomolecular edge, it slices armour like butter," Zapan said in a melodramatic tone. "Forged before the Fall by the lost arts of Urm metallurgy—"

"Oh, really?" Alita sounded bored, but Hugo knew her ears had pricked up as soon as Zapan mentioned Urm. "So who'd you kill for it?"

Zapan peered over the top of the blade at her and didn't like what he saw. He sheathed the sword and put his arm around her shoulders in sham camaraderie. Hugo started calculating how many seconds he'd need to get behind Zapan and plant the paralyser in the back of his neck.

"Cupcake, you're a cutie," Zapan said. "But a Hunter-Warrior is a solitary predator—a lone wolf, if you will. No offence!" he added as the Hellhounds growled again. "What this means for you is, every time you go out for a kill, you're competing with us—*all* of us. Do you see what you're up against here?"

Much to Hugo's delight, Alita shrugged his arm off as if it were nothing and stepped away from him.

"Listen to me," she said to the room at large. "I came here because I want your help. We have a common enemy. You know who I mean: Grewishka. Once he was a Paladin, a champion, even a contender to be Final Champion. Even now, everyone says he's the best there ever was. But he blew every chance he was given. He's not a champion any more—now he's a thief and a murderer. He murders women and he steals from Hunter-Warriors—from *you*. He takes your weapons and he uses them to kill people!"

She turned back to Zapan. "Do you want to lose your sword to him? Or you—" she looked at McTeague. "Do you want him to take your Hellhounds?"

McTeague looked uncomfortable but he didn't say anything. No one did. The place had never been so quiet while it was still open, Hugo thought. Most of them were actually *listening* to her.

"Grewishka's being protected by the system," Alita went on, her expression serious. "He can go on rampaging, killing, doing anything he wants, and nobody's even trying to stop him. Now he's after Ido—and me." She turned in a slow circle, looking at all of them, and Hugo noticed more than one had trouble meeting her gaze. "So I've come to you, my Hunter-Warrior brothers, to ask you to help me. If we band together, we can take him down and get rid of him once and for all."

Zapan gave it two seconds before he stepped up beside her. "No takers? What a surprise. A shock, even! Too bad, Cupcake." He put his arm around her shoulders again and Hugo felt another surge of white-hot rage.

"Look, sweetheart, I wouldn't normally take a rookie under my wing and give them the benefit of my vast knowledge and experience and wisdom. But your story is so touching that for you, I'll make an exception." Zapan gave Alita's shoulders a little squeeze. "All you have to do is cut meat-boy over there loose—" He jerked his over-chiselled chin at Hugo, who had begun to vibrate with fury. "And let me buy you a drink or two and we'll see where the night takes us? How does that sound?"

Hugo thought it sounded like someone really needed a paralyser in the back of the neck.

"Hey, watch it," he said in a warning tone and took a step forward, intending to stick the slime ball like a pig and see where the night took him then. But Alita made a small gesture at him with one hand—*back off*—and he stayed put. But only for now, he told himself. The paralyser's charge was good for another eighteen hours; he could wait.

Alita turned to Zapan and gave him a long look of appraisal, up and down, that took in the various designs carved into his steel body. "That's really some offer," she said finally. "But what could *I* possibly learn from some jumped-up, loudmouth pretty-boy who obviously spends all of his money on his *face*?"

There was a moment of shocked silence. Then everyone in the bar burst out laughing. Even McTeague's Hellhounds were laughing. Guys Hugo had never seen crack a smile, hunters he'd thought were too scarred to change expression, were pounding their fists on tables or stamping their feet. Cyborgs were bent double, holding their middles and howling. Hugo was laughing pretty hard himself until he caught sight of Zapan's face. His jumped-up, loudmouth, pretty boy features were twisted with rage. He was so angry he actually forgot to pose.

Hugo's heart started to pound. Alita had really done it now. A guy like Zapan didn't let anyone get away with humiliating him, not even a cupcake. *Especially* not a cupcake.

When the room finally quieted down enough so Zapan could make himself heard, he loomed over Alita and said, "Maybe I oughta rip out your pretty little arms and legs and kick your head around the block a few times. Teach you some manners."

"Better not. You might mess up your hair," Alita retorted, and stuck out her tongue at him.

And there went Zapan's last nerve, Hugo thought as the Hunter-Warrior lunged. Alita sidestepped him effortlessly. Moving in a manner that appeared casual, she grabbed his arm, twisted it up behind him, and struck him hard in the middle of his back with her open palm. Zapan crashed into the pillar Hugo had been leaning against. Hugo stepped away just in time, sneaking a look at Master Clive White-Hot Palm Lee to see if he was taking notes; he should have been.

Zapan whirled, heart's-blood dripping from a gash in his no-longer-perfect forehead, and whipped out his sword. Alita ducked his wild swing and popped up close enough to give Zapan two more hard blows with her open palm. The first knocked the sword out of his hand, the second landed squarely on his nose. Before Zapan could holler with pain, Alita leaped into the air with a dancer's grace and thrust one leg out in a kick that sent Zapan flying across the room to land on the floor like a pile of dirty laundry.

Alita used her toe to flip the Damascus Blade up into her hand and hurled it at the far wall, where it stuck. "You don't deserve such a magnificent weapon," she told Zapan, marching across the room and looking down on him as if from a great height before she turned her attention back to the rest of the bar.

"I heard you guys were supposed to be the 'heroes of Iron City'. *Heroes*." She spat the word. "That's not what *I'd* call you—*any* of you."

Oh, God, no, Hugo thought and was on her in two giant steps. "Okay, I think that's enough excitement for tonight," he said, trying to pull Alita towards the door. "We'll just be going now—"

Alita shook him off. "*Real* life and death, remember?" she said in a low voice. "I need you to stand way back."

Hugo gave ground until he felt a wall behind him. He had a feeling that wasn't going to be far enough.

"Listen up!" Alita shouted, openly angry. "I'll take on anyone in this room—*anyone*! If I win, you agree to fight alongside me. Deal?" She waited a beat. "Okay, who's first?"

On the floor, Zapan sat up with one hand cupped over his face. "Bitch broke my nose," he whined.

"Buy a new one," Alita said without bothering to look at him. She took a running leap and landed on top of a table where half a dozen Hunter-Warriors were nursing beers. "*Heroes*," she jeered, looking down at them. "There aren't any heroes in this dump. All I see are junkyard punks, assorted cyber-trash, and Motorball burnouts too slow to cut it against *real* Paladins."

And there went everyone else's last nerve, Hugo thought, watching the room explode as a lot of very pissed-off Hunter-Warriors decided to let their inner homicidal maniac come out and kick her ass. Two of the guys at the table lunged for Alita; she stepped back and stomped hard on the edge, flipping the tabletop up like a coin. Beer mugs went flying; a few well-aimed kicks and punches sent them into the faces of Alita's nearest attackers.

Hunters at the edge of the room were getting up now, Hugo saw. Guys who never let themselves get drawn into anybody else's drama were leaving drinks unfinished, wanting to get a piece of the upstart who had dared to impugn what few shreds of honour they had left. Or thought they had left.

But they weren't going to do any better than Zapan, Hugo thought, watching them lumber towards the centre of the room where all comers were getting their asses handed to them. Because in this fight, size *wasn't* an advantage, something none of these guys were used to. They were powerful but not agile, tough but not fast, set in their ways instead of adaptable, while Alita was all those things and more, not to mention sober. It was easy for her to evade their wild swings and clumsy lunges, knocking them down before they even knew where she was. Two hulking Hunters thought they had her trapped between them; she did one of her dancer-style leaps, as strong as it was graceful, and they smashed into each other, knocking themselves out.

Hugo looked over at the barkeep, who was also the owner. He was watching the free-for-all with a look of sad resignation on his saggy face. There probably wouldn't be much furniture left after this. Hugo felt a sudden rush of pity for the man, then frowned. That wasn't much like him at all.

A chair suddenly flew towards the bar. The barkeep ducked in time but the chair hit the liquor shelf, breaking every bottle. The barkeep popped up again, drenched in booze and decorated with bits of broken glass in his hair.

"Aw, son of a *bitch*!" the barkeep said miserably and disappeared behind the bar again.

Ido ran all the way from the clinic, Rocket Hammer in hand, hoping what he'd heard about the fight in the Kansas Bar had been exaggerated. People always exaggerated bar fights, blowing everything out of proportion.

Like saying a pretty young girl had started it. Ido was sure that pretty young girls had been the catalyst for lots of bar fights. But in all the bar fight stories he'd heard over the years, none of them had involved a pretty young girl offering to beat up every guy in the place and then throwing the first punch. That had to be totally made up—maybe some muscle-head's fantasy of being a slave to a pretty young dominatrix.

And for all he knew, the whole thing might be over by the time he got there. The Kansas Bar's owner, fed up with having to buy new furniture all the time, had said anyone who started trouble would be thrown out.

Ido made himself stay hopeful all the way from the clinic. But just as he reached the bar, the front window exploded outwards and two cyborgs landed on the sidewalk. Probably not what the owner had meant by "thrown out", Ido thought. Stepping around one of the cyborgs, he edged up to the broken window to have a look, then ducked as a third cyborg came hurtling out, flying all the way across the street to land on the opposite sidewalk.

"Oh, dear God, no," Ido moaned and rushed inside.

The whole place was in chaos. The first thing he saw clearly was Hugo using a paralyser bolt on a Hunter who'd been about to swing a chair at Alita. Alita herself was oblivious; she was busy giving two Hunters the kind of beating that would have scarred normal people for life.

Ido shoved Hugo aside and waded in, prying fighters apart with the shaft of the Rocket Hammer and yelling for them to stop. Several turned to him with raised fists but backed down immediately when they saw who he was. Ido struggled through the room until he reached the bar and climbed on top of it.

"Knock it off *right now*," he bellowed, "or *no more free repairs!*"

Everything stopped as if someone had flipped a switch. For a second, the only thing Ido could hear was Alita breathing just a bit heavily from all the exertion. She stood in the centre of the room in a fighter's stance: knees slightly bent, arms up with her hands ready to protect her face and her shoulders down. Her shiny black hair was slightly mussed but otherwise she seemed none the worse for wear. Ido glared at her, then at everyone else. When he was sure they all understood the party was over, he climbed down off the bar.

Hugo sidled up to him, holding the paralyser bolt. "I'm with her," he said to a nearby cyborg with a chair-leg in one hand. "And him, too," he added, nodding at Ido.

There was a discordant chorus of grunts and groans as hunters began pulling themselves together, getting up to look around for lost weapons, armour, clothing and anything else that had gone missing during the period of temporary insanity that had swept over them. "Hey, anybody seen my arm?" a battered cyborg asked plaintively as he plodded past Ido. "It's a long metal thing with a hinge in the middle and a hand on one end."

"Try retracing your steps, Cronie," someone called to him.

"Where'd you last see it?" asked someone else.

"Someone was hittin' me with it," the cyborg muttered and plodded away to keep looking.

Ido turned to Alita. She was no longer looking for a fight but, to Ido's dismay, she didn't seem even faintly sorry about all the trouble she'd caused, not to mention all the damage. Ido turned to look at the owner, who was now leaning on the bar and watching the night limp to an abysmally unprofitable conclusion.

"I'm so sorry," Ido told him.

The owner wasn't impressed. Ido looked around and found a chair lying on its side but miraculously intact. He righted it and pushed it up to a table. The owner was still underwhelmed. Ido couldn't blame him.

"You and I are going to have a little talk," Ido said to Alita, taking her arm.

Alita shrugged him off. "We *had* our talk. You left me no choice."

Before Ido could argue, there was a deafening *clang!* of something announcing itself with metal striking metal, followed by an explosion that blew the front door to fragments.

"Why, God? Why?" moaned the barkeep softly.

The creature that came through the ragged hole of the entrance was bigger than any cyborg in the place. Every part of its metal body was deliberately exaggerated, overdone, intentionally monstrous. The metal itself had a brutal look, as if the body were made of parts taken from weapons by someone who had wanted to build something that would be the antithesis of humanity.

The face, however, was very familiar, and not just to him. Every Motorball fan in Iron City would have recognised that face. It was older, a lot more scarred, and quite a bit uglier than the last time Ido had seen it, which was somewhat remarkable, considering that had only been a few days ago.

"Grewishka!" said a Hunter in a shocked tone. "Damn, that's *Grewishka*!"

"Yeah, but what the hell happened to him?" the Hunter beside him said.

Grewishka pointed at the second Hunter-Warrior. "To answer your question—" His finger zoomed out from his hand, trailing a long metal coil. It whistled through the air, flying around the Hunter too quickly for the eye to follow, then snapped back to Grewishka's hand.

The second Hunter-Warrior's face went from amazed to confused. A moment later, his body came apart, the pieces making nauseating wet sounds as they slid away from each other and fell to the floor.

"I've had a little upgrade," Grewishka said conversationally.

Ido was lost for words. Out of the corner of his eye, he saw all the blood had drained out of Hugo's face; the kid seemed to be on the verge of passing out. Poor little bad boy, Ido thought; he'd probably told himself he was a black-market badass, unaware of how black things could get or how evil people could be.

And, as if fate or karma needed to remind him of the same thing, Chiren stepped out from behind the monster, looking antiseptically and frostily beautiful, and quite proud of her upgraded toy.

"Impressive, isn't he?" she said, giving the monster an admiring, practically worshipful, look.

"My God, Chiren," Ido breathed. "What have you done?"

"Let's find out, shall we?" she said brightly, as if this were just a funny little game, no more innocuous than Motorball.

Grewishka took a step forward, and then another, his angry eyes fixed on Alita. "I only want the girl," he said in a gravelly purr.

"'S far as I'm concerned, she's yours," said a very nasal voice. Everyone turned to look at Zapan, still holding his ruined nose.

Ido switched on the Rocket Hammer. Hugo produced a fire-bottle. He stood beside Ido with his head up and his shoulders back, but he was still extraordinarily pale. Poor kid was obviously scared out of his mind. Ido looked around at the rest of the Hunter-Warriors, or at least those who hadn't sneaked out of the ragged hole Grewishka had made coming in.

His gaze came to Clive Lee, who shook his head. "No bounty on Grewishka," he said to Ido. "If there's no bounty, he's not our problem."

A surge of anger sent heat rushing into Ido's face. "This—this *beast* has been killing women. Not just killing them, vivisecting them. And he's acquired weapons he has no right to. Or don't any of you remember whom you last saw using grind-cutters? Kinuba won that night—he was in here celebrating and you were all buying him drinks. Have any of you seen him since? *Anybody?*" Ido looked around, his anger intensifying. "And any one of you could be next. But here he is, on your home turf, laughing in your faces because he knows no one here will do a thing about it. Because *he's not your problem.*"

Ido looked around again, but the room seemed to have somehow stretched out in every direction so that all the other hunters seemed to be far away.

"Sorry, Doc," Clive Lee said from his now-distant table. "You're on your own."

Ido turned to Alita. She *wasn't* far away. She was very close—very, *very* close—and her wide-eyed face had a calm composure that Ido found utterly frightening.

Then, because things still weren't bizarre enough on this planet, a small dog barked.

Ido turned to give McTeague a baffled look and saw a little mongrel that wasn't even remotely hellish or houndish spring out of the man's lap. He landed on the floor in front of Grewishka and bared his teeth in a snarl.

"The only one with courage," Grewishka sneered. "An innocent." He pointed at the dog.

Ido turned his face away. Metal whistled through the air. There was one startled yelp, followed by terrible slicing noises, and then the sound of the grind-cutter snapping back into place.

"There's no place in Iron City for innocence," Grewishka said smugly.

Ido forced himself to turn his head and look at Grewishka, trying not to see the mess on the floor, and failing.

A chair scraped back from a table as McTeague got to his feet. The Hellhounds rose with him, growling low and dangerous; they'd caught the scent of heart's-blood in the air. Beside Ido, Alita was watching the pool of blood spread out from the little stray's body. When it reached the toe of her boot, she knelt and dipped one finger into it.

Grewishka laughed at her. "Time for us to play, little flea."

The sensation spreading through Alita now was not unlike what she'd felt a few minutes earlier when she'd been kicking asses and taking names and generally showing a bar full of Hunter-Warriors that they weren't as big and bad as they thought they were. But this time the feeling was intensifying far more quickly. It was a power and intent that came from a deeper place, from her true *self*, from the very stuff of which she, Alita, had been made.

Words suddenly flitted through her mind, a memory that had come loose from its moorings, something from long ago in her life:

De profundis clamavi ad te. Out of the depths I cry to you…

What cry did she make out of her depths?

It came to her immediately: "I do not stand by in the presence of evil."

Alita dragged her blood-covered fingertip in a straight line across her right cheek under her eye, and then did the same on the left. The blood was still warm. Heart's-blood from a heart braver than a roomful of men who called themselves heroes.

She raised her head. Grewishka loomed over her, his ugly face made even uglier by his certainty that there was nothing in the world stronger than cruelty.

Alita got to her feet, aware of all the eyes on her, aware of who they all were and their locations in the room, aware of Ido and Hugo and Chiren.

"*I do not stand by in the presence of evil,*" she said again, louder this time, to make sure they could all hear this cry from her depths, this promise from her soul.

The grind-cutter flew out from Grewishka's hand and everyone dived for cover.

Go ahead and hide, you junkyard punks, Alita thought as she sprang into the air, *but keep watching, you don't want to miss what's coming up next.* At the top of her leap, she twisted to dodge the grind-cutter blade, then segued into a backflip that put her squarely on her feet again, out of reach of the grind-cutter as it chopped up the last unbroken table and the chair Ido had righted earlier. Bounty hunters scrambled away, trying to find safer hiding places, some of them diving behind the bar with the owner.

As if there really were any safe places in this world, Alita thought. Ido's Rocket Hammer roared into high gear; she turned to see him rear back to take a swing at Grewishka. Grewishka whirled and fired another grind-cutter at him. Only Ido wasn't there any more because Hugo had tackled him, sending the two of them tumbling across the dirty, splintered floor.

Hugo was big on tackling, Alita thought, feeling a surge of affection she had no time to indulge.

"Hey, ugly!" she yelled at Grewishka and cartwheeled across the floor, took a flying leap over the ruins of a table and made a three-point landing on the bar. The sight of the Hunter-Warriors cowering behind it sent a wave of pity through her and made her want to destroy Chiren's monster more than ever. "Over here, you pile of pig iron!"

Grewishka smiled nastily and fired another grind-cutter at her. She leaped away as it made kindling of the bar and scattered everyone who had been hiding behind it—everyone, that was, except the owner. He stayed where he was, looking at the wreckage.

"Last call," he said glumly. "You don't have to go home but you can't stay here. Because there's nothing here any more. Why am I talking? Nobody's listening."

Alita didn't tell him she was listening, although she heard everything. She took another leap and aimed a kick at Grewishka's wretched face. He swatted her away and sent her crashing into a post and then the floor.

Grewishka laughed at her and mocked her with a flying leap of his own. Alita rolled away as he fired his grind-cutters at the place where she had just been. Deliberately, she realised; he had deliberately missed her.

She rolled to her feet and assumed her usual fighter's crouch, watching the grind-cutters throwing up clouds of dust and splinters as they savaged the floor. Grewishka laughed and jumped again, landing on the spot his grind-cutters had just been working on—and then kept on going *through* the floor, leaving a gaping hole.

Alita scurried over to it and peered down into the darkness. It was too dark to see anything, but she heard Grewishka's voice, mocking and evil. "What are you waiting for, little flea? Come and get me!"

She raised her head for a quick look around, assessing the situation in the bar. Everyone was still alive. But where were Ido and Hugo? It took a couple of seconds for her to spot them extricating themselves from a pile of plaster and broken furniture. They had a few bruises and cuts but neither of them were seriously injured. They were all right for now.

Alita had a brief glimpse of their horrified faces, and heard them both yell, *"Noooooo!"* in unison as she jumped into the hole.

 CHAPTER 15

Alita fell through the darkness and kept falling. *Out of the depths I cry, and into the depths I fall*, she thought with the wind buffeting her face and blowing her hair back. The earth was swallowing her, and it was a very long way to the belly of the beast, a long way to fall and fall and fall and fall and fall—

A heap of refuse rushed up to meet her. Landing in trash piles was getting to be a habit, she thought as she slid down from the top and assumed her usual fighter's crouch. *Yeah, pretty long fall. What else you got?* she said silently.

Laughter boomed through the darkness, seeming to come from everywhere around her. There was a metallic reverberation, as though she had landed in a tank. Alita blinked, willing her eyes to adjust more quickly to the dark as she searched the shadows for her enemy.

"Welcome to the underworld—*my* world." Grewishka's rumbling laughter was louder and even more aggressive down here. Now Alita could make out damp, cracked walls with enormous patches of mould growing on them and on the rusty pipes running in rows of four and five.

Sometimes the pipes curved upwards and vanished into the shadows; others ran away into murky tunnels through openings that were vaulted, like the empty windows in Hugo's cathedral.

But this was no cathedral, or any other kind of holy place. If Grewishka were here, this place was the very opposite of sacred.

"From here, there are worlds above worlds above worlds," Grewishka said, melting out of the darkness in front of her. "They go further up than a little flea like you can imagine." His rumbling voice had become a jeer. The way it echoed made it even more repellant, every word a physical blow. "And the trash and refuse of each world falls down on the one below, and so on and so forth, until it all ends up here. This is the land of the unacceptable, the unwanted, the rejected." Grewishka had moved closer so she could see him grinning at her like a cyborg gargoyle. "This is where I used to live—"

"And it's where you're going to die," Alita promised.

She leaped at him and, dodging his fist, flew over his ugly head, rebounded from a wall, and drove herself feet first into his shoulder, intending to take his arm off again. Instead, she bounced off and fell to the filthy concrete without hurting him. Chiren had fixed that flaw in his joint, made him stronger and tougher. But he probably couldn't get any nastier, she thought as he thrust out his right hand, fingers splayed.

All five grind-cutters shot out, the pointed ends stabbing at the concrete, throwing up damp, greasy fragments. Alita flipped to her feet and did a series of somersaults as the grind-cutter blades flashed in the gloom, whistling as they sought her out.

"That's it—dance, little flea, dance!" Grewishka laughed, as if her every move really were made at his command, for his amusement. She flipped from side to side, gradually getting closer to him, then launched herself straight at him. She hit him with her whole body, slapping him hard with both hands.

Grewishka hurtled backwards into a mouldering wall. It crumbled on top of him, burying him in boulder-sized fragments of damp concrete. Alita flipped backwards into a series of tumbles, and bounced up to assume her ready stance, only to have her right leg buckle under her. She looked down to see bright-blue cyber-blood dripping from her knee while sparks of energy flickered and buzzed around the joint. Glitching servo—damn, wasn't *that* just perfect.

Abruptly, she felt a change in the foul air and snapped her head to the right. Grewishka was charging at her, grind-cutters writhing and twisting. Alita somersaulted away, intending to build up momentum for a double airborne tumble. If she moved fast enough, her bad leg wouldn't have a chance to give. Instead, she touched down and staggered to one side. Her knee had lost too much cyber-blood. A grind-cutter blade flew at her, overshooting by several feet, but twisted and sliced a deep gash in her hip on its way back to Grewishka. *Damn!* She was going to have a hard time compensating for both that and her knee.

Hard time? More like, *no chance.* She ducked behind a thick concrete column standing between the openings to two diverging passageways to give herself a chance to breathe and think.

If she was going down, she was taking that son of a bitch with her. She just had to figure out how.

❧

"This is all *your* fault!" Ido said angrily as he climbed down a ladder.

Below him, Hugo snatched his hand away from a rung just before Ido stepped on it. "Hey, *you're* the one who drove her to this, not *me*," he said. They had come down half a dozen filthy levels so far, and Ido had spent the whole time blaming Hugo for every bad thing that had happened. It reminded Hugo of how Alita had complained about Ido the night he'd taken her to her first Motorball game. Like sort-of father, like sort-of daughter, he thought. He smiled at the memory, but only for a second. That same night, his crew had jacked Kinuba for Vector, leading directly to their current state of deep shit. Dammit, maybe this really *was* his fault, Hugo thought miserably. The only way it could get worse would be if Ido found out about the jacking.

Hugo shook the thought away and kept going down the ladder to the bottom. Ido had said the ladders were access for maintenance workers, but Hugo was pretty sure the last time a maintenance worker had accessed anything here was before he was born. The ladders were crusted with years of greasy dirt and who knew what else. And just to make the experience really special, the garbage smell became stronger at every level. If it went on till they reached the bottom, they'd puke themselves to death before they could even look for Alita.

Ido climbed down and brushed past him roughly. He'd twisted his shirt into a makeshift back carrier for the Rocket Hammer so he could have both hands free, but it was clumsy to walk with. He'd be lucky not to trip and fall before they got to the bottom.

The doc had already found the next ladder down—they were staggered in what seemed to be a random way. "Hey, *you*! Mr Black-Market Badass!" Ido snapped. "Wake up and let's go!"

Alita stood with her back to the column. The gash in her hip was still bleeding heavily and her knee was about to short out and die any moment, while Grewishka was too in love with the sound of his own voice to shut up for even a second. What the hell was *that* about?

"I was forgotten," the ugly beast was saying in a solemn rumble, like this was the most important origin story ever told. "I was unwanted, left to rot with the rest of the garbage. I thought it was my fate to rot, to disappear into decay and putrescence, unmourned by the uncaring world that produced the very garbage I had been consigned to."

Can we speed this up? Alita thought. *I'd like to kill you before I die myself.* She peeked around the column, saw Grewishka grinning at her, and drew back quickly.

"But then, someone saw me—saw *me*, just as I was, and embraced me. And so I was saved, remade by the same hand that shapes *your* destiny even now at this very moment!"

Alita felt the world tilt as if the monster had kicked it off its axis. And then kicked her in her stomach, so she couldn't catch her breath.

No. She kicked the world back where it belonged, straightened up, and stepped out from behind the column.

"*Whose hand?*" she demanded. "You wanna talk? Answer me right now—*whose hand?*"

Grewishka's gargoyle grin widened. "My master." He raised his fist. "My master, Nova."

"What do you know about me?" Alita shouted.

Grewishka splayed his fingers and the grind-cutters flew out from them. Alita leaped into the air, twisting and flipping, but the grind-cutters seemed to anticipate her moves now. The long blades converged on her and she felt something sharp pass through her torso, severing one arm. Another blade sliced her in half at the waist while a third cut off her legs at mid-thigh.

She was falling again, not as far as before but somehow it seemed to take a long time before she and the filthy concrete rushing towards her finally met. The smell of dirty water and damp stone fought the clean, bright fragrance of cyber-blood splashing out of her limbs as they fell around her. Somewhere in the darkness a voice very like Ido's cried out in horror. Alita supposed everyone made their own cry from the depths and the darkness.

Raising her head, she flexed her remaining arm and began to drag herself away. She could only manage a few centimetres at a time. It was like when they were in the van waiting to get out of Iron City the day Hugo took her to the Badlands; what a wonderful day that had been. She was going even more slowly now, but she refused to lie down. She wasn't dead, not yet—

A silent explosion of white light obliterated the damp, grimy darkness and she was—

Flying. She was flying, weightless in the zero-g training sphere, completely free, nothing resisting her movements, nothing to stop her twisting and turning and tumbling.

And she was young, very young—ten years old. She was a ten-year-old cyborg and she already knew how to use the fighting stick in her hand. The stick was more than familiar in her grip; it was perfect. She knew the mass, the length, how to counterbalance, and she knew how to defend herself against the woman coming at her with her own fighting stick.

Gelda. The woman was Gelda, and one day they would fight side by side on the moon, but now Gelda was her *sensei*.

"They're telling me you're too young, too small," Gelda said, her face alive and glowing with physical exertion and fierce warrior pride. "But they're wrong!"

Alita met her attack with a flurry of kicks and strikes, parrying Gelda's stick and scoring a few blows of her own—but only a few.

"I saw what you lived through," Gelda said. "You have the soul of a warrior!"

Alita's heart swelled with joy as she struck at Gelda, wanting to be worthy of her *sensei*'s praise.

"You'll never give up," Gelda told her, only slightly winded as she countered Alita's move. "You'll never stop. Never. Stop."

Gelda made a move to one side and Alita started to make the proper defensive parry. Gelda's arm shot out and pulled her close. Their faces were only centimetres apart and Alita felt the cold flat blade of Gelda's knife against her throat.

"Know what is hidden," Alita's *sensei* said sternly.

Gelda watched Alita closely as she let her go. Alita met her gaze steadily, composing her face into a stony, expressionless mask that wouldn't show her defeat. You never showed defeat to an opponent, never let them see you felt conquered, never let them into your head, not even if you were dying.

"Always ask: what is it that you are not seeing?" Gelda said.

Alita saw him then, the man in the observation gallery. He had been watching, but he had no eyes. Instead, he had chrome surgical optics. Chrome was the highest grade, reserved for the most elite of the elite, a social class so rarefied they were never actually seen by any of lesser stature, including people like her.

Only she *did* see him, and she saw him seeing her. As exalted as his chrome optics were supposed to be, they looked like they had been pushed into his head by a careless surgeon who had left too much sticking out of his face.

The man was smiling, but not at her. It was more like he was enjoying a private joke no one else would understand.

"Only when you see what is hidden can you win!" said Gelda. "Again!"

Alita twisted in the air—

And she was back on the filthy concrete floor, trying to drag herself away with her one arm while Grewishka knelt beside her and laughed.

He dug his fingers into her hair and lifted her up so she dangled like a broken doll.

"Aw, my little toy doesn't want to play any more?" His face was so close she could feel his fetid breath as he spoke.

Alita stared back, letting him see her refusal to give out, give in or give up. Ever.

"I'm going to turn you into a living pendant to adorn my chest," Grewishka said in a demented croon. "I'll wear you all the time so that every moment of every day, I can hear you screaming and pleading for mercy."

Alita drew back from him, and he pushed his face forward—just as she'd hoped he would. She thrust her open palm into his face and tore herself out of his grasp as he fell back. With her decreased mass, one arm was all she needed. She guided herself into a perfect landing on her open hand, then lowered herself slowly to the cement. Bright-blue cyber-blood was still pouring out of her, although it was starting to slow. She was in a pool of it now but she knew there was enough left for what she wanted to do.

Grewishka struggled to his feet, roaring with rage. Good; anger made him stupid. As he came thundering at her, she raised her body up, flexed her elbow and launched herself into the air. Sending herself into a spin, she aimed herself at Grewishka. Keeping her arm straight out, she flattened her hand like a blade and plunged it into his eye.

Now his scream was high and shrill, full of pain and terror. Alita smiled as she steadied herself so she could look directly into his other eye.

"*Fuck* your mercy," she told him.

She tried to yank her hand free but it was caught on something inside, probably one of his enhancements. In a way, that was even better, she thought. She twisted hard until her forearm cracked and broke just above her wrist and she dropped away from him.

Enjoy the souvenir. It's better than a pendant. There's a flower on it. I left a flower in your eye, a beautiful flower. You're welcome.

Grewishka's scream deepened with outrage, but not a lot—there was still more pain than anything else in his voice. Alita watched him lumber towards her, his hand over the eye with the flower in it. The flower would always be there, she thought; even after they took it out and gave him a new and better eye, he'd still feel the pain of her pretty little flower for as long as he lived.

She smiled up at him as he raised his foot to stomp her.

The next thing she knew, Grewishka was staggering sideways. Joy surged through her as she heard the unmistakable sound of the Rocket Hammer. In the next moment, a fire-bottle broke over Grewishka, engulfing his upper body in flames, making him scream again.

Alita caught a glimpse of Hugo before something fast and vicious slammed into Grewishka, snarling and growling as it drove him back. Then the rest of hellhounds were on him, ripping his armour, going for his exposed innards, biting and snapping.

Still screaming, Grewishka tore the Hellhounds away from himself and fled into a passageway. The Hellhounds went after him, barking furiously until McTeague appeared and hollered, "Break off! Come! Now!"

The Hellhounds came galloping back to him and formed a protective circle around him, Ido and Hugo. Alita remembered her friend, the little stray, and felt her eyes well with tears. McTeague met her gaze with eyes shiny with empathy.

"He wasn't a dog-lover," McTeague explained grimly. "I hate that."

Ido barely heard McTeague's pronouncement. He fell to his knees beside Alita's torn and shattered form and brushed her hair back from her face.

She looked up at him; and he discovered his heart could still break after all.

His little girl. She was his little girl, and it had happened again. A demon he was responsible for had gone on a rampage and his little girl had been caught in its path. That Chiren had actually made this monster was only a technicality—he had set all the things in motion that had led to this, and he had done nothing to stop this horror from getting loose.

His little Alita. She hadn't been helpless; she had fought the creature with everything she had—literally everything—and she had damaged it badly and driven it off. But the demon had been too strong, too crazed and too evil. For all that she'd hurt him, she'd never really had a chance against Grewishka. Ido had failed to protect her—even though he could have.

His little girl. The very thing that could have protected her was lying on a table in his lab, but he'd refused to give it to her. Instead he'd been a self-righteous, moralising fool, convinced that *not* giving her the power of the Berserker body was the best way to protect her from evil.

It might have been—in any other world but this one.

His little Alita. After everything that had happened, he'd managed to remain in denial about the nature of this world and the dangers around her. Worst of all, he'd been in denial as to who *she* really was, trying to make her—*remake* her—into a sweet, beautiful young girl adorned with flowers. As a result, he had failed her completely.

Ido gathered her up in his arms.

❧⟞⟝❧

Once they were on the street, Ido had Hugo run ahead, sweeping the Rocket Hammer back and forth to clear the way for him and the precious burden in his arms. He held Alita to his chest protectively, feeling his breath coming in great, ragged sobs, not caring about anyone or anything except getting his little girl back to the lab.

Then Chiren stepped out of the shadows near the boarded-up Kansas Bar.

If Hugo hit her with the Rocket Hammer, Ido thought, he would pretend not to notice.

"You think it'll be that easy?" Chiren called to him. "Bring her back all you want, but we can do this indefinitely—forever if we have to! Can you? Can you, Dyson?"

Ido pushed past her like she wasn't there. He felt her staring after him and imagined her wilting, shrivelling, collapsing in on herself because there was nothing inside, nothing at all.

Ido was running but Chiren didn't try to kid herself—he wasn't running from her. Now he had something to run *to*. She'd lost that a long time ago—they both had—and nothing would ever change that.

But there he went.

And here she stayed.

CHAPTER 16

The operation was a marathon procedure that took twice as long as the first one, although much of that time was spent disconnecting Alita's cyber-core from the wreckage that had been Ido's work of art.

When Gerhad had seen what Grewishka had done to Alita, it had been all she could do not to break down, not just for Alita, but also for Ido. He'd been here before and, although Chiren had made the monster that had destroyed his little girl, Gerhad knew Ido was blaming himself. She hadn't thought anything could happen that would make Ido punish himself any more than he already had, and still did. But apparently she'd had no idea what Chiren was capable of. That woman had to be the coldest, most heartless person in Iron City—and that was saying something. It was hard to believe she had ever been a mother—of a human being, anyway.

Gerhad looked at the girl on the operating table. After almost two days, most of the re-embodiment procedure was finished; all the nerves were physically connected, and both circulatory systems—cyber-blood and heart's-blood—were functioning. In fact, Gerhad had never seen a face pink up so quickly. It was as if this was the body Alita should have had all along.

And yet Ido had been so dead set against uniting her with it. Gerhad had been afraid this would drive a permanent wedge between him and Alita, pushing them so far apart that they'd never find their way back to each other. Worse, Gerhad suspected Ido didn't realise what he doing. After Chiren had left, alienation had become his default setting. Gerhad was close to him only in a professional capacity, as his nurse. Given the nature of his practice, the relationship involved a certain amount of intimacy—the wellbeing of their patients depended on their understanding each other. But it wasn't the personal intimacy shared by good friends.

For a while, Gerhad had thought it was. A surgical team was a well-oiled machine, and its members were the moving parts, all working for the same goal. It was easy to feel closer to your team than anyone else, including your family, which was a quick way to lose your family. Neither she nor Ido had families to lose; the only problem would have been if Ido had shown a romantic interest in her. Fortunately, he hadn't. Before long, she realised he wasn't interested in anything beyond their professional relationship. He tolerated her personal disclosures without impatience but didn't volunteer any of his own.

Ido would always be the man who had given her back her life, and she would always love him for that. Even if it was solely pragmatism on his part, his complete acceptance of her, no questions asked, was more than she'd ever had in any other relationship, professional or personal. And so she continued her nursing career in circumstances that were less than perfect but more fortunate than most.

Gerhad had never considered doing anything that might disturb the equilibrium between her and Ido. But then he had brought Alita's cyber-core home, and Gerhad had wondered what it would do to him. He had seemed happy to be a father again, but Alita was not his daughter. Supposedly he knew that. But as time passed, Gerhad realised this Alita was going to become less and less like his daughter. How would that play out?

Then Alita had brought the Berserker body home and turned Ido's world upside down. The argument between them had started while Gerhad was still cleaning up after the usual long day. Gerhad knew Ido expected her to make an inconspicuous exit as soon as things got heated, but instead she had gone down to the basement and pretended to sort laundry, not coming back upstairs until Alita had run out.

Ido had retreated to the kitchen to sulk over a cup of tea. Gerhad knew he wouldn't want company so she'd taken a close look at the Berserker body. It was a magnificent thing—Gerhad had never even imagined anything like it. Under different circumstances—if, say, she had been a former nurse with one arm and no prospects—she might have been strongly tempted to roll it up in a carpet and try her luck on the black market.

She had tried to imagine wide-eyed, angel-faced Alita embodied in it and couldn't. This wasn't a young girl's body.

And maybe that was the *real* problem, Gerhad thought. Ido could go on about not wanting blood on Alita's pretty flowered hands, and advanced weapons, and how lucky she was to start over with a clean slate. But Gerhad suspected that, in truth, he didn't want to let his little girl go. He'd given her the lovely young-girl body his little girl should have had, with the beautiful flowers and the silver and gold inlays, and he wanted her to stay that way.

When he'd lost his daughter, he had lost the chance to see her grow up. His Alita was fourteen, now and forever.

Gerhad had come very close to going into the kitchen that day, sitting down at the table with him, and telling him this. But it would have been the last thing she ever told him. Ido wouldn't have argued or yelled at her or told her to mind her own business; he simply would have fired her, effective immediately, and even if he regretted it later—even if he decided she'd been right—she would never be welcome in his clinic again.

Well, if this had been a more typical argument between a father and daughter—something less drastic that didn't involve having her entire body replaced, maybe just an enhancement, or even contraception— would she have hustled her bustle in there to have a word with him?

Hell, no. She wasn't a parent. For all the insight she might have, the only advice she was actually qualified to give anyone about their kids was first aid, good nutrition, and how to take their temperature. Suggesting they might be having a problem with the idea of a kid growing up was not her business, even if she was right.

But now circumstances had forced Ido to unite Alita with the Berserker. To his credit, he hadn't hesitated, hadn't substituted one of the other TRs in cold storage. He'd given her what she'd wanted and he hadn't seemed a bit reluctant about it. He had leaned over and whispered, "No one will dare harm you again."

Gerhad moved closer to the table and saw that Alita's eyes were moving back and forth below her closed lids. What could the girl be dreaming about? she wondered. Not Grewishka, certainly—her face was far too peaceful.

She appeared to be engrossed in whatever dreams her mind had conjured up. Maybe her lost memories were playing like movies in her head. But when she awoke, she'd forget them all, because nothing was that easy for anyone, not even a girl in a Berserker body.

And it would be even harder for Ido, Gerhad thought. At the moment, he was all cyber-surgeon, surrounded by display screens and swivelling on his chair from one to another, then rolling over to the table to check on the patient. But soon he would be Ido the grieving father again.

Gerhad frowned and moved closer to the table. Was she seeing things or were Alita's fingers longer than the last time she'd looked? Yes, they *were*, and they gained another millimetre as she watched. That was a relief. Going crazy was pointless in Iron City, which was itself the most insane place in an insane world.

Of course, she didn't have to be crazy to start seeing things, just tired. Two major cyber-surgeries in such a short period of time—that was pushing the limits of human stamina and technology both. Gerhad decided to run a quick diagnostic on her cyborg arm. It would flag any problems with the human operator.

Her arm checked out fine. In fact, it was more than fine. Ido had built it to perform more complex tasks and procedures than those they usually had to deal with in the clinic. Re-embodying Alita had made full use of its capabilities. Gerhad also seemed to be fine, although the diagnostic flagged her fatigue as something that needed her immediate attention. It recommended a minimum of eight hours of uninterrupted sleep. Gerhad thought twenty hours was more like it.

Fatigue was one of the reasons cited most often by people opting for a cyber enhancement. In many cases, one enhancement led to another—improvements in one area tended to make people dissatisfied with their unenhanced parts. Gerhad had never suffered from new-part fever herself but that was probably because her cyber-arm hadn't been an optional upgrade. Or maybe she just wasn't tired enough yet.

Now she could see that Alita's shoulders were measurably broader and her chest was becoming less androgynous by the second. Gerhad found this unsettling enough that she had to look away. In her time as a nurse, she had seen all kinds of things—gory, weird, eerie, scary, absurd, even miraculous—but nothing as trippy as advanced Urm technology.

Gerhad gave it a minute before looking back at Alita. Yeah, those were breasts. Alita's waist had narrowed and her hips were now quite womanly. No delicate flowers on creamy pink skin, no gold and silver inlays etched with lovely scrollwork. The biomechanoid body was beautiful, but it was a strong and formidable beauty that also happened to be anatomically correct.

"It's the adaptive technology of the Berserker body," Ido said. Gerhad jumped; she had all but forgotten that he was in the room. "The corporeal shell is reconfiguring to match her image of herself—her *new* image, that is. Her brain knows there's been a change in her embodiment. This body registered as more mature biologically, with increased capabilities, and the brain reacts accordingly. It's mutual feedback between her core and her corpus as they progress towards a state of unity."

Gerhad nodded. Re-embodiment could be tricky. If the cyber-core held onto anything from its previous incarnation, it would have trouble adjusting to a new form. Sometimes all it took was a couple of faulty pH readings and a patient would wake up with a bad case of dysmorphia or even outright rejection.

"I've never seen anything like this," Ido went on. "The body's doing most of the work, making micro-adjustments to all the systems on every level." He tilted his head at the displays. The sheer volume of data on them would have overwhelmed anyone else—and it wasn't a tea party for Ido's big brain, either, Gerhad realised, taking in his puffy, bloodshot eyes and overall haggard look. This had pushed him to the limit of his capability, and he was probably so busy relishing the challenge that he didn't know how tired he really was.

"Well, however this works, I'd say Alita isn't your little girl any more," Gerhad told him cheerfully. "She's all grown up. Officially a woman."

Ido's face went bright red and he averted his gaze. "Indeed she is. And in that spirit, we should respect her, uh, privacy. Would you mind, uh—"

Gerhad had already taken a surgical sheet from the shelf under the table. She shook it out and draped it over Ido's erstwhile little girl.

"Thank you, Nurse," Ido said in a stiff, professional tone and went back to the displays.

Gerhad put a hand over her mouth to keep from laughing. The poor guy had no idea what he was in for. Alita really *wasn't* a little girl any more. Kids here grew up too fast anyway. Iron City was that kind of place. But the social and psychological forces that acted on the average kid didn't include being maimed to within a millimetre of their lives by a monster in a sewer.

Even when Alita had been down to one arm with her hand broken off and jammed into Grewishka's eye, she had defied him, refusing to be defeated even when the monster was about to kill her. After something like that, the standard Iron City resident would probably spend the next few years curled up in the foetal position, crippled with PTSD. But not Alita—she'd have been back on her feet and looking for payback *without* a Berserker body.

But *with* one—

Urm's advanced science may have strained Ido, but he was about to discover that when it came to his little girl—who was *not* a little girl any more—he was completely out of his depth.

Welcome to the next phase of fatherhood, Gerhad thought. *You poor bastard.*

Someone kissed his forehead.

Ido woke to find himself stretched out on the sofa. He should have given it to Gerhad, he thought guiltily as he sat up blinking, trying to make his eyes open wider. He had to check on his little girl. Alita was— she was—

She was not his little girl any more, he remembered, looking at the lovely young woman standing in front of him. He looked at her sleekly muscled arms and legs and her easy, graceful stance. At least she's got good posture, his mind babbled. Without taking his eyes off her, he reached over and shook Gerhad, who was asleep in the chair beside the sofa. She slapped his hand away, started to say something, and then saw why he'd roused her.

"Well," Ido said after a bit, when he was sure he wasn't going to cry. "Look at you."

Alita gave him a warm smile. She bent casually to one side as if to pick something up off the floor and just as casually went into a one-armed handstand. Ido watched her draw her fingers together; the handstand became a one-fingerstand. Slowly, with no visible effort, and remaining perfectly balanced, she lowered her legs into a split.

Ido was still giving thanks that Gerhad had thought to put underwear on her when Alita flexed her elbow and flipped herself back up on her feet.

"You were right, Alita," he said humbly. "A warrior's spirit needs a warrior's body."

She held up her right hand, showing him the small vents on her forearm; they were breathing while a small blue flame danced over her fingertips.

"The vents draw in air to generate arc plasma," Ido said. "But don't ask me what's controlling it. I mean, you are, of course, but the exact mechanism involved—" He shrugged. "You didn't come with a manual, I'm afraid." He pointed to intake ports higher up, on her bicep. "That's part of some kind of weapon, probably also arc plasma.

And that's pretty much all I can tell you. Now you know as much about who you are as I do."

Alita sat down beside him on the sofa. She was still smiling but there was a hint of uncertainty in her face.

"You know, all this—" Ido gestured at her body. "All this beauty and strength and ability—this is the shell. It's not bad and it's not good. That part's up to you."

She surprised him by resting her head on his shoulder. *Not my little girl any more, except when she is,* Ido thought, putting his arm around her shoulders. For some unmeasured period of time, they stayed that way, watching the late afternoon rain running down the windows in rivulets. He and Gerhad had slept most of the day, but Ido felt like he could sleep a few more hours. He'd almost dozed off again when Alita suddenly spoke up.

"Grewishka told me someone from up above saved him and turned him into who he is." Pause. "He said it was his master, Nova."

Ido sighed. "Grewishka is a crazed monster, spawned to play a corrupt game by an even more corrupt system. Actually, he's just the latest in a series. They've made a lot of monsters like him that roam the streets until people like me take them out."

"It's not the game or the streets that are the problem," Alita said. "The problem is up above. Up there."

"But we're all down here, in this world. Our world," Ido replied. He drew back a little to smile at her. "You know, I told Hugo I'd call him when you were awake."

Alita bounced to her feet with a thousand-watt smile. "I'll go find him!"

"Not dressed like that, you're not," Gerhad told her firmly. "Let me find you some clothes that aren't quite so—" She hesitated. "—in-patient."

Walking—the simple act of putting one foot in front of the other—was so much better now, Alita thought as she strode along the crowded night-time streets. The rain had stopped, although rain seldom had much effect on Iron City's nightlife. The Berserker body made it a lot easier to make her way through the crowds, although that may have been due simply to her being taller. It helped to be on eye-level; people gave way for a woman more readily than for a kid. Being more substantial helped, too. Not that she'd ever been easily moved, but now she looked like someone you couldn't push around.

Part of her felt a little bad about what had happened to her old body—Ido's labour of love. Maybe it was the relief of finally being who she was that gave her a deeper understanding of what that pretty little cyborg body had meant to Ido. It had deserved better—much, *much* better.

On the other hand, if *Ido* had understood what the Berserker body had meant to *her* and done what she had asked, his work of art wouldn't have been sliced up by a monster in a sewer. So they each had some responsibility, and if she understood that, Ido probably did, too, even if he didn't say anything. Some grown-ups were like that—as Gerhad had pointed out to her once: some people wouldn't say *shit* if they were standing neck-deep in it.

Ido wasn't really like that, though. As soon as he had realised what the Berkserker body meant for her, he hadn't hesitated or tried to palm a different TR off on her. Nobody was perfect, but Ido tried to be; she had to give him that. It was a lot more than she could say for most people, especially the ice queen who had sicked Grewishka on them. Her heart had to be a frozen lump, Alita thought; maybe she'd freeze over completely and be nothing but a bunch of parts on ice. Which might be pretty soon, if those cold blue eyes were any indication.

Alita pushed the thought away, unsure how her mind could have turned to Chiren when she simply wanted to enjoy her new physicality. She couldn't remember what it had been like to be completely organic, but she thought that it must have been a lot like this—well, if the organic body in question happened to be in peak condition.

But it was more than just physical. The power she felt in her arms, her legs, her shoulders, her torso and back, seemed like something that had always been within her, waiting for her to find it. Or to wake it? Maybe she just had to realise she had it at all. Strength and endurance were things of the body but something in her core—in the core of her core— gave them life. Her memory of what had happened to her hadn't come back completely yet, but this was her muscle memory of being alive, conscious and embodied. She was a warrior spirit in a warrior body.

Alita paused, looking around. The traffic on the sidewalks as well as the streets was increasing. The crowds wouldn't start thinning out till sometime after one A.M. As convenient as it was to get around in her new, grown-up form, it might take her almost that long to find Hugo, especially in the busier parts of town. But there was a better way.

She stepped off the sidewalk into a narrow passageway between two buildings. For a minute, she studied each structure's outer surface, looking at the various protrusions—windowsills, narrow wrought-iron balconies, drain pipes, old bits of fire escapes half stripped away by scavengers. Then she launched herself upwards.

The sheer physical pleasure of the leap seemed to give her extra momentum. As she rebounded between the two buildings, from drain pipes to windowsills to wrought-iron bars, it crossed her mind that what she was doing had been known at one time in the dim, distant past as *parkour*, although she had no idea how she knew that. It didn't worry her—a tidbit of information shaken loose from some obscure nook or cranny. There was plenty she *couldn't* remember and she didn't know why that was, either, but she kept on keepin' on anyway, so what the hell.

On the roof, Alita stopped to breathe deeply, not because she was winded but because she liked the smell of rain in the air. She looked up at the overcast sky and saw something twinkle brightly. Not a star, but a light from one of the tall buildings at the edge of Zalem. The city was a slightly darker shadow in the night-time rain clouds. It was almost as if Zalem had caught something of what she'd been feeling and wanted to remind her that there was always a ceiling, always something out of reach, even for her.

We'll see, she told the shadow silently.

The bodysuit Gerhad had found for her was really a good piece of clothing, Alita thought as she bounded from rooftop to rooftop, pausing to scan the streets below. The plain black fabric was light but tough, and it breathed so she didn't get overheated when she exerted herself. (Which was a good thing, as Ido had insisted she wear a raincoat over it.) It was a lot like skin, minus the pain receptors.

Not that she knew much about human skin or pain receptors. A warrior spirit didn't give two craps about pain. She'd conquered pain so long ago, she couldn't even remember what it felt like. How she could know that, when she hardly knew anything at all, was another one of those little mysteries, along with why she could shake a memory loose only by spitting in death's face. Or poking it in the eye.

She had so many questions; she even had questions about questions. But she'd worry about that later. Right now, all she really wanted to do was find Hugo. Was he ever going to be surprised!

Alita finally spotted Hugo hanging around in front of the CAFÉ café with Koyomi and Tanji and a few other members of his crew. Seeing him made her feel like the sun had come out inside her, filling her up with light. And warmth. She had to take a steadying breath before she made her way back down to street level, going from window ledges to drain pipes to bare centimetres of uneven brick. Finally, she dropped from an old-fashioned faux-neon sign to make a three-point landing on the sidewalk, startling a couple who had been looking dreamily into each other's eyes. She gave them a thumbs up and headed towards Hugo.

Tanji was talking to him about something. His gaze passed over her without recognition—she could tell because his face didn't immediately curdle. A couple of seconds later, he looked at her again, frowning a little, and started to say something else to Hugo. Koyomi had recognised her; she gave Hugo a hard nudge and pointed.

Hugo's double take was faster. Recognition didn't come right away, but she watched it dawn on him as she approached, until finally his face lit up with joyful relief and he ran to meet her. He swept her up in his arms—with an effort—and swung her around—with even more of an effort.

"Alita! You're all right! You're—" Hugo put her down as he discovered there had been some changes since he'd last seen her. Standing back, he gave her a long look from head to toe.

"Wow," he said, noticing what she had on under the raincoat. "You're all—"

"Back together?" she suggested, making them both laugh.

"Yeah, you're *way* back together," he said. "You look real, uh—"

Alita could practically see the little gears and wheels turning in his head as he tried to find the right word.

"Different," he said finally.

Behind Hugo, Koyomi was grinning broadly as she gave Alita two thumbs up. Tanji looked unimpressed, but it took so much effort that he couldn't manage his usual sour face. Alita almost felt sorry for him. She winked at Koyomi and took Hugo's arm. He put his hand over hers and they walked off together.

"It's all nanotech this and nanotech that," Alita told Hugo. She wasn't sure how long they'd been walking or where they were and she didn't care. "I don't understand it and Ido says there's a lot about it even he hasn't been able to figure out yet."

"So you're stronger now?" Hugo asked.

She nodded. "And faster. And I feel so much more—well, *me*."

Hugo gave her a thoughtful, sideways look. "You know, some guys would be intimidated by a girl like you."

"Really?" Alita blinked at him. "Why?"

"Oh, probably because you could rip out my arm and beat me to death with the wet end," he deadpanned.

"Well, there's an easy solution to that," she said, smiling. "Don't piss me off."

Hugo threw back his head and roared with laughter and she laughed with him, delighted (and a bit relieved) he thought it was funny.

"I always knew there was a warrior in you, Alita," he said when he wound down. "And now the rest of the world gets to see that, too."

Alita. He said my name.

It wasn't the first time, not even the first time that evening. But it was the first time he'd called her Alita and meant Alita the warrior. She had never thought she would be this happy, about anything.

When they came to the bridge, Alita realised they must have walked in a large circle and they were now back near the CAFÉ café. But she had no sense of time passing or distance travelled. For all she knew, time had stopped altogether. If so, she had no problem with that.

When they were halfway across the bridge, they stopped to look down at the river. It had risen quite a lot and was flowing more energetically than usual. It must have rained practically non-stop while she'd been down for repairs, Alita thought. She was about to ask Hugo about it when he took her hand and twined his fingers with hers.

Did he miss the flowers, she wondered, or the silver and gold inlays with the pretty patterns etched on them? Or the swirling lines on her fingertips?

"I'm more sensitive now, too," she told him. "Ido says it's due to the much higher density of force feedback and texture sensors. What that means is—" She took her hand away and slipped her arm out of her coat, then held her hand out to him again. "Well, try it."

Hugo turned her hand over and ran his fingers over the back, past her wrist and all the way up to her shoulder. "Can you feel that?" he asked.

She nodded, wondering if he could feel how she was loving his touch.

"Close your eyes," he said and she obeyed. A moment later, she smiled as his fingertip moved gently along the side of her neck. "Where am I now?" he said.

Eyes still closed, she put her fingers over his. He stroked her cheek with his other hand and she sensed his face moving closer to hers, so close she could feel the warmth radiating from his skin.

"And where am I now?" he asked and kissed her. His lips were surprisingly soft and tender and she kissed him back, hoping he could tell how much she loved this, the feel of him. The young girl covered with flowers had stood up to a monster, but she had not been ready for this; the woman she had become.

"You're with me," Alita whispered when they moved apart. All at once, she felt self-conscious and dropped her gaze. "As you can see, I can do anything a regular girl can do."

"Anything?" Hugo said.

"Anything," she promised, smiling as his finger traced a line from her temple down to her chin. "Does it bother you that I'm not—well, you know—completely human?"

He used the finger under her chin to lift her head so he could look into her eyes. "You're the most human person I've ever met."

They went on kissing and then it was raining again, coming down hard and straight so they were both drenched within a minute, Hugo in his light jacket and Alita with her raincoat half on and half off, and no night had ever been so utterly, wonderfully perfect.

Sitting by the window in CAFÉ café, Tanji made a contemptuous noise. Koyomi looked up from her wrist-cell screen and followed his gaze. The sight of Hugo and Alita kissing made her grin from ear to ear. Tanji shook his head.

"God, what's your damage?" Koyomi asked him, annoyed. "Why don't you like her?"

"I just never got that whole hardbody thing," he said, making his usual disapproving face. "And that Urm body she's wearing fits her like it was made for her. Which probably means she was the enemy."

Koyomi rolled her eyes. "Oh, sure—three hundred years ago. Get over it already, why dontcha?"

CHAPTER 17

Her body was stretched out on Vector's desk, but Chiren's eyes were fixed on Zalem.

She had a good view of it through the tall windows behind the desk. A few lights from the skyscrapers near the edge of the disc showed through the rain clouds. Eventually, the clouds would blow away and she'd be able to see Zalem unobscured. She needed to see it; she had to keep her eyes on the prize, no matter what happened, either to the world in general or to her in particular.

Like this business on the desk—some kind of masculine power thing, she supposed. It was uncomfortable as hell but she put up with it. At least Vector didn't play rough. And it was easy to see Zalem.

Abruptly, Vector took his hands off her. Annoyed, she was about to tell him to scratch on his own time. Then she saw his eyes.

"You." Her stomach turned over, and for a moment she thought she was going to throw up on the spot. She scrambled off the desk in revulsion, buttoning her blouse and tucking it back into her skirt.

"Why aren't you rebuilding Grewishka?" the Watcher behind Vector's eyes, Nova, wanted to know. The sound of his voice made Chiren sure Vector's throat was going to hurt when the Watcher was through with him.

"He won't let me touch him," Chiren said. "I can't even get near him. That's a problem."

"Well, then, why don't we go see him?" Nova said, and Chiren knew it wasn't a request.

She also knew he wasn't going to like what he saw.

Chiren stood in the doorway of the laboratory with Nova. The lab was fairly large, three times the size of the sad, shabby place Ido called a clinic. The equipment was also superior—everything from scanners to test tubes to surgical tech was high quality, not jerry-rigged and held together with duct tape and spit.

Or rather, it had been, before Grewishka had crashed his way in through the bedroom window again, with iridescent-blue cyber-blood leaking from cyborg-dog bites and a hand sticking out of his eye. By the look and smell of him, he'd spent the previous couple of days hiding in the sewers and doing unspeakable things to vermin.

Having finally found his way home, he had proceeded to express his existential displeasure by demolishing the entire laboratory. When Chiren and Vector realised he would also demolish anyone who got near him, they had used the blast doors to shut him up in the place and waited for him to run down and pass out. Or die.

A day later, Grewishka was still rampaging around the room, even though there was nothing left to break. Although he had managed to do more damage to himself; the grind-cutter hand was in pieces, more of his armour had been torn off, and his internal organs were starting to spill out of his chest. And the damned hand was *still* sticking out of his eye.

Nova turned to Chiren and raised one eyebrow. It was something Vector himself did from time to time but the Watcher made it freakish.

"I told you. I can't get near him," Chiren said, hating the defensive note in her voice. "He won't even let me fix his eye. Says he *wants* the pain."

Grewishka whirled at the sound of her voice. What the hell *was* keeping Alita's hand there, Chiren wondered—Grewishka's desire for pain or Alita's fury? Chiren wouldn't have been surprised if it were the latter. The girl should have been like an ant trying to take on a Centurian. She shouldn't have had a chance against Grewishka, and yet she had hurt him badly. Worse, she had incited others to help her. All of that should have told Nova to write Grewishka off as a lost cause and get a new hobby— something that didn't involve him riding Vector like a gyro-wheel.

"*Enough!*" Nova bellowed suddenly, making Chiren jump. But no, he hadn't read her thoughts. He was speaking to Grewishka. The cyborg roared in outrage and stumbled towards him, his one good hand raised in a fist. Chiren drew back, trying to pull Nova with her. Grewishka might be mostly wreckage but there was still enough power left in him to cripple them or worse. Nova didn't have to care what happened to the body he rode, he could just re-patch himself into another. But if she lost Vector, she lost her best chance of going home to Zalem.

The bastard refused to move, just stood there while Grewishka rushed at him. Before the monster had closed half the distance, however, he suddenly fell to his knees and bent forward until his head touched the floor. He was actually whimpering, Chiren realised. Somehow Grewishka in submission was more disturbing than Grewishka in full homicidal frenzy.

Nova shook Chiren's hand off his arm and went to stand over the cyborg, who was now weeping. "Grewishka, my poor, tortured child," Nova said tenderly.

Chiren's stomach did a slow forward roll. She bit her lip, commanding herself not to be sick or even to make a sound. Nova was still convinced he needed her, but that could change if she made him angry. She straightened up and composed her face into the expressionless mask of a disinterested party merely observing events as they transpired. Right now, she was observing blue cyber-blood and oil ruining Vector's trousers and shoes. Vector would be furious, until she told him how it happened. Or maybe he'd already know.

"When your mother abandoned you to die in the sewers," Nova said in a bizarre silky purr, "who reached out to take your hand?"

"You did, master," Grewishka replied in a small voice.

"Because I saw rage burning in your eyes, like a flame defying the darkness," Nova went on. "Your rage cried out for a body of equal power. And who gave you that body?"

"You did, master," said the cyborg even more meekly.

"And in return, you have *failed* me!" Nova suddenly shouted. "Stand up!"

Grewishka obeyed, head still bowed, tubes and internal organs dangling from his open chest.

"You will *never* triumph until you understand *what she is*!" Nova thundered at him. Chiren saw Grewishka flinch. "There hasn't been anything like her in three hundred years—*three hundred*! She's the last of her kind and the finest weapon ever produced by the Urm Technarchy!"

As if Grewishka had any idea what a "technarchy" was, Chiren thought, still queasy. If this went on for much longer, she really would throw up. She told herself to wait till she could do it on Vector's expensive shoes.

"She's dangerous by her mere existence!" Nova was saying. "She's a variable that threatens the very order of the world!"

"Then why not just send some Centurians to hose her down with some twenty-mill shells?" Chiren blurted, unable to help herself. "Case closed."

Nova turned to her with a twisted expression she had never seen on Vector's face and hoped she'd never see again. "Because I want her *dead*, not *obliterated*," he said, over-enunciating as if he were talking to a child. "Her core contains technologies that have been lost to us for *centuries*."

He turned back to Grewishka and his tone softened. "Doctor Chiren is going to make you faster and stronger than ever. And *you* are going to *let her do her work.* Aren't you?"

"Yes, master," Grewishka said, utterly chastened.

"I need you to *destroy* Alita," Nova said. "I need you to bring me *her heart.*"

Grewishka knelt again, a grotesque knight pledging himself to an even more grotesque king. "Master, I live only for her death."

They stayed like that for a long moment. Then Vector—only Vector now—turned on his heel and rushed past her into the bathroom. Chiren heard the water running and let him have a few seconds by himself before she followed.

"Damn, I *hate* it when he does that," Vector said, still splashing cold water on his face. He spoke softly and left the tap running so Grewishka couldn't hear.

"Well, on the upside—" She gave a weak laugh as she handed Vector a towel. "He's a better kisser than you are."

Vector finished drying his face and tossed the towel on the floor. "Joke all you want. Just keep in mind this isn't someone who tolerates failure."

Except for creatures he finds in sewers, Chiren added silently.

"I'm not inclined to bet my entire future on a piece of iron that won't even let you pull a spear out of his eye," Vector said.

"Actually, it's a hand," Chiren said, remembering her composure, "with the wrist and part of the forearm. Do you have something better in mind?"

Vector looked thoughtful for a few seconds, then smiled. Chiren went into one of two stalls, knowing that would make Vector leave immediately, and just sat, listening to the water still running in the sink. Her stomach had already settled but she stayed a while longer, thinking about Vector and his future—that he'd said *my future* and not *our future* wasn't lost on her. She thought about how to rebuild Grewishka and wondered how long it would take to replace everything he'd wrecked in the lab. Why did Nova have an intense desire to have *Grewishka* bring Alita's heart to him, after the girl had already kicked Grewishka's ass twice, and when there were any number of other ways he might get to her through Ido? What was Nova trying to prove? And why was he trying to do it with a blunt instrument like Grewishka when there was a precision instrument like herself available?

Maybe he was crazy. Not a normal-for-Iron-City whack job, but clinically psychotic, of the variety that were a danger to others, especially since he had the power to indulge any obsessions or delusions he might have.

The safest thing to do, she decided, was to get to work on rebuilding Grewishka. At the very least, it would keep her out of Vector's office. And off his desk.

But it was another five minutes before she could persuade herself to leave the empty bathroom.

"To dreams," Vector said, raising a glass containing a generous shot of dark-gold whisky. The glass was one of a set of six genuine pre-Fall antiques he had found stashed in a forgotten corner of the Factory. The glasses were thick and curved in a way that made them a pleasure to hold in the hand. Vector only brought them out on occasions that demanded conspicuous consumption, and tonight he needed only two of them.

"To dreams," agreed Hugo, raising the other glass, which held an even more generous shot. He was ensconced in the biggest, cushiest chair in Vector's palatial office, gaping at his marble floor, his sensational view and his polished desk that was probably bigger than the sad rat-hole the kid called home.

Hugo looked a lot more comfortable now than he had earlier when Vector had picked him up in the limo for an impromptu private meeting. They had arrived at the Factory at shift change, just in time to see one long line of workers going into the Entrance and another long one coming out of the Exit.

It wasn't the most heartening sight in the world—the people coming out were so tired and lifeless, they might have been robots rather than cyborgs. The ones going in were a bit livelier, but only a bit. You could tell they weren't looking forward to the next eight hours.

Most of them were TRs, and the rest were almost there. But they weren't sporting flashy, shiny Paladin bodies—these people were all walking toolkits, tailored for a particular purpose, whatever that might be. No one in this group had any conspicuous adornments like a custom paint-job or a fancy etched design. The Factory frowned on customisation not required for the job as a possible safety hazard; it could distract other employees, and a distracted employee was an accident waiting to happen. It might also confuse sensors monitoring employees on duty, which might cause mistakes in attendance records. As a result, an employee might not be paid, and nobody wanted that. Payroll mistakes were notoriously difficult to straighten out, sometimes taking as long as six months, which was a very long time to go without a pay cheque.

The expression on Hugo's face at the sight of these two sorry groups gave Vector the idea that this could be what they called an object lesson or a teachable moment.

"If you're not the lead ant," Vector said, "the view never changes."

Hugo had turned to him with wide eyes and Vector knew instinctively the kid had been thinking something very similar. He might as well drive the point home, Vector thought, and decided to take a little detour on his way up to the office.

When they reached the executive elevators, Vector had made a business of waving the Centurians aside just before they read his internal ID. He knew how it would look to Hugo, like he had more power in his fingertips than regular people could even imagine.

Then they made a stop at the control booth high above the Factory floor so Hugo could see what it was like to look down on operations through the floor-to-ceiling windows.

Seen this way, it was actually quite amazing. Cyborgs worked among much larger robot arms, their machine attachments performing tasks in perfect rhythm. The human workers were so integrated into the mode of production that it was actually hard to tell where they left off and the machines began, even when you saw their faces, which sort of bobbed around near the assembly line like balloons with unhappy, careworn faces painted on them.

While the unhappy expression on Hugo's face suggested he might throw up, Vector decided he'd suffered enough and took him up to his office.

Vector wasn't especially fond of letting street trash sit on his expensive furniture—he'd have to have everything shampooed and maybe fumigated to get rid of the stink of poverty and failure. But if you wanted something from one of these little weasels, you had to give them the idea that if they pleased you, they actually had a hope in hell of climbing out of the hole they'd been born in.

"Smooth, isn't it?" Vector said, as if he thought Hugo would know.

"This is the stuff they send up to Zalem, not the watered-down rat piss they serve locally."

"So it's like tasting Zalem," Hugo said happily. As if he really believed it.

"You know, Hugo, I was born in a poor village on the outskirts of the Badlands," Vector said chattily, pumping sincerity into each word. No one could do honest like he did. "I came to Iron City when I was nine, and I was surrounded by scum. Everywhere I looked, it was all scum, all the time. But I survived. I worked hard, and pretty soon I gained a reputation. People knew me, knew who I was." He paused to look out of one of the windows and the kid looked too. *His* view, although the kid probably didn't understand that yet. But he would, unless he was stupider than he looked.

"The poor in this world, they suffer and work, work and suffer," Vector went on. "That's how it's always been and how it always will be. Insects never know they're insects." He turned to the kid, looking wise. "But we know the truth, don't we?" As if "we" would ever mean him and Hugo.

"Well—" Hugo frowned a little. "*I'm* no worker ant, I know that."

No, you're a worm. "I like your drive," Vector told him, enthusing a little, as if he didn't usually but Hugo was so special he couldn't hide his admiration. "You have the determination not to fail. You could have a pretty solid future with my organisation."

Hugo took another sip of the whisky Vector was wasting on him. "*My* future's in Zalem," he said confidently. "I remember your promise every day."

Vector's smile never faltered. His policy was to forget promises as soon as he made them, sometimes even *while* he was making them. Whenever some fool came around expecting him to cough up a reward, he always found a way to show them they'd failed to hold up their part of the bargain and were therefore entitled to nothing except an ass-kicking for trying to con him.

But somehow the kid picked up on the fact that he'd drawn a blank. "You know, to send me up?" Hugo prodded. "You said when I bring you a million credits, you'll send me straight to Zalem."

Vector covered his surprise by taking a hefty swig from his glass. "Of *course* I remember," he lied amiably. "And you have that many? A million credits?"

"Almost," Hugo said, beaming with pride. "Just a couple more months and—" He looked through the window and pointed up at Zalem. "I'm there."

"*Really.*" Vector refilled Hugo's glass more generously. "Hugo, I do believe I'm *impressed*. You don't see that kind of spirit in kids these days. Not in too many adults, either." He gave himself a refill. "Let's drink to Zalem."

They clinked glasses and Vector watched him throw back a healthy gulp. The little shit-bag had to be living on next to nothing, Vector thought, careful not to show his amazement. He could have been living high in a nice apartment—well, nice for Iron City—dressing like royalty and taking pricey companions to restaurants and bars where fights *didn't* break out every night. Instead, he was living like a beggar while he saved up for his big dream. It was almost enough to make him *like* the kid. He could use someone like that on his payroll.

On the other hand, guys like Hugo could suddenly grow a conscience at the worst possible time. Although, Vector reminded himself, the kid jacked cyborgs for a living; he knew damned well he wasn't an angel. But he was smart; he was more likely to start second-guessing every order he was given. Either way, Vector would end up having to get rid of him, because you couldn't buy someone like that off.

Still, he wouldn't have minded having someone with a real work ethic to do the heavy lifting; it would be good while it lasted. Maybe he could talk the kid into reconsidering his plans.

"I agree that Zalem's great," Vector said before Hugo could say anything else about his real dream, "but personally, I'd rather rule in hell than serve in heaven. If you see what I mean." The kid nodded but he was starting to look a little bleary. Vector gestured at the tiny lights in the night sky. "If we went up there right now, we'd have to start all over again, at the bottom of the food chain. Down here, though—" He gestured at their surroundings with both hands. "Down here, we can live like kings. We can make our own rules—they look the other way because they need me to keep the wheels turning at the Factory and keep the Games running. Someone's gotta keep the masses distracted; bread and circuses, you know the drill." Hugo didn't; Vector gave him a thousand-megawatt smile as if he did. "Might as well be me. And you, if you're up for it."

He gave the kid another unnecessary refill, then brought over one of the other, slightly smaller and less cushy chairs and sat down so they were eye to eye.

"So, tell me about this girl of yours," Vector said, his voice low and confidential. "The one you brought to the track the other night."

"You mean Alita?" Hugo looked a bit surprised at the sudden change of subject.

"Oh, is that her name?" Vector said innocently. "Word on the street is she's a pretty good Motorball player. Left a lot of guys eating her dust." As if she were the talk of the town.

"Oh, she's the *best*!" Hugo's face was flushed with good booze and impossible dreams. And, if Vector wasn't mistaken, puppy love, too. "She's got more natural talent than anybody I ever saw. I swear, she could play for the Second League right now. Tonight!"

Vector made an impressed face. "Well, if she's *that* good, bring her to Second League tryouts and I'll see to it she gets a shot."

"You mean—you mean at the *stadium*?" If the kid's eyes got any bigger, they'd pop out of his head and drop into his whisky. "Are you *serious*?"

"Hugo, you and I have a common trait," Vector assured him, his tone even more confidential. "We can both spot talent in its natural habitat."

"You won't regret this," Hugo promised him.

"Oh, I know I won't," Vector replied. The kid was so boggled that the compliment had gone right by him. That was some bad case of puppy love he had. He raised the level in Hugo's glass to make sure he was too drunk to think of running off to give Alita the good news right this minute. The tryouts were weeks away; she could use the time to train. Vector wanted both him and the girl all pumped up on faith, hope and puppy love so that when she went down in flames, Hugo would be too destroyed to say the word *Zalem* ever again.

CHAPTER 18

Eventually, Hugo realised the warmth on the side of his face was sunlight. He guessed it must be morning. Furthermore, judging by the angle of the light and by how sweaty he felt, he realised he had belly-flopped onto his mattress fully clothed last night.

The sun was getting brighter, like it was nagging him to get up and do something to justify his existence, when all he wanted to do was go back to sleep. The only way he could avoid the monumental hangover waiting to strike him down was by not moving. Ever.

All at once, a shadow fell over him, and he felt himself smile at the blessed relief. A second later, it was gone and he winced as the sun threatened to cook him where he lay. The hangover decided it could wait no longer; his brain turned into a big bass drum and started beating itself.

The shadow returned and this time it stayed where it was. The relief from the sun was welcome but it did nothing to alleviate the pain in his head. It occurred to him that the shadow expected something from him. Hugo hoped it was the Angel of Death, come to put him out of his misery. He opened one eye.

Not the Angel of Death, but his head hurt too much to let him smile. "Hey," he croaked.

"What *happened* to you?" Alita asked with real concern. Like she'd never seen a guy with a hangover before. Then he remembered she probably hadn't.

Moving slowly, he sat up, holding his head so the big bass drum wouldn't pound it off his neck and send it rolling across the floor.

"Oh, nothing." He tried to sound casual. "I wound up hanging with Vector last night. Alcohol was involved. Apparently. He said it was the good stuff." Everybody claimed the good stuff wouldn't give you a hangover. Obviously everybody was a big fat liar. So what else was new?

"Vector?" Alita squatted down to peer into his face. "Is he your connection for getting up to Zalem?"

"Yeah."

"Oh," she said, and Hugo watched her wilt like she'd just lost the last thing she'd ever had to be happy about. "I was hoping you'd want to stay."

God, sometimes he could be such a boob. "Well, it's not right away," he added quickly. "I've still got—"

"No, it's okay," she said and he saw her forcing herself to perk up. "It's your dream. What you've always wanted."

"Used to be." Hugo got to his feet and kicked through the clothes lying around on the floor, searching for a shirt that might be even just marginally cleaner than the one he had on. "I was always so sure about that. Then you come along and nothing's clear to me any more." He paused to look out the window at the Factory complex. Alita followed his gaze, then looked quizzically at him.

"All I know is, I'm not gonna end up like my dad," Hugo told her. "A Factory drone who had to replace himself piece by piece."

The night his father had come home with the extendable arm, Hugo had been frightened by all the metal and rubber, and when his father had hugged him with his real arm, the smell of oil and plastic cement had made him gag. He'd just been a little kid but he still felt ashamed of the way he'd run away crying.

"And for what?" Hugo gave a harsh, humourless laugh. "So he could drop dead on the assembly line one day making things he could never have. He never even *tried* for anything better. But I'm getting the hell out of here before it's too late." He paused. "My dad always used to joke about Management having a rule that if you felt yourself passing out, you had to fall *away* from the machines. Otherwise it made a mess and it took longer to replace you. Some joke, huh? Or maybe the joke is, he didn't have time."

Alita was silent for a long moment. Then she said, "How much more do you need before you can go?"

"Ninety K." Although the way he felt now, he'd have had trouble making nine credits.

"But I can earn that in bounties!" Alita said, perking up again. "I'll just see who's got the highest bounties on their heads and take 'em out!"

Hugo stared at her incredulously. Even his head was too surprised to throb. "I'd *never* ask you to do that for me," he said.

"I'd do *anything* for you," she told him cheerfully, like it was no big deal. She pulled up her shirt and pressed a spot at the base of her throat, which opened her chest cavity.

Hugo was horrified. "What are you *doing*?"

Alita reached into her ribcage with one hand, removed her heart, and held it out to him, like she was offering him a sandwich. Or a bar of chocolate. For the first time in his life, Hugo couldn't speak, couldn't move, couldn't do anything except stare at the exquisite white ceramic heart beating away in her hand, pumping heart's-blood and cyber-blood through the vessels attached to it.

"I'd give you my heart," Alita said, and Hugo knew it was a promise. He had never fainted but he was starting to feel like he might. Unless he woke up first.

"I mean it," she went on. "And it's a good one. It's got an Urm micro-reactor for a power supply. It's worth *millions*."

Tanji appeared suddenly in Hugo mind's eye, looking as grim-faced as ever. *Don't just stand there, dumbass—jack that shit and run! We'd get enough to live on for the rest of our lives.*

"With your connections, you could find a buyer easy," Alita was saying. "You could get enough so we could *both* go to Zalem. Then you could find me a cheap replacement."

The memory of the crew heaving Kinuba's cyber-core replayed in his head. But when it hit the street, in his mind's eye it was Alita, looking up at him with those big eyes. *I told you I'd do anything.*

"No!" Hugo snapped.

Alita gave him a nudge. "Oh, come on. You buy and sell pieces all the time."

When you gonna tell your hardbody you jack cyborgs?

"No," he said again, more quietly but just as firmly. "Look—don't just *do* things for people, no matter how good you think they are or how deserving or—or anything else. Especially not things like this."

"It's all or nothing with me, Hugo," she said, her big eyes serious. "That's just who I am."

Hugo pushed her hand gently back towards her chest cavity. For a moment, his fingertip touched her heart and he *felt* it beating. "Please put it back," he begged her. "*Please.*"

Alita did so without further argument. Hugo watched her close up her chest and pull down her shirt, knowing the sensation of her heart beating was going to haunt him for a very long time, possibly forever.

"Okay, see?" she said brightly. "All gone. That was pretty intense, though, wasn't it?" she added.

"Yeah, *very* intense," he agreed and went back to hunting for a shirt so she wouldn't see how freaked he still was. But at least it seemed to have scared off his hangover.

Outside, Hugo was about to start his gyro when he paused to look up at Zalem. "Maybe there's another way to get there," he said. "I meant to tell you, Vector wants you to try out for Second League."

"*What?*" Alita wasn't sure she'd heard him right. "What did you say?"

"Hey, if you become a big-deal Motorball star, you'll make a fortune and we can go up together."

Alita burst into hearty giggles. "What are you talking about? I can't be a pro Motorball player!"

Hugo twisted around and took her head in both his hands. "Alita, you *could* be a champion. For real. No kidding. You win the Second League tryout and scouts'll be killing each other to get to you. We'll be home free—home in Zalem."

Alita frowned. "Well, let's ride while I think it over."

Shrugging, Hugo turned around to start the gyro and Alita burst out laughing again. She grabbed him around the waist and squeezed.

"Okay, I'll do it!" she said. "But *only* if *you'll* be my coach!"

"If that's what it takes—" He gave her a quick kiss. "I'm your man!"

She was leaning back as she rode behind the kid, stretching out, letting the wind blow her hair around like she didn't have anything to worry about. Like nothing bad could ever happen to her. Like this wasn't Iron City, where all good things came to a bad end, often before they even had a chance to begin.

"You gonna kill her?" asked the cyborg in a whiny voice.

"Worse," said Zapan, keeping his gaze on the happy couple as they sped away. He rubbed the bridge of his nose, which would never be the same again. "I'm gonna break her heart."

"Come again?" the cyborg said.

Zapan had to force himself not to take the cyborg's head off and drop-kick it into traffic. He had, after all, tracked the kid down for him. But Zapan was damned if he was going to call the guy Cronie, even if that was his name. People could get the wrong idea.

"Okay, let me break it down for you," Zapan said. "Shut. Up."

Cronie nodded. "That's what I thought."

CHAPTER 19

The weeks Alita had been sure would never pass finally went by. The day of the tryout seemed to last as long as the previous month. Several times, Gerhad made a point of assuring Alita that the sun would set and night would fall. Ido promised he would go with her to the track and help her with her armour and her wheel-feet and everything else. And Hugo, to her immense disappointment, promised to meet her there because he had an errand to run. But he would definitely be there. After all the time he'd spent coaching her, he wasn't going to stand her up. Gerhad promised her the same thing, saying that Hugo would miss it only if he were dead.

"I didn't rebuild you just so you could end up as wreckage on the Motorball track," Ido complained as Alita led him along the access tunnel.

"You're right," Alita said. "Let's just go bag ourselves a couple of heads. Easy money."

"All right, all *right*," Ido said grumpily.

"Thought you'd see it my way," Alita replied, smug and happy as they walked up to the SECURITY guy. The pride she had felt at giving Ido a pass on a lanyard was completely undercut when the SECURITY guy waved them both through without even looking. Well, it was only a tiny letdown, she told herself. Hugo would be waiting for them on the pit lane.

But he wasn't.

Hugo's phone rang as he whipped through traffic on his gyro. He didn't have to look at the display to know who was calling. "What's up, Alita?"

"'What's up?' What do you think? Where *are* you?" she demanded.

"On my way," he assured her cheerfully. "Just gotta make this one stop and—"

"If you miss this, I'll *kill* you."

"Hey, I'll be there, trust me! I just gotta—" There was a hard click as she hung up on him. "Do one thing," he finished lamely and pushed the gyro faster, dodging in and out of traffic on both street and sidewalk.

Trust him? Of course she trusted him, Alita fumed, feeling more dangerous than usual. She'd spent all that time training with him; he should know that she trusted him absolutely. And that he could trust her unconditionally—to *kill* his ass if he didn't get there on time.

A moment later, she forgot all about Hugo as Jashugan appeared before her, a vision of Motorball royalty with his black-and-gold armour, while his pit crew scrambled and flitted around him with scanners and sonar wands and thermo-readers, calling out to each other.

"The camber's still off in the right bogey," Jashugan said, serene with authority and wisdom, while the crew went into a frenzy of note-taking, one guy writing on his own arm in marker.

Jashugan was about to say something else when his gaze fell on Alita and time stopped.

Then it started again as his noble, godlike features broke into a broad, sunny smile that made his grey eyes twinkle. *Jashugan was glad to see her.*

It only took a fraction of a second for the story to unfold in her head. Hugo had told Jashugan about her tryout and about what a tremendous talent she was, and Jashugan wanted to meet her. And to befriend her! Mutual respect of competitors. Brotherhood of the Paladins. Heroes of the Game. She could see it all in his face as he came towards her and reached out to shake her hand.

And then his hand went past her to Ido.

"Doc!" said Jashugan, his dignified tones warm and delighted. "I haven't seen you in ages! Really glad you're here!"

"Hi, champ," Ido said, shaking hands with him, all casual. "And here." Ido put his arm around her shoulders. "I'd like you to meet Alita."

"Hello," Jashugan said politely, absolutely and definitely offering his hand to her now. "I'm Jashugan."

"Oh, I know who you are!" Alita bubbled, grabbing his hand with both of hers and pumping it up and down. "I'm a *big* fan, *really* big—the *biggest*! I'm trying out for Second League tonight!"

He looked down at her with benign curiosity and she suddenly felt a lot more like pretty young Alita covered in flowers, not the fierce warrior who had been training with Hugo to be the next Motorball badass.

"I see," Jashugan said. "So you intend to play the greatest game that ever was?"

"Yes, sir," Alita said, pride in her voice.

"And what do you want from my game?" Jashugan asked. "Fame? Wealth? Glory?"

Alita met his gaze with confidence and certainty. "I follow the path of the warrior."

She must have said the right thing, Alita thought; he was smiling and there was a twinkle in his eye, but he seemed genuinely pleased by her response.

"Then perhaps the next time we meet," Jashugan said, "it will be on the track."

"Okay, yeah, good!" Alita enthused, waiting for him to go off with his crew. Why was he still standing there? Maybe he was waiting for her to say something more intelligent than *Okay, yeah, good*?

No, she realised, he was just waiting for her to let go of his hand.

Mortified, she released him and he inclined his head towards her. (He *bowed* to me! she thought ecstatically. Jashugan *bowed to* me!) He gave Ido another big smile and then rolled off towards the locker room area with his pit crew scurrying after him.

"*Wow*," Alita breathed, staring after him in star-struck wonder. Did his crew have any idea how privileged they were to be in the service of such a magnificent Paladin? She turned back to the pit lane and bumped into a stout man in greasy mechanic's overalls. The top of his head came to just under her nose.

"So you're Hugo's hot prospect," he said in a flat, almost bored voice. "I'm Ed, how ya doin'?" Before she could answer, he shoved a large, lumpy duffel bag at her. "Here's some loaner gear I scraped together for ya. You're welcome." He stumped away, leaving her and Ido nonplussed.

Vector looked around at the rough, scarred men in the locker room who were currently cursing and speculating on each other's parentage. His bodyguard was stationed just inside the door, although Vector wasn't concerned about anyone walking in on them. Any Paladin would take one look at who was in there and find somewhere else to be. Real Paladins didn't mix with street thugs who couldn't get even one sponsor to sticker them. Several of them were banned from every bar in town, on the grounds that their presence could decrease property values.

But this was nothing Vector had to worry about. Owning the Game afforded him a lot of privileges. Final Champion was the best a Paladin could hope for, but Vector was the king. And it was good to be the king, better than anything.

Vector cleared his throat and they quieted down. "I'd like to thank you all for coming in at such short notice," he said. "You—well, I hesitate to use the term 'players' because, frankly, you're the scum of the Game."

They let him know they didn't like that a whole lot. There were catcalls and jeers. But no one threw even a towel at him, and not only because his bodyguard would make garbage out of them with the automatic under his jacket. You didn't have to be the sharpest knife in the drawer to know that life could get very bad for everyone when you disrespected the king.

Grinning, Vector held up both hands and they all shut up. "Tonight, however, you're *hand-picked* scum—*my* scum. Because tonight, it's not a game, and it's not a tryout. It's a hunt. And I'll pay five hundred K to whomever kills the girl called Alita."

Now he had their attention.

Alita stopped fumbling with the connections on her leg armour and looked up at Ido so plaintively, it was all he could do not to take her in his arms, stroke her hair, and tell her everything was going to be all right. But that was no way to treat a Motorball badass.

"Can a human love a cyborg?" she asked, her voice wistful.

"Why do you ask?" Ido asked with a gentle smile. "Does this cyborg love a human?"

She sighed. "I love Hugo."

It wasn't exactly news to Ido, given all the time they'd spent together. The way she talked about him, the way she looked when she came back after training sessions, not to mention the mornings she'd pretended she'd got up very early when she had really just come home—he might have no experience with a grown daughter, but he wasn't stupid. Gerhad had advised him to stand back, give her room to move, and let her come to him, if and when she wanted to talk. And now here she was, confiding in him. If only her timing had been better.

"Well, that's wonderful," he told her. "But right now you have to keep your head in the Game. It can get crazy-rough out there on the track, even when it's just a tryout." Ido took a pair of wheel-feet out of his own bag and swapped them for the loaner wheels she'd been about to put on. "Here, use these."

Alita's face lit up with surprised delight. "Did you make these for me?"

Ido nodded as he put the loaner wheels back in the duffle bag. "They won't give you super-speed—regulations—but they'll be a lot more reliable."

Ed had actually put together some pretty good gear for her but borrowed wheels could be iffy for anyone, especially for Alita with her technologically advanced body. Ido had done his best to make this pair more compatible with the Urm connectivity. They weren't Urm-level, but there wouldn't be even a microsecond of lag between her nerves firing and the action of her wheels. Ido had watched Hugo's videos of their practice sessions so he could match the shape and wheel placement to her rolling gait and style of movement. And they were durable—they'd hold up for tonight. He could see about making an even better pair later.

Watching Alita put them on, Ido had a sudden, powerful urge to sweep her up in his arms and run for home. Gerhad had reminded him more than once that Alita wasn't his little girl any more—except she *was*, dammit, and she had no idea how brutal it could get out there. She *thought* she did, just because she'd seen a few games and she'd been training hard for weeks. But the Paladin-bodycam view they showed on the big stadium screens didn't convey what it was really like to be in the thick of things.

"What is it?" Alita asked, looking up at him curiously.

"Nothing," Ido said and forced himself to smile as if he didn't think this was a terrible idea. "Now, look—here's our deal: you go out there, you win, and then you skate right back to this locker room. And you wear *all* the protection—*all* the pads, *all* the armour. And this." He pushed the helmet down on her head and adjusted the sizing.

Alita's smile turned to a grimace as she looked from him to the padding and body armour piled on the floor. "I don't *really* need all that crap, do I? It'll slow me down."

"You *do* need every bit of it," Ido told her firmly. "Remember, if you wreck *this* body, you're outta luck. It's Urm technology; I can't fix it."

Alita immediately began padding up, and Ido helped her while congratulating himself on finally saying exactly the right thing. She didn't even mind him double- and triple-checking everything to make sure nothing would come loose or fall off. He took a few extra minutes to give her wheels one last pre-game check. They really were good wheels; in a previous lifetime, he would have been proud of this work. Now his only concern was that it was the best he could do for his little girl. His little girl, the Motorball badass.

As soon as they were finished checking everything, Alita surprised him by asking him to leave.

"I need a little time to myself," she told him, her voice gentle. "You know, to think about what I'm gonna do, compose myself."

Ido stood back and looked her over, his little girl, the warrior spirit in the warrior body. Even in borrowed padding and armour, she looked formidable.

"Good luck, honey," he said.

"Thanks," she said absently. She had found a marker in the duffel bag and was too busy scrawling "99" on each shoulder to see him leave.

Alita plumped down on the bench with relief as the door closed behind Ido. It wasn't really that he'd been making her nervous, although his checking and rechecking had started to feel more than a little obsessive-compulsive. She wanted him in the stadium so he could watch as she made her entrance onto the track. Then he'd see she was ready for anything and there was nothing to worry about.

She gave herself a few quiet seconds before rolling out of the locker room into the hall where she almost collided with Ed, as stout as ever but even shorter when she was wearing wheel-feet. He didn't look at all impressed; maybe because she didn't have her game face on yet, she thought.

"Have you seen Hugo?" she asked him.

"I've seen everyone," Ed assured her. "Track's this way." He started down the hallway without looking back to see if she was coming. "Unless you changed your mind and you wanna go out for ice cream."

She'd show him ice cream, Alita thought as she rolled after him. She'd show them all.

CHAPTER 20

Hugo heard them even before he turned the corner into the alley.

"Please, just stop!" the cyborg begged Tanji and Dif. They had him on the ground tangled up in a net. "I haven't done anything to you, I just wanna go home and catch the game highlights!"

That was pretty much what all the cyborgs said when they got jacked. In the past, it hadn't meant a thing to Hugo, just the noise an unlucky cyborg made while he and the crew made a living.

"Hey, this is *just business*," Tanji was telling him in an exasperated tone of voice while he pried off the cyborg's actuator mount from the back of his neck. It came away with a loud wrenching pop that made Hugo feel sick, even though he'd done the same thing himself more times than he could count. "It's nothin' personal. *Really.*"

Hugo skidded to a stop and hurriedly leaned his gyro against a wall. He was barely aware of hearing the gyro topple over as he ran to Tanji.

"Tanji, *stop!*" Hugo yelled, pulling him off the cyborg on the ground.

Tanji's astonishment was plain even though his face was completely hidden behind his goggles and bandanna. He dropped the actuator, turned back to the cyborg and bopped him on the head with the pry bar, knocking him out. Dif seemed to be frozen in place with a bundle of wires in one hand; cheap stuff they'd probably have to give away.

"You said my *name*, you idiot!" Tanji said angrily. "What the hell's wrong with you?"

"Nothing's wrong with *me*," Hugo replied. "I can't do this any more. I *won't*."

Tanji gave him a hard shove. "So *that's* your damage now?" He shoved Hugo again, making him stagger backwards so he almost tripped over his fallen gyro. "You been gone for weeks and now you show up with this line of crap? It's your little hardbody, isn't it?"

Hugo grabbed him by the front of his jacket, whirled him around, and slammed him against the wall. "It's over for me, got that? *I'm out*—done, finito, thank you and good night! And if you had half a brain, you'd get out, too!"

Tanji batted Hugo's hands away. He raised his goggles and pulled down his bandanna. "You shoulda jacked that bitch. You'd be on your way to Zalem right now!" As Tanji made a move towards the still-unconscious cyborg, Hugo punched him.

The blow surprised Tanji more than it hurt him. He hit the wall behind and bounced back swinging. Hugo knew Tanji had the advantage just by virtue of experience—Tanji had been in lots of fights and won most of them. By contrast, Hugo always tried talking his way out of a tight spot, and if that didn't work, he ran like hell. Right now, however, he didn't want to talk *or* run, he wanted to pound Tanji into the pavement, and the feeling was mutual.

Tanji had him in a headlock and Hugo was trying to bite him through his jacket when someone burst out laughing. It wasn't Dif, who was still standing by, uselessly clutching the wires. Hugo and Tanji let go of each other to see a familiar pampered face grinning at them.

"Bravo!" Zapan said, clapping his hands as he stood over the cyborg on the ground. "A magnificent display! *Very* professional!"

Breathing heavily, Tanji wiped his bloody mouth with his sleeve. "Hey, we don't want no trouble with you." He gestured at the cyborg. "If this is your mark, we're sorry. He's all yours."

Zapan ignored him. "Really, Hugo—jacking cyborgs? Your little girlfriend might take this kinda personally, don't you think?"

Hugo took an unsteady breath. He didn't want to imagine Alita's face if she were here. His whole life had been a waste until she had come into it. He'd sworn he would never be a drone on a Factory assembly line like his father. But there were all kinds of assembly lines, and they weren't only in the Factory. He'd told himself it was all just so he could get to Zalem, but jacking cyborgs had really been just another kind of assembly line, and he'd been a dedicated drone. It hadn't been pieces of his body he'd been replacing, but bits of his soul, swapping them for empty modules labelled *Zalem*. All this came to him as a single, fully formed thought, and then Zapan was running his mouth again.

"You know how girls are," the hunter said in an exaggerated, blasé tone. "First, she'll go all weepy and oh-Hugo-how-*could*-you. But in the end she'll forgive you—" The Damascus Blade flashed as Zapan drew it from its sheath. "When I show her your head!"

"There's no marker out for me." Hugo kept his eyes on the sword.

"Don't worry, there will be." Zapan's over-done face made his smile even nastier. "Murder pulls a pretty good bounty, even on gutter trash like you."

"I never killed *anybody*!" Hugo said hotly.

The Damascus Blade swept a gleaming path through the air, dipping downwards and then rising. On the ground, the cyborg's head rolled away from his body, trailing a mix of heart's-blood and cyber-blood.

"You just did," Zapan informed him.

In the next moment, Hugo found himself against the wall with the edge of the Damascus Blade under his chin and Zapan's face centimetres from his own. Up close, he could see how badly Alita had ruined the perfection of his nose. It really *wouldn't* ever be the same.

"She thinks she can punk *me* and get away with it?" the Hunter snarled, digging his metal fingers into Hugo's shoulder.

Oh my God, this is all about Alita! Hugo thought as the cyborg's fingers pushed through his clothing to break his skin. Blood welled up and spilled down his jacket, and he couldn't help crying out in pain, just as Zapan let go of him and fell sideways.

"Run, Hugo!" Tanji turned to Zapan with the pry bar in one hand but Zapan was faster and kicked him against the wall where Hugo had been. The Damascus Blade flashed again and there were two distinct thuds as Tanji hit the ground.

Hugo had one fire-bottle left on his belt; he flicked the fuse with his thumb and hurled it straight at Zapan. The Hunter-Warrior turned away but Hugo's aim was too good, even with a wounded shoulder. Zapan screamed and cursed as flames enveloped his entire body. He tore his clothes off, and Hugo wondered briefly if all the cyborgs in Iron City were really too stupid to drop and roll when they were on fire. Hugo pelted out of the alley and into the street.

Tears spilled down his face as he ran and he smeared them away roughly, telling himself he could cry for Tanji later, when Ido collected the bounty on Zapan. But not now, not while Zapan's screams and curses were echoing in his head.

He glanced back and discovered he wasn't hearing Zapan in his head—the son of a bitch was chasing him, even though he was still on fire! People gave ground quickly to a madman holding a sword with his arms in flames—Zapan was actually *gaining* on him.

Hugo sprinted off the sidewalk and into the middle of the road, dodging traffic. He narrowly missed losing the top of his head to the side-view mirror of a lorry going the other way, just before a pedal-car driver tossed a cup of something cold, brown and sticky at him. Everyone on the road was cursing him, but he could still hear Zapan coming after him.

His chest was starting to feel tight now and he was vaguely aware of pain in his shoulder. If he could get down to the old highway interchange, he'd have a better chance of losing the Hunter. It was only a few more blocks. He doubted Zapan knew his way around the shadowy area under the remnants of flyovers that now stood broken and disconnected.

Hugo began zigzagging his way towards the opposite side of the street, infuriating more drivers until he ran up onto the sidewalk to earn the wrath of pedestrians, as well as the people in the outdoor seating area of a café. They were all watching a big screen feed from the stadium, which reminded Hugo that Alita was going to kill him.

But only if Zapan didn't kill him first. The hunter was pacing him on the other side of the street, bellowing curses in between descriptions of what he was going to do to Hugo's head. God, didn't he *ever* shut up?

Hugo reached the edge of the interchange area; all he had to do was find the right place to jump. Zapan was coming across the street and there wasn't time to be choosy or careful. He went another half-block and hoped he remembered the layout below correctly as he vaulted over the guard rail.

The fall was longer than he expected but a lot more trash had piled up on the slope below. The landing knocked the wind out of him but no bones snapped and no joints twisted. He scrambled to get out of sight and tumbled down the incline into a dead-end lower-level street where the homeless found shelter from the rain.

As Hugo got to his feet, he saw a few of them look up from sorting through the stuff they'd collected that day, but only briefly and without interest. People down here had their own problems and they didn't need any more, especially not the kind on Hugo's tail.

Gerhad had found a spot for them with a good view of the pits as well as the track. It proved once again what an excellent friend she was, Ido thought as he sat down beside her.

The stadium was still emptying out. Most people didn't hang around after a game to watch tryouts. Usually, the spectators were mostly friends and family of the prospects and some of the Factory team jobbers, a few trainers and scouts looking for someone with potential, and a small group of hardcore fans who felt it was their sacred duty to jeer at aspiring players in an attempt to break their spirits and crush their dreams.

Ido was more concerned about who would be on the track attempting to break and crush more substantial things. He looked around, listening to the roar of motors and the higher, whining sound of cheap turbines. For some people, players as well as fans, motors were the best thing about Motorball. He could remember building in a sound-effects attachment for—

Abruptly, he felt Gerhad's hand on his knee, pressing down hard until his leg stopped jiggling.

"Thanks," Ido said. "You know, I haven't been to the track since..." His voice trailed off. Still couldn't say it.

"I know," Gerhad said kindly. She studied his face for a moment. "You gonna be okay tonight?"

Ido was about to tell her yes, of course he would. Instead, he heard himself say, "I *hate* this game." Pause. "Almost as much as I love it."

256

Gerhad patted his arm. "You think our girl has a chance?"

Ido sighed mournfully. "I'm afraid so."

"Next up this evening!" the announcer boomed over the PA, making Ido jump a little. "Tryouts for the Second League! *Anything* can happen— we might witness the birth of *the next champion*! Will the Factory practice team please assemble at the starting line and show us what you've got!"

Ido frowned at the players streaming onto the track in the distance. The big screen directly in front of him and Gerhad showed only clouds of dust and smoke, arty camera angles of spinning wheels that looked suspiciously like stock footage put in to sweeten the video come-on, and a few glimpses of some very scarred armour seen mostly through heat shimmers.

This was a lot of camera-tease for a tryout, Ido thought as he adjusted his glasses for long-range. The players were still throwing up a lot of smoke and dust, but now he could see their battered armour and their even more disfigured faces and they told him everything.

"That's no Factory team!" Ido said angrily.

"What?" Gerhad pulled a small pair of binoculars out of her coat pocket.

"See for yourself. Those two punks on the far right in red and blue? There are bounty markers on them."

"Damn," Gerhad said.

"And the rest of them—they used to be players but now they're bounty hunters or worse. This is nothing but a gang of street iron!"

"What the hell are hunters doing lining up with marks?" said Gerhad, appalled.

"Because it's rigged." Ido hopped over the rail and ran for the pits.

"And here come our new prospects!" sang the announcer, as if he could barely contain his excitement. Then: "Oh, wait a minute. It seems we have only one prospect trying out tonight. I guess the rest of them went out for ice cream. Well, okay then, everybody, give it up for *Alita*!"

The pessimists in the stadium gave her the traditional greeting for newcomers—i.e., thumbs down and a chorus of boos, interspersed with calls of "Go home, punk!" and "Die in flames!"

Ido saw he was too late. Alita was already on the feeder lane. Her face appeared on the big screen; she looked tough, focused, determined. It crossed Ido's mind that he wouldn't bet against her, even in borrowed armour. He pushed his way through the crews milling around on the pit lane, hoping he could get her attention before they started. He saw her scanning the stadium. Looking for Hugo, of course. Where the hell was he, anyway? This was *not* the night to play Disappearing Boyfriend. If he didn't show up, Ido was going to kill him twice before Alita got her hands on him.

"Since we have only one prospect," the announcer enthused, "there will be *no teams*! I repeat: *one* prospect, *no* teams! The name of the game is Cut-Throat! Ten laps. All players to the starting line now."

Ido climbed onto the pit-lane railing. "Alita!" he yelled, waving his arms frantically. "Alita, wait!"

Vector was enjoying some Zalem-restricted whisky along with the elevated view of the track from his glassed-in box. Part of the back wall was an enormous screen that showed feeds from any of a number of cameras Chiren controlled remotely. The picture slewed back and forth until Chiren finally found the right subject. She kept the camera on Alita as she skated onto the track. Vector had to admit the bitch actually looked a little scary.

"Hugo brought her right to us," he said, momentarily pleased with the state of the world and anticipating its imminent further improvement.

"And what did you promise him?" Chiren asked.

Vector had another sip, savouring the taste. "I'm sending him to Zalem, of course," he said and laughed, because it really was funny. No, not just funny—hilarious. Strangely, though, he was the only one laughing. He turned to Chiren and saw she was giving him her trademark Ice-Queen-Death-Ray glare.

"You're sending *me* to Zalem," she said.

"Yeah, yeah, of course I am," he said breezily, wishing she'd just shut up and have some whisky. Whisky always put her in the mood to lie down on the desk, or anywhere else he told her to. Onscreen, he saw she was now zooming in on the last person he wanted to see. Ido seemed to be having hysterics about something, yelling and hollering at someone who obviously didn't want to look at him either.

Vector helped himself to some more whisky. He was so tired of Chiren's bullshit that he couldn't even be bothered to tell her to get the camera off her pathetic ex and focus on Alita.

Chiren would pull herself together, Vector thought; she had as much at stake as he did.

Ido stared helplessly as Alita rolled onto the track. He tried calling out to her, but he couldn't even hear his own voice over the roar of turbines and engines.

They must have called out the toughest practice guys they had, Alita thought as she squeezed between two hulking cyborgs in the centre of the line-up. She smiled tentatively at them; they scowled back at her. Or maybe that was how really tough guys smiled. She gave a small, nervous laugh.

"Hey, guys, go easy on me, okay?"

"Oh, sure, kid," said the guy on her left. "We'll give you the cream-puff treatment." His name tag said "Antioch", and she wondered why she'd never heard of him. Or seen him on the track. In fact, she didn't remember any of these guys being in games she'd seen recently. The two guys down at the end in red and blue looked familiar, but she wasn't sure from where. Maybe the practice team didn't play much?

As she put her left wheel on the starting line, the internal phone in her helmet rang. If that was Hugo saying he couldn't make it, she'd kill him. "What?" she growled.

"Get out of there!" Ido yelled in her ear. "It's a set-up!"

"Players!" the announcer said ecstatically. "Ten-second warning. Hope you went before you left!"

"They're going to *kill* you!" Ido wailed.

Alita sneaked a glance left, then right. "Which ones?"

"All of them!" Ido cried.

One of the guys on Alita's right started up a device on the end of his arm: whirring blades instead of a hand. The name on his armour was "Stinger".

"Good to know," Alita said and broke the connection.

There was an enormous framework in front of her with a vertical row of lights. They began to flash one at a time, starting at the top with red and moving downwards to yellow.

The very last one flashed green and Alita felt her heart leap with excitement as she surged forward.

CHAPTER 21

During the weeks she had spent training with Hugo, Alita had learned a great deal about her Berserker body. She had to become accustomed to its adaptability. Once she got used to her body, she was more prepared to deal with the unexpected, which, according to Hugo, was what Motorball was all about.

This was why they put actual motors in the ball, Hugo explained; lots of little motors acted on its centre of gravity to make its trajectory unpredictable. Even if some of the motors malfunctioned, the ball's movements wouldn't be easy to anticipate. Plenty of rookie Paladins had learned that the hard way when the ball they thought they were about to get their hands on suddenly popped back at them so hard it cracked their helmet or knocked them out, or both.

The players, however, were a different story. People were full of surprises—but unlike a randomly bouncing Motorball, you could get to know your competitors. When you were playing a game without teams, you had to assume that everybody was out to eat you for dinner, because they were. There was no way to see where everybody was at once, unless they were all lined up across the track and coming at you together, in which case, you were fast or you were toast. But that was pretty unlikely to happen. Players were all over the place, and you had to learn how to locate them without seeing them.

You gotta know how to listen, Hugo had told her. *When you're on the track, it might sound like just a bunch of machine noise, but it isn't. Every motor or turbine sounds a little different because of how a player moves as well as what kind of tech they go for. Some players accelerate then slow down repeatedly— zoom-brake, zoom-brake. The wear and tear that puts on a motor makes it sound different than, say, Jashugan's, because Jashugan uses things like steep banking on the track to slow down rather than stomping his brakes all the time.*

Then Hugo had talked about habits. *Everybody's got 'em, and a lot of guys don't even know it. Twice around the track will tell you a lot about your competition, even if you've never seen them before. Besides zoom-brake, there are guys who always swoop in front of you right after a banked turn. Then there are the tail-waggers—guys who tailgate you and keep faking coming up on one side, then the other, over and over again. Get away from them. They'll make you crazy.*

Hugo had showed her feints and fake-outs, get-outs and work-arounds, jump-ups and slide-unders. There was so much to think about, all kinds of strategy. But if you wanted to win on the track, Hugo said, you had to win in your head.

Alita had been amazed at all his knowledge and insight. He'd told her it was all just stuff he'd picked up hanging around crews and finding parts. But after her tryout was over, Alita was going to suggest he become a professional coach. He'd probably argue with her, but she was going to get through to him if she had to take his head off and pour in everything she knew by hand.

At present, however, she was certain that none of the scarred and beat-up thugs on the track with her tonight had ever been much for strategy or winning games in their heads. Hell, they weren't even playing the same game she was. She was here to play Motorball; they had come to play Murderball. And she was the ball.

Something else Hugo had said popped into her mind in her last half-second at the starting line: *No matter what you do, just be faster.*

Then the green light flashed, and she was faster.

Faster reaction time was one of the best things about the Berserker body; it was also her best chance of surviving the night.

The sound of Stinger's blades rose slightly as he swung them at Alita's head. At the same moment, she heard Antioch grunt with effort as he leaped for her. A human sound, even a grunt, had a completely different quality to the sound of a machine, and her Berserker hearing could pick it out from the cacophony around her, just as it could detect the infinitesimal rise in pitch that meant it was approaching.

Berserker reaction time put her three metres down the track before the rest of them got all their wheels past the starting line. A quick look over her shoulder was all she needed to know each player's position; she only had to listen to know when they moved. She hoped, for example, that the one whose name tag said "Gangsta"—whose legs formed a single big wheel and had smaller wheels running the lengths of his forearms—didn't really think he could sneak up on her, because he sounded like Hugo's gyro (which reminded her: she was going to kill Hugo).

Then there was Screwhead, the one with four arms. If having four arms was a real advantage, wouldn't she have been a champion by now? Her weapon of choice was a deadly-looking chain with multiple blades on one end, but Alita could picture her getting all four arms tangled up in it.

Another one, labelled Exploder, had two right arms and what looked like a small cannon on his left shoulder. He had wheels rather than legs, but they looked like they belonged on a baby carriage or maybe a tricycle. Even Stinger, with his double-threat blade-arms, had weird oval-shaped wheel-feet—the treads rolled around the stationary rims. Maybe the blade arms were supposed to distract attention from wheel-feet that looked like a malfunction waiting to happen.

And the two guys on the far end, identical except one was all in blue and the other in red—her borrowed gear looked to be in better shape than theirs. Taken altogether, the whole group looked like a bunch of mutant animals stampeding in slow motion.

But they weren't animals and they weren't in slow motion, either. Her Berserker body was pumping nutrients into her brain to accelerate her thought processes, but that wasn't going to last much longer. She had to remember everything was always happening fast and she always had to be faster.

When she broke the century—when her speed passed one hundred miles per hour—the mortar fired, snapping the Motorball into play. Alita heard the ball whistle through the air over her head before it hit the track several metres ahead of her, bounced once and flew five metres farther on, lurching from side to side, as if it were daring all of them to try catching it.

Alita didn't have to take another look over her shoulder to know the pack was gaining on her. Stinger was in the lead, waving his whirring blade-hand around. Time to show a little dominance, she decided, and pushed herself faster, keeping her eyes on the Motorball, observing the way it bounced. As she came to within three metres of it, she took a long leap of faith to the left: good guess. It bounded into her hands as if she had called it to herself. But just as she leaped for the ball, Stinger leaped for her.

"And the new kid, Alita, gets possession practically right off the snap!" yelled the announcer, on the verge of hysteria.

Alita smiled. If he thought that was exciting, he was going to wet his pants over her next move. Still airborne, she rotated her body around the ball, and then, a second before she touched down, drove the ball straight into Stinger's brutish face.

Stinger flipped backwards into the herd of murderers. Four went down immediately, including the guy with one large wheel—Gangsta—and the guy with the nuts and bolts sticking up out of his head—Mace. *He* should have been called Screwhead, Alita thought, watching the carnage as she skated backwards.

Screwhead herself somehow managed to avoid going down in the pile-up, although she barely missed tripping over someone's loose arm sliding across the track. The thug in red wasn't as lucky. He jumped over the arm as it crossed his path but tripped as he landed and did an inadvertent cartwheel. Despite the fact that he was obviously no acrobat, he might have recovered if his fuel line hadn't ruptured. Sparks flying up off the track set him ablaze, turning him into a Catherine wheel of napalm. The crowd screamed ecstatically.

And it really was a crowd now, Alita saw; seats were filling up and more people were coming in all the time. Apparently word had got out that tonight's tryout was going to be a slaughter. Maybe it would be, Alita thought with a grin that would have scared Ido.

She turned her attention back to the track and everything slowed down again as her would-be murderers disentangled themselves from each other, got back on their feet, and aimed themselves at her. Two of them, Mace and another called Kumaza, pulled ahead of the pack with Exploder right behind them.

Mace was twirling a mace over his head. The dense metal club on the end of the chain was studded with thick, flat shards and circular saw blades, as well as spikes. It had to weigh at least as much as the Motorball itself, and Mace seemed to have no problem spinning it and skating at 100 mph. He might be unimaginative about his name but his balance was almost as good as hers. Almost; not quite.

Exploder was coming up on her other side—another less-than-creative type with pretty good balance. From this angle, his weapon looked a bit more like a jet engine than a cannon. Either way, he was carrying a hell of a big chip on his shoulder, Alita thought. The way he and Mace were positioning themselves relative to each other, it looked like they wanted to make an Alita sandwich.

Sorry, boys, that's not on the menu.

Time speeded up to normal. Alita saw the small change in the position of Mace's arm that meant he was going to let fly. She ducked just as Exploder blasted a fireball at her, or rather, where she had been. Mace ducked the fireball but his weapon slammed into Kumaza's head and they both went down, taking Exploder with them, sliding sideways across the track just as it began to curve.

Still holding the Motorball, Alita sprang up onto the outer railing, skating along the top so she could see more of the track as well as the stadium crowd, which had swelled to several hundred, with still more coming in. No one was booing her any more, although she knew a lot of the cheers were for the spectacular crashes. But she could work with that.

Alita came down off the railing into a position low enough that the Motorball scraped the track and threw up a flurry of sparks. The motors in the ball made it twitch in her grasp, as if it were trying to get away. She could sense the rage and desperation radiating from the killers behind her almost as clearly. Had they told Vector they'd leave her dead at the starting line? And how much was she worth anyway—100 K? 500 K? A whole million?

Hugo needed a million to get to Zalem. Would Vector offer that much for her? Somehow she didn't think so. She had a feeling that Vector, like most wealthy people, was a tightwad. It was probably why he'd hired this sad bunch to take her down, because he knew they'd work cheap. But that was okay. Even if he'd offered ten million, it wouldn't have mattered. Vector could buy them, but he couldn't buy her.

She heard Screwhead panting behind her. Alita slowed very slightly, letting her get almost within arm's reach, then leaped up into a spinning roundhouse kick, sending her flying into Gangsta, who rose up to knock her away into Exploder. Gangsta was upright long enough for Alita to deliver an open-hand blow to the chest, which put him flat on his back with his one large wheel spinning uselessly in the air and his motor making the kind of high-pitched whine that meant serious mechanical trouble.

Stinger suddenly drew even with her on her left. No doubt he thought that was more likely to be her weak side—except Berserkers didn't have weak sides. She was still grinning as her arm shot out and popped him before he could raise one bladed arm. He skidded sideways and Exploder skidded into him. *Get a room, you two,* Alita thought, laughing to herself as Screwhead swerved to avoid them and bashed into Antioch. Alita kept going, kept moving faster.

"A slow Tuesday night just got hotter than the playoffs, folks!" sang the announcer, thrilled to have lucked into what would probably be the most memorable tryout of all time. "The fans have got themselves a new favourite to cheer for, an underdog with the face of an angel and a body built for battle!"

Yeah, sing my praises, Alita told him silently, beaming as the guy all in blue drew even with her. She sprang into the air, performed a showy body twist, and swung the ball into the back of his head. Head and body parted ways, the head soaring off the track while the body rolled on briefly before collapsing. Maybe that would go viral, Alita thought.

"We've been calling it Motorball," the announcer rhapsodised, "but in *her* hands, it's a *wrecking ball!*"

Someone kicked the guy's head back into the track, where it came to rest on its side, facing the oncoming pack of thugs.

"Aw crap," the head said, and then disappeared in a flurry of wheels and armoured legs while the crowd went insane.

Alita swivelled around to skate backwards and saw that the murderers were rolling towards her in a single line across the track. And Hugo had said that would never happen, she thought; she couldn't believe he was missing this.

Antioch pulled ahead and Alita marvelled at how his face and body communicated his every intention. He was planning to come straight towards her, feint right—his right—then left, and then lunge low. No wonder he'd never made it as a pro; she almost felt sorry for him, except he was the one who had promised her the cream-puff treatment. Well, she'd show him a cream-puff—

Then she was watching his body divide in two, the parts spraying bright-blue cyber-blood everywhere as they slid away from each other. Stinger moved into his place, his blades dripping with Antioch's cyber-blood.

That was some weapon he had there, Alita thought, but the guy himself was as dumb as a box of pig iron. He seemed to have forgotten what had happened the last time he'd tried to take the ball from her. But what the hell, if he wanted it that bad, she might as well give it to him.

Alita hurled the Motorball straight into his midsection. It knocked him backwards, but most of the other killers managed to avoid piling up on him. Alita noticed they also managed to avoid taking possession of the ball. Apparently no one felt the need to keep up the pretence that this was anything like a game.

"Hey, let's keep watching, folks, and maybe a little Motorball will break out in the middle of this street-fight," said the announcer with a nervous laugh. Poor guy, Alita thought—maybe he was finally getting the idea that this hot ticket wasn't a game after all. He probably didn't know how to call the action for Murderball.

Tough stuff, kid, and it only gets bloodier from here, so try to keep up.

The obstacle course ahead was called "the traps", Hugo had told her, and it could turn good luck into bad. The traps consisted of a transparent tube full of random problems—that was what Hugo had called them, problems—but not always the same ones from game to game. Sometimes they even changed things up during a single game.

The tube itself was the biggest problem because it limited the range of movement. Being able to jump high wouldn't help her in the traps unless she fell into a really deep pit—and if she did, she'd have to get herself off the stakes at the bottom first. Reaction time would be even more crucial and so would flexibility—mental as well as physical.

Guys with big showy weapons were at a disadvantage in the traps unless they could retract them or somehow fold them away for easier manoeuvring. Alita grinned, thinking of Exploder, the tricycle with the giant chip on his shoulder, Gangsta with his big wheel, and the guy with the chainsaw arms who had done little except hang back and try not to get caught in any pile-ups. This might actually be entertaining.

Chainsaw arms was currently chasing her around pillars and potholes but he couldn't balance too well in tight quarters. Alita slowed up to let him take a swing at her; she dodged and his arm went into the pillar beside her, where it stuck, revved briefly, then died. He was trying to free himself by sawing the arm off when she side-kicked him, knocking him out. She lured another thug into a tar pit, jumping over it at the last moment when it was too late for him to do the same, then stuck a third to a ramp using his own nail-gun hand.

Exploder reappeared, much to her delight. It took her all of five seconds to get behind him, twist the fuel feed to maximum, and detonate him. Dodging shrapnel and body parts, she let the shock wave blow her towards the end of the tube. Just before she emerged, she heard the familiar whirr of spinning blades, the sound of Stinger cutting his way through the last few obstacles as well as a few of his competitors. Well, that was one way to get through an obstacle course.

The very last obstacle was actually outside the tube: an enormous metal spike with a deep groove in its surface that forced players to spiral up to the sharp point at the top. Alita knew Stinger was going to stay on her tail, intending to do to her what he'd done to Antioch. He wanted to make a big flashy kill. She powered her way up the spiral to the top where she tucked into a triple backwards somersault to land on the track.

Stinger tried to do the same, but acrobatic movement wasn't his forte; neither was physics. His blade-arms threw him off, and instead of flying through the air to the track, he belly-flopped onto the spike. Alita hoped that would go viral, too; she was pretty sure he'd never be able to do it again even if he tried. Not even if he *practised.*

She skated backwards slowly, watching to see who else would come out of the traps. Mace, Kumaza, and Chainsaw Arms appeared, followed by Screwhead, who bumped into them because they had all stopped to stare at Stinger trying to wiggle himself free. Then they turned to glower at her. Were they going to *scowl* her to death?

"Well?" Alita couldn't help laughing at them. "Did you guys come here for blood or quiet time? What're you waiting for?"

Stinger finally managed to heave himself off the spike, slid down to the track and rolled at her with his blades whirring, although the motor sounded a bit rough and overworked. He wasn't bleeding nearly as much as she'd have thought—he must have been packing sealant. *Did he even know that stuff was only temporary?*

Her phone rang.

"Ali, it's me! I got a big problem!" Hugo shouted.

He had a big problem? "Not a good time, Hugo," she growled, turning to skate forwards and accelerating.

"He's trying to *kill* me!" Hugo said.

Immediately, nothing else mattered. "*Who* is trying to kill you?" Alita asked, skating faster, widening the gap between herself and the killers.

"Zapan, the Hunter-Warrior! He killed Tanji!"

The sob in his voice sent a wave of fierce protectiveness and outrage through her. Tanji was part of her life with Hugo, sour face and all, not a mark for a Hunter-Warrior. She remembered what Hugo had said about Zapan when she'd first seen him: *Scanning for his mark. I wouldn't want to be* that *guy.*

If Zapan had killed Tanji, Hugo didn't stand a chance.

"Oh, shit, here he comes!" There were sounds of traffic and Hugo panting as he ran.

Alita turned to look at the killers behind her. They were lined up across the track again, with Stinger slightly ahead on the inside in case she had any thoughts about calling it quits and leaving the track. She wasn't supposed to get out of this alive, no matter what happened.

The hell with it—she was tired of this stupid game.

"Where are you?" she asked Hugo.

"Heading for the old cathedral," he said breathlessly.

"On my way. I'll meet you there."

Alita did a full turn, checking out her pursuers, then scanning the stadium until she found the area she wanted—no seats, no concessions, just plain wall.

Okay, you guys, this next move is a little something I call "Takin' It To The Streets". Alita kept her gaze fixed on the wall and went faster.

At first, people on the street thought a bomb had blown out part of the stadium. Debris sprayed in all directions for a half-block radius; a large chunk of cement and drywall crashed through a coffee-shop awning, scattering the people sitting underneath but without causing any serious injuries. Another large fragment landed in the middle of an intersection in front of a small gyro-lorry, precipitating a chain reaction of bumper-to-bumper collisions. Luckily, no one was seriously injured in this incident either. But those on the scene saw a young woman also land on the street nearby, hitting the ground hard enough to leave an indentation twenty centimetres deep. Seeing her armour and the number 99 on her shoulder, bystanders believed her to be a Motorball player caught in the explosion and thrown to her death.

Before anyone could check, however, the young woman picked herself up and skated off into the night as if she thought she were still on the Motorball track. Moments later, cyborgs also wearing armour poured out of the hole in the stadium and skated after her in pursuit.

Witnesses to this remarkable turn of events were divided as to how they felt. Many declared Motorball had obviously got out of hand, while others approved of this fresh new direction for a game that had shown signs of stagnating. A few others, believing they were hallucinating, went to the nearest emergency room to seek medication.

Alita zoomed around a corner and into a narrow alleyway just ahead of a skinny black truck and realised she'd made a mistake. The alley let out on another main road and she would almost certainly skate right into an ambush. But as skinny as the truck was, the alley was too narrow—not enough room for her to turn around and go back. Then, ten metres from the end, she saw the building on her left had a small recessed area. As soon as she reached it, she flattened herself against it and held her breath; the truck passed her with centimetres to spare and reached the end of the alley just in time to meet her killers and spoil their ambush.

Two of them bounced off the front bumper but the other two leaped up onto the cab and skated the length of the trailer. Alita was already speeding back the way she had come, looking for the turn she had missed. It was actually a space between two buildings, not even wide enough to be called a passageway. Not wide enough for her pursuers, either; she rolled through it sideways.

Hang on, Hugo. I'm coming.

Hugo knew every nook and cranny in Iron City, every hiding place, every place good for lying low. The problem was, Zapan did too. But Hugo had an additional problem: there was no way he could go on running flat out indefinitely. By contrast, cyborgs could run for days and they'd only have to stop if their legs fell off.

But worst of all was Zapan's hunting ability. The man was damned good, almost like one of McTeague's Hellhounds with their talented noses, keen hearing and sharp eyes. Hugo had tried going back to the upper level and Zapan had spotted him almost immediately. For some reason, the Hunter didn't come down to the lower level, either because the territory was too unfamiliar, or—more likely—he wanted to keep Hugo trapped below. There was nothing down here except abandoned buildings, the homeless, and some kind of strange Factory building with few windows and no doors, guarded by Centurians. *How long was Zapan going to keep this up?*

Zapan's words popped into his mind: *She thinks she can punk* me *and get away with it?*

The Hunter wasn't going to stop until he killed her, Hugo realised. As far as Zapan was concerned, everything began and ended with Alita's humiliating him. Nothing else mattered.

Hugo kept moving through the lower-level streets, staying in the shadows as much as possible. He had intended to find a way back up and double-back past the place where he'd found Tanji and Dif jacking the cyborg. But Zapan seemed to be a step ahead of him—maybe Zapan's hunting instinct told him Hugo would return there and he'd figured the odds on where Hugo was most likely to emerge. Or maybe he didn't have to do the math at all—maybe he had flunkies with night-vision goggles watching Hugo run around like a bug in a bottle.

He had to get out of here.

❧∽❧

Hugo sheltered for a little while in the shadow of a set of stone steps leading to the upper level. They came out on a side street in a spot so obscured by the surrounding buildings that you couldn't find it unless you already knew it was there. A lot of black-market goods went up and down those stairs. Zapan would know that, but with any luck his flunkies had gone home for the night and he was still expecting Hugo to double-back to the scene of the crime.

Or not. It didn't matter. Hugo couldn't stand being down here a moment longer. The only chance he had of getting away from Zapan was to meet Alita at the cathedral.

He took a couple of steadying breaths and then climbed the steps, dropping low as he reached the top, and held still, listening for crazed cursing and death threats. But all he heard was traffic and the hurried footsteps of people on their way home. Hugo stood up slowly, wincing as his thigh muscles complained about all the running and crouching. He kneaded them briefly, working his fingers the way Tanji had showed him when he'd got a cramp during a pick-up game of Motorball.

The thought of Tanji made his throat tighten and his vision blur with tears. He had to move now or Zapan would find him just by following the sobs. A block away on his right, the main road was still busy although the traffic was starting to thin out as night-time segued to early morning. There wasn't much to his left but a few businesses closed for the night and, farther down, another Factory distribution centre with a shipment tube growing out of the roof. The graveyard shift would be clocking in soon to dutifully sort and categorise goods for shipment to Zalem. He had to risk the main road if he wanted to get to Alita.

Hugo moved quickly, sticking close to the buildings until he got to the corner, and paused to look up and down the main road before stepping out on the sidewalk. Nothing happened. He put up his hood, stuck his hands in his pockets and kept his gaze down to avoid making eye contact with anyone as he headed for the cathedral.

He managed to go an entire block before he heard Zapan's laugh.

"Got you now, you criminal!" Zapan yelled, standing directly across the street from him. People around him ducked and ran as he waved the Damascus Blade in the air. "You murderer, I'm gonna take your head!" Smiling evilly and pointing at him, Zapan was about to step off the sidewalk and cross the street when Hugo finally caught a break. Or more specifically, a bumper.

Hugo hadn't bumper-jumped for years but he didn't have time to wonder if he could still do it. Traffic was heavy enough that the driver didn't notice he had a passenger riding his front bumper; even better, no one ratted him out. All the good citizens were probably home in bed by now.

Hugo peeked around the side of the bus and for a moment he was afraid he'd see Zapan grinning at him from the rear bumper. But for once, his luck held; Zapan was still standing on the sidewalk, turning around and around and looking pissed off.

Hugo's phone rang.

"I'm almost there," he said. "Almost."

"Got it," Alita said. She had reached the marketplace, which seemed to be very different late at night. People didn't notice very much that happened around them, no matter how weird or unsavoury, and they were even less inclined to help anyone.

She parkoured her way up to roof level, hoping her pursuers wouldn't be as skilled. To her dismay, a few followed her example with no trouble and shouted directions to the ones pacing her on the street. But she was still faster up here. Jumping from roof to roof was actually easier with wheel-feet because she could build up more momentum. She kept moving from building to building faster and faster, until finally she didn't hear them calling out her location to each other. Hoping she really had lost them, she rebounded from windowsills to drain pipes until she got to ground level—

—and found herself boxed into a dead end where they were all waiting for her. She hadn't lost them; they'd herded her. There were more of them now, several who hadn't been on the track, and they seemed to be organised into two groups, one led by Antioch who had somehow managed to staple himself back together, and one led by Screwhead. They surrounded her slowly, as if waiting for her to beg for her life.

Did they really think she would?

Stinger suddenly dropped down on her from somewhere overhead and started spinning his blades.

Alita threw him off, thinking absently that he wasn't as heavy as she'd thought. The moment she was on her feet again, Screwhead body-slammed into her, sending her crashing into the wall. The rest of Screwhead's gang piled on, forcing her to the ground with punches and kicks.

It was like being pelted with lots of little stones; Alita drove a wheel-foot into Screwhead's middle and she flew all the way across the alley to land on some overflowing trashcans. Alita sent the rest of her gang with her— *So you won't be lonely, bitch.* This discouraged them, and Antioch's gang as well. Antioch himself looked somewhat shamefaced as he backed off, even though he must have known those staples would never have held.

Then she heard the sound of spinning blades; one person *still* hadn't given up on trying to kill her. Alita groaned, catching Stinger as he tried to throw himself on top of her again. She slammed him down on the street, straddled him, and tore his head off.

"I do *not*—" She banged his head on the pavement. "—have time—" Another *bang*! "—for *this*!" *Bang, bang, bang-bang!*

If he didn't get the message now, he was too stupid to live, Alita thought. She dropped his head in a trashcan and took off for the cathedral.

CHAPTER 22

Hugo jumped off the bumper just as the bus started to turn right. He tucked, rolled and stayed on his belly, looking at the empty street straight ahead of him. The cathedral was only half a block away. With any luck, Alita would already be there. He was going to tell her everything; then they'd figure things out together. Hugo looked around and saw nothing but shadows. Maybe his luck was still holding, he thought as he got up and ran towards the cathedral.

Or he tried to run. It was more an uneven lope as his aching legs told him they'd had enough of his bullshit. His burning lungs agreed and his shoulder chimed in to remind him it was going to hurt a lot now that he was out of adrenaline. Hugo tried to focus on what he and Alita could do about the mess he was in. Doc Ido would help. He wouldn't be too happy to find out how Hugo had come by some of the parts he'd got for the clinic, but the doc would never believe he was a killer. If anyone could get him out of a false murder rap, it was Ido.

But first, he just wanted to see Alita. She wasn't here yet—he knew because he was almost at the entrance and if she'd been there,

she'd have come running out and—

Abruptly he found himself on his back looking up at the dark sky. Something had hit him hard at the base of his throat. He was trying to sit up when he heard a familiar voice say, "Hey, where you goin', huh?"

Zapan loomed over him, holding his arm straight out to show Hugo how he'd clotheslined him. Hugo scuttled backwards from Zapan but the Hunter advanced on him, one hand on his sword, grinning with delight. He'd had his teeth re-done, Hugo realised. How crazy did a person have to be to get his teeth re-done while he was hunting a mark?

Hugo felt a solid wall behind him. He was out of room, out of time, and out of luck.

The Hunter was eyeing Hugo's neck avidly as he raised the Damascus Blade. But Zapan just stayed that way, holding the sword high in the hair, unable to complete the stroke, because a metal hand was gripping his arm. Zapan's chiselled jaw dropped as Alita ripped the sword out of his hand and flung it away.

Alita rolled to Hugo and knelt down beside him. She started to say something and then froze, staring past him in disbelief and horror.

Hugo raised himself up to follow her gaze. The motion detectors on the street had registered the presence of more than two people and activated the flatscreen mounted on the building across from the cathedral. It was the Factory's way of making sure everyone in Iron City could keep up with the latest news.

Tonight the latest news showed Hugo's face in glorious high definition and very much larger than life, unmistakable and unmissable. The caption scrolling sideways below it was equally clear:

Number 9107/HUGO—wanted for jacking and murder—bounty 30,000 credits.

There was a price on his head already.

For a moment, Hugo almost wished Alita had arrived too late to catch Zapan's arm. Except it would have put 30,000 credits in that bastard's pocket.

"Looks like your Hugo hasn't been entirely honest with you," Zapan said with fake concern, then laughed.

Alita was vaguely aware of Zapan saying something but it sounded too far away to make sense of. She turned from the screen to Hugo.

"Is it true?" she whispered.

"It's—you don't understand—"

Alita made a frustrated noise and drove her fist into the wall beside Hugo's head, letting her hand remain in the cracked indentation.

"I *never* killed anyone, *never!*" Hugo said desperately, almost sobbing. "We only—we jacked *parts*. We paralysed cyborgs and stripped them for parts but *that's all.* We never—" He cut off and looked away from her. "I needed the money for Zalem. But I wanted to quit. I was trying to quit when—" He stopped and raised his eyes to her again. "I'm sorry," he whispered.

Mission accomplished, Zapan thought triumphantly, picking up his sword. Better yet, he'd got a two-for-one deal: he'd broken Hugo's heart as well as the girl's. Brute force execution was all well and good when it was just a bounty you were after, but when things got personal, there was nothing sweeter than devastating an enemy's soul. Criminals deserved to suffer as much as possible anyway, and he was just the Hunter-Warrior to dish it out.

"Step aside," he told the girl imperiously, "and let me do my job."

Zapan felt an explosion of pain as he hit something cold and hard. A cracking sound thundered from the point of impact behind him as Alita picked him up and held him against the stone of the cathedral with her forearm jammed against his throat. Her other hand was drawn back and flattened as blue light swirled and throbbed around it, a halo of unearthly fire.

"Touch him again," the girl warned in a voice that might have come from the dark depths of a bottomless pit, "and I'll kill you."

Not an empty threat, Zapan thought uneasily, watching the blue glow. That looked an awful lot like a plasma weapon. How she could have got one, he had no idea. But he always had the code on his side: "Interference between a licensed Hunter-Warrior and a claimed kill is a violation of Factory Law and the Hunter's Code," Zapan informed her.

"He's *mine*!" she snapped.

"Oh, so *you're* claiming the bounty?" Zapan gave her his all-business, professional-to-professional smile, as if she weren't still holding him up against a wall by his neck. He felt her hesitate, and for a moment the pressure on his neck let up. Then it came back stronger than before.

"I had him first," she cried. "*You* are in violation!"

"Then make the kill, Hunter-Warrior," Zapan said, genial but still all business. "You have the licence. I've seen it myself." The blue glow around her hand was fading. She couldn't argue. "Become one of us."

Alita let him drop and turned back to her boyfriend, Hugo. Hugo the Magnificent, jacker and murderer extraordinaire. The kid was up off the ground now but he had his back to the wall, like he was too scared to move. What a coward. Not to mention ugly.

"You know there's no room in the Hunter's Code for love or mercy," Zapan went on. "But just because I know you're new to this, I'll make it easier for you." He stepped past her and lunged.

The Damascus Blade slid ten centimetres into Hugo's middle before it struck something solid, possibly his backbone although Zapan really hoped it was the wall behind him. What most people didn't know about stab wounds was that the real damage wasn't always from the blade going in. Quite often, what killed someone was yanking the blade out again. Especially from the gut. Zapan stood back, sword in hand, and watched Hugo crumple like a pile of rags.

And if that wasn't melodramatic enough, the tragic heroine scooped her doomed lover up in her arms and rushed into the cathedral with him. As if *that* would help either of them. Zapan looked down the street and saw the lights of approaching Centurians, responding to the message he'd sent them. Took them long enough, although their slow response had allowed him extra time for entertainment.

He was also happy to see his buddies coming along behind the Centurians. Good—he didn't want them to miss this next part, because it was going to be one hell of a show.

"Hey, Cupcake!" he called, wiping the Damascus Blade clean of blood. "You better finish him before I do!"

No answer. Well, she couldn't say he hadn't warned her.

Alita had never seen so much heart's-blood. It didn't seem possible that Hugo could lose so much and still be alive, and yet he was. But she didn't think he could last much longer.

"I have to get you to Ido," she said, holding him close so he wouldn't see how bloody her hands were.

Hugo turned his head to look at the lights flashing on the walls from outside. "Centurians," he said. "If you go out there with me still alive, they'll kill us both."

Alita's eyes welled with tears. "Oh, God, Hugo, what did you *do*?"

But he was looking past her up through a gap in the roof at a bright star in the sky. "Hey, you see that star up there?" He smiled and tried to lift his hand and point but couldn't manage it. "All my life, I wondered why all the other stars move across the sky but that one never does. I think I just figured it out." He gave a weak laugh. "I guess there's nothing like imminent death to focus the mind."

Alita looked from him to the star and back. "What do you think it is?"

"Zalem is *hanging* from it," he said with another feeble laugh. "That's what's been holding it up all these years—something big and far away. Maybe it's as big as Zalem—or bigger, even—way out in space."

"A star city," Alita said.

"Going to Zalem—it was never *just* about the promised land," Hugo said. "It was getting answers to so many questions."

"I need answers too," Alita told him. "I need to know what's in your heart—*right now.*"

Hugo gazed into her eyes. "I didn't kill that guy," he told her, and everything in her knew it was the truth. "But it doesn't matter. I tore people apart—for *money.* People like you."

"Where were you tonight?" Alita asked, her voice gentle.

"I went to stop the others, to tell them I quit." Pause. "Because I love you, Alita." He managed to lift his hand and touch her cheek. "I'd give up my dream for you."

Alita bent forward and pressed her lips to his, tenderly, lovingly.

"*Never* give up your dream," she said and bent to kiss him again.

"*Never* give up your dream."

Hidden on the other side of a broken wall, Chiren stood very still with her face buried in her hands to keep herself from breaking down in sobs. It wasn't that she'd given up on her dream, she thought. Her dream had died and left her with nothing; nothing to dream, nothing to give up.

Unbidden, the memory of looking down at Iron City from Zalem with Ido rose up in her mind. It had been the night before they had been forced to leave. The dark landscape dotted with tiny lights had offered no hints as to what they could expect. It was simply unknown and, when she looked at it, she'd suddenly been unable to breathe as a hard lump of panic congealed in her chest and began spreading tendrils to every part of her. She had reached out blindly for Ido and he had gathered her into his arms so securely it damped down her panic.

"We'll be together," he said in a low, loving voice. "Nothing else matters."

And for a few hours, she'd believed that without a shred of doubt.

The cell phone on her wrist flashed. Vector's face appeared on the tiny screen. "Did you find them?" he demanded, impatient. Always demanding, always impatient, and she had nothing.

"No. They're gone," Chiren whispered and broke the connection. Then she picked up the case at her feet, stepped out from behind the wall and walked the short distance to where Alita was now rocking Hugo in her arms like a child.

"Don't die, Hugo. Please don't die," Alita begged. "You're so cold but don't die, okay? Please? Don't. *Don't.*" She looked up at Chiren, showing no sign of recognition, only pain and loss and sorrow. "I'd give him *my life* if I could," Alita said.

Chiren knelt beside her and pushed her hair back from her face. She hadn't seen anyone so devastated and lost since the night she had walked out on Dyson. After her dream had died.

"Maybe you can," she said. "Alita."

It wasn't until close to dawn that the tragic heroine finally came out to play her final scene. Maybe she'd been praying, Zapan thought. The idea of a cyborg praying was as hilarious as that of a cyborg in love. Neither would do her any good now.

She stood squinting against the spotlights the Centurians had on her, clutching a backpack to herself. Zapan recognised it as Hugo's. Bless— she was sentimental. A sentimental cyborg who was in love and prayed. This was going to be more fun than three marks trying to get away on one gyro, and that one had been a *hoot*.

Zapan stepped forward and pointed at the girl. "You have violated Factory Law and the Hunter's Code," he announced loudly.

A Centurian marched over to stand in front of him. "Where is the criminal Hugo, Bounty 9107?" it asked in its flat, mechanical voice.

The girl lowered the front of the backpack just enough to show Hugo's head. His eyes were closed and he looked peaceful. "Hugo is dead," she said dully.

Zapan's jaw dropped. The girl had actually done it! The other Hunters with him couldn't believe it either.

"I claim the kill," she added in the same lifeless tone. "Hunter-Warrior 26651."

"Damn," said a Hunter on Zapan's right. "She really did it. She killed him."

"Man, that is *hardass*," said someone else, sounding more uneasy than impressed.

Another Centurian scanned the head. "Claim confirmed," it said. "Case closed."

No, Zapan thought, something was off here. The girl had been completely in love with this jackass, and then suddenly kills him? Zapan knew women like that, and this cupcake wasn't one of them.

He lunged at her and tried to pull the backpack away. For less than half a second, he saw how the tubes of heart's-blood and cyber-blood ran from her partially open chest and disappeared under Hugo's chin. Then she raised the backpack to cover his head and pulled it closer to herself.

Zapan was baffled. How the hell could she have done that? It wasn't like she was any kind of a brain surgeon—

Then he spotted the tall woman sneaking out of the side of the cathedral with a case in one hand. That was Victor's pet Tuner—the one he claimed could turn a chunk of scrap metal into a Second League champion. But what the hell was *she* doing here? And carrying a case that looked a lot like the one Doc Ido used to carry medical supplies—

The little *bitches—both* of them! "Oh, that's a real cute trick," Zapan yelled. "You think that's gonna fool anyone? Gimme that—" He made a grab at the girl's backpack; she shrank back from him as a Centurian rotated its gun turret in his direction.

"Hunter-Warrior Zapan, registration number F44-269," the Centurian said loudly. "Stealing another Hunter's bounty is against Factory Law and the Hunter's Code."

"Thank you," the girl said politely. She took a step towards Zapan and he automatically recoiled; she had a look on her little face that he didn't like one bit. He forced himself to stand his ground; he wasn't going to let anyone think a girl could make him flinch. Then she made some kind of gesture at him—no, not a gesture. That little cupcake had the Damascus Blade!

Zapan reached for her, intending to take his sword back, when a terrible pain exploded at his left temple. Something was on fire or burrowing under his skin and oh, God, now it was moving all around his face, across the top of his forehead at his hairline to his other temple, down the other side of his face, under his jawline, his chin, and coming up the other side and why the *hell* wasn't anyone trying to help him? Couldn't they see—

Something fell at his feet with an obscenely wet smack. Zapan looked down and saw his own face staring up at him. Except it had no eyes. His face had no eyes—

Because he had no face!

Screaming in pain and horror, Zapan turned to the other Hunters for help. But all they did was wave him off and back away, refusing to look at him, some of them even gagging. Meanwhile, the bitch who had done this to him was escaping with his Damascus Blade and no one was even *trying* to stop her. Were they all afraid of her because they thought she'd killed her own boyfriend for a bounty? Or was it that weird blue fire dancing along the length of the sword?

But she was just *a girl*, just a *stupid little girl*; any of them could take the sword away from her easy and give it back to him, the rightful owner. What kind of Hunter-Warriors would just stand by and let a girl walk off with a brother Hunter's weapon, especially after she'd just used it *to flay him alive*?

What kind of Hunter-Warriors wouldn't help one of their own save face? It was a very special face, too, not cheap plastic hackwork; it was expensive, worth more than all of those lame-assed so-called Hunters put together! They weren't his brother Hunters—they weren't even his friends. And now they were all walking away, like this was just another night in Iron City and he was just some faceless nobody.

CHAPTER 23

Alita had no idea how long she had been sitting on the bench outside the OR. Ten hours, ten days, ten centuries—she couldn't tell one period of time from any other. If she'd had to guess, she'd have gone with centuries. She would have waited that long for her Hugo. Ido said she was three hundred years old—what were a few more centuries between friends? As long as Hugo lived, she didn't care how long it took.

When she finally heard the OR door open, she bounced up in front of Ido, tears welling in her eyes, ready to spill down her cheeks.

"How— How is he?" she asked, afraid to raise her voice above a whisper.

Ido dabbed at her face with a soft cloth. "You can see for yourself. He's in Recovery now."

Alita dashed past him.

Even if the body wasn't a Berserker, it was A-grade, a composite that Ido had made himself, using the best parts and materials he could find. It was his own design, and when he had finished it, he had put it away carefully in cold storage, refusing to raid it for parts, no matter how depleted the clinic's inventory was. He'd had a hunch that someday this body would save a life, and when the time came, he didn't want anything missing.

Gerhad had been watching over Hugo since they'd wrapped up the cyber-surgery. In the past few weeks, they had done more embodying procedures than most reputable doctors did in a year. When things quieted down, Ido was going to suggest to Gerhad that she go for certification as a doctor—i.e., just take the test. She had enough experience in cyber-surgery to count as coursework.

Now she stepped aside with a smile as Alita went to Hugo's side. "He's good," Gerhad told her. "He's stable. No question, he'll be all right."

Alita touched Hugo's steel hand, so much like her own now. It wouldn't be as sensitive because it wasn't Urm technology, but it was the best work in Iron City, state of the art, top of the line. And maybe it wasn't such a bad thing that it wasn't as good as Alita's, Ido thought; the prospect of two Urm Berserkers running around together was a little scary.

"I'm sorry, Alita," Ido said. She looked up from Hugo, her expression mildly puzzled. "This city—eventually it finds a way to corrupt even the best of us and somehow the wrong people pay too dearly for other people's sins. Hugo didn't deserve what happened to him. Fortunately, Chiren's surgical technique was brilliant—genius actually, rigging your circulatory system to include Hugo as part of your body. There's no brain damage at all. And that brilliant heart of yours was strong enough for both of you."

"Chiren knew how to do it," Alita said, smiling through her tears. "If it weren't for her, he'd be dead."

Ido had a sudden mental image of Chiren in the cathedral, helping Alita and Hugo, and his heart skipped a beat, the way it had when he'd seen Chiren holding their daughter, talking to her, playing with her, rocking her to sleep. Chiren's blue eyes hadn't been cold then, they'd been bright, full of life and love. During those years when Motorball had been the outlet for their talent, they had been busy and happy, creating champions for a game they both couldn't get enough of, and he had constructed a new body for their daughter, hoping to replace the one that wasn't strong enough.

But when the game had betrayed them and destroyed their beautiful girl, Chiren's heart had frozen and she had gone over to the kind of life that they'd promised themselves they'd never live.

Well, *he* had promised. He'd thought she had, too. But, to Chiren, life had broken its promise, rendering any promises she'd made null and void. As time passed, Ido had begun to wonder if there was something in Chiren that had always been drawn to the worst that Iron City had to offer, and losing their daughter had simply freed her to follow.

Either way, he'd thought the spirit of the woman he had loved had died with their little girl. But apparently, he was wrong—there was still a spark of his Chiren alive inside the ice queen.

"You had her heart in your hands—*in your hands!*—and you let her live." Vector came around his desk to grab Chiren by her upper arms and look into her face. "Why? Just tell me that. *Why?*"

She didn't try to twist away, didn't even yell at him for putting his hands on her when he was angry. Maybe she'd finally lost her mind. Entirely possible—she'd always been a little off. If he could sell Nova on the story that his Tuner had gone mad, and if Nova would give him a break for his past loyal service, he'd have Alita all boxed up and delivered within twenty-four hours. With whipped cream and a cherry on top.

"*Well?*" Vector gave Chiren a hard shake. "Do you even *know* why?"

Chiren was silent for so long he thought he was going to have to shake her a whole lot harder. Then she straightened up and looked him right in the eye.

"Because I'm a doctor. And a mother." She lifted her chin in defiance. "Somehow I'd forgotten that."

Vector pushed her away and threw his hands in the air. "And what the hell am I supposed to do with *that*?"

Chiren turned her back on him, on the view of Zalem, and on his enormous shiny desk. "I can't do this any more. It was one thing when it was just big stupid beasts fighting each other in the streets or on the Motorball track. But this—" She shook her head and walked towards the door. "I'm leaving."

"Chiren, *wait*!" It came out sounding more desperate than he'd have liked. She stopped, although she only turned her head a little instead of turning around.

"I understand now I can't keep you here any longer," Vector said slowly, doing sincere as if his life depended on it, because it probably did. "But if you're going to leave, don't you think it's time—past time, really—that you left for Zalem?"

Now she did turn around, and for a moment he wondered if she had seen the shadow behind the opaque glass of the door. But the way she was looking at him, her eyes too bright with tears of joy and her face alive with hope and gratitude, he knew she hadn't.

❧

It had been hard, but Ido finally managed to get Alita out of the OR so Hugo could get some rest. She couldn't stop herself from talking to him, and if she kept it up, he would wake up too soon. Hugo needed all the rest he could get before he faced the world in this new and different body.

O brave new body, that has a Hugo in it.

Ido shook the thought away. His mind always generated nonsense when he was overtired. But sleep would have to wait; his patient was going to need him. Two patients, really—somehow he had to make Alita understand that what was normal, even exhilarating, for her would be traumatic for someone who'd been completely organic before waking up as a Total Replacement cyborg.

On the plus side, Hugo was young enough that his brain was still growing, so his central nervous system would probably adjust more easily to its new embodiment and accept it as natural. On the other hand, what had happened to his father would make it very difficult for Hugo to accept what had happened to him. And then there was what Ido would have to tell him about his grand dream of going to Zalem. He was going to take that hard—once he got Hugo to believe him, anyway. He was having a hard enough time convincing Alita of the truth.

"Vector was running a scam on Hugo," Ido said wearily. "I told you, if you're *born* on the ground, you *stay* on the ground—no exceptions, not for any amount of money. And the only way to get from down here to up there is to become Motorball Final Champion. That's it. You can*not* buy your way up there. No one can."

"How do you know that?" Alita said.

"Because *I'm* from Zalem," Ido said finally. "I was born there," He pointed at the small pale scar in the centre of his forehead. "I used to have the same mark Chiren has—the mark of Zalem. I removed it myself. Because our daughter wasn't perfect, because she was ill, Chiren and I were forced into exile with her down here. The magnificent floating city doesn't tolerate the weak, the sick, the defective. The man responsible is

Nova, the Watcher behind the eyes. And because I fathered something imperfect, I couldn't go back up there if I wanted to."

Alita was staring at him wide-eyed and open-mouthed.

"And *that* is how I know Hugo was never going to get to Zalem. Hugo was conned. Vector's nothing more than a jumped-up con artist who doesn't care about anyone. He just strings them along with promises so they'll keep doing whatever he wants."

Alita peered at him with a searching look, as if she were trying to find some evidence in his face that he was wrong, even as her shoulders slumped and her eyes lost their brightness. She knew he was telling her the truth.

"I'm sorry," Ido added, wishing he were apologising for being wrong instead of right. He was about to say something else when there was a loud crash in the OR.

"*No!*" Hugo yelled. "*Nooooo, noooo!*"

Hugo had fallen off the table and was pulling IV lines and the nutrient tube out of his chest. Now he was struggling to his feet, still groggy despite his shock. Alita bit back tears; she had to help Hugo, not cry over him. But when she moved towards him, he backed away, waving her off with a wild movement that took out a shelf of beakers and equipment, sending broken glass, sensors and shattered bits of circuit board all over the floor.

"This was all for *nothing*?" Hugo cried, his cheeks wet with tears. "Everything I did, all the people I hurt—all for *nothing*?" He staggered to one side and knocked over a tray of surgical instruments, scattering calipers, retractors and scalpels. He kicked the tray across the room where it smashed into the far wall, dislocating a shelf of scanners and biochemical tracers, which fell on a freestanding cabinet below. The cabinet wobbled and tipped over with a terrible crashing sound of metal and glass.

Hugo didn't know his own strength, Alita realised. She had to calm him down.

"And now, *look* at me!" he sobbed, holding his metal hands out. "Look at what I've become—*look*! I used to make fun of them when I was ripping them apart—and now look at me!" He raised his metal hands and looked at them. "It's too perfect. It's exactly what I deserve."

As he dropped his hands and turned away, Alita wrapped him up in her arms. He was strong but he was no match for a Berserker. She hugged him tightly, keeping him still until Ido could sedate him. Hugo bristled when he felt the needle go into his neck, then slumped in Alita's arms.

"It will be better tomorrow," Ido promised gently.

Hugo raised his eyes and looked at Ido in despair. "What good is tomorrow to a dead man?"

"*I* see you," Alita told him as she carried him back to the table. "As long as we have each other, nothing else matters." She held his hand while Ido reconnected the IV lines and the nutrient feed. They hadn't broken, at least.

It wasn't supposed to be like this, she thought sadly. Only a few short weeks ago, he'd been helping her train for her big tryout. Her big tryout—what a joke *that* turned out be. Before that, he'd taken her out to the crashed spacecraft in the Badlands, to show her something that might help her with her memory. To help her, to help her—he'd done everything he could to help her. And in return, he'd been framed for murder and, for the grand finale, run through with a Hunter's sword. And he owed it all to her and her insistence on remembering her past.

"I wish I'd never found out who I was," Alita blurted suddenly. "It's only made everyone I love suffer! I'm sorry. I'm so sorry."

Ido turned her around to face him. "Don't you *ever* apologise for who you are," he said, his face intent and serious. "This is why you're here. You're the only one built for this."

She nodded, smearing away tears with the back of one metal hand. "And I have to face it all head on." Suddenly she caught sight of herself in the mirror over the sink. For a moment, she stood very still, feeling the Damascus Blade in her hand, feeling a purpose in herself that was slowly making itself clear to her.

Staring at her reflection, Alita became aware of a drop of water shimmering at the lip of the tap. It hung there for another second before it fell. The Damascus Blade was a bright streak in the air as she cut the drop in half.

"I want to thank you," Ido said as she turned back to him. "Because of you, I got to see my little girl grow into an exceptional woman. One who's going to save the world."

"Thank you, Father." Alita said as Ido dried her tears again. She leaned over and kissed Hugo gently on the forehead before she left.

❧

The Factory doors rumbled open. Alita stood with the daylight at her back, wondering how she must look to the Centurians lining the walls—a small silhouette standing in a rectangle of brightness. Something long and slightly curved extended down from her right hand, heat shimmers rippling in the air around it. Blue plasma cast no shadow but it was as real as anything—as real as the Damascus Blade, as real as she was and what she had come here to do.

"Vectorrrrrrr!" she roared.

The Centurians' gun turrets swivelled around to point at her. Her Berserker reaction time put her ten metres into the hall by the time they fired at the spot where she had been. Still firing, the guns swivelled again, shooting chunks out of the floor, the walls, the ceiling as they tried to get a fix on her. More Centurians stumped into the hallway, spraying the place with bullets and taking out other Centurians in the process. Someone had adjusted their programming from KILL-INTRUDER to KILL-INTRUDER-AT-ALL-COSTS, and Alita was pretty sure she knew who that was.

Unhurt, she vaulted onto the back of one of the reinforcements and plunged her plasma hand into its brain case, causing it to freeze. The others registered her location but she had already leaped away as they shot the frozen Centurian into scrap. She bounced up beside another, sliced off its gun with the Damascus Blade and dragged it along with her.

"Violation! Violation!" A deckman came down off the bounty platform and rolled towards her.

Oh, come on—seriously? It really was no more than a tin can, and not a very good one. Alita used the Centurian's gun to blow it to pieces.

Past the bounty platform, she saw a bank of three elevators. Two went no higher than the floor where Vector's office and penthouse suite were located. The third stopped on the level below, where there was maintenance access.

❧

Vector had already been waiting several hours for dispatch to pick up the cabinet in his office and send it up to Zalem when the alert came in from Security. The cyborg girl his hired thugs had failed to kill, Alita, was coming up the front steps, and she was obviously loaded for bear.

After the past couple of days, he wasn't in the mood for any more of her steel-assed bullshit and he'd set the Centurians to "Overkill". After they obliterated her, he intended to send whatever was left up in a plastic bag to the Watcher. If Nova wanted her heart so bad, he could piece it back together like a jigsaw puzzle.

Vector was pretty sure the Centurians would close Alita's case before she got as far as the bounty platform. But the gunfire went on and on and Vector began to get annoyed. It was one thing for a gang of hired killers to screw up—it wasn't like any of them were geniuses. But Centurians had big guns, a perfect aim, and they couldn't be outsmarted or distracted in a limited space like the entry hall.

When the sound of gunfire finally died away, Vector stabbed the intercom key.

"Security, report!" he barked. "Did you get her?"

He waited for someone to babble apologies for the noise, but there was no response.

"Security, dammit, report!"

Still nothing. Someone was definitely going to die before the day was out. He was trying to decide who and how many when his skylight exploded.

Shards of glass rained down on him, cutting his face and hands, sticking in his hair and clothing. He tried to brush himself off and ended up pushing the glass even deeper into his skin. A whole bunch of people were going to die for this, Vector thought, momentarily blind with rage. The stupid skylight was supposed to be shatterproof, made with the same kind of glass they used in Zalem. Obviously someone had swapped out the good stuff and left him with Iron City crap while making themselves a fortune on the black market. When he found out who, he was going to kill them so hard it would wipe out everyone in a six-block radius—

Then he saw her in the middle of the room, and all thought ceased.

Alita assumed a fighter's stance: knees slightly bent, hands up to protect her face as she glowered at him. Like she felt she mattered to him—like she mattered *at all*. She looked around, straightened up and walked over to his desk. "You were never going to send Hugo to Zalem," she accused him, her big eyes as dark as her voice. "Were you?"

"I *always* keep my promises to send people up," he said, but he could tell she didn't buy that. What the hell—the girl wasn't getting out of his room alive; it wouldn't matter if she knew. "Like Dr Chiren here," Vector added, gesturing vaguely at the cabinet in the corner of his office. Alita looked at where he gestured, then back at him with a puzzled expression.

Vector walked over to the cabinet and rapped his knuckles on it, but the girl still didn't get it. He shrugged and deactivated the seal so he could open the front. If dispatch came now, they could just wait a few minutes, he thought, as a little vapour snaked out of the refrigerated interior. As long as he didn't leave the door open too long, nothing would spoil. A minute or two would probably do it. Alita wouldn't be able to distinguish any of Chiren's packaged internal organs from the mystery meat they sold in the market, and she probably wouldn't recognise Chiren's hands, as lovely as they were. But he was sure she'd know those blue eyes. They were packaged separately in transparent containers and secured side by side, to indicate they were a set. They were as beautiful and as cold as they had ever been. Literally cold.

"If dispatch ever get their asses in gear, she'll go up with the rest of tonight's shipment." Vector gave the girl another few seconds to be thoroughly horrified before he closed the cabinet up and reactivated the seal. "Who the hell knows what the boss does with any of this." He rapped his knuckles on the case again. "And *that* is the only way anyone *ever* gets to Zalem."

Vector smiled, seeing the shadow through the opaque glass in the door behind Alita. This was going to be good.

Alita saw Vector start to duck just as the door crashed inwards. Berserker reaction time let her protect her face from the various fragments, which bounced harmlessly off her body. But the grind-cutter didn't bounce. It sliced through her side and she fell to the floor, holding the wound as bright-blue cyber-blood poured out between her fingers.

"I knew you would not wait for your fate to find you," Grewishka said, towering over her in ugly triumph.

Then he vanished.

They were under attack.

Zalem was under attack. The wind was screaming past her ears as the supply tube she was climbing with the rest of her squad shivered and rocked—not much, but enough to make it tricky to hang on. They were up pretty high but they still had some distance to go. Gelda was leading them, urging them upwards, reminding them every metre, every centimetre, every millimetre was a gain.

At this height, they had to be ready for the bladed rings that appeared without warning and slid down along the supply tubes. These were the floating city's defence against any ground-dwellers foolish enough to think they could simply climb to a better life in a better place, neither of which they had any right to. Alita and her squad had already fired on a few with plasma rifles and shoulder-mounted missile launchers, blowing them into fragments that went spinning off into the void.

The squad had just destroyed another one when the side of the tube blew out.

Earth and sky slewed crazily as Alita clung to the tube, dragging herself forward until she was clinging to the jagged, still-hot edge of the hole. The wind was quickly drying splashes of heart's-blood and cyber-blood on the tube and on the parts of dead and dying cyborgs still stuck to the metal.

Her whole squad was gone, she realised. *Now* what was she supposed to do?

A hand reached down and clamped onto her wrist. Alita looked up to see Gelda's torn face, bleeding blue in some spots, seeping red in others.

"You know Zalem's defences!" Gelda shouted at her over the wind. *"Finish the mission!"*

Finish the mission—

Grewishka was back, looming over her. Under her fingers, Alita felt the wound in her side closing up, healing itself, and she knew it wasn't just temporary sealant.

How about that? She got to her feet.

"I know who you are," she said to Grewishka, her voice low and dangerous. "You're a child of the underworld, taken to live up here as a slave. And I'm just an insignificant girl." As she spoke, she felt a sudden profound pity for Grewishka, for the utter tragedy of the life he had been forced to live. "Die knowing this—the people who did this terrible thing to you will suffer. I'll *make* them suffer."

Grewishka laughed at her and she found it in herself to pity him even more. Chiren had rebuilt him into something like a walking truck. His thick arms and bulky shoulders were vaguely suggestive of a gorilla but there was no life in them, only machinery. His torso was a distinct triangle, made so his lower body could be attached easily. His thick metal legs were shaped like a human's, but such exaggerated musculature didn't exist organically; his feet were more like a Centurian's.

And all of this was topped off with the last vestige of his humanity. His head and face were protected by his over-built shoulders. To Alita, however, it looked less like protection and more like the machinery was swallowing him.

The body was no good for anything except killing—killing *her*, to be precise. Grewishka had become nothing more than a Centurian with more metal and less purpose.

"My master Nova is *so* eager to meet you," Grewishka said. "Allow me to introduce you!"

The intake doors on Alita's arm opened with a discreet hushed noise as they drew air in. Blue fire blossomed on her hand, flowed over the pommel of the Damascus Blade and ran along its length like a living thing.

Sneering, Grewishka pointed and his grind-cutter flew out from his hand. There was a blinding flash of blue light and then the grind-cutter was writhing impotently on Vector's shiny marble floor.

The cyborg bellowed with rage and fired all the rest of his grind-cutters at once. Alita leaped into the air, performing a whirling dance with the brilliant blue flames, moving too fast for Grewishka's brute eyes to follow. But afterwards he had no trouble seeing the other four grind-cutters dying on the floor like headless snakes.

Grewishka raised both fists and charged at her. She dodged him effortlessly and one fist demolished one of Vector's absurdly ostentatious pillars, leaving a pile of rubble below the ragged piece of stone hanging down from the ceiling like a weird stalactite.

Time slowed as she somersaulted over Grewishka's head. In his bewildered, upturned face, she caught the barest hint of the innocent he'd never really been, before she dropped straight down, driving the Damascus Blade so that it bisected him from top to bottom. Alita landed on one knee with her back to the monster, not wanting to see the two pieces fall away from each other.

This city—eventually it finds a way to corrupt even the best people.

Ido had said that, and she had told him the problem wasn't the streets or anything else in the city, but up above. There was no pleasure in knowing she was right, she thought as she got to her feet and turned to Vector, who was cowering behind his desk.

"No, no, wait!" he pleaded, backing away from her as she moved towards him. "Please, just wait—" He tripped on nothing and fell on his expensive ass. Alita walked around the desk, watching him try to scuttle away from her like a bug. She raised her arm and drew it back so the point of the Damascus Blade was aimed at his left eye.

"Speak," she commanded.

"Sure, what do you want me to say? I'll say anything, tell you anything," Vector babbled. He was backed up against another of his stupid classical-knock-off pillars. "Anything, just tell me what to say—"

"Not *you*," Alita said. "*Him*."

Vector had a fraction of a second to look terrified before his eyes went dead and his face lost all expression.

"So we finally meet, Alita," he said in a calm, inhuman voice.

"Nova." The name felt like a profanity.

"May I?" asked the Watcher, making a small gesture at the space between them. When she didn't move, he shrugged, got to his feet, and made a business of smoothing Vector's clothing and brushing off any remaining bits of glass, ignoring the cuts and scratches they left on Vector's skin.

"Where are you?" Alita asked.

"Home, as we speak. Feet up. Very comfortable." He glanced out of the window at the floating city, then moved past her to sit Vector's body on the edge of the desk. He was looking at her with what she realised was supposed to be a mischievous grin. But implanted optics didn't twinkle, and neither did Vector's dead eyes.

"Well, my girl, you've certainly exceeded all expectations, mine included," he said. As if he were complimenting a small child on their homework. "Killing my champion Grewishka—most impressive! And turning a selfish creature like Chiren to your side—I never saw *that* coming. You're definitely more interesting to me alive than dead. And we're from the same place, which in these hard and perilous times makes us practically *family*."

She waited, her sword ready and unwavering.

"You can go ahead and walk out of here and the Factory will not stop you." The Watcher made Vector wink at her—a neat yet nauseating trick for someone who hadn't had eyelids in centuries. "*This* time."

"I don't need *your* permission to live," she said evenly.

"Ah, but others might." He chuckled. "Your precious Dr Ido, for example. And what about your beloved Hugo? Yes, I know he's still alive. Although not for long—we'll track him down." Nova laughed again. "I've found the best way to enjoy immortality is to watch others die."

Fury surged through her. She gave Vector's body a hard shove that put him flat on his back on the desk with his legs dangling, then raised the Damascus Blade with both hands. All at once the Watcher vanished and it was just Vector on the desk, looking terrified.

"Please, *don't*!" he begged. "I'll do anything! I'll make you a champion in the Game. You're good. The crowd loves you! I'll give you anything you want, just *please don't kill me!*"

And then as Alita was staring at him in uncertainty, the Watcher was back. "See? No character. None whatsoever."

In answer, Alita drove the Damascus Blade through the centre of his chest, pinning him to the wood.

"Then you'll enjoy losing your puppet," Alita said.

Nova lifted Vector's head to look at the sword sticking out of him. "That does look fatal," he agreed. "Well, no matter. Vector was getting tiresome." He coughed; heart's-blood leaked from his mouth and he began to tremble. But still the Watcher kept his eyes clear and focused. "Oh, Alita, you poor child. Everything you've gone through and still no answers."

"And you've just made the biggest mistake of your life," Alita said matter-of-factly.

"What would that be?" asked the Watcher, as if indulging a clever but insolent child.

"You let me live."

Nova made Vector smile, exposing blood-soaked teeth. "Then adieu, until our next meeting. And remember—" He was losing his hold on the last shreds of Vector's life. "*I see everything.*"

He was gone. Alita pulled the Damascus Blade free, letting Vector's body slide to the floor. She stared at his corpse, but there was no pity in her for the man who had lied so egregiously to Hugo, to Chiren, and to all the other sad, lost souls who'd thought they could get out of Iron City in one piece.

Her phone rang, making her jump. For a moment she was afraid it was *him*, with one last word. But her relief at hearing Ido's voice was short-lived.

"Factory enforcers came looking for Hugo," he told her. "Somehow they found out he'd been kept alive. I sneaked Hugo out of here but they've sealed the city. The Factory's determined to find him."

"Do you know where he went?" Alita asked.

"He—oh, God, Alita, he's trying to go up."

Y'know, if I were as strong as you, I'd climb that tube to Zalem right now.

Alita ran to the window and looked out, scanning each of the spider-leg supply tubes until she made out a tiny figure working his way upwards to the flying city he thought was heaven. Only because he didn't know what really lived there.

You know Zalem's defences—

CHAPTER 24

Finish the mission.

Gelda's voice echoed in Alita's head as she made her way up the supply tube after Hugo. The sense memory of the climb she'd made with her squad seemed to echo the same way in her body. She went faster this time; it wasn't easy but it wasn't as hard as before.

It would be more difficult for Hugo. The increased strength and coordination of his cyborg body would have made the first part of the climb easy. But as he went higher, it would become more of an effort for him to hang on in the wind. To withstand the forces of wind and rain, all very tall structures need some give to them, but the supply tubes had a lot more than most, something that wasn't obvious from ground level.

Finish the mission.

Alita knew she could do that; she always had. She couldn't remember the missions themselves but she knew she had finished all of them, and she would finish this one, too.

It was after the first third of the length of the supply tube that Hugo would have begun to struggle. Even hardcore adrenaline junkies willing to gamble that Centurians would be too busy to show up and shoot them down had never gone higher and never, despite their claims, scratched their initials into the tube. They couldn't have—they'd have needed both hands to hang onto the bucking, swaying pipe.

If they actually *had* gone higher, however, they'd have found themselves in real trouble. The middle stretch of every tube had sensors to detect pressure and movements produced by someone engaged in purposeful climbing. The sensors would then trigger the bladed rings, sending them down towards would-be trespassers. They were virtually impossible to avoid, and the only way to get rid of them was to destroy them. Few climbers were strong enough to carry weapons that powerful. Even if they were, there was still the possibility of being blown to smithereens by a mine left over from the War. Even a squad of Berserkers could get chewed up and spit out.

Anyone foolhardy enough to try scaling a supply tube usually attracted a Centurian before going any higher than twenty feet. The Centurian would invite the daredevil to dismount under penalty of law, allowing thirty seconds for compliance. After that there was no further warning before the penalty of law kicked in.

Hugo had picked the one time in the history of Iron City when, thanks to the spectacular snafu of Vector's "Overkill" command, there were no Centurians available to shoot him down. The handful of still-functioning Centurians were aware that Vector's life-signs had ceased, and were currently on standby, awaiting orders from his successor.

Alita realised that Hugo had made his choice when he was unaware of all this, that this option was the only one he had left.

"Hugo!"

At first, he thought his ears were playing tricks on him again. When the wind had started to pick up, Hugo had thought he'd heard voices calling to him—first Tanji's, then Doc Ido's, even Vector's. But he hadn't heard Alita's until just now. Clinging to the tube, he twisted his head around to find it was no trick; she was really there, her beautiful face serious as she pulled herself towards him.

"You have to come down!" she shouted. "You can't stay up here! *We* can't stay up here!"

"This is the only way!" he called back to her. "I'll never make it out of this city alive!"

Alita moved a little closer. "Zalem isn't heaven, Hugo!"

"It has to be!" he told her.

"But you don't even know what's up there!" she replied.

Hugo looked down over the long, snaking supply tube to the ground below. "It doesn't matter."

"Don't you do this!" Alita shouted, and he saw her eyes were welling with tears. "Don't you dare leave me behind—" she looked past him towards Zalem with pure hatred in her face. "For *that*!"

Hugo shook his head emphatically. "I'm trying to set you free!"

"Please—*please* listen to me, Hugo! I've been here already—I mean, *here*, in this spot—and it's right where Nova wants us! Nova's the Watcher behind the eyes and he's using you to get to me! We have to go back down *now*!"

Hugo shook his head. "If I go back down there, I'm dead! Don't you understand that?"

"I can fight them off!" Alita was almost close enough to touch him.

"We can make a run for the Badlands. They'll never follow us!"

The Badlands; Hugo thought of the day he'd taken her to the Urm ship (with Koyomi and Tanji, and for a moment the memory of his friend was a knife in his heart). He looked past her, down the length of the supply tube, and then up to where it disappeared into a low-hanging cloud. What was the Badlands or any other place compared to a city in the sky?

"We belong up there!" he called to Alita.

Alita shook her head vehemently. "We don't belong *anywhere*! You and I are the same, Hugo. You're the only one who sees *me*, and I'm the only one who knows you for who you really are!" Her eyes welled with tears, not because of the wind, and it occurred to Hugo that he was always making her cry.

"We'll always be on the run!" he called to her.

"We'll be *together*!" she yelled. "Please, come back down with me so we can go home—wherever that is—*together*!"

The love shining in her face was wide, deep and unconditional, and he finally understood that without it he had nothing. Hugo stretched out his arm to her.

Alita moved up a little more and reached for him. "We can go home," she said, straining to touch him.

I almost threw away the only thing of value in my life, Hugo thought as his heart filled with every feeling he had ever wanted.

The hideous roar and clang from above startled him so much he almost lost his grip on the tube. He looked up to see a horrific circle of metal burst through the cloud and bear down on him in a halo of spinning teeth.

This time, she had no squad, no plasma rifle, no missile launcher. Alita reached for Hugo, intending to leap over the ring, and found that somehow she was already in his arms and *he* was lifting *her* over the bladed ring. Their combined weight should be enough to keep them from being blown away, she thought, and aimed herself so they would touch down on the tube again together. Always together.

Except something had gone badly, terribly, horribly wrong—Hugo was suddenly so light, he almost flew out into empty space. From the chest down, his body had been chewed away, and heart's-blood and cyber-blood streamed out from him on the wind. Berserker reaction time let her catch his hand just in time.

With her other hand, she drove the Damascus Blade into the supply tube as an anchor, and there they stayed.

"Hold on, Hugo, please!"

Hugo looked up at her. She was beautiful even like this, clinging to the side of a supply tube with the wind blowing her hair every which way while she strained to save him. He would have gladly held on for as long as she wanted him to—an hour, a year, a thousand years—except his arm wasn't going to last another minute. The ring had chomped him good, killing every connection in his cyber-body. His arm was going to come apart before he could even bleed to death.

Show's over, thank you and good night.

"I love you, Hugo!"

He realised that Alita was trying to pull him up and shift him onto her back. It wasn't going to work. He was going to let her down again and this time he couldn't help it.

"I'm glad I had the chance to know you. To love you," Hugo told her. His arm came apart. "Goodbye—"

She shot away from him at high speed. Still, Hugo went on looking into her eyes even after he couldn't see her any more.

Hugo's face was dreamy as he fell away from her, as if he were flying off to somewhere beautiful, like the Zalem he'd always believed in, and not falling to his death in a place he'd spent his life trying to escape.

Or as if she'd find him waiting for her at the cathedral, so they could climb the tower and look up at Zalem and the bright, unmoving star.

As if his arm hadn't fallen to pieces in her grip.

As if he hadn't been chewed up by a machine made by a man who needed the suffering of others to relieve the terrible boredom of his immortality.

Alita threw back her head and screamed defiance and rage and loss at the sky and everything in it.

CHAPTER 25

Nova heard her.

Chrome optics weren't his only enhancements, and there had been many upgrades since the young battle prodigy had first spotted him watching her spar with her sensei Gelda in the zero-g sphere.

That hadn't been the first time he had watched her, nor the last. He had kept track of her over the years—the centuries—and when she had finally fallen, he'd thought she had met her end.

In hindsight, he should have known better. Gelda herself had said it: this girl, this Alita as she was known now, would never give up, never stop. *Never. Stop.*

And after Dyson Ido had lifted her out of the trash pile, she never had. She had opened her eyes in a completely different world, with only a few fragmented memories of her life, but she was still who and what she had always been: the warrior who would never give up, never stop. This was bound to bring a great deal of suffering to everyone around her.

But the best, most entertaining, part was that she had no idea. She was completely unaware that she caused more suffering by persevering than she would have by giving up. Resignation was merely constant, ongoing misery that never waxed or waned, a treadmill where people were not so much alive as they were simply waiting to be dead. But then she had come along, shaking everything up, making people believe there was more to life. And there was—just not for them. When they realised that, their pain was ineffable.

Immortality was definitely less boring with her in the picture.

The uncaring stars travelled the same courses they always had through the darkness, except for the brightest one, which never moved. That wasn't *strictly* true, of course. The star never moved relative to any observers on Earth, in Iron City, or the Badlands, or in the one city still floating above the surface of the Earth, where observers' feet never touched the ground.

The residents of Zalem enjoyed the prolonged sunsets and sunrises that came with their elevated status. They also soared above the low-lying clouds characteristic of local weather conditions so they saw the stars more often, and many of them had become stargazers. Their interest was more about appreciating beauty rather than technical astronomy or astrophysics. Why the brightest star in the night sky never moved wasn't something that concerned them. Nor did they feel compelled to investigate the bright beam of light that ran from the centre of the city up into the sky where, somewhere out in space, it ended at that very same bright star. The beam was only visible at night, and it was most easily seen from the edge of Zalem. The people in Iron City couldn't see it at all, which was just as well. They might start asking questions they'd never get answers to. No one in Zalem knew why the beam of light was there or what was on the other end, and it really didn't concern them. They were all too busy with their own pursuits and amusements.

The man in the silvery suit watched the very end of the sunset from his usual spot on the observation deck at the edge of Zalem. He knew how important things like aesthetics, beauty and amusements were to maintaining a stable society, suspended in the air or otherwise. Currently, the most popular amusement in Zalem was Iron City Motorball. The people just couldn't get enough of it. Bread and circuses; it had ever been thus; and as above, so below. Iron City couldn't get enough Motorball either, especially now.

His own taste in amusement had evolved to include a lot of abstract concepts and conditions over the course of his long life. Fortunately, cyborgs provided entertainment that went well beyond their bashing each other to pieces. It was incredible how cyborgs that were more machine than organic flesh could spend most of their waking hours *emoting*. The tragic death scene he had enjoyed thanks to his enhanced sight and hearing—*that* had been exceptional. The cyborg girl who saved her boyfriend's life by turning him into the thing he was most afraid of becoming, which was, in fact, exactly what his one true love happened to be—oh, the drama, the humanity! And her scream of anguish at the end!

Better yet, she was *still* screaming, with everything she did, with every fibre of her being. It was a different kind of screaming, not audible to the ear, perceptible only to those with a true appreciation of human nature, who knew that it was the nature of humans to suffer. Now *that* was entertainment.

Tonight he was using his enhanced hearing to listen to the Motorball stadium announcer wax rhapsodic about tonight's game.

"The Second League waited for a long time for a new hero, someone they could follow, someone worth cheering for, who would never let them down! Well, I'd say they found their hero in a rookie who came out of nowhere! In the first five games of the season, her point record has been *outstanding*, a record-breaker—ask anyone, they'll tell you! There isn't a soul in Iron City who doesn't know this little beauty's name!"

The man at the railing smiled. A smile which, on his face, was terrifying, without warmth or humour or humanity, an expression of pleasure taken in the kinds of things that should never happen, or even be imagined.

He hoped the little heroine remembered what he'd told her: that he saw everything. He wondered how long it would take before she understood that all of it, bread and circus, belonged to him and, being part of the circus, so did she.

These days, the pads and armour she strapped on were custom-made for her by Ido and Gerhad, with a little help from a walking toolbox of a man named Ed, who would say, "You're welcome," whether you thanked him or not. All of it was beautiful and it fitted not only her body but her style of movement, with preternaturally responsive nano-sensors that reinforced the material at points of impact. Wearing it made her feel invincible without slowing her down.

"—her team's facing a pretty tough line-up tonight," the announcer was saying in a tone that suggested he was tickled to death about this and all of life in general. "With Skamasakus *and* Massiter traded to the Vipers to shore up their offensive game, our girl will have her work cut out for her—"

Alita tuned him out and had a look at the Damascus Blade strapped to her forearm. Every time she used it, she did her best to be worthy of it. It had never let her down. She popped on her helmet; the feel of the lining adjusting to the contours of her head was Ido's doing. It was like getting an extra hug from her father before every game.

She revved her wheels, did a quick burn-out and whispered *Hugo* to herself before she left the locker room and headed for the pit lane. Sell-out crowd again tonight, and she thought she could hear every single one of them individually as well as together.

"She's new, she's white-hot and she's captured all our hearts!" enthused the announcer. "If anyone's got a chance of becoming First Champion, it's Iron City's very own sweetheart, number ninety-nine, the Battle Angel herself—*Alita*!"

The cheering seemed to make the whole stadium vibrate, all the way down to the track beneath her wheels. She raised her hands to acknowledge the crowd and looked to where Ido and Gerhad were sitting in their usual seats. Then she slid the Damascus Blade down into her grasp and turned to point it straight at Zalem. Blue flame danced around her hand and along the length of the sword to flare at the tip.

So you see everything, Watcher? Then see this: I have declared war on you and war is the one thing I'm even better at than Motorball. I was made for war and I will not stop, I will not give up, and I will not be defeated. I will finish the mission: I will come for you and I will break you and throw the pieces off the edge of Zalem, to land in the trash pile below. Where you belong. Because I will not stand by in the presence of evil.

Ten thousand fans screamed their approval of the angel who dared to challenge heaven, loving her defiant strength, giving themselves to it, and embracing it as their own.

ACKNOWLEDGEMENTS

My thanks to: Ella Chappell, for being the kind of editor every writer wants to work with; Joshua Izzo and Adrienne Ogle at Lightstorm for helping me see the world of Iron City and Alita, and for their encouraging words; Amanda Hemingway for ongoing support and friendship; my amazing, brilliant son Robert Fenner, who makes me proud every day of his life, and his lovely and talented girlfriend, Justyna Burzynska, who is quite the Battle Angel herself; Jo "Mutha Hydra" Playford, who has come to our rescue so many times, and Colin Harris, a true friend for many years; George R. R. Martin and Parris Phipps, for more than I can say; and Mic Cheetham and Simon Kavanagh, my absolutely indispensable agents.

ABOUT THE AUTHOR

Pat Cadigan is a science fiction, fantasy and horror writer, three-time winner of the Locus Award, two-time winner of the Arthur C. Clarke Award, and one-time winner of the Hugo Award. She wrote *Lost in Space: Promised Land*, novelisations of two episodes of *The Twilight Zone*, the *Cellular* novelisation, and the novelisation and sequel to *Jason X*. In addition to being the author of the novelization of *Alita: Battle Angel*, Pat is also author of the official prequel novel, *Iron City*.

IRON CITY

THE OFFICIAL PREQUEL TO ALITA: BATTLE ANGEL

A long time ago there was the Great War. The reasons for the war have been lost to time. On the shattered surface of the Earth, there is a metropolis that lives amidst the garbage thrown down from the inhabitants of a sky city floating above it. Welcome to Iron City.

A lonely doctor specialising in cyborg repair, Ido, is doing his best to help the citizens of Iron City. But Ido has a double life, another persona born from the pieces of his broken heart. Hugo, a young man surviving on a life of crime, spots the ultimate steal; an object that will unearth secrets from his own past. And Vector, the most powerful businessman in the city, has his sights set on a new technology that will change the future of Iron City forever.

For more fantastic fiction, author events,
competitions, limited editions and more

Visit our website
titanbooks.com

Like us on Facebook
facebook.com/titanbooks

Follow us on Twitter
@TitanBooks

Email us
readerfeedback@titanemail.com